HUME'S MORALITY

Feeling and Fac

Rachel Cohon offers an original interpretation ___ ... moral philosophy of David Hume, focusing on two areas. Firstly, his metaethics. Cohon reinterprets Hume's claim that moral distinctions are not derived from reason and explains why he makes it. She finds that Hume did not actually hold three 'Humean' claims: 1) that beliefs alone cannot move us to act, 2) that evaluative propositions cannot be validly inferred from purely factual propositions, or 3) that moral judgments lack truth value. According to Hume, human beings discern moral virtues and vices by means of feeling or emotion in a way rather like sensing; but this also gives the moral judge a truth-apt idea of a virtue or vice as a felt property. Secondly, Cohon examines the artificial virtues. Hume says that although many virtues are refinements of natural human tendencies, others (such as honesty) are constructed by social convention to make cooperation possible; and some of these generate paradoxes. She argues that Hume sees these traits as prosthetic virtues that compensate for deficiencies in human nature. However, their true status clashes with our common-sense conception of a virtue, and so has been concealed, giving rise to the paradoxes.

Rachel Cohon is Associate Professor of Philosophy at the University at Albany, State University of New York

Hume's Morality

Feeling and Fabrication

RACHEL COHON

OXFORD
UNIVERSITY PRESS

OXFORD

UNIVERSITY PRESS

Great Clarendon Street, Oxford OX2 6DP

Oxford University Press is a department of the University of Oxford.
It furthers the University's objective of excellence in research, scholarship,
and education by publishing worldwide in

Oxford New York

Auckland Cape Town Dar es Salaam Hong Kong Karachi
Kuala Lumpur Madrid Melbourne Mexico City Nairobi
New Delhi Shanghai Taipei Toronto

With offices in

Argentina Austria Brazil Chile Czech Republic France Greece
Guatemala Hungary Italy Japan Poland Portugal Singapore
South Korea Switzerland Thailand Turkey Ukraine Vietnam

Oxford is a registered trade mark of Oxford University Press
in the UK and in certain other countries

Published in the United States
by Oxford University Press Inc., New York

© Rachel Cohon 2008

British Library Cataloguing in Publication Data

Data available

Library of Congress Cataloging in Publication Data

Data available

Typeset by SPI Publisher Services, Pondicherry, India
Printed in the United Kingdom by
Lightning Source UK Ltd., Milton Keynes

ISBN 978–0–19–926844–3 (Hbk.)
ISBN 978–0–19–959497–9 (Pbk.)

For Randy and Jeremy, my narrowest circle,
and for my parents, Baruch and Claire Cohon

Acknowledgments

Many, many people have provided valuable assistance throughout the writing of this book and during the preceding years when I labored over the texts and devised interpretations that ultimately did or did not find their way into it. Because the book has been long in the making, I am likely to leave people out inadvertently, for which I apologize in advance.

My first debt is a collective one, to the Hume Society, for affording such a wonderful forum for discussion at its conferences and other meetings, year after year, and for fostering a culture of mutual encouragement, intellectual challenge, and excitement about the study of Hume. Too frequently for it to be a coincidence, Hume Society sessions exemplify the best of philosophic exchange: people giving smart papers and asking and answering well-informed and often ingenious questions with civility and respect, adhering to the highest intellectual standards without the contemptuous tone and with little of the personal competitiveness that so often mar contemporary philosophic discourse. It has been my intellectual incubator.

I am deeply grateful to the National Endowment for the Humanities, whose Fellowship for University Teachers gave me a year of uninterrupted work on this book (2002–3), and whose Summer Stipend (1993) supported my first efforts at what later became Chapter 7. I thank the Stanford Humanities Center for its support of my work on Hume's artificial virtues (1992–3) that culminated in Chapters 6–8. I also thank the Department of Philosophy at the University at Albany, under the leadership of Jon Mandle, as well as the College of Arts and Sciences under then-Dean Joan Wick-Pelletier, for preserving my precious sabbatical time for me after I was sidelined by illness in 2005–6, even though the department was short-handed.

There are many specific individuals whom I am eager to thank. I gratefully acknowledge the debt I owe Timothy Schroeder for offering me a Ulysses contract for the completion of the first draft of the manuscript. I thank Charlotte Brown and Robert Shaver, who read and criticized that draft with care, and Donald Ainslie, Vere Chappell, Mary Clayton Coleman, John Corvino, Stephen Darwall, Stephen Finlay, André Gallois, Ernesto Garcia, Don Garrett, James King, Tito Magri, Jon Mandle, Alison McIntyre, Robert Meyers, William E. (Ted) Morris, David Owen, Herlinde Pauer-Studer, John Perry, Gerald Postema, Elizabeth Radcliffe, Debra Satz, Geoffrey Sayre-McCord, Eric Schliesser, and Jacqueline Taylor for reading and providing constructive comments (in writing, and in some cases at symposia) on various chapters at various stages in their development, whether as papers or as parts of this book. Two anonymous readers for Oxford University Press read the manuscript with care and provided me with thoughtful feedback that enabled me to correct and improve it, for which I am grateful. I thank Richard McCarty for the magic words "modular structure" that provided a mantra for organizing the first half of the book. I thank Bradley Armour-Garb, Michael Bratman, Robert Howell, Rosalind Hursthouse, Robert G. Meyers, Elijah Millgram, Corliss G. Swain, and Christine Swanton for discussions that helped me clarify my thinking in certain places. The book is much better for all these people's efforts, though unfortunately deficiencies persist in spite of them.

Audiences at many universities and conferences have provided helpful discussion of pieces of various chapters. I am grateful to participants in the Hume Society conferences at Nantes, France (1992), Park City, Utah, USA (1995), Nottingham, UK (1996), Monterey, California, USA (1997), Cork, Ireland (1999), Las Vegas, Nevada, USA (2003), Tokyo, Japan (2004), and Boston, Massachusetts, USA (2007); the American Philosophical Association conferences of March 1995, April 1996, December 2002, and March 2003; the first Stanford Early Modern Philosophy conference organized by Marleen Rosemond, 1995; the Creighton Club meeting of 2002 in Ithaca, NY; the Western Canadian Philosophical Association meeting of 2005 in Winnipeg; the Sixth Hume Readings organized by Tito Magri, Rome, Italy, June 2006; the Upstate New York Early Modern Philosophy Workshop organized by Eric Schliesser, September 2006; and the New Philosophical Perspectives on Hume conference at the University of San Francisco organized by Jacqueline Taylor, February 2007. I have learned from audiences at Wake Forest University, Columbia University, the University at Albany (SUNY), the University of Binghamton (SUNY), SUNY New Paltz, the University of Rochester, Washington University in St Louis, Occidental College, the Stanford Humanities Center, Union College, the University of Maryland at College Park, the University of Connecticut (Storrs), Bowling Green University, Rice University, the University of Washington, and San Jose State University.

Students in my graduate seminars on Hume's ethics at Stanford, the University of Southern California, and the University at Albany have read and commented on many of the papers that eventually became chapters of this book, and I thank them for their perceptive contributions.

I am also grateful to Keith Donnellan, who taught the only Hume course I ever took, on Book I of Hume's *Treatise*, in my Ph.D. program at UCLA, and to Thomas E. Hill, Jr., who first directed me to read *Treatise* 2.3.3 and 3.1.1 and discussed them with me in a graduate tutorial there, enticing me (for good or ill) to try to figure out what Hume's moral philosophy is all about.

I am grateful to the following journals for permission to include material I previously published there in whole or in part: *Hume Studies*, for both "Hume's difficulty with the virtue of honesty", 23 / 1 (1997), 91–112, which provides much of Chapter 6, and "On an unorthodox account of Hume's moral psychology", 20 / 2 (1994), 179–94, for a couple of points I use in Chapters 2 and 3; *Philosophy and Phenomenological Research*, for "The common point of view in Hume's ethics", 57 / 4 (Dec. 1997), 827–50, on which Chapter 5 is based; *Journal of the History of Philosophy*, for "Hume on promises and the peculiar act of the mind", 44 / 1 (Jan. 2006), 25–45, which forms most of Chapter 7; *History of Philosophy Quarterly*, for "The shackles of virtue: Hume on allegiance to government", 18 / 4, (Oct. 2001), 393–413, which provides the core section of Chapter 8; *Pacific Philosophical Quarterly*, for "Hume and Humeanism in ethics", 69 (1988), 99–116, some of whose arguments appear in Chapter 1 in a new guise; *Philosophical Studies*, for "Is Hume a noncognitivist in the motivation argument?", 85 (1997), 251–66, for some arguments similarly discussed in Chapters 2 and 3; and the Brazilian journal *Manuscrito* for R. Cohon and David Owen, "Hume on representation, reason and motivation", 20 / 2 (1997), 47–76, for some arguments discussed in Chapters 1, 2, and 3.

I thank David M. Krueger for compiling the index.

Contents

References to Hume's Works

References to Hume's works include the following abbreviations:

Hume's *Treatise of Human Nature* is cited with notations of the form *T j.k.m.n* / SBN *pqr*, the lower-case letters here standing for arabic numerals. Numerals immediately following *T* indicate book, part, section, and paragraph nos. in David Hume, *A Treatise of Human Nature*, ed. David Fate Norton and Mary J. Norton (Oxford: Clarendon Press, 2000); numerals following 'SBN' indicate page no. in David Hume, *A Treatise of Human Nature*, 2nd edn., ed. L. A. Selby-Bigge and P. H. Nidditch (Oxford: Oxford University Press, 1978).

Hume's *Enquiry concerning the Principles of Morals* and *Enquiry concerning Human Understanding* are cited similarly. *EPM* followed by two numbers gives the chapter and paragraph in David Hume, *An Enquiry concerning the Principles of Morals*, ed. Tom L. Beauchamp, The Clarendon Edition of the Works of David Hume (Oxford: Oxford University Press, 1998). *EHU* followed by a number refers to *An Enquiry concerning Human Understanding*, ed. Tom L. Beauchamp, The Clarendon Edition of the Works of David Hume (Oxford: Oxford University Press, 2000). And in each case numbers paired with these, following 'SBN', indicate the corresponding page in David Hume, *Hume's Enquiries*, ed. L. A. Selby-Bigge and P. H. Nidditch, 3rd edn. (Oxford: Oxford University Press, 1975).

Hume's "A Dialogue" is cited similarly, with 'D' or '*A Dialogue*' followed by a paragraph number (the numbering is printed in "A Dialogue" in *An Enquiry concerning the Principles of Morals*, ed. Tom L. Beauchamp, The Clarendon Edition of the Works of David Hume (Oxford: Oxford University Press, 1998)), followed by 'SBN' and a page number indicating the page in "A Dialogue" in *Hume's Enquiries*, edn. L. A. Selby-Bigge and P. H. Nidditch, 3rd edn. (Oxford: Oxford University Press, 1975).

EMPL followed by a number indicates a page in David Hume, *Essays Moral, Political, and Literary*, (1st edn. Edinburgh, 1777), ed. Eugene F. Miller, (Indianapolis: Liberty Fund, 1987).

'DoP' followed by a number gives the part and section numbers in Hume's "Dissertation of the Passions", which appears as "Dissertation II" in John Immerwahr, John Valdimir Price, and James Fieser (eds.), *Four Dissertations and Essays on Suicide and the Immortality of the Soul* (South Bend, IN: Thoemmes Press, 1992, 1995).

In all quotations, emphasis is original unless otherwise indicated.

Introduction

Hume's startling arguments about causation and personal identity have fascinated scholars without interruption since the eighteenth century. Not so his ethics. For the first two-thirds of the twentieth century, Hume's moral philosophy was neglected, apart from a few celebrated paragraphs. In the last thirty-some years, however, the moral philosophy has inspired an explosion of well-deserved attention from philosophers. But interpreting Hume's writings presents many challenges. Recent interpretive work too often treats Hume's ethical theory as a prototype for one or another present-day theory of the nature of moral thought, or as a version of commonsense moral philosophy, Hellenistic ethics, or another historical view. How we interpret Hume makes a difference to how we assess Hume's greatness as a moral philosopher, and also to what we can learn from him that is applicable to contemporary philosophical debates about moral judgment and virtue and vice.

In this book I hope to reveal aspects of Hume's program in moral philosophy that have not been noticed, showing him to be as subversive a moral philosopher as he is a theorist of the mind. If I can do the job properly, we will see the originality of Hume's genius in ethics and will alter what we take away from his ethical writings. I hope experts in ethics and in Hume will find arguments and interpretations here that stimulate and persuade them. But I hope the book will be of broader interest as well, to students of philosophy or anyone who wishes to know why Hume is an important moral philosopher, and to those interested in the foundations of our ethical judgments and the nature of vice and virtue.

Eighteenth-century philosophers and theologians debated whether values arise from reason, are handed down by God, or are products either of human nature or of human ingenuity. They also discussed the nature of the virtues and vices, and whether virtue was man-made. Hume takes positions on these questions that, correct or incorrect, are dramatic, carefully reasoned, and important for anyone thinking systematically about these topics. If my interpretation of Hume is sound, he makes a rather different contribution to this discourse about values than prior interpreters have believed. Thus my main hope is to contribute to our understanding of Hume.

But I draw out some modest consequences from Hume's positions that are instructive for ethical theory in general. Where Hume has an attractive proposal that has been overlooked before, we have something to learn about virtue and vice. Where Hume's theses are unpalatable but ingeniously defended, he poses a challenge that moral philosophers must meet. The doctrines I claim to find in Hume will thus be important in their own right for reflective thought about the nature of morality.

The book centers on two related theses: that for Hume all virtue and vice are discerned by feeling, and that for him certain virtues and vices are collectively fabricated to compensate for deficiencies in our natural human endowments. Hence it is divided into two parts: "Feeling Virtue" and "Fabricating Virtue".

The first of the two main theses is about Hume's theory of moral discovery and judgment. While all agree that for Hume it is emotion and not reason that discerns good and evil, in what follows I argue that for Hume our moral sentiments of approval and disapproval, with which we make our ethical assessments, are a non-rational source of cognition, in many ways analogous to the senses, and give rise to beliefs about quasi-sensible qualities. The moral sentiments differ from the senses in that approval and disapproval, unlike our sense impressions, are triggered only by a fairly large body of information about a person or a character trait. The moral sentiments resemble the senses in conveying new impressions into the mind from which new ideas and beliefs may be formed. This thesis, which I call the moral sensing view, goes between the horns of a traditional interpretive dilemma: does Hume think moral judgments are mere expressions of emotion, or descriptions of the observer's sentiments? On the moral sensing view, the answer is "neither". Our moral *reactions* are occurrent sentiments, but our moral *judgments* are beliefs: lively ideas copied from the felt sentiments. In developing the moral sensing view and the interpretation of Hume's moral psychology that grounds it, I will argue that the main traditional interpretations of Hume's theory of moral judgment are seriously flawed. The moral sensing view will be found to have affinities with the view that for Hume moral qualities are analogous to secondary qualities (defended by other interpreters such as Stroud and Sturgeon), and also some affinities with the view that for Hume moral qualities are dispositional properties of persons (as others, including Falk, maintain); but it avoids the internal conflicts introduced into Hume's thought by either account of moral judgment. On the moral sensing view, moral judgments are capable of truth even though they arise from sentiment, while moral evaluation remains necessarily connected with motivation. This is a new twist.

There are certain principles that are widely taught as composing Hume's moral psychology and theory of moral judgment.

1. Beliefs alone cannot move us to act.
2. Evaluative propositions cannot be validly inferred from purely factual pro-positions ("Hume's Law").
3. Moral judgments are mere expressions of emotion and have no truth value (noncognitivism).

Each of these views is so closely associated with Hume that it has been called Humeanism, and those who hold one or more of them are called Humeans. As a consequence of the version of Hume's moral psychology developed in the next few chapters, and of the moral sensing interpretation based on it, we see that the historical Hume holds none of them.

The second main thesis of the book concerns Hume's distinction between the natural and the artificial virtues, a distinction that has puzzled Hume scholars and attracted only slight attention from ethical theorists in general, with a few important exceptions. I will argue that this is a distinction between traits that meet the requirements of our commonsense conception of virtue and those that do not. The commonsense conception of virtue is rooted in human nature and based on our natural proclivities to prefer and to approve (and thence to judge good), so we may call it the *natural* conception of virtue. It fits the particular character traits that Hume labels "natural virtues", such as benevolence, parental attentiveness, and gratitude. Successful social life, however, requires us to invent and acquire other character traits that are in tension with these natural proclivities, traits that involve impartiality and enable us to cooperate with people to whom we have no affectionate ties. Among these are honesty with regard to property, faithfulness to promises, and respect for the civil authorities. These do not come naturally to human beings—indeed, to some extent they go against the grain—but without them we cannot get along together. According to Hume, as I interpret him, human beings must devise these new traits and must engage in a beneficial but covert program of systematic social deception to cause these traits to be taken for virtues. On the natural conception, they are not. But Hume himself has a more inclusive definition of virtue according to which they are. Thus the artificial virtues are prosthetic character traits, ones we build to remediate our natural disabilities; and our approval of them is likewise engineered. This fabrication is all to the good. Given Hume's causal account of how moral approval is generated, once the prostheses have been seen to work, we approve them, and so they become Humean virtues. Each artificial virtue bears marks of its synthetic origin in the form of paradoxes about motivation and obligation which Hume investigates. The existence of these paradoxes gives Hume his primary evidence that the virtues in question are man-made and are not virtues in the ordinary sense. In so interpreting Hume's doctrine of the artificial virtues, I challenge the main existing interpretations, which either construe the artificial virtues as manifestations of self-love or greed that has been redirected, or interpret them as being, on Hume's own view, fictions incapable of sustaining scrutiny.

In the recent past it was common to treat Hume as a sloppy writer with prosaic things to say about ethics, except for a few famous points that could safely be evaluated out of context. I think, on the contrary, that Hume is a careful writer with radical things to say about ethics throughout his writings. Consequently, I scrutinize the texts closely, and argue against the positions of other interpreters, in part based on Hume's logic and at times based on his use of particular expressions. Hume is as likely to use a term inconsistently or commit a fallacy as is the next genius of Western philosophy, but not more so.

Hume's ethical theory is built upon his general theory of human nature and knowledge, with all its eighteenth-century peculiarities, and so I keep those doctrines in view in parsing his ethics, in spite of the fact that some of them are very far from what we would accept today. Hume really does think that the mind is furnished with impressions and ideas, and that every simple idea is copied from some impression. He does think that the affections or passions (the emotions or feelings, as we would say today) are impressions, and so are all immediately available to consciousness, though at one point I consider what happens if he relaxes this requirement. He is committed to the thesis that causal connections can be discovered only by experience, and that causal inference is fundamentally different from demonstration. (Here we would be inclined to agree today, but the challenge is to make all Hume says about ethics compatible with this commitment.) He does really think that some passions are direct and some are "indirect" in that they have a more complicated provenance involving not only a cause but also an object, and that the four indirect passions he analyzes are made possible by a double relation of ideas and impressions; and he does think that these four indirect passions do not themselves cause actions. He does actually think (following a tradition dating back to Aquinas) that anger is the desire for harm to those we hate. Some of these positions strike us as quaint, and it is very tempting to recast them as something more palatable to the contemporary philosopher. But if we do this, we may utterly miss the point of arguments he makes about ethics that are based on the original eighteenth-century theses; and these arguments might prove interesting and fruitful to us today. Sometimes a great author can reach important insights starting from premises or concepts we are inclined to reject at the outset, and if we do reject them at the outset, we miss those insights. So where Hume expresses a position, I do my best to pay heed to it and make my interpretation consistent with it if I can.

The *Treatise of Human Nature* is the main focus of this investigation, with a very secondary emphasis on both the *Enquiry concerning the Principles of Morals* and Hume's essays, including the *Dissertation of the Passions*. Occasionally I draw on the *Enquiry concerning Human Understanding*. The *Treatise* is the focus because its treatment of moral matters is detailed and fully argued, and it serves as Hume's springboard for his later moral thought. It is important not to assume that his view does not change over time, however. Where Hume seems to have changed his mind in the moral *Enquiry*, I consider that possibility and speculate about potential reasons; but the paucity of arguments there leaves us with less to go on.

The eighteenth-century Hume of this book does not teach us what twentieth-century emotivists thought he did, but nonetheless he has some lessons for present-day ethical theory. One example is Hume's implicit (and idiosyncratic) understanding of truth in ethical judgment that nonetheless permits a non-contingent connection between ethical evaluation and motivating feelings, something present-day philosophers have thought impossible. Another point, one that follows from Hume's arguments about the artificial virtues, is that we cannot provide a satisfactory account of the virtue of justice without a place for the motive of duty, which is an interesting complication for virtue ethics. Other insights emerge along the way.

In Part I, "Feeling Virtue", the first chapter ("Our Common Reading of Hume's Metaethics") sketches a shared understanding of Hume's metaethics that I believe most philosophers today have absorbed in their training on that subject, parts of which have been elaborated and defended by a number of scholarly interpreters. I call it the *common reading* of Hume's metaethics, because it is our default understanding, one that has shaped the way in which most readers of Hume who have a philosophical education read his text. I include myself in this. Part of the challenge in writing this book has been to free myself from this understanding sufficiently to devise a different one. The common reading is supported in many works one can peruse, and for the most part I do not rehearse the arguments that have been or might be made in its favor (though I do briefly indicate its textual basis). In this chapter I argue that if we accept the common reading, we must concede that there are a great many puzzles and also errors and contradictions in Hume's ethical writings. The problems for the common reading may not be insurmountable, but they certainly provide good reasons to develop a different interpretation that can make better sense of the moral psychology of the *Treatise*.

Chapter 2, "The Causes of Motivating Passions", considers a topic usually called motivation to action, although I argue that the term 'motivation' obscures distinctions that are better made evident. This chapter considers two ways to interpret Hume's understanding of the roles of pleasure and pain, desire and aversion, in the production of motivating passions and so of actions. Its upshot is that even on the most subtle interpretation of the text, the best evidence shows that for Hume beliefs about available pleasure and pain cause new motivating passions and do not merely direct existing passions. Since this is his position, we must rethink what he means when he argues that reason alone is not a motive to the will, and we must reinterpret his arguments to show that moral distinctions are not derived from reason. For on the common reading, those were all based on the claim that no belief can cause a motivating passion without the causal assistance of some prior passion not of its making. And that is not Hume's view.

Chapter 3, "Reason Alone and Moral Discrimination", offers a new account of why Hume thinks reason alone cannot be a motive to the will, and also a new explanation of his claim that moral distinctions are not derived from reason. 'Reason' for Hume is the name of a process or activity, one of comparing perceptions, and given the nature of this activity, no new impression can be its outcome. When he says that no passion or action can be produced by reason alone, he means that none can be produced by the reasoning process without another process. Passions, however, are made by a different process, even when they are caused by beliefs without any independent causal assistance. Thus, although causal inference produces the belief that drinking the cold beverage before me would give me pleasure, and that belief causes me to want to drink it, and this desire in turn causes me to act, neither the desire nor the action is produced by reason alone. Discerning the difference between virtue and vice, good and evil, is also a distinct process from reasoning, since the process of moral discrimination is one that can result in new passions, and the reasoning process cannot do so. The two processes, reasoning and moral discrimination, are not identical.

Chapter 4, "Feeling Virtue and the Reality of Moral Distinctions", considers whether Hume is a moral realist or anti-realist, and presents the moral sensing view as an interpretation of his positive theory of moral judgment. On the moral sensing view Hume is not a noncognitivist; he regards moral sentiments themselves as lacking truth or falsehood, but moral ideas for him can be true or false and are often true, in the full-blooded sense in which any ideas are true. However, the evidence shows that Hume is not a moral realist as that present-day term is most widely understood; and this is consistent with his cognitivism. Thus we see that one form of ethical cognitivism is compatible with moral anti-realism. This position captures some of what appeals to many philosophers about moral anti-realism without having to make the counter-intuitive claim that our moral assessments are without cognitive content, and without having to invent for them a weaker notion of truth than the one we apply to other sorts of discourse.

Chapter 5, "The Common Point of View", addresses the question how an emotion-based theory of moral discrimination, one that in many ways assimilates moral cognition to color sensation, can explain the fundamental expectation that moral evaluations will be widely shared within a community. Hume explains the causal origin of our moral sentiments by means of the mechanism of sympathy, and he completes his account of moral evaluation with an appeal to our use of the common point of view to compensate for the variations in sympathy's workings. The account threatens to become inconsistent, first because it sounds as if Hume is backing off from his claim that moral discrimination is not an activity of reason, and secondly because he seems tacitly to retract his claim that passions (including the moral sentiments) have no representative character. I offer a two-feeling interpretation that removes these inconsistencies. But there is a further puzzle: why do we take the trouble to imagine ourselves to occupy the common point of view? I resolve this by showing that for Hume there is a considerable pressure to filter our moral assessments through the common point of view that comes from the practical demands of social life. We need skill in adopting that imaginative perspective if we are to make reliable predictions about the human beings with whom we interact; and if we cannot make such predictions, we will find ourselves in all sorts of trouble.

This brings us to Part II, "Fabricating Virtue", which is about the artificial virtues and their differences from the natural virtues. Chapter 6, "The Difficulty with the Virtue of Honesty", considers the problem of circularity that Hume claims to find when he attempts to analyze the character trait of honesty with respect to property. It offers an explanation of the paradox Hume identifies and of his solution that, I hope, sheds light on his entire theory of the artificial virtues, showing it to be rather radical at its foundations, though not in its consequences. One of the questions to answer is in what sense honesty is artificial and in what sense it is a virtue. I argue that it is artificial in the sense that the attitudes and behavior that embody it are socially invented and this manufacture is then concealed, so that once the trait is widely internalized, it provides a prosthesis that lets human beings overcome their natural deficiencies. It is a virtue in Hume's own sense, but not according to the natural conception of virtue.

Chapter 7, "Fidelity to Promises and the Peculiar Act of the Mind", considers the artificial virtue of fidelity to promises and contracts. In our commonsense and philosophical thinking about this virtue Hume discerns yet another paradox, besides the circularity problem it shares with honesty about property. The problem with fidelity is that if we understand it as a natural rather than a conventionally created virtue, we have to pretend that the obligation of a promise is the result of some mysterious (and indeed impossible) mental act. I argue that an analysis exactly parallel to the one that allows us to explain what Hume says about honesty explains his remarks about fidelity. It shows why the paradox arises about the "peculiar act of the mind" in the case of fidelity to promises, and how Hume proposes to handle it. The solution emerges from understanding fidelity as another prosthetic virtue whose conventional status is covered up by our tendency to assimilate it to natural virtues. Here I also draw some general conclusions relevant to virtue ethics about the motives or reasons for acting characteristic of someone who has the virtue of fidelity, which seems to me to be a real and important virtue whose nature should be explained by any satisfactory ethics of virtue.

In Chapter 8, "The Shackles of Virtue: Allegiance to Government", we turn to a virtue that is obviously created after the founding of human governments: deference to the civil authorities. There are difficulties in conceiving this as a virtue or even a character trait at all. There is also a fundamental puzzle in political philosophy that interests Hume: that of how masses of people can ever, by any means, be induced to obey the laws or their rulers, given that the people are so much more numerous than the enforcers. I argue that Hume's account overcomes these difficulties and is consistent with the rest of his understanding of the artificial virtues. In this case Hume identifies yet another fundamental human disability (the preference for the near-term good over the distant but greater good) that can be outmaneuvered by collectively fabricating a character trait and manufacturing approval of it (using our natural tendencies as raw materials). The disability is different, and so the prosthesis is different, but the basic strategy is the same. In a coda to this chapter, I propose that Hume's general picture of the artificial virtues could be expanded to include others. Since each artificial virtue is an invention designed to remedy some natural human deficiency, it might be possible to fabricate other artificial virtues to remedy further natural inabilities to cope well with changing conditions.

Finally, in the concluding chapter, "Criticizing Hume's List of Virtues and Vices", I take up the question whether Hume sees himself as merely a psychologist describing the human mind and its moral proclivities, or also as an advocate for a particular way of life or list of virtues and vices that should replace its competitors, and so a potential critic of socially accepted lists of virtues and vices. This is one of the most difficult interpretive questions about Hume's ethics, and I do not investigate all its ramifications. But I argue that Hume makes normative claims on behalf of the traits he lists as virtues and vices, and that his moral theory provides readers with some grounds on which to criticize the shared ethical standards of a particular society or historical era, though not adequate grounds to enable a reader to make all the criticisms he or she might wish to make.

PART I

FEELING VIRTUE

1

Our Common Reading of Hume's Metaethics

We philosophers are confident that we know Hume's metaethical position. We are sure that for Hume moral evaluation is a matter of sentiment, not reason. And most of us believe that Hume is committed to three more specific positions:

1. Mere cognitive states such as beliefs cannot move us to action; we also need a desire or other connative or affective state. (Call this thesis the Motivational Inertia of Belief.)
2. Moral judgments are not cognitive states or representations, but mere feelings or expressions of feeling; they do not assert propositions or represent states of affairs, and can be neither true nor false. (This is ethical noncognitivism.)
3. Evaluative judgments cannot be inferred or deduced from any set of purely factual premises. (This is the logical fact/value gap.)

Whatever we take to be the merits or demerits of these theses, most philosophers claim to find them in Hume's *Treatise of Human Nature*. The first, the principle of the motivational impotence of belief, is standardly called Humeanism about motivation, and is usually treated as an obvious truth in the philosophy of action. The second is reverently attributed to Hume by almost all who call themselves noncognitivists or expressivists (or emotivists, or non-propositionalists), and also (less reverently) by their opponents. The third thesis has been called "Hume's Law", and the fact–value gap it articulates is almost universally traced to Hume's paragraph about 'is' and 'ought' at *Treatise* 3.1.1.[1]

---

[1] Some of the many interpreters who attribute the Motivational Inertia of Belief to Hume are Foot (1963); Harrison (1976: ch. 1); Stroud (1977: ch. 7, e.g., pp. 167–8) (though he argues that Hume does not succeed in establishing it); Mackie (1980: ch. 3); Snare (1991: chs. 2 and 3); Bricke (1996: ch. 1); Shaw (1998: ch. 2; see, e.g., p. 56); Radcliffe (1999); and Baillie (2000: ch. 4). (Some but certainly not all of these authors attribute all three features of the common reading to Hume.) Among the systematic "Humeans" about motivation who are committed to the Inertia of Belief Thesis or a refined form of it are Davidson (1980: 3–4) (at least with regard to explicable, intentional actions); Goldman (1970); Williams (1981a); Smith (1987; 1994: ch. 4; 2004: Part I, *passim*, e.g. chs. 1 and 8); and various writers influenced by rational choice theory. Among the variety of noncognitivist interpreters of Hume are Antony Flew (1963); Blackburn (1984: ch. 6; 1993); Snare (1991); Bricke (1996); and many other writers who interpret Hume this way *en passant*; e.g., Thomson who rejects noncognitivism, quotes Hume in *T* 3.1.1 as giving the most promising defense of emotivism, a species of noncognitivism (Harman and Thomson, 1996). A number of Hume scholars have questioned the noncognitivist interpretation, as we shall see, but it remains dominant among non-specialists. Systematic noncognitivists who cite Hume as their role model

These theses are attributed to Hume by a widely shared interpretation that has shaped our understanding of the text for a long time. It is a relatively recent one—for the most part less than 100 years old—but so dominant that it is difficult to read Hume's metaethics without experiencing its influence. These three specific claims have certainly not gone unchallenged; interpreters have given arguments over the years to show that Hume is not committed to each of them. But these claims are consequences of an over-all reading of Hume's works that nonetheless retains much of its influence over how we understand his ethical writings. Even those who challenge one aspect of it tend to preserve the rest of the picture, and it is striking how much it still shapes present-day scholarship and teaching. In this chapter I sketch the shared interpretation from which these three claims follow, which we may call the *common reading*, and point out some of the fissures and tensions it appears to leave in the text of the *Treatise*. If Hume is arguing as we suppose in the common reading, then his discussions of moral psychology and metaethics are at various points puzzling, sloppy, conceptually discontinuous, fallacious, self-contradictory, or in conflict with other parts of his philosophy. Of course, this may simply be so. Hume may be a great iconoclastic genius in metaphysics and epistemology, but a clumsy and inconsistent ethical theorist. However, one hopes to do better for Hume. Most of the problems raised by the common reading (and mentioned in this chapter) have long been noticed by Hume's interpreters, who try to remove them with inventive variations on the common reading, with limited success. A few have not received attention before. Some are less severe than others, but as a group they give us a powerful reason to seek a different interpretation, one according to which Hume's ethical thought is less flawed. In the succeeding chapters I offer an alternative way to read Hume's discussions of motives and morals that I believe does him more justice. It reveals him to have a metaethical theory that is original, precise, and largely coherent and consistent with the rest of his philosophy, whether or not we find it ultimately satisfactory—one that is rather different from what we supposed.

Of course, Hume does, without doubt, espouse some theses that sound to the present-day reader a great deal like the three claims above. Hume does deny that *reason alone* can produce or prevent actions, or on its own cause emotions (passions) that generate action. He vehemently rejects moral rationalism, the view that moral good and evil are discovered by reason alone and consist in the accordance or conflict of actions with reason. And he denies (or dramatically

include Hare (1952 and 1963), Blackburn 1984, and Gibbard (1990), though in their later works (Blackburn 1998 and Gibbard 2003) Blackburn's and Gibbard's versions of expressivism no longer count as noncognitivism, since they propose a special sense of 'truth' according to which moral judgments can be true. On reading the is–ought passage as proclaiming Hume's Law (the Logical Fact–Value Gap), see Nowell-Smith (1954: 36); Hare (1952: 28–9; 1963: 108–9); Mackie (1980: 69), and Flew (1986: 148–9). So many philosophers assert the impossibility of inferring evaluative conclusions from purely factual premises that it is treated as an axiom of moral philosophy in many introductory textbooks.

doubts) that solely by reasoning from the relations of propositions typically expressed with 'is' we can infer relations of propositions typically expressed with 'ought'. But these three positions need not be equivalent to the three listed above. The common reading so construes them, but perhaps it gets Hume wrong.

THE COMMON READING

Like others who were trained as academic philosophers, I was educated to take the common reading of Hume's metaethics for granted. I have found it very hard to break free of its hold, and can slip back into reading Hume that way without noticing it. For philosophers it is rather like the views of "the vulgar" about sense perception or causation—when we leave our studies, we resume those ways of thinking. However, unlike the latter beliefs, the common reading of Hume can be resisted.

First it helps to know its general basis.

The common reading focuses on an argument in *Treatise* 3.1.1 that we may call Argument M.[2] In one of Hume's many statements of it he says:

1. "Morals . . . have an influence on the actions and affections."
2. "Reason alone . . . can never have any such influence."
3. "It follows, that [morals] cannot be deriv'd from reason . . ." (*T* 3.1.1.6 / SBN 457).

It is tempting to read Argument M as follows:

A. Moral judgments move us to act.
B. Beliefs alone cannot move us to act.
C. Therefore moral judgments are not (mere) beliefs.[3]

This is a simple, valid argument, although its premises need support. But the common reading cannot emerge this quickly. First, this is not what Hume's premises literally say. Argument M quoted above (and which he gives over and over, with slightly varying wording) never mentions belief, but is about *reason*. For Hume reason and belief are not identical; the connection between them must be explained. Furthermore, Hume's stated conclusion in Argument M is not about the content or representational status of moral judgments (thought of as beliefs, opinions, or expressions of propositions). In its many repetitions, it talks only about the *origin* or *derivation* of *morals* or *moral distinctions*,

---

[2] In my articles since 1989 I have called this the Motivation Argument, but as we will see in the next chapter, the use of the term 'motivation' is ill-advised. The argument intends to show that morals cannot be derived from reason. Snare calls it the Influence Argument.

[3] For example, Harrison says that it is "fairly obvious" that Hume was right in thinking that "beliefs cannot alone move us to action, but simply inform us how desires can be satisfied" (1976: 6), which gives us premise B.

and not about the status of moral judgments, opinions, or sentences. So the common reading has to explain how it is that what Hume really means is not so different from the quick caricature in (A)–(C). Although the textual and philosophical grounds for this assimilation are not always given, they can be made explicit.

One premise of Argument M says that reason alone cannot "influence", or "produce or prevent", passions, volitions, or actions. Call this the Inertia of Reason Thesis, since Hume at one point summarizes it by saying that "reason is perfectly inert" (*T* 3.1.1.8 / SBN 457–8). (Note that it is distinct from the Inertia of Belief Thesis—so far.) The common reading understands this Inertia of Reason Thesis as supported primarily by an argument from *Treatise* 2.3.3, paragraphs 2–3 (SBN 413–14). There are two kinds of reasoning or operations of the understanding, this argument says: demonstrative inference and causal or probable inference. Neither of these actually generates an impulse to act. Demonstrative reasoning confines itself to the domain of ideas, which is removed from that of realities, where the will resides; hence it generates no motives. It provides believed ideas that are used by probable or causal reason. Causal inference is of course useful in determining efficacious means to our ends; but we find that if we are indifferent both to the cause and its effect, discovery of their connection by causal reasoning produces no passion or action. Rather, causal reasoning simply directs desire or aversion to the means of satisfaction it has identified. Therefore reason alone cannot cause passions or actions. This argument we may call the DC Argument, for demonstrative and causal (reasoning), or "divide and conquer".

The Inertia of Reason Thesis that results from this DC Argument is construed by the common reading to say not only that the faculty of reason itself cannot produce passions or actions, nor only that the process of reasoning or inference alone cannot produce passions or actions, but also that the *products* of that faculty or process cannot do so. Reason, on the common interpretation, produces our beliefs; those are its outcomes. When Hume claims in the DC Argument that the discovery of a causal relation alone cannot produce actions or the passions that give rise to them if we are indifferent to the cause and to the effect, the common reading interprets him as intending at least the following: a *belief* that A causes B cannot produce any passion or action by itself, without the help of some separate and causally independent passion directed to object A or object B—some emotion or feeling that is not caused by the belief that A causes B but comes into existence in another way. Thus, beliefs on their own have no access to the will. The Inertia of Reason thesis becomes the Inertia of Belief Thesis.

On the common reading, the other premise of Argument M, that morals have an influence on the actions and affections, is construed to say that the moral evaluations we make—the states of mind constituting our moral judgments—do produce passions and actions, and do so *alone*. What this appears to mean is that they do so without assistance from any (distinct) passions such as desires or aversions. This is a view sometimes called moral judgment internalism. It says that when we judge that an action is obligatory, the recognition of obligation is sufficient on its own to motivate action. So, for example, if we recognize that it is obligatory to save a child from drowning, that in itself can move us to do so; we do not need a separate desire to do whatever is morally obligatory, or any other separate desire, in order to be moved to save the child.

The conclusion of Argument M is then taken to say that moral judgments (or evaluations, or convictions) are not produced by reason. Since the Inertia of Reason premise was construed to assert or imply the Inertia of Belief Thesis, that the products of reason—beliefs—cannot cause passions or actions, what Hume must mean by the concluding claim that moral judgments are not products of our reason is that they are not beliefs. For if moral judgments were beliefs, they would be produced in us by reason, the common reading supposes. Since no moral judgments are produced by reason, they are not beliefs. Since they are not beliefs, they are not representations of any reality, but psychological states of some other sort. Hence they cannot be true or false. So the conclusion of Argument M, on the common reading, is ethical noncognitivism.[4]

The common reading finds confirmation of its interpretation in the paragraph about 'is' and 'ought' that ends *Treatise* 3.1.1. There, according to this reading, Hume says that it is fallacious to infer moral or other evaluative conclusions from purely factual premises. It is evident to inspection that such inferences are logical *non sequiturs*. But if moral judgments were beliefs or factual assertions, then they could be inferred from factual premises. Therefore they are not beliefs or factual assertions. Unlike beliefs, they lack representational content, and are not truth-evaluable. This insight "subvert[s] all the vulgar systems of morality" (*T* 3.1.1.27 / SBN 469–70).

On this interpretation, Hume is indeed committed to the three metaethical positions with which I began: the motivational impotence of belief without desire or aversion, ethical noncognitivism, and the logical fact–value gap.[5]

---

[4] As an anonymous reader rightly points out, over the last several years a number of Hume scholars (perhaps the most explicit is Sturgeon (2001)) have rejected the noncognitivist interpretation of Hume. It has long had a competitor in the propositional descriptive interpretation as well (that moral judgments describe the speaker's actual or hypothetical feelings—see ch. 4). So in the common reading, noncognitivism is less common than the other theses. But what such commentators generally have not done is explain how to avoid this way of construing the premises of Argument M. If this is what the premises are taken to mean, then the argument commits Hume to noncognitivism, even if this is not the best way to understand the rest of his moral philosophy.

[5] What I call the common reading is (of course) a distillation of the interpretations of many philosophers, including both Hume scholars and philosophers not primarily interested in textual interpretation. Obviously my sketch of the textual basis for it is brief and superficial. For a more thorough defense of it as an interpretation, see Harrison 1976; Mackie 1980; Stroud 1977 (to some extent); Snare 1991 (to some extent); and Bricke 1996. For an exposition for students with many marks of the common reading, see Radcliffe 2000. Many objections have been made to parts of it in recent years, though not, to my knowledge, to the whole picture.

DEFICIENCIES IN THE COMMON PICTURE

So far the common reading looks reasonable. But we will find that it leaves many of the things that Hume says unexplained, and also leaves him either making weak arguments or contradicting himself. When we attempt to provide explanations for the lengthy, related discussions in the *Treatise* that surround the DC Argument, Argument M, and the is–ought paragraph, more tensions and incoherencies emerge. There are five main areas to which we should attend.

1. The DC Argument

On the common reading, the DC Argument is Hume's chief support for his thesis that reason is inert. But while its form is that of a disjunctive (or separation of cases) type of inference, it is more a re-description of what occurs in motivation to action than an argument. It simply claims that neither demonstrative nor causal reasoning generates any impulse. This sounds plausible enough, and we find ourselves nodding. But what proof does it offer?

Looking for the proof, we face an interpretive dilemma. Is the DC Argument intended as an argument a priori to the conclusion that reason as such cannot possibly cause any motivating passion? Or is it intended as an empirical argument to the effect that we do not observe any impulses to arise from reason alone? Either option leaves Hume in difficulties.

If the argument is offered a priori, then in using it Hume contradicts his conclusion in Book 1 that no causal relation can be discovered or ruled out a priori, and that no causal relation holds necessarily (at least for all we can know). For the DC Argument is an argument about what the two kinds of reason, demonstrative and causal, can *cause*. Motivation to action, for Hume, is a species of causation. The argument says that neither kind of reasoning can cause any impulse to act or motivating passion. But in principle, Hume has said, "[a]nything can cause anything. Creation, annihilation, motion, reason, volition; all these may arise from one another" (*T* 1.3.15.1 / SBN 173). At *T* 3.1.1 he wields this against his rationalist opponent, reminding us that "it has been shown, in treating of the understanding, that there is no connexion of cause and effect . . . which is discoverable otherwise than by experience, and of which we can pretend to have any security by the simple consideration of the objects" (*T* 3.1.1.22 / SBN 466). Thus if we are to read this passage about the two types of reasoning as a proof that reason alone *cannot* cause passions or actions, in principle, then we must suppose that Hume argues in a way he classifies as unsound, not only in the previous book but also in the next one.

The alternative is to read the DC Argument as an empirical observation, a Humean thought-experiment about the passions and the will, in which we find that in fact there is no regular conjunction of reason and the impulse to act. Its conclusion in that case is contingent: while it is not a conceptual truth that reason generates no impulse, we have no experience that it ever actually does. But in that case the argument is both slapdash by Hume's standards and unconvincing. When Hume sets out in Book 2 to argue from experience that a passion of a certain type (pride or hatred, for example) has a particular cause or directs the mind to a particular idea (its object), he proceeds with great care. He confirms his elaborate introspective analysis of the causes and effects of pride, humility, love, and hatred with detailed "experiments" that require us to vary systematically the nature of an imagined object and its relation to the observer, and to take note of what passions result. In these experiments we draw on our extensive experience of our own prior passions, but not willy-nilly; we hold certain features of the situation fixed and imagine that others are altered so as to perceive the changes that would occur. In the DC Argument we see none of that; just a breezy observation that "'tis evident . . . that the impulse arises not from reason", and that "It can never in the least concern us to know, that some objects are causes, and some others effects, if both the causes and effects be indifferent to us" (*T* 2.3.3.3 / SBN 414). Doesn't it concern us, though, if the connection is singular and surprising? (Suppose I learn that a cat's sneezing in Albany, New York, causes a volcanic eruption on one of Jupiter's moons. Each is indifferent to me, but discovering their relation might well move me to act.) More importantly, there seem to be many experienced instances of choosing a course of action on the basis of what we take to be reason rather than passion, "following the head rather than the heart", as we often say, and also of using our reason to resist the promptings of passion. The descriptions of opposition between reason and passion made by "the greatest part of moral philosophy, antient and modern" are plausible because of the familiarity of such experiences. Until now it has seemed to us that reason triggered an impulse to act or at least blocked one on many occasions. Certainly the conclusions of various stretches of reasoning have been correlated with impulses and actions. If in those experiences we conflate reason with calm passion, as Hume goes on to claim, how are we to observe by experience that we make this mistake? Where is the perceptible difference here between reason and a calm passion? There may be one, but Hume does not point it out. As an empirical argument, then, this one is inadequate.[6]

2. The Inertia Thesis and the Causal Power of Belief

As we saw, the common reading attributes to Hume the Inertia of Belief Thesis: not only does the reasoning faculty or process alone not cause passion, but also beliefs (its products) alone can neither cause any actions directly nor cause any motivating passion (such as desire or aversion) that might in turn cause action.

---

[6] Most of these criticisms appear in Cohon 1988.

But Hume seems to say explicitly that belief causes desire and aversion as well as other motivating passions. In the DC Argument itself, at the start of his discussion of causal reasoning, he says that "when we have the prospect of pain or pleasure from any object, we feel a consequent emotion of aversion or propensity, and are carry'd to avoid or embrace what will give us this uneasiness or satisfaction" (*T* 2.3.3.3 / SBN 414). The prospect of pain or pleasure would certainly seem to be the belief (the lively idea) that pain or pleasure is available from an object, and this belief causes motivating "aversion or propensity". Before our rational discovery of causal relations can come in to direct the aversion or propensity that is present in us to appropriate means of fulfillment, the impulse itself apparently arises from a belief. He repeats this later in the same paragraph, and says similar things later in *T* 2.3.3. He remarks that in certain cases "a passion, such as hope or fear, grief or joy, despair or security, is founded on the supposition of the existence of objects" (*T* 2.3.3.6 / SBN 416). And abandoning a belief that we discover to be false eliminates the motivating passion and volition entirely. While reason and passion can never "dispute for the government of the will and actions, . . . [t]he moment we perceive the falsehood of any supposition [of the existence of a pleasant or painful object], or the insufficiency of any means, our passions yield to our reason without any opposition" (*T* 2.3.3.7 / SBN 416). Thus when reasoning reveals the falsehood of our belief, we cease to believe, and once we do, passion consequently disappears. Now if we cease to believe that a certain means is efficacious and so cease to desire that means, our desire for the end may remain. But if we cease to believe that the end is pleasant, our desire for the end ceases also. Belief alone entirely silences passion.

We find the same thought in *Treatise* 3.1.1, where Hume grants that "[a] person may be affected with passion, by supposing a pain or pleasure to lie in an object", and even that "reason, in a strict and philosophical sense, can have an influence on our conduct . . . when it excites a passion by informing us of the existence of something which is a proper object of it" (*T* 3.1.1.12 / SBN 459). Apparently *reason* can excite a passion by generating a belief.

Nor is the acknowledgment of the motivating power of belief limited to Books 2 and 3. Hume apparently embraces it in 1.3.10, "Of the influence of belief". He observes that *impressions* of pleasure and pain "actuate the soul", and notes that some *ideas* of pleasure and pain do so as well. The difference between ideas that generate motives and those that do not is that those that cause motivating passions are beliefs—in particular, ideas of the likely existence of future pains and pleasures, but ones that approach impressions in their force and liveliness.

We find by experience, that the ideas of those [pleasant or painful] objects, which we believe either are or will be existent, produce in a lesser degree the same effect with those impressions, which are immediately present to the senses and perception . . . . The effect, then, of belief is to raise up a simple idea to an equality with our impressions, and bestow on it a like influence on the passions.   (*T* 1.3.10.3 / SBN 119–20)

If Hume really concludes from the DC Argument that beliefs alone do not (or perhaps, cannot) produce motivating passions, it seems that he contradicts what he says within that argument, as well as in Books 1 and 3.[7]

It may be possible for the common reading to explain away these passages, but it will take some ingenuity. The usual strategy is to grant that Hume of course thinks that belief has some influence on passion and action, but to assure us that even in these passages no impulse is produced by belief *alone*. In the next chapter I consider the prospects of success for such an effort. On the surface, however, there is a serious tension here.

3. The Representation Argument

The common reading tends to view the Inertia of Reason Thesis through the lens of the DC Argument in the way indicated. But there is another argument in support of the Inertia of Reason Thesis, the Representation Argument, on which Hume himself seems to place greater weight. In its first and simpler version it appears as follows:

> A passion is an original existence, or, if you will, modification of existence, and contains not any representative quality, which renders it a copy of any other existence or modification. When I am angry, I am actually possest with the passion, and in that emotion have no more a reference to any other object, than when I am thirsty, or sick, or more than five foot high. 'Tis impossible, therefore, that this passion can be oppos'd by, or be contradictory to truth and reason; since this contradiction consists in the disagreement of ideas, consider'd as copies, with those objects, which they represent. (*T* 2.3.3.5 / SBN 415)

In *Treatise* 3.1.1 Hume repeats this argument in an expanded form. He supplies more detail about the work of reason and the nature of truth: "Reason is the discovery of truth or falsehood. Truth or falsehood consists in an agreement or disagreement either to the *real* relations of ideas, or to *real* existence and matter of fact." And he applies the argument not only to passions but to volitions and (importantly) actions: "our passions, volitions and actions . . . [are] original facts and realities, compleat in themselves, and implying no reference to other passions, volitions and actions" (*T* 3.1.1.9 / SBN 458).

It is fairly clear how Hume is arguing. Passions, volitions, and actions as such are not signs or symbols of a reality beyond them. They do not stand for anything else. In particular, they are not copies of other items, as ideas are copies of the impressions that cause them (and that they consequently represent). Passions and volitions, of course, are impressions and not ideas, in Hume's system (*T* 2.1.1.1 / SBN 275; *T* 2.3.1.2 / SBN 399). Actions are certainly not ideas either, and in general do not purport to represent anything (though of

---

[7] On the continuity of *T* 1.3.10 with *T* 2.3.3, see Tweyman 1974: 134, and especially Baier 1991: 157–9. For the allegation of inconsistency between this and the Inertia of Belief Thesis, see Cohon 1997*c* and Persson 1997.

course there are some symbolic actions). But truth and falsehood consist in the agreement or disagreement of their possessors "consider'd as copies" with the originals they are thought to represent. Therefore passions, volitions, and actions cannot be true or false, logical or illogical, conformable with or contradictory to reason, for they are not representations. They are not the sorts of items that can be conclusions of inferences, whether demonstrative or probable.

This argument, Hume claims,

> proves *directly*, that actions do not derive their merit from a conformity to reason, nor their blame from a contrariety to it; and it proves the same truth more indirectly, by shewing us, that as reason can never immediately prevent or produce any action by contradicting or approving of it, it cannot be the source of the distinction betwixt moral good and evil, which are found to have that influence.   (*T* 3.1.1.10 / SBN 458)

In the part of this passage following the semicolon, Hume claims that the Representation Argument shows that reason cannot produce or prevent action (that it establishes the Inertia of Reason Thesis). The Representation Argument is supposed to establish this key premise of Argument M, the argument he here calls the "indirect" proof and states for at least the second time here and once more in this paragraph.

But the conclusion of the Representation Argument is merely that passions, volitions, and actions cannot be reasonable or true, unreasonable or false. On the common reading, however, the Inertia of Reason Thesis says more: that reason and belief cannot cause passions or actions. How are these related? The Representation Argument is manifestly not an argument about the causes or effects of passions or actions. It is not empirical but explicitly conceptual; it points out that passions and actions are of the wrong ontological category to be true or reasonable. All this could be so even if reason and beliefs had the capacity to *cause* both passions and actions. Presumably reason is a faculty of the mind and beliefs are mental states; and these might well cause other occurrences in the mind and body, regardless of whether those events can be classed as reasonable or unreasonable, true or false.[8] Nothing in the Representation Argument rules this out. Hence this supposedly "conclusive" argument for the Inertia of Reason Thesis (understood as the Motivational Inertia of Belief Thesis) falls far short of establishing it. Indeed, given the common reading, the Representation Argument, far from proving a necessary premise for Argument M, as Hume claims, is irrelevant to it.

Hume's additional claim (before the semicolon) that the Representation Argument also proves *directly* that actions do not derive their moral merit from conformity to reason underlines its irrelevance to the Inertia of Reason premise. That little proof says:

---

[8] Stroud 1977: 161; Cohon 1988, 1997*c*.

Actions may be laudable or blameable; but they cannot be reasonable or unreasonable:
Laudable or blameable, therefore, are not the same with reasonable or unreasonable.
(ibid.)

Here he makes explicit use of the precise conclusion of the Representation
Argument, that actions cannot be reasonable or unreasonable. It works perfectly
well here, as a premise in the "direct" argument. But this is somehow supposed
to be the same thesis that figures as a premise in Argument M as it appears in
Hume's next three sentences:

The merit and demerit of actions frequently contradict, and sometimes controul our
natural propensities. But reason has no such influence. Moral distinctions, therefore, are
not the offspring of reason.

So the claim that actions cannot be reasonable or unreasonable is supposed to be
equivalent to the claim that reason "has no such influence"—that is, that it does
not contradict or control our natural propensities. On the common reading, the
latter claim is that it is impossible for a belief to cause a passion or an action;
but this is certainly not equivalent to the claim that no passion or action can be
reasonable. Thus Hume is just wrong about that.

   Now, we could attempt a solution to this puzzle within the context of the
common reading. Might Hume perhaps think that causation by reason or by
belief, if there were such a thing, would have to be a species of entailment or, more
precisely, an instance of being caused to believe some conclusion as the result of
noticing an entailment? The moral rationalists claim that reason produces desires
and actions; but reason is the faculty of inference, so perhaps they mean by this
that some rationally supported premises we possess entail or imply passions and
actions, and so reason produces passions and actions that way. If this were Hume's
intent, it would make the Representation Argument relevant to Argument M.
We could read the Representation Argument to say that the special form of
causation belonging to reason, the causation of a new belief by the recognition
that an idea is entailed by other believed ideas, is not a type of causation that
can produce passions or actions, since these, not being representations, are of the
wrong ontological category to be entailed by any ideas. So far this seems a good
prospect, and would reflect credit on Hume. But if this is what Hume means in
Argument M by the Inertia Thesis—that reason cannot cause passions or actions
as it causes beliefs, by proving to us their truth, then Argument M contains a
fatal equivocation between its two premises, an equivocation on the concept of
production or influence. For Argument M would now read as follows:

1. Moral judgments produce passions and actions.
2. Reason alone cannot produce passions and actions by entailment from
   premises.
3. Therefore reason alone cannot produce moral judgments by entailment from
   premises.

The Inertia of Reason Thesis (premise 2) on this construal says that reason is not able to cause actions by proving their truth—by entailment. If premise 1 said that moral judgments do produce actions by proving their truth (whatever that might mean), then the argument would be valid, because entailment is transitive. That is, if moral judgments entail actions, but reason does not, then it would follow that reason does not entail moral judgments (for if it did, reason would entail actions, in two steps). But the first premise, which says that moral judgments can cause actions, surely does not mean that moral judgments cause actions by proving their truth! Hume thinks that moral judgments or distinctions influence the will; but since he has just argued in his Representation Argument that actions have no truth to be established, he cannot mean by this that moral distinctions give rise to actions by establishing those actions' truth—not to mention that to say this would be contrary to his whole spirit. What Hume must mean, then, in saying that moral judgments produce actions is that they bring them about in some other way, not by proving their truth. But if that is what the premise about the potency of moral judgments says, then it does not follow from these premises that reason cannot produce moral judgments. Reason might prove the truth of moral judgments, deriving them from premises we accept and making us believe them; and those moral judgments might in turn cause us to act by way of a different causal mechanism. So this attempt to construct a logical connection between the Representation Argument and Argument M proves unfortunate for Hume.[9]

Another puzzling feature of this text is that Hume claims that the Direct Argument and Argument M prove "the same truth", "that actions do not derive their merit from a conformity to reason, nor their blame from a contrariety to it". So he also thinks their conclusions equivalent. But while the conclusion of the Direct Argument is that goodness is not the same property as reasonableness, on the common reading the conclusion of Argument M is something quite different: that moral judgments are not caused by reason and (so) are not beliefs. There are two discontinuities here—two confusions of which Hume is guilty on the common reading. First, he would have to conflate something's being itself reasonable with something's being the causal product of the faculty of reason or its activity. One might naturally suppose that "X is a product of reason" and "X is reasonable" are equivalent, and perhaps this is what the common reading unwittingly does. But we have seen that for Hume they cannot be equivalent, since the faculty of reason or its activity could, for all we know, cause something (such as a passion or a bodily change) that is incapable of truth or falsehood, and so is neither reasonable nor unreasonable. Secondly, Hume would have to

---

[9] I point out this equivocation problem in Cohon 1988, 1997c, and we point it out in Cohon and Owen 1997. Ingmar Persson (1997) identifies it independently. Stroud (1977) is helpful on many of Hume's arguments in these passages, but as far as I can tell does not try to explain the alleged connection between the Representation Argument and Argument M. Mackie (1980: 55) identifies a different but related problem regarding how the first of these arguments is to provide a premise for the second.

conflate a claim about the properties of good and evil with a claim about which states of mind have propositional or representational status. For on the common reading these two conclusions (of the Direct Argument and of Argument M) are not even about the same subject: one is about the properties of good and evil and what they consist in (the non-identity of the properties goodness and reasonableness, evil and unreasonableness), the other about the semantic status of moral judgments (whether moral judgments are truth-evaluable). The common reading presumably must say that Hume confuses these.

4. The Epistemic/Ontological Arguments

On the common reading, when Hume asserts that morals are not derived from reason, what he means in part is that the moral judgments we make do not have cognitive content. Thus our moral judgments do not actually predicate any properties of the people and actions that we judge. But more than half of the section of the *Treatise* where he ostensibly advocates this thesis is devoted to two extended arguments intended to make an epistemic point: that reason alone cannot discover moral properties (virtue and vice, good and evil, right and wrong) because of some key ontological features of moral properties that he tries to establish. He argues that the moral goodness and evil of actions do not essentially consist either in (the making of) certain true or false (non-moral) judgments related to them or in any relations discoverable by reason; and because this is not what moral properties are, they cannot be known by reason alone.

This yields a puzzle. If Hume takes himself already to have shown in Argument M that moral judgments do not describe any properties of actions or persons at all (since they do not describe anything), why does he devote many pages and much ingenuity to arguing that the essence of moral properties cannot consist in the truth and falsehood of various causal or existence judgments and cannot consist in various types of relations? If the common reading is correct, Hume has already proven in Argument M (in its many repetitions) that moral judgments do not describe any properties, since moral judgments are not beliefs and do not express propositions. So there is little point to his extended efforts thereafter to prove negative theses either about the ontological status of moral qualities (they are not relations) or about their epistemic status (they are not known or discovered by reason alone).

Consider the nature of two specific arguments in the *Treatise*. The first is Hume's rejoinder to something he supposes a moral rationalist might say in his own defense:

But perhaps it may be said, that tho' no will or action can be immediately contradictory to reason, yet we may find such a contradiction in some of the attendants of the action, that is, in its causes or effects. The action may cause a judgment, or may be *obliquely* caus'd by one . . . and by an abusive way of speaking . . . the same contrariety may . . . be ascribed to the action. How far this truth or falsehood may be the source of morals, 'twill now be proper to consider.   (*T* 3.1.1.11 / SBN 459)

Hume argues that while the judgments that cause and are indirectly caused by actions can indeed be called unreasonable or false, " 'tis impossible such a mistake can ever be the original source of immorality" (*T* 3.1.1.14 / SBN 460). The falsehood of the judgment is not what makes the action immoral.

The second, longer argument intends to show that it is not the case that "the understanding [is] alone capable of fixing the boundaries of right and wrong". It shows this by noting that if the understanding were capable of doing so, then "the character of virtuous and vicious either must lie in some relations of objects, or must be a matter of fact, which is discover'd by our reason" (*T* 3.1.1.18 / SBN 463), and then demonstrating in great detail that moral properties cannot consist in relations of this sort, whether abstract or causal. One of his chief sub-arguments here is that were vice and virtue to consist in abstract relations that can be known by reason alone, the relations that constitute them would need to fulfill certain specific requirements, and no relation can satisfy those requirements. When a particular relation is proposed, Hume notes its failure to fulfill one of these requirements by observing that if this relation were what constituted vice, nonhuman animals or plants would be capable of vice, which is absurd.

The problem for the common reading here is not that there is any incompatibility between the noncognitivist conclusion attributed to Argument M and the gist of these ontological/epistemic arguments. The theses that, on the one hand, there are no such properties as virtue and vice, and that, on the other hand, virtue does not consist in any relation and cannot be discovered by reason, are logically compatible. The first entails the other two.[10] The problem is that once Hume has established the first, global thesis, his effort to refute the specific points of detail seems entirely otiose. It is as if he had proven something to be true of all even numbers already, and then spent the next six pages proving some small portion of that theorem to hold for the numbers 12 and 42, using different arguments. Why bother? Furthermore, the concepts he deploys in those later arguments, such as that of the "essence" or "first spring or original source of all immorality" (*T* 3.1.1.15 / SBN 461), seem to have been ruled out as without referents by Argument M. It is strange to reintroduce such concepts in order vigorously to defend some very small-scale corollaries of the sweeping thesis that was already proven. It is true that he is directly challenging the positions of some of his contemporaries and recent predecessors in this passage, such as William Wollaston and Samuel Clarke, but why whittle away at them with minutiae if he believes he could refute them in a single grand stroke?

---

[10] Strictly speaking, the common reading attributes to Hume not the thesis that there are no such properties as virtue and vice (as I say in the text), but that in predicating virtue and vice of objects we do not attribute any properties to the objects or describe any facts. I substitute this simpler phrase for the more cumbersome one.

5. The Is–Ought Paragraph

It was noted long ago that Hume himself seems to make inferences from factual statements to moral evaluations, in particular reasoning from the premise "justice is beneficial to all members of society" or "justice, on reflection, produces the sentiment of approbation in those who consider it without bias", to the conclusion "justice is a virtue".[11] The same type of inference is very evident in some of his more controversial claims about individual virtues and vices, as where he argues in some detail that well-concealed pride is actually a virtue and no vice because it is beneficial to oneself and does no harm to others, and so is in fact approved, while abject humility (as distinct from modesty) is in fact a vice, since it is harmful to its possessor. It is also implicit in his attention to the potential objections to his sympathy-based account of the generation of the moral sentiments in *Treatise* 3.3.1, where he worries that since we sympathize more with a nearby victim of murder than with one far away, this seems to imply (on his theory) that we feel a stronger sentiment of disapprobation toward the nearby perpetrator, and therefore it might follow that a murder in our own neighborhood is more vicious than one far away. Hume takes himself to be arguing that since a trait or action evokes disapprobation in human beings, it is therefore a vice, and its vice is proportioned to the amount of disapprobation it evokes; that is why the variations in sympathy pose a problem. The tendency to make inferences from factual observations about human sentiments to moral conclusions is also revealed in his argument that justice, though artificial, is nonetheless a virtue, because while it is indeed created by human ingenuity, it naturally produces approbation by means of sympathy with the whole of society. Indeed, much of the *Treatise* and of the second *Enquiry* is in each case an extended inference from factual premises (ones that describe what all agree are facts about human character and sentiments) to moral conclusions (ones that make crucial use of the word 'virtue' or 'vice'). Yet, according to the common reading, Hume argues in the final paragraph of *Treatise* 3.1.1 that no moral judgment may be validly deduced from purely factual premises. Since he seems to do just that throughout his ethical writings, this is fairly dramatic and obvious self-contradiction, and should give the interpreter pause.[12]

---

[11] MacIntyre 1959.

[12] Hume's alleged conclusion from the fact–value gap, that moral evaluations are not factual (in the present-day sense of 'factual')—that they do not state any facts—is also thought by some interpreters to contradict remarks in many places that certainly seem to say that moral evaluations are equivalent to statements that describe human sentiments. (Whether that is what they mean, however, is controversial.) For example, Hume says in the paragraph just before the one about 'is' and 'ought' that "when you pronounce any action or character to be vicious, you mean nothing, but that from the constitution of your nature you have a feeling or sentiment of blame from the contemplation of it". A recent example is Sturgeon 2001: 4–5. He does not think that Hume really contradicts himself; he offers a subtle reading of the paragraph and of Hume's understanding of moral evaluation that reconciles these passages and has many affinities with my own in the coming chapters.

First, does the paragraph really assert that no evaluative conclusion can be inferred from purely factual premises? The term 'fact' and the notion of a purely factual premise do not appear there. The paragraph says that propositions (sentences) linked together with 'ought' express an entirely different relation or affirmation from that expressed by propositions linked with 'is', and that it "seems inconceivable" (no doubt Hume means that it *is* inconceivable) that the former relation could "be a deduction" from the latter.[13] 'Is' and 'ought' express relations by joining sentences or phrases. Is-relations (those expressed by 'is') are different from and do not entail ought-relations. This much he says. But this neither asserts nor shows that 'ought'-expressed relations are not factual. For all he says, sentences joined with 'ought' might describe facts as well, but different facts, ones not deducible from the sorts of facts described by 'is'. Many facts are not deducible from one another; from the fact that glass is transparent we cannot infer that moss grows on the north side of trees. There is not much evidence that Hume intends to assert what is called "Hume's Law" rather than simply to say that moral facts cannot be deduced from certain other sorts of facts.

The common reading gets its purchase from the following consideration. Of course ought-judgments and other moral judgments can also be expressed with 'is'. "We ought to help people in need", for example, could be restated as "it *is* obligatory to help people in need". The version of this sentence containing 'ought' can certainly be validly inferred from the version containing 'is', since they are equivalent. But surely this sort of inference is not what Hume objects to when he says that it seems inconceivable that 'ought' can be deduced from 'is'. In this the common reading is clearly right. Then what does he object to? On the common reading, what he objects to is a certain use of words. 'Ought' in his pronouncement stands in for all moral words, including such words as 'good' and 'obligatory'. On the common reading the paragraph says that no sentences containing such words can be validly deduced from those that do not. Why not? He does not say. The claim is apparently supposed to be self-evidently true, and is unconnected with the arguments that precede it. But some support seems called for, and the common reading leaves Hume without it.

There is a further concern about this interpretation. Even if we were to grant this much of the common reading (which in the end we will not do), it would not yet show that sentences devoid of moral words, and only those, are to be identified with *factual* sentences. That is, even if the common reading were right about the linguistic point that sentences containing moral words cannot be inferred from sentences lacking moral words, the claim that moral sentences cannot be inferred from factual sentences would not be established. But this is what Hume would need to be saying at a minimum if he were asserting that

---

[13] Note: Hume is not a (translated) Fregean; by 'proposition' he does not mean some abstract entity. Since he is discussing the *words* 'is' and 'ought', presumably 'proposition' here is a synonym for 'sentence' and refers to a linguistic entity.

there is a logical gap between *fact* and value, as opposed merely to a gap between the non-moral and the moral, or the non-evaluative and the evaluative.

Another strain in Hume's position emerges if we try, as some versions of the common reading do, to identify an *argument* in this paragraph whose premise is "Hume's Law" (no inferring value from fact) and whose conclusion is ethical noncognitivism. Francis Snare maintains that either there is no argument there, but only dogmatic assertion, or there is an argument that is blatantly question-begging, assuming the truth of noncognitivism in order to prove it. A further possibility that Snare considers is that the paragraph is not supposed to be an argument for noncognitivism, but rather is supposed to draw out a consequence of the noncognitivism that was established earlier.)[14]

The common reading is quite right that if Hume is to argue for ethical noncognitivism in this paragraph, he would do so by first asserting a logical gap between fact and value. He would then, presumably, use this to show that moral assertions do not represent any facts. If we are right that there is no evidence that he has established such a gap, this robs him of a crucial ingredient in the argument. Now, I suppose we could interpret Hume as *assuming* that ought-judgments (and moral judgments generally) do not express facts; that assumption, together with the claim that moral sentences cannot be inferred from non-moral sentences, would give us the logical gap between moral sentences and factual ones. But of course, if the paragraph is supposed to contain an argument for noncognitivism, then he cannot make *that* assumption, as it would beg the question.

Although there is no textual evidence for this, he might make the weaker assumption that every fact can be expressed in sentences that contain no moral words—is-sentences, for short. Since 'ought' expresses a different relation not deducible from any set of is-judgments, it would seem to follow that ought-judgments cannot be expressed in non-moral terms. (If they could be, then they would be equivalent to some of those non-moral is-judgments and so deducible from them.) That is, perhaps according to the common reading Hume assumes that all facts can be expressed in non-moral terms and whatever we express in moral terms cannot; therefore moral judgments or sentences do not express facts. But even this assumption is tendentious. For what grounds are there to assume that every fact can be expressed in non-moral terms? There might well be facts expressible only in moral words, just as there might be facts expressible only in scientific terms, or perceptual or psychological ones.

It remains very difficult to discern either any assertion or defense here of a fact–value gap or any consequent argument for noncognitivism.

An alternative way to read the paragraph is not as an argument for noncognitivism, but rather as an observation that assumes the truth of noncognitivism and draws out a corollary from it. Perhaps noncognitivism was proven previously. Since moral judgments do not attribute any properties to objects and in

[14] Snare 1991: 38–40.

general do not assert or represent anything, of course they cannot be inferred from statements containing 'is', for they cannot be inferred from any statements whatsoever. That would provide support for the thesis that no moral judgment can be inferred from a non-moral judgment and for the logical gap between fact and value. This would be perfectly legitimate provided noncognitivism was established before. The only possible place is Argument M, however; and we have seen the interpretive difficulties that ripple through the rest of the text when that is construed as an argument for noncognitivism.

CONCLUSION

On the common reading, then, Hume's account of moral judgment is rather flawed. The DC Argument is either an impermissible form of argument (an inference a priori to a necessary conclusion about cause and effect) or an unmotivated and unpersuasive empirical generalization. The Representation Argument shows us that Hume's theory depends on the confusion of a causal Inertia Thesis (that reason and belief cannot cause any impulse to act) with the very different thesis that passions, volitions, and actions are not bearers of truth-value or reasonableness; and in context Argument M, which is supposed to show that moral judgments are not beliefs, at one point depends on that confusion for one of its premises.[15] An attempt to remove the confusion by restricting the type of causality that reason might be thought to have, however, renders Argument M invalid. Although (on the common reading) the is–ought paragraph asserts a general principle that moral or evaluative judgments do not follow from factual premises, such a principle is incompatible with Hume's efforts later in the *Treatise* to prove that certain traits of character are virtues by showing that human beings (in fact) approve them under specified conditions; and the paragraph offers no argument for a logical gap between fact and value, and lacks the resources to make any new argument for noncognitivism that is not obviously question-begging.

Thus, given the common reading, Hume's metaethical theorizing is not very deep and not very good. Defenders of the common reading might find various ways to reinterpret the text to remove some of these difficulties. I have tried to do so in the past and mostly failed, but this does not prove that others cannot succeed. However, it looks unpromising.

Not all who hold the common reading of Hume think the three theses that it attributes to Hume are true. But for some they have a profound resonance, and these philosophers are pleased with the common reading because it attributes to a great philosopher of the past claims they find intuitively convincing. If

---

[15] This interpretation of Argument M also assumes that all beliefs are products of reason, something rejected in Hume's own discussion of the understanding. I take this up in Ch. 3.

the common reading is correct, however, and if my observations about his arguments are correct, then Hume's moral philosophy is not the best place to seek argumentative support for these claims, since he does a poor job of defending them. One cannot simply invoke Hume in defense of the Inertia of Belief Thesis or the others. One must find other premises with which to argue for these three theses, or support and use the premises that the common reading finds in Hume in ways not available to Hume.

As I said at the outset, this may all simply be the case. Hume's metaethics may be internally incoherent, and some of its key claims may be unsupported. He was very young when he wrote the *Treatise*, and it is tempting to think of it as his dissertation—written by an individual of towering talent, to be sure, but also without the guidance of more experienced philosophers who could point out the errors even a genius might make. I cannot refute this way of understanding the *Treatise*. I will argue that the metaethics does not change in Hume's mature work; but that would not show that it is not riddled with errors.

Instead of trying to make the common reading work, or shrugging off the difficulties as Hume's mistakes, however, it is worth devising a different interpretation and seeing whether it can make the text more consistent and more convincing. I offer such a reading in the next four chapters. The result, interestingly enough, is an interpretation according to which Hume does not accept any of the three metaethical theses with which we began. He does not argue that belief cannot produce a motivating passion without the help of some prior passion; he is not a noncognitivist; and he does not assert an unbridgeable logical gap between fact and value. The challenge to us as interpreters will be to block the interpretive assumption that he is committed to them which results from our training. He is a quirkier, more eighteenth-century figure than the common reading would make him, and we need to give him the chance to be that. If we do, what we learn from him will be different as well.

2

The Causes of Motivating Passions

We saw in the previous chapter various internal flaws that emerge in Hume's metaethics when construed according to the common reading. Next we must break free of received assumptions and see the text afresh. We begin with Hume's motivational psychology, on which he grounds his positions on the role of reason in morals and the status of moral judgments.

The topic of this chapter is how, according to Hume, intentional actions are produced. The answer may seem obvious: they are caused by certain passions or affections, guided by factual (largely causal) beliefs. Beliefs alone cannot act as proximal causes of intentional actions on Hume's view, so passions are needed. This obvious answer, as far as it goes, is correct. However, it masks a more difficult and pressing question, both of textual exegesis and of philosophy of action. What is the cause of those passions or affections that give rise to our actions? What produces *them*? It will be argued here that for Hume beliefs of a particular sort—beliefs about forthcoming pleasures and pains—are the immediate causes of (new) motivating passions.

Elizabeth Radcliffe (1999) argues that the key point at which Hume's motivational psychology diverges from that of his moral rationalist opponents is probably not whether a belief, unaided by any passion, can directly produce action. According to Radcliffe, moral rationalists agree, or could consistently agree, that a passion is needed. Hume and his rationalist opponents disagree, instead, about what could produce the needed passion: might a belief, unassisted by any causally independent passion, produce a passion that would in turn cause action? The rationalists think a belief about the good, without further causal assistance, can cause such a motivating passion. According to Radcliffe's interpretation (and the common reading), Hume thinks no belief can do this. In this chapter I shall argue the converse: that for Hume, apart from those motivating passions that arise from instincts, all our motivating passions are caused directly by beliefs, without help from a separate, prior passion.[1] The beliefs in question are not, however, beliefs about what is abstractly or eternally good, or about the good for man. They are beliefs that some situation or object holds pleasure or

---

[1] As we will see below, among the instinctive (motivating) passions that make up the exception to this generalization are benevolence and anger, which arise from love and hatred respectively.

pain in store for the agent.[2] But this interpretation does not make Hume a moral rationalist or commit him to the view that reason alone causes action. (We see why not in the next chapter.)

First a word about terminology. In present-day common parlance people talk loosely about "motivational speakers", a "motivating teacher", or "how to motivate the team". In philosophy of action and Hume exegesis we are not quite so loose, but we nonetheless talk about "motivation" in an overly vague and potentially misleading way. We dispute whether belief or reason motivates, whether general desires (for success, for pleasure) motivate specific actions, and so on, typically without saying what the process consists in. It is left undetermined, first, whether for X to motivate an action A is for X to be a cause of A or for X to be something else (instead, or in addition)—for example, what the agent takes to be A's rational ground. And if X is a cause, we often fail to say whether it is a proximal or remote cause, a partial or complete one. In some cases we do not even specify whether X is an actual cause of action or merely a potential one; some say that X motivates (or is "a motivation") when they mean that X is or produces some inclination to act that *might* result in A, or might just as easily be overmatched by an opposite inclination, so that A does not occur. By contrast, Hume does not use the terms 'motivation' or 'motivate' or even 'move to act'. He has a specific understanding of what occurs when a person acts intentionally as the result of an "influencing motive". The process is causal: something in the mind causes the person to act intentionally. Hume provides details (which we trace in this chapter) about what sorts of items do this and how they originate. So I propose to eschew the questions "Which mental states motivate, for Hume?", "Does Hume think reason can motivate?", and "Does Hume think beliefs can motivate?", and substitute more precise questions that Hume would find comprehensible, such as these: "For Hume, can a belief cause action proximally, or only mediately, by first causing something else?", "Can a belief cause a new passion or only direct an existing passion?", and "Can a belief cause a passion without causal contribution from a prior passion?" However, I will keep the term *motivating passion* to refer to a Humean passion or affection that is the *proximal cause* of an intentional action—a passion that excites us to action directly, without intermediary.

I. THE BASIC PSYCHIC EQUIPMENT

In the paragraph that opens Book 2's "Of the direct passions" (*T* 2.3.9.1 / SBN 438), we learn that pain and pleasure are sufficient to stimulate passions and necessary for the occurrence of all or most of them. If pain and pleasure

---

[2] This apt phrase I borrow from Karlsson 2000.

are removed from the human mind, "there immediately follows a removal of love and hatred, pride and humility, desire and aversion, and of most of our reflective or secondary impressions". Not only are pain and pleasure needed for the occurrence of passions or affections, but they are also needed for the occurrence of intentional actions. At the start of the section "Of liberty and necessity" Hume describes the will as the most remarkable immediate effect of pain and pleasure, suggesting that every volition has pain or pleasure as its cause. Hume puts the point especially emphatically in his summary at T 3.1.1.2 (SBN 456):

The chief spring or actuating principle of the human mind is pleasure or pain; and when these sensations are remov'd, both from our thought and feeling, we are, in a great measure, incapable of passion or action, of desire or volition.

To understand the "springs of action", then, we must discover how, for Hume, pleasure and pain are involved in the generation of motivating passions, those passions that directly produce action.

It seems to be Hume's view in Book 2 that all actions are proximately caused by a passion or sentiment. At least, he never mentions any action that comes into being without the prompting of some sentiment or other; nor does he mention any other sort of mental state or process that causes action without the mediation of passion. (The one possible exception is active habit, which "not only gives a facility to perform any action, but likewise an inclination or tendency towards it" (T 2.3.5.5 / SBN 424). Even here, though, he may think of the inclination as itself a feeling.) Hume assumes this without support, and one may well wonder why someone whose theory of causation entails that "[a]ny thing may produce any thing" (T 1.3.15.1 / SBN 173) should assume that no mere belief can be the proximal cause of action. Most likely he supposes that there is overwhelming empirical evidence that a feeling of some sort precedes each action, though he never exhibits this evidence, and it may be more difficult to amass than he imagines. Perhaps Hume makes no effort to support the assumption because, as Radcliffe suggests, he finds it uncontroversial. But for good or ill, he *does* make it, and it will not be challenged here.

Officially, Hume treats all the passions as simple, uniform impressions that cannot be analyzed directly but are familiar to everyone. A philosopher can only enumerate "such circumstances, as attend them"—that is, their (perhaps defining) causes and effects (T 2.1.2.1 / SBN 277). And every passion is an impression of reflection: a lively or forceful perception caused by other impressions or (more commonly) ideas (T 1.1.2.1 / SBN 8; T 2.1.1.1 / SBN 275). Consequently, passions have causes within the mind that can readily be traced. The passions properly so called are the (characteristically) more violent reflective impressions (T 2.1.1.3 / SBN 276), which means they occasion more "disorder in the temper" or "sensible agitation" (T 2.3.4.1 / SBN 418–19) than the (characteristically) calm ones. But Hume does not always restrict the term 'passion' to violent reflective impressions; sometimes he speaks of calm passions (*T* 2.3.3.9 / SBN 417; *T* 2.3.4.1 / SBN 418–19). So we may use the terms 'passion' and 'affection' interchangeably.

Not all passions actuate the will. Pride and humility do not "immediately excite[ ] us to action" (*T* 2.2.6.3 / SBN 367). Nor do love and hatred, properly speaking. Rather, love is naturally conjoined with the passion of benevolence, defined as the "desire of the happiness of the person belov'd, and . . . aversion to his misery", while hatred always produces anger, the "desire of the misery and . . . aversion to the happiness of the person hated" (*T* 2.2.6.3, 6 / SBN 367, 368); and these latter cause actions. However, the direct passions—joy, grief, hope, fear, desire, and aversion—all do produce action.

Hume provides some causal explanation of the occurrence of the direct passions. He says that they, as well as the will or volition, arise from what he calls "good and evil". It is abundantly clear that by "good and evil" in non-moral contexts he means simply pleasure and pain (*T* 1.3.10.2 / SBN 118; *T* 2.1.1.4 / SBN 276; *T* 2.3.1.1 / SBN 399; *T* 2.3.9.1 / SBN 438; *T* 2.3.9.8 / SBN 439; DoP 1.1). For example, the opening sentence of *T* 2.3.1, "Of liberty and necessity", reads: "We come now to explain the direct passions, or the impressions which arise immediately from good or evil, from pain or pleasure."[3] Not only the direct passions and the will, but indeed the indirect passions as well, all arise from pleasure and pain (*T* 2.3.1–2, 2.3.9).

Hume suggests that the non-motivating indirect passions at times facilitate the direct ones in causing action. Suppose an object that gives us immediate pain or pleasure also happens to be one that qualifies as a cause of pride or love, humility or hatred, as Hume analyzes these. For example, suppose we receive an immediate impression of pleasure from driving our own luxurious carriage (or convertible). We feel joy, a direct passion, while driving such a well-designed and beautiful conveyance, for example, or we feel a desire (another direct passion) to drive it again tomorrow. At the same time, because the carriage is our own, the immediate pleasure we take in it combines with "certain dormant principles of the human mind" to help excite an impression of pride, a further and qualitatively distinct pleasure. This pride (an indirect affection) "returns back to the direct affections, and gives new force to our desire or volition, joy or hope" (*T* 2.3.9.4 / SBN 439). So while the indirect passions alone cannot cause action, they can strengthen the direct passions, making them more potent motives.

Hume says that "by the *will*, I mean nothing but *the internal impression we feel and are conscious of, when we knowingly give rise to any new motion of our body,*

---

[3] In this use of the terms 'good' and 'evil' he follows an established precedent. See, e.g., Hutcheson on natural good and natural evil (1971: i. 101–4), and Locke (1959 [1690]: 303). Both define the terms 'good' and 'evil' as that which causes pleasure and pain, but in practice extend the labels to the feelings themselves.

or new perception of our mind" (*T* 2.3.1.2 / SBN 399). In Book 1's discussion of the influence of belief (*T* 1.3.10) and in the discussions of the influencing motives of the will at 2.3.3 and the direct passions at 2.3.9 Hume freely refers to the will and to individual volitions, but gives no further account of what these are. He seems sincere in saying that we do knowingly give rise to some of our own bodily motions and mental happenings, and that there is some impression we feel when we do so. This impression is impossible to define and unnecessary to describe, apparently because it is simple yet familiar to everyone (as is each of the passions). This leaves open the possibility that a volition is simply identical with a motivating passion (a desire or aversion, feeling of hope or grief, or the like)—that each of the direct passions becomes a volition when it causes action. But since "properly speaking, [the will] be not comprehended among the passions" (ibid. par. 2), Hume may instead think the will is an impression *sui generis*, perhaps one caused by a motivating passion. Hume does not indicate what causal role the will plays in the production of action. As the definition shows, at times he seems to treat it as epiphenomenal—as an awareness of the fact that intentional action is taking place, a phenomenon without any causal role. Elsewhere this is not so clear. But usually he makes little use of it, instead explaining actions simply by appeal to their motivating passions. When he does refer to volition, though, we may at least take him to be thereby labeling the actions under discussion as intentional rather than, for example, automatic (like breathing) or inadvertent. Since Hume gives the will no independent role in action causation, we will largely ignore it in what follows, apart from treating his references to volition as indications that he is talking about intentional action. The "influencing motives of the will" are simply those motives that produce intentional actions.

Although on Hume's view the pleasure and pain of other people besides the agent can influence an agent's passions and actions, the main leverage comes from the agent's *own* pleasure or pain. That is what Hume talks about explicitly when he discusses goods and evils. The enjoyments and sufferings of others, when relevant, must first become the agent's own via sympathy before they have causal impact. (Likely exceptions to this are the passions of benevolence and anger. The mere thought of the possibility of happiness or misery for one's friend or enemy (*T* 2.2.6.5 / SBN 367) leads to benevolence or anger, and Hume does not say that the other's happiness or misery is sympathetically felt by the agent.) Here we will focus on pleasure and pain for oneself and beliefs about these; the adjustments to the theory to accommodate the feelings of others are straightforward and need not detain us.

For Hume the natural impulses or instincts form a separate category of motivating passions that do *not* arise from pleasure or pain. These instincts are hunger, lust, and some other bodily appetites, desire of good to friends and harm to enemies (*T* 2.3.9.8 / SBN 439), and perhaps also the love of life and kindness to children (*T* 2.3.3.8 / SBN 417). The two instincts of anger and benevolence ("desire of punishment to our enemies, and of happiness to our friends" (T 2.3.9.8 / SBN 439)) that standardly accompany love and hatred directly cause us to aid or harm those we love or hate, without the help of any expectation of pleasure or pain for ourselves. They do *result* in pleasure and pain for the agent, but "proceed not from them, like the other affections" (ibid.). Although one might read Hume in T 2.3.9 ("Of the direct passions") as saying that these instincts are themselves distinct direct passions, what he literally says is that the very same direct passions he has already listed there (joy, grief, hope, fear, desire, and aversion), besides arising from pain and pleasure, "frequently arise from a natural impulse or instinct, which is perfectly unaccountable" (T 2.3.9.8 / SBN 439). So desire, for example, might arise either in the ordinary way from pleasure "consider'd simply" (T 2.3.9.7 / SBN 439) or from the instinct of hunger or revenge. Presumably this means that I might desire to eat a chocolate because I think it will be pleasant (good considered simply), or I might desire to eat it because I am hungry or because I wish to pain my enemy (by keeping it from him, perhaps).[4]

Clearly, even though the natural instincts play some part, pleasure and pain take the dominant role in the generation of the motivating passions. Hume contrasts the natural instincts with those passions that arise from pleasure and pain by calling the instincts "perfectly unaccountable" (T 1.3.9.8 / SBN 110), meaning that we are not in a position to explain their origin. While Hume describes each passion as a simple impression that cannot be defined, his strategy in Book 2 is to offer causal analysis in place of conceptual analysis of the various passions. So while it need not be a conceptual truth, for Hume, that we are proud of good things linked with ourselves, on his view this is nonetheless

---

[4] As far as I can tell, Hume's accounts of the two instincts of benevolence and anger are not consistent. In T 2.2.6 he defines each of them as a pair consisting of a desire and an aversion, and says they are produced by love and hatred respectively; but in grouping them with hunger, lust, and the other instincts he commits himself to the claim that their causes are not discoverable by the scientist of the mind and that they are the causes of direct passions such as desire and aversion rather than being desires and aversions themselves.

Alison McIntyre points out (in correspondence) that Hume's claim that the instincts "produce good and evil, and proceed not from them" is far from clear in general, and involves a duality. Above I interpret the claim to mean that our having a certain instinctive urge (such as vengefulness) makes some occurrence (e.g., someone's suffering) pleasant for us that would not otherwise be so. But something further occurs with instincts when they are in play: they render the *thought* of some object pleasant or painful in prospect that would not otherwise be so. Anger (the vengeful instinct) does not merely make my enemy's real suffering give me pleasure, but makes the idea of the future suffering of my enemy attractive to me. This is another sense in which an instinct produces pain or pleasure. But in this case the idea of pain or pleasure might well go on to give rise to a desire or aversion in the usual way, from the contemplation of good or evil considered simply; it is different only in that the good or evil in prospect depends for its existence on the instinct. These desires or aversions that arise from thinking how lovely it would be if my enemy should suffer (or how wretched it would be if my loved one should, or how lovely it would be to have a drink when I am thirsty), however, do in a sense proceed from good or evil (pleasure or pain). McIntyre is more optimistic than I that Hume's position on these phenomena can be rendered consistent.

universally the case with the passion of pride, because good things (that is, pleasure-inducing things) that are associated with the self are the *causes* of pride, and pride *causes* us to attend to the idea of the self (*T* 2.1.2.4 / SBN 278).[5] This causal analysis of the passions, in every case where he thinks an account can be given, is in terms of pleasure or pain. We see the importance of pleasure and pain to the explanation of the passions in, for example, the central distinction between the direct and the indirect passions. The indirect passions are so classified because they arise from complex relations among pleasures or pains, in conjunction with other items, whereas the direct passions arise from pleasure or pain by a simpler mechanism (*T* 2.1.1.4 / SBN 276–7). Pleasure and pain, then, are thought to provide a ground-level explanation of the generation of passions.

Hume regards *desire* and *aversion* as (potentially) inherently motivating passions: impulses that can immediately cause action (e.g., *T* 3.3.1.2 / SBN 574). Apparently the other direct passions (such as hope, fear, joy, and grief) can directly cause action as well.[6] I shall use desire and aversion to make my arguments, which can easily be extended to the other motivating passions. We have seen that as Hume describes them, desires and aversions are simple, conscious, and often fairly intense feelings (often "violent" passions)—presumably cravings, longings, felt urges, or feelings of revulsion.

While the direct passions are the proximal causes of action, clearly Hume does not think of them as sufficient to cause all our actions without the aid of other mental states. It is clear from the outset that some beliefs are involved in the *production* of at least some of the motivating passions themselves: joy and grief, for example, occur only when the pleasant or painful object is thought to be probable or certain.[7] In addition, once one of these passions is produced, in order for the will to be engaged—in order for the person to act—a belief about means is often needed. Desires and aversions and all their kin are the proximal causes of actions, but they do not produce them unassisted.

---

[5] Here I follow Árdal 1966, who interprets Hume as accounting for the intentionality of passions in terms of their causes and effects. Also see Cohon 1994.

[6] Thus he lists hope and fear, joy and grief among the "propense and averse motions of the mind" (*T* 3.3.1.2 / SBN 574), suggesting that they cause us to pursue and avoid objects. It seems that joy or grief, which on Hume's account arise when pleasure or pain are certain, could only cause expressive behavior such as jumping for joy or weeping. But perhaps Hume also thinks of grief as the cause of suicide, e.g., as in Shakespearean tragedies.

[7] Hume actually says: "When good is certain or probable, it produces JOY. When evil is in the same situation there arises GRIEF or SORROW" (*T* 2.3.9.5 / SBN 439). But surely one does not feel joy at a certain good without *believing* that the good is certain, and surely a false belief that a good was certain would be sufficient to evoke joy. So it is reasonable to read this as indicating that the belief about likelihood is what is crucial to the production of joy and grief. And this may be built right into Hume's words, since what he calls certainty and probability are not objective features of events but subjective states of mind regarding them (*T*, Book 1 *passim*, e.g., 1.3.11.2 / SBN 124, 1.3.12.2 / SBN 130–1, and *T* 2.3.9.10 / SBN 440).

II. HOW PLEASURE AND PAIN GENERATE MOTIVES:
TWO MODELS

How do pleasure and pain give rise to such motivating passions as desire and aversion? Hume's remarks about this are scattered about the *Treatise* and need to be assembled. Below we consider two possible models of how motivating passions "arise from" or are "deriv'd from" pleasure and pain. Although they have many features in common, one lends support to the common reading of Hume's metaethics while the other undercuts it.

Note Hume's remark above that when pleasure and pain are removed both from our *thought* and feeling, we are for the most part devoid of passion and action. Thus not only sensations but also thoughts or ideas of pleasure and pain appear to have a role in the generation of motivating passions. "The mind by an *original* instinct tends to unite itself with the good, and to avoid the evil, tho' they be conceiv'd merely in idea, and be consider'd as to exist in any future period of time" (*T* 2.3.9.2 / SBN 438). And surely this must be what most often happens in the generation of intentional action. We are far more frequently moved by the prospect of future pleasure or pain than we are by the pleasure or pain we actually feel before or at the moment of acting. But just what is the role of ideas of future pleasure and pain in producing action? The two models differ on this.

Both models are, to some extent, oversimplifications: themes on which individual interpreters have composed variations. Although the difference between them is subtle, their consequences diverge significantly. I shall argue that one model is definitely superior. It makes sense of more of the text, and, unlike its competitor, is consistent with Hume's tacit and quite plausible understanding of certain features of pleasure and pain.

In the section "Of the influencing motives of the will", before he introduces the motivating passions, Hume describes the role of causal or probable reasoning (reasoning pertaining to matters of fact) in the generation of actions. This paragraph forms the second stage of what we earlier called the DC Argument, one of the arguments to show that reason alone is not a motive to any action of the will. The ambiguities in the paragraph nicely raise the crucial question about the role of ideas of pleasure and pain in the causation of actions.

'Tis obvious, that when we have the prospect of pain or pleasure from any object, we feel a consequent emotion of aversion or propensity, and are carry'd to avoid or embrace what will give us this uneasiness or satisfaction. 'Tis also obvious, that this emotion rests not here, but making us cast our view on every side, comprehends whatever objects are connected with its original one by the relation of cause and effect. Here then reasoning takes place to discover this relation; and according as our reasoning varies, our actions receive a subsequent variation. But 'tis evident in this case, that the impulse arises not from reason, but is only directed by it. 'Tis from the prospect of pain or pleasure that the aversion or propensity arises towards any object: And these emotions extend themselves to the causes and effects of that object, as they are pointed out to us by reason and experience. It can never in the least concern us to know, that such objects are causes, and such others effects, if both the causes and effects be indifferent to us. Where the objects themselves do not affect us, their connexion can never give them any influence; and 'tis plain, that as reason is nothing but the discovery of this connexion, it cannot be by its means that the objects are able to affect us.   (*T* 2.3.3.3/SBN 414).

Call this the *key paragraph*. For now, set aside the issue of what Hume means by the conclusion that it is not by means of reason that the objects affect us, and consider the account he sketches of the origin of motivating passions.

Both candidate interpretations below are premised on the following assumption: that for Hume desires and aversions, and the other motivating passions, are impressions, as he claims, and so are felt, at least to some degree. They may be very calm, and custom may inure us to their presence, or emotional turmoil from other sources may divert our attention from them; but still, they are available to consciousness. Call this the *occurrence assumption*. So assume for now that Hume does not have a purely dispositional theory of desire, aversion, and their ilk. Once we have considered the two models under this constraint, we will see whether it can be relaxed without doing too much violence to the rest of Hume's theory, and whether doing so favors one model over the other.

A. The Background Impulse Model

What happens when we have the prospect of pain or pleasure from an object? According to the first interpretation, the Background Impulse model, Hume assumes that we have in our minds, at all times, two general impulses or passions: the desire for pleasure as such and the aversion to pain as such. Empirical reasoning, on this view, at times provides us with what we may call *hedonic beliefs*—beliefs about the existence of particular objects that (we believe) are potential causes of pleasure or pain. In so informing us, reason enables the basic desire for pleasure, or the basic aversion to pain, to comprehend or include in its scope the particular means of satisfaction that are then available. So, for example, on this view, I, like all other human beings, have a desire for pleasure at all times. At a given moment, when a tray of chocolates is being passed at a party, reason informs me that eating one of the chocolates is a means to satisfy my background desire for pleasure. And thus, reason enables my desire for pleasure to encompass the eating of a chocolate. As Hume says in the key paragraph (*T* 2.3.3.3 / SBN 414), "the impulse arises not from reason, but is only directed by it". According to the Background Impulse view, then, the desire for pleasure and the aversion to pain are present in the mind at all times, although they are not always given more specific direction.[8]

Some additional passages offer support to this first model of how motivating passions arise "from the prospect of pleasure and pain." In *T* 2.3.3.8 (SBN 417) Hume refers to two passions that he seems to think we possess: "the general appetite to good, and aversion to evil, considered merely as such". He describes these as "calm desires and tendencies, which, tho' they be real passions, produce little emotion in the mind". This suggests that the two general appetites might be in constant residence in the mind. Also, as we saw, in *T* 2.3.9.2 (SBN 438) Hume says that "The mind, by an original instinct, tends to unite itself with the good and to avoid the evil". And in passing, in a discussion of why power evokes joy, he remarks at *T* 2.1.10.8 (SBN 314) that "all men desire pleasure".

The Background Impulse view can be used to interpret Hume's claim that reason alone does not produce the impulse to act. The key paragraph says that "It can never in the least concern us to know, that such objects are causes, and such others effects, if both the causes and effects be indifferent to us. Where the objects themselves do not affect us, their connexion can never give them any influence." According to the Background Impulse view, what Hume means when he says that objects "do not affect us" is either that we do not desire them and are not averse to them, or that they do not move us to act. Probable reason reveals causal connections between things—for example, that high humidity causes moss to grow on trees, or that eating chocolate causes pleasure. This alone, we observe, does not move us to act in the absence of an already present, occurrent desire or aversion. Thus causal *beliefs*, whatever their subject matter, are incapable of generating any motivating passion, but contribute to the production of action only by directing an existing, occurrent impulse. We always have within us such

---

[8] Hume's commentators do not often consider how the ideas of pleasure and pain figure in the causation of actions. The Background Impulse view is an attempt to fill in what they would need to say if they attended to ideas of pleasure and pain specifically, given what they say about desire and aversion. Jonathan Harrison (1976: 5) attributes to Hume the view that "belief could not move us to action, unless it was relevant to the satisfaction of some passion, desire, or need"; and he seems to see these as being causally independent of the belief, though he does not take up the issue explicitly. Barry Stroud (1977: ch. 7) interprets Hume along the lines of the Background Impulse view, as being committed to the claims both that propensity or aversion is needed for action and that beliefs are not themselves and do not by themselves cause propensities or aversions (though without specifying the propensities and aversions in question to be the desire for pleasure and aversion to pain specifically); but Stroud criticizes Hume for espousing a position that is inconsistent with a number of other theses he accepts. Francis Snare (1991: chs. 2–5) interprets Hume as committing himself to the thesis that no belief alone can generate a motivating passion, which he thinks is built into what he calls the Influence Argument (what in the last chapter we called Argument M), and spends chapters exposing the bad reasons for accepting this thesis and arguing against it. For all these commentators, if Hume indeed thinks that the prospect of pleasure (the belief that there is pleasure to be had from an object) causes action, it can only do so by directing an antecedent desire for pleasure; hence there must be one present. Many systematic philosophers take it for granted that no belief can generate a new motivating passion, and so would have to explain our appetitive and aversive responses to hedonic beliefs in much the way the Background Impulse view does.

an impulse directed at pleasure, but we need not have any such impulse directed at high humidity or moss on trees. So beliefs about pleasure lead to action (by directing our existing desire), while beliefs about moss on trees often will not. In this sense of 'alone', neither piece of information (neither belief) alone causes an impulse to act. The one about pleasure is followed by action because it directs a desire that was there from the outset.

According to the Background Impulse view, how are the motivating passions of desire and aversion "deriv'd from" pleasure and pain? Hedonic beliefs do not generate the motivating passions. But we have background impulses constantly aimed at pleasure and away from pain. These impulses are then directed to (or away from) particular, anticipated future pains and pleasures as those become available. Any prospective pleasures or pleasant objects of which we are informed (and which seem sufficiently probable) can engage the ever-present desire for pleasure as such, and any prospective pains can engage the similar aversion to pain. Belief about the availability of a particular future pleasure or pain directs the general background impulse, and this enables that impulse to cause action.

B. The Spontaneous Creation Model

But this is not the only way to read the text. According to the second interpretation, the Spontaneous Creation model, there is no constant background desire for pleasure or aversion to pain present in the mind at all times, awaiting direction. Indeed, there may not be any motivating passion in permanent residence. Rather, particular desires and aversions are brought into being by certain thoughts that come at particular times, thoughts to the effect that we can expect pleasure or pain from an object that now exists or will exist in the future.[9] The desires and aversions generated by such thoughts are not a desire for pleasure (as such, or in general) or an aversion to pain (as such, or in general). They are desires for particular objects or events (such as eating chocolate) that one expects to be pleasant, and aversions to objects that one expects to be painful. According to the Spontaneous Creation view, Hume thinks that desires and aversions (and the rest of the motivating passions, when not generated by instinct) are created spontaneously by thoughts about the prospect of pain or pleasure from particular objects. When such thoughts are sufficiently enlivened, they become hedonic beliefs.

This view, too, draws support from the key paragraph. As we saw, its first sentence says, " 'Tis obvious, that when we have the prospect of pain or pleasure from any object, we feel a *consequent* emotion of aversion or propensity, and

---

[9] Baier (1991: 158–9) points out that for Hume hedonic beliefs actuate the will, and argues that they influence our passions, though she does not say explicitly that such beliefs cause entirely new passions. Elements of the Spontaneous Creation model are suggested in Cohon (1997*c*) and Persson (1997). It is explicitly endorsed by Mikael Karlsson (2000 and 2001, esp. 2001: 36–7). Nicholas Sturgeon (2001) is also a supporter of something like the Spontaneous Creation model.

are carry'd to avoid or embrace what will give us this uneasiness or satisfaction" (emphasis added). And later in that paragraph, " 'Tis from the prospect of pain or pleasure that the aversion or propensity *arises* toward any object" (emphasis added). Thus the desire is for the *object* that we think will be pleasant, on this view, and arises spontaneously in response to the expectation that it will give pleasure. The expectation or prospect of pleasure is the belief that pleasure is forthcoming; it is not a desire, nor is it a feeling of pleasure. This belief that pleasure is available from the object causes us to desire the object. This desire in turn causes us to try to obtain it, and here we use causal reasoning to learn how that may be achieved. According to this account, I come to expect that eating one of the chocolates on the tray will give me pleasure, and from this belief or expectation arises a newly formed desire to eat a chocolate, which (given that I know exactly how to achieve the eating of chocolates under the circumstances) causes me to take one from the tray and put it in my mouth.

Clearly the difference between this and the Background Impulse model is subtle. On the Background Impulse model the belief that the chocolate will taste pleasant directs a standing desire for pleasure; on the Spontaneous Creation model this belief generates a new desire to eat the chocolate.

Several passages strongly suggest the Spontaneous Creation account. It is in evidence at the very start of the *Treatise*, when impressions of reflection are first introduced and explained.

An impression first strikes upon the senses, and makes us perceive heat or cold, thirst or hunger, pleasure or pain, of some kind or other. Of this impression there is a copy taken by the mind, which remains after the impression ceases; and this we call an idea. This idea of pleasure or pain, when it returns upon the soul, produces the new impressions of desire and aversion, hope and fear, which may properly be called impressions of reflection, because derived from it.   (*T* 1.1.2.1 / SBN 7–8)

On the Spontaneous Creation reading, this says that when we taste chocolate for the first time, pleasure of a certain kind strikes upon our senses. The mind takes a copy of this to form an idea of that type of pleasure. When we see the tray at the party, this idea "returns upon the soul", and causes the new impression of desire. Indeed, the very point of classing desire with the impressions of reflection is that it is generated by or from ideas or impressions that precede it in the mind. The causes of our sense impressions (primary impressions) are not available to introspection, but the causes of our secondary impressions are. We can observe that the idea of the pleasure of eating chocolate is the cause of our desire to eat some.

The basic account of the causation of desire and aversion in Book 2 can be read in accordance with the Spontaneous Creation model as well. There we read:

DESIRE arises from good consider'd simply, and AVERSION is deriv'd from evil. The WILL exerts itself, when either the good or the absence of the evil may be attain'd by any action of the mind or body.   (*T* 2.3.9.7 / SBN 439)

Since desire *arises* from the consideration of good (that is, pleasure), then, says the Spontaneous Creation view, it is not present all along, but comes into existence anew when one considers the prospect of pleasure. When one also believes that one may acquire the good or avert the evil by acting, the will exerts itself.

Perhaps the strongest support for the Spontaneous Creation view comes from a part of Book I discussed in the previous chapter, *Treatise* 1.3.10, "Of the influence of belief".[10] There Hume says that, apart from occurrent pleasures and pains (such as those that make us pull our hand out of a fire here and now), what gives rise to passion and action is the *belief* that pleasures or pains "either are or will be existent".

Nature has implanted in the human mind a perception of good or evil, or in other words, of pain and pleasure, as the chief spring and moving principle of all its actions. But pain and pleasure have two ways of making their appearance in the mind: of which one has effects very different from the other. They may either appear in impression to the actual feeling and experience, or only in idea, as at present when I mention them. 'Tis evident the influence of these upon our actions is far from being equal. Impressions always actuate the soul, and that in the highest degree; but 'tis not every idea which has the same effect.   (*T* 1.3.10.2 / SBN 118)

If it were only impressions of pain and pleasure and not their ideas that could "influence the will", we could not protect ourselves from future calamities, for our ideas of their approach would not provide any impulse to avoid them. But of course not every "idle conception" of a good or an evil should move us to act either. The happy medium is that

Tho' an idle fiction has no efficacy, yet we find by experience, that the ideas of those objects [pleasures and pains], which we believe either are or will be existent, produce in a lesser degree the same effect with those impressions, which are immediately present to the senses and perception. The effect, then, of belief, is to raise up a simple idea to an equality with our impressions, and bestow on it a like influence on the passions. (*T* 1.3.10.3 / SBN 119)

Here Hume seems to say that just as currently felt pleasure or pain actuates the will, moving us to let go of a burning hot pot or to prolong enjoyment with another sip of wine, so does the *idea* of a pleasure or pain that we believe does or will exist. Taken together with our other quotations, the passage suggests an account of how a believed idea of available pleasure influences action. I see the chocolates; I then not only have the mere idea of pleasure that I associate with them, but my idea is believed—I believe that if I eat some, such a pleasure will really be mine. This belief causes a desire to eat some chocolates that is sufficiently strong to cause me to act.[11]

---

[10] Tweyman (1974: 134) and Baier (1991: 157) point out the close connection between this passage and the discussion of the influencing motives of the will.

[11] What Hume says in all these passages is compatible with the thesis that mere ideas of pleasant objects can cause desires even if the objects are thought unattainable. E.g., daydreams

Hume further presses the analogy between hedonic beliefs and impressions of pleasure and pain to explain his empirical observation that believed ideas move us, while mere fictions do not. It is only with respect to vivacity that impressions differ from ideas, and so only differences in their vivacity can account for differences in their influence, and only similarities in vivacity for similarities in their influence. Therefore, Hume argues, believing that the pleasure or pain exists gives the idea of that pleasure or pain an impression's power to produce passion by increasing its vivacity.

To summarize, on the Spontaneous Creation view motivating passions are derived from pleasure and pain as follows. Painful and pleasurable *impressions* cause motivating passions to spring into being in the mind; and beliefs that pain or pleasure can be had from available objects, because of their comparable vivacity, likewise cause passions such as desire and aversion to become "strong enough to produce action.

Not only the violent desire for chocolate, but the calm passions, particularly the appetite to (remote) good and aversion to (remote) evil as such, are likewise generated in response to the belief that pleasure or pain is to be had or avoided. Thus the calm appetite to my own good is not constantly present in my mind. It is intermittent, and arises when I think of something that might redound to my benefit. If I contemplate the choice between a comfortable and a penurious retirement (which from my present perspective is a reasonably remote consideration), then I will feel a preference for the former; if I am not thinking about such matters but only about a philosophical problem, I have no such calm passion at all. The calm passions can become habitual in certain contexts; I can learn to think of my retirement every month and so be moved to save for it regularly. (Calm passions are perfectly capable of causing action, as indicated for example at *T* 2.3.4.1 / SBN 418–19.) And Hume may think that ultimately the habit of saving can persist by its own inertia without the recurrence of a triggering passion. But according to this model the calm passion of prudence (desire for one's own long-term net advantage) is not constantly present, even in a prudent individual.

We should note that on the Spontaneous Creation interpretation, in the passage at *T* 2.3.3.8 (SBN 417) Hume does not mean by "the general appetite to good and aversion to evil" a generic, background, and universal desire for pleasure and aversion to pain of any kind whatsoever. Where he mentions this "general

of wealth and leisure evoke longing in a poor laborer. Hume says that desire arises from good considered simply—not from good that is thought to be existent. Belief that one can obtain the good by some action of mind or body is needed only to enable the desire to engage the will (cause action). But this passage from Book 1 articulates the effect on the passions when the idea of pleasure is believed. The vivacity of the idea is sufficient to engage the will, yielding a *motivating* passion. Given Hume's account of the strength of a passion (*T* 2.3.4.1 / SBN 419), it is fair to understand his remarks in *T* 1.3.10 as claiming that when the idea of pleasure comes to be believed, this strengthens the desire for the pleasant object enough to make it efficacious in causing action.

appetite", he is writing about calm passions that are of the same species as certain violent ones. The calm passion that he describes as "the general appetite to good" is the desire for one's own long-term well-being, or interest; its violent cousin is the desire for immediate pleasure (or the aversion to immediately threatened pain). This is clear two paragraphs down, where he says (evidently referring to the calm and the violent appetites for good) that "men often act knowingly against their interest: For which reason the view of the greatest possible good does not always influence them. Men often counter-act a violent passion in prosecution of their interests and designs: 'Tis not therefore the present uneasiness alone, which determines them." What is general about the general appetite to good, on this interpretation, is that it is the desire for overall, long-term, net advantage rather than for any specific pleasant object—not that it is an appetite merely for *pleasure*, of some kind or other to be specified later, as hunger is an appetite for something or other to eat; and not that it is constantly present and waiting to be specified. The general appetite to good is not directed to its object by the belief "this object will yield (some) pleasure", but by the belief "this course of action will yield the most net pleasure over all". The general appetite to good, when present, can thus conflict (as Hume claims it does) with desires for specific goods whose attainment will not yield the highest total.

These two interpretations are not the only ones possible. But if Hume means what he says about tracing the roots of motivating passion to pain and pleasure, then any interpretation must see him as taking one of two stands on the issue of the generation of motivating passions: either the prospect of pleasure creates passion anew, or it directs existing passion. There does not seem to be any third alternative. So, while other interpretations will differ in their details from the two views just described, they will fall on one side of this divide or the other.[12]

---

[12] Radcliffe (1999) denies both that on Hume's view a hedonic belief by itself (without assistance from a passion) can generate a new motivating passion and that we have a background desire for pleasure and aversion to pain constantly in residence in the mind. So how does a motivating passion occur, for Hume? Radcliffe proposes a third option: in each case a belief about matters of fact is assisted by some affective principle in the passionate nature of the individual. These items vary from one person to the next; among her examples are a nervous or calm temperament, a fear of heights, and a passion for sweets. Hume does, of course, allow differences in individual temperament to explain differences in behavior (e.g., at T 2.3.3.10 / SBN 418). But he does not seem to regard people's individual passionate natures as necessary for the causation of all motivating passions. Both the Background Impulse and Spontaneous Creation accounts can explain most of Radcliffe's examples without invoking the individual's emotional constitution as an independent affective causal factor. Instead, according to both models, given the person's emotional constitution, he will have evidence in support of, and so form, a particular hedonic belief. Thus if someone has a passion for sweets or a fear of heights, typically he will remember enjoying sweets or suffering discomfort at high vantage points in the past. Consequently he will believe that a sweet pastry or a trip up a ladder has pleasure or pain in store for him; and this will either trigger a new desire or aversion or activate one of the general background impulses, according to the relevant model. Someone without such individual proclivities will have no comparable expectation of forthcoming pain or pleasure. The individual's distinctive emotional constitution thus plays no separate role in producing the motivating passion. One of Radcliffe's examples seems harder to explain in this

III. MINOR DISADVANTAGES OF THE BACKGROUND IMPULSE MODEL

In a number of respects, the text fits the Spontaneous Creation view better than the Background Impulse view.

Although Hume says that we are naturally drawn to pleasure and repulsed by pain, he never says that a generic desire for one and aversion to the other are constantly resident in the mind. He does, however, say that all the motivating passions arise from or are derived from pleasure and pain, even when these are present merely as ideas, and that a new impression of desire or aversion is produced when an idea of pleasure or pain "returns upon the soul".

Also, for Hume pleasures and pains are phenomenologically quite diverse. There are the pleasures of delicious wine, harmonious music, contemplation of beautiful objects, and so forth. On Hume's view these feel different. He even classifies the bodily pleasures and pains as impressions of sensation, while the rest are impressions of reflection. This makes it difficult to imagine a constant background desire for pleasure as such to the satisfaction of which these fundamentally different experiences are merely the means. Such a desire seems to lack an object.

Furthermore, since desire and aversion are only two of Hume's motivating passions, the Background Impulse model would have to explain the possibility that a belief about imminent pain or pleasure might direct our joy, grief, fear, or hope when these (rather than desire or aversion) move us to act. There is no textual evidence that these other motivating passions are constantly present in the mind, and if they were, Hume would have to explain why they do not either annihilate one another or convert one another into one or two more powerful passions, as his theory of the passions would require. A more plausible reconstruction by the Background Impulse view would limit the latent passions

way: the coward and the hero may have the same beliefs about a dangerous situation, and both are naturally averse to pain and drawn to pleasure (whether we analyze these as constant background impressions or tendencies for episodic beliefs about pain and pleasure to cause new motivating passions). Yet one stays, and the other flees, because one is courageous, and the other is a coward—a difference in their passionate natures. Surely, one might think, this shows that individual passionate natures determine which or how much motivating passion we feel, and beliefs about pleasure and pain (and/or desire for one and aversion to the other) are not sufficient to produce motivating passions. However, this example at most shows that passionate natures *can* play a causal role in the generation of motivating passions (or more precisely, in their interaction with other passions and resultant causal efficacy). Motivating passions are typically caused in a certain way, by pleasure and pain in prospect; but yes, there can be additional causal factors on some occasions. It does not follow that some distinctive passionate nature is necessary if one is to have a motivating passion at all. Given Hume's frequent references to pain and pleasure (which are common to all human beings) as the origin of motivating passions, the only reason to appeal to individual passionate natures in every case is if Radcliffe is right that we cannot salvage either of the two models. But this will not prove to be so.

to just the two, desire for pleasure and aversion to pain, and would explain the genesis of the others in terms of these. So joy, which is also a motivating passion, is generated (this account might say) from the background desire for pleasure, by means of the belief that this background desire will surely be satisfied in a particular way. This is a reasonable theory in its own right, but there is no textual evidence that it is what Hume has in mind. Hume treats desire and joy as mutually independent passions. "When good is certain or probable, it produces JOY" (*T* 2.3.9.5 / SBN 439), he says; and after that, "DESIRE arises from good consider'd simply" (*T* 2.3.9.7 / SBN 439). He never traces the origin of joy to desire.

Finally, if the occurrence assumption is correct, then the sentiments postulated by the Background Impulse view would need to be felt at least faintly all the time in order to be present. Presumably, the background desire and aversion postulated by this model would be among Hume's calm passions, even though on occasion they flare into violence. The occurrence assumption, however, mandates a particular understanding of Hume's "calm desires and tendencies": these too, when they are present, are always available to consciousness as feelings. This applies to those of the instincts that he thinks possess a calm manifestation, and to the "general appetite to good, and aversion to evil, consider'd merely as such", on those occasions when it causes no disorder in the soul (*T* 2.3.3.8–9 / SBN 14).[13] At times, of course, these passions (or others of the same kind) become quite violent and produce a "sensible emotion"; but when they operate with calmness and tranquility, they produce so little emotion (that is, feeling or disturbance) in the mind, that their activity may be confused with the affectless operation of reason. Nonetheless, in assuming that Hume means these calm passions, too, to be impressions, we assume that when they occur in the mind, they are available to consciousness. By this I mean that whenever they are present, we have episodes of mild feeling on which we can focus attention should we wish to. If we experience no such feelings even when we are attentive and not distracted, then we do not have the calm passion. Consequently, if there are times when we cannot find in our minds any felt appetite for our own pleasure, at those times we lack the "general appetite to good". So that appetite, while it is universal in human nature, is intermittent in its presence. This, however, is incompatible with the Background Impulse model.

But these textual considerations are not completely decisive. One can construe the passages I quoted so that they better accommodate the Background Impulse interpretation. For example, to say that desire *arises* from the thought of pleasure might mean not that desire is caused by it, but merely that this thought enables

---

[13] Hume is explicit that the calm version of this appetite occurs when we think of remote goods and evils. "Both these kinds of passions [the calm and the violent] pursue good, and avoid evil; and both of them are encreas'd or diminish'd by the encrease or diminution of the good or evil. But herein lies the difference betwixt them: The same good, when near, will cause a violent passion, which, when remote, produces only a calm one" (*T* 2.3.4.1 / SBN 419).

a preexisting desire to be directed or applied. And "Of the influence of belief" could be read more favorably for the Background Impulse model by assuming that Hume gives only half the story there. Perhaps he is telling us only what sort of *cognitive* state we need in order for a motivating passion to be activated: namely, not an idea that is merely entertained, but one that is believed. His topic in the section is the role of belief, so he might not see fit to mention the role of background desire or aversion. After all, he does not explicitly mention the generation of new desires either, as the Spontaneous Creation view would lead us to expect; he describes only the generation of action. So one might, with reason, argue that the motivating passions (whether new or already extant) are not on his radar screen here. His expressed view, it would seem, is compatible with either model: it is the believed idea of pleasure or pain, rather than the merely entertained idea, that makes the production of intentional action possible, with the help of passion in some capacity or other; but the passion in question may be either a background desire (or aversion) or a new one caused by the hedonic belief.

Furthermore, while Hume's official position is that all impressions, including not only passive feelings but also motivating desires and aversions, are conscious episodes, many suppose that he gradually relaxes his commitment to that view as the *Treatise* progresses, and allows desire and aversion to be dispositional properties.[14]

IV. A MORE IMPORTANT DIFFICULTY

However, the problems with the Background Impulse view run deeper. Hume says at T 1.3.10 that the believed idea of a painful object produces, on the passions and the will, the same effect as does an actual painful impression, though in a lesser degree. The two fulfill the same causal role, in virtue of their vivacity. Take, for example, the believed idea that pain will come to me by touching a hot pot. If we analyze it in accordance with the Background Impulse view, this believed idea provides information that directs my background aversion. That sounds plausible enough: I am averse to pain, I believe that touching this hot pot will be painful, and this belief directs my general aversion so it can move me to

---

[14] Shaw (1998: ch. 2) interprets Hume as ultimately holding a dispositional account of desire and aversion (largely in light of his remarks about the calm passions). Bricke (1996: chs. 1 and 2) understands desires in Hume as end-setting psychological states with a characteristic direction of fit, rather than conscious episodes. Ingmar Persson (1997), who argues for a version of the Spontaneous Creation view (or at least goes part of the way with it) as an interpretation of Hume, suggests that Hume may have incorrectly assimilated desires and aversions, which really are dispositional properties postulated as commonsense placeholders to explain behavior (in the absence of neuroscientific knowledge of the actual causes), to genuine passions such as anger that are more plausibly understood as impressions subject to the occurrence assumption.

avoid touching the pot. It is not the belief that moves me, but the background aversion to pain, which is merely guided by the belief. So far, so good.

But Hume says at *T* 1.3.10 that my *belief* that touching the pot will be painful works the same way as does the *sensation* of pain, because of its similar vivacity. Does the effect of a sensation of pain parallel the effect of the believed idea as this is understood on the Background Impulse model? Suppose I touch the hot pot. If we take literally the claim that the impression works the same way as the belief, the impression must work merely to guide my general background aversion toward a specific object. That is, the Background Impulse view would entail that when I touch the pot and feel pain, that feeling does not create a new motivating passion, but rather directs my background aversion to pain toward this experience I am now having. What moves me to snatch my hand away is not the pain itself; nor is it a sudden aversion brought into existence by the pain. What happens instead is that the occurrent feeling of pain provides the *information* that pain is present (just as the hedonic belief provided the information that pain was forthcoming), and this information directs my previously existing aversion, so that *it* (the background aversion) can move me to pull away. The sensation of pain, like the belief about future pain, is just a piece of information guiding my existing aversion.

But surely *that* is not how we are moved to pull back from a hot surface. The painful sensation is not just a source of information that guides the aversion. And it is unlikely that Hume thought it was. It is in part because of the spontaneous aversive power of feelings of pain and the spontaneous attractive power of feelings of pleasure that Hume traces nearly all motivating passions to origins in one's own pain and pleasure. He surely does not think the sensation of pain itself an "indolent judgment of the understanding". Rather, pain is the sort of experience that inherently generates an impulse to retreat. Its characteristic impact on passion and action is independent of any aversion or desire that might have been present in the mind before the pain began. (Of course, a feeling of pain might interact with background passions as well; but that would be a further effect.) Pain itself makes one want it to stop; pleasure itself makes one want it to continue. This is what makes Hume's motivational hedonism plausible in the first place.

Hence, if Hume is serious in saying that the believed idea of pain has an influence on the passions similar to that of an actual feeling of pain, he would not think the believed idea entirely without influence of its own. What Hume must actually have in mind with the analogy between the effects of feelings of pain and of beliefs about forthcoming pain is rather this: present pain generates passion, and belief in the existence of a painful object does likewise. He is not saying that present pain activates a latent aversion to pain. He may, of course, call it an instinct in us to be averse to pain—anyone might say that. But for him this means not that we have a background impulse to flee pain that is directed from time to time by information, but that pain is *the kind of experience* that moves creatures such as we are to flee. Since belief in forthcoming pain resembles the sensation of pain in its effect on the passions, belief that a painful thing exists is likewise the kind of experience that moves one to flee.

The Spontaneous Creation view, then, has an important advantage over the Background Impulse view: unlike its rival, it gives a plausible account of the parallel Hume draws between the influence of actual pain and pleasure and the influence of the belief that they will occur, one that draws on the significance of pain and pleasure in Hume's psychology.

V. DOESN'T HUME RULE OUT THE CAUSATION OF PASSION BY BELIEF? INDIFFERENCE TO CAUSE AND EFFECT

At this point anyone schooled in Hume's ethics will be inclined to protest as follows: according to the Spontaneous Creation view, a belief or judgment that a pain or pleasure exists or is pending causes a new aversion or desire to come into being. That aversion or desire in turn generates action. But this would be an instance of belief, unaided by any causally independent affection, generating a motivating passion. And Hume cannot say this! We have seen that according to the common reading of Hume's metaethics, he commits himself to denying this thesis in the DC Argument (indeed, right in the key paragraph). And even some who do not espouse the whole common picture think he denies it.[15] So if the Spontaneous Creation interpretation were right, and these interpreters were right, then Hume would contradict himself. This thought, indeed, is what drives interpreters to assume that Hume *must* have the Background Impulse picture in mind.

Of course, Hume does claim that *reason* alone cannot generate a motivating passion: ". . .the impulse arises not from reason". He says this explicitly in several ways, and nothing said here opposes taking him at his word. The question to raise is whether he in fact denies that *beliefs* alone can do so. He does not actually say that the impulse arises not from a belief; rather, interpreters think he is *indirectly* committed to this. Eventually we will see that he is not, in spite of misleading appearances. The main argument that he is not must be reserved for the next chapter, where I examine why Hume thinks reason alone is not a motive to the will, and where we determine what Hume means by reason "alone" or "of itself". Here I will only briefly dispel one misapprehension that might arise from the key paragraph.

One reason to think Hume is committed to the inertia of beliefs alone, including hedonic beliefs, is his remark in the key paragraph that where cause

---

[15] Radcliffe, who does not interpret Hume as a noncognitivist, nonetheless defends his commitment to the inertia of belief (1999: 109–10). I take up her argument in the next chapter.

and effect are both indifferent to us, the discovery that they are causally linked cannot concern us. One might read this as saying that where we have no background desire for or aversion to either of two items, the belief that they are causally linked cannot cause any impulse in us. That is, "indifference" to X is construed as the absence of a prior desire for or aversion to X that is causally independent of the belief that X exists. Thus only with the help of background impulses of the kind employed in the Background Impulse model can a belief about cause and effect—even one about the causal relations between objects and our own forthcoming pleasure or pain—give rise to passions or actions.

However, there is good evidence that this is not the right way to read the remark about indifference. In the part of the "Dissertation of the Passions" where Hume reworks the key paragraph, we find the point stated in such a way as to suggest a different reading. (I will address the omitted words later.)

It seems evident, that reason, in a strict sense . . . can never, of itself, be any motive to the will, and can have no influence but so far as it touches some passion or affection. *Abstract relations* of ideas are the objects of curiosity, not of volition. And *matters of fact*, where they are neither good nor evil, where they neither excite desire nor aversion, are totally indifferent; and whether known or unknown, whether mistaken or rightly apprehended, cannot be regarded as any motive to action.   (DoP 5.1)

So matters of fact are indifferent not across the board, but only *where they are neither good nor evil.* In the Dissertation he defines goods and evils as pleasant and painful objects. Where a matter of fact is likely to be neither pleasant nor painful, and where it (consequently) excites neither desire nor aversion, it is of course indifferent—that seems to be what 'indifferent' means here—and so *it* is no motive to action. It is implicit but obvious that there is an alternative scenario: where the matter of fact is or pertains to something pleasant or painful, it is not indifferent. Thus the point of saying in the key paragraph that we are indifferent to the cause and the effect in a given case is not that we have no *antecedent* desire or aversion to either of them, but rather that we do not think either the cause or the effect is pleasant or painful, and so the causal belief linking them does not *create* aversion or desire. In contrast, a causal discovery with respect to something pleasant or painful will. In particular, the discovery that something available to us will cause us pleasure or pain (where pleasure or pain is its *effect*) concerns us very much. Thus, the key paragraph too (if we read it consistently with its restatement in the "Dissertation of the Passions") does not say that *no* causal belief can generate new desire or aversion. It does not say that in order for a causal belief to trigger an aversion to the believed effect, we must have a prior, background aversion to that type of effect, whatever it may be—even if the effect in question is pain. So it does not deny that the belief that pain will come from touching a hot pot can generate a new aversion. Rather, it denies that a causal belief that is not about *pleasure or pain* can produce a desire or aversion. Hedonic beliefs presumably can.

We find a similar passage in the *Enquiry concerning the Principles of Morals*: "where the truths which [inferences and conclusions of the understanding] discover are indifferent, and beget no desire or aversion, they can have no influence on conduct and behaviour" (*EPM* 1.7 / SBN 172). This leaves open the possibility he mentions explicitly in the *Dissertation*, that such truths might pertain to goods and evils and so might not be indifferent and might beget desire or aversion.

We should thus read the key paragraph as follows. It is not the judgment's status as a causal judgment that gives it the power to produce desire. It is not the relation of cause and effect it expresses that stimulates passion. We know this because, when the cause and the effect are unrelated to our pain or pleasure, a causal judgment stimulates no motivating passion. Inferential discovery of the relation of cause and effect is what reason contributes. That operation of reason—causal inference—functions in the same way whatever its subject matter may be. So in the special cases where a causal belief gives rise to a passion, *reason* is not what generates the passion. What stimulates passion is the resulting belief's unique subject matter: pleasure or pain. Not all subject matter can do this. The ideas of pleasure or pain, when sufficiently lively, have a special power to produce passion. Indeed, vivid and lively thoughts of pleasure and pain give rise to desire and aversion no matter how their vivacity is increased, whether by reasoning or by another process such as the psychological response to eloquence (*T* 2.3.6.7 / SBN 426–7).[16]

Again, this is only one small reason why Hume has so often been thought to be committed to the claim that causal beliefs alone cannot produce motivating passions. The more substantial grounds for this interpretation will, I hope, be seen to disappear once the concept of reason alone is explicated in the next chapter.

Thus far, we have seen significant textual reasons to reject the Background Impulse model of the generation of motivating passions, especially given its implication that current pain behaves as a belief does—merely directing an existing background passion rather than provoking a new passion. Furthermore, we have seen that if Hume thinks of desires and aversions as impressions (if we preserve the occurrence assumption), then the Background Impulse view is not a plausible interpretation. We have seen no reason so far to construe Hume's claim that causal reason alone cannot produce a passion to entail that a hedonic belief cannot cause a passion, although the full discussion of and rejoinder to this type of objection has been postponed until later. Thus we see that the first thesis of the common reading of Hume, the Inertia of Belief Thesis that beliefs alone cannot "motivate" action, when explicated to eliminate its initial vagueness, is incorrect. Hume does indeed hold that a belief does not directly cause action without the intervention of a passion; but he also holds that a hedonic belief itself causes a

---

[16] See the next chapter for more about representation and its relation to reason.

motivating passion that in turn causes action, and so a hedonic belief is (in the ordinary case) sufficient to initiate a causal chain that terminates in action.[17]

VI. RELAXING THE OCCURRENCE ASSUMPTION: THE DISPOSITIONAL VIEW

Finally, we must consider one last competitor to the claim that for Hume hedonic beliefs cause motivating passions.

So far the occurrence assumption has been a vital interpretive premise in the reconstruction of Hume's practical psychology. But there is at least one good reason why one might wish to relax this assumption, and if we are warranted in relaxing it, this will make a difference to which model we should accept. Without the occurrence assumption, one of the criticisms of the Background Impulse model is removed. And this would offer us a chance to read Hume as denying that any sort of belief alone can cause a motivating passion. Perhaps Hume is committed to the existence of a general appetite to pleasure and aversion to pain present in the mind at all times but often unfelt. Then it is possible that these *unfelt* passions really do join together with hedonic beliefs and are directed by them, as the Background Impulse view claims, so that it is desire and aversion together with belief that engender a motivating passion, not belief (in this sense) alone.[18] Such an interpretation seems implicit in much traditional thinking about Hume's moral psychology. Its evaluation requires some investigation of how such a picture would fit into Hume's overall philosophy. (Readers who are not interested in such an interpretation can skip this last section of the chapter without loss of continuity.)

So why might we relax the occurrence assumption, and what effect would it have to do so?

Hume's official account of desires and aversions has an evident philosophical weakness. It classifies every desire and aversion as an impression, and hence a

---

[17] Eugene Heath, in conversation, worries that if this is Hume's view, then he cannot explain the complete apathy to opportunities for pleasure sometimes experienced by the clinically depressed. The objection is important, but not decisive. The Spontaneous Creation model, for its part, might explain their lack of desire in various ways, depending on what goes on in clinical depression. Perhaps the depressed individual does not really believe that an activity he enjoyed in the past will produce pleasure here and now, since of late he enjoys nothing. Or perhaps he believes it will, but his melancholy acts as a separate cause that blocks the belief's production of desire. He may, for example, feel unworthy of pleasure, or feel that any pleasure he gains will be hollow and insignificant; and these thoughts might derail the causal mechanism. In general Hume's claims that some item is the cause of another allow room for exceptional circumstances when hidden causes prevent the effect from following upon the usual cause (*T* 1.3.12.5 / SBN 132).

[18] This is what the common reading understands by "belief alone". No commitment to this use is intended here.

conscious feeling, an episode or period of inner sensation. But this is the correct phenomenology of only *some* of what we ordinarily call desires and aversions. If on a steaming hot day I glimpse a cold glass of water, ice cubes within, a mist of condensation forming on its exterior, I feel a pang of longing, and this is my desire to drink the water. But there are many occasions on which we have a desire or want but have no such conscious feeling. Someone who wants a secure retirement does so not only when she thinks longingly of financial security in her old age, or thinks with dread of penury, but even when she is hunting for her car keys or fast asleep. In a poignant moment a parent's desire for her child's future success may generate a wave of feeling, but she desires his success all the time, even when she is fully engrossed in grading midterm examinations or struggling to remove stains from the careless lad's shirt. At such times the desire for the child's future success is not felt, and so presumably is not an impression at all. Hume's explicit account of desire entails that at such moments one *does not have* a desire for a secure retirement or one's child's success. But this is quite implausible.

If Hume were to countenance unfelt desires and aversions, then the Background Impulse view, according to which there is a generic desire for pleasure and a similar aversion to pain in constant residence in the mind, becomes more attractive. While we do not always *feel* any longing for pleasure or dread of pain, it might nonetheless always be true of us that we desire the one and want to avoid the other. Now perhaps, even on Hume's own account (his doctrine "between the lines", though not acknowledged), the general desire for pleasure and general aversion to pain (and perhaps other desires and aversions as well) are not occurrent impressions. Then what are they? The most natural proposal, both from interpreters of Hume and from philosophers of action, is that they are dispositional properties of us: tendencies for us to have certain feelings and act in certain ways in response to particular stimuli. For you to have the general desire for pleasure, then, is for you to be disposed to feel a prick of longing when you have the belief that something close at hand is a potential source of pleasure, and also for you to be disposed both to feel other things (hope, fear, disappointment, perhaps joy) and to act in certain ways whenever you form other specified beliefs under the right conditions—beliefs, for example, about the availability or unavailability of things you expect to yield pleasure or pain. The general desire for pleasure and the general aversion to pain are thus roughly analogous to magnetism, brittleness, and solubility in water. For a glass object to be brittle is for it to be likely to break if struck, dropped, or interacted with in certain other ways under certain conditions. Of course, it is more difficult to specify the behavior that the general desire for pleasure is a disposition to exhibit—the behavior analogous to breaking in a brittle object. Unlike breaking, this behavior will be quite varied, and will include having feelings as well as acting. But a mind that has this dispositional property (the general desire for pleasure) will, at the very least, be disposed to pursue objects once it comes to believe that they are attainable sources of pleasure, at least subject to some restrictions.

The dispositional property that (according to this view) *is* my general desire for pleasure is of course distinct from the feelings and actions to which I am disposed in having it; that is why I can have the desire while feeling and doing nothing. The general desire for pleasure is the dispositional property; hence the prick of longing, the urge to act, and the action that one performs when the right beliefs are present are *other* things. Those that are occurrent feelings might be *other desires*: perhaps the category of desires contains items of diverse ontological types, some dispositional properties and some occurrent longings. And perhaps, then, one who has the general desire for pleasure (a dispositional property), faced with the sense perceptions of the glass of cold water I described above, would come to feel a desire (a prick of longing) to drink the water, for example. Or perhaps the feelings to which one is disposed are not desires at all but something else, such as volitions. In any case they are not identical with the general desire for pleasure, on this account; for they are fleeting impressions, and the general desire for pleasure is by hypothesis a constantly present dispositional property. This is the present proposal for how to understand Hume's deeper view, his unofficial doctrine of desire and aversion.[19]

Plainly Hume does not *say* that desires and aversions are dispositional properties. However, it remains possible that a dispositional conception of this pair of mental states underlies his overall thinking about the causes of motivating passions and action. He does talk in other contexts about tendencies and about powers, so there is some reason to interpret him as acknowledging dispositional properties in his ontology (although, as we shall see, there is also some reason not to). He even describes some mental qualities, and beauty, in ways that are

---

[19] An aside is needed here. The dispositional account of the general desire for pleasure will not allow us to attribute to Hume a view that often *is* attributed to him: that the general desire for pleasure *becomes* a specific impulse to pursue a particular pleasure-promising object when we come to believe the object can be obtained, or is *directed* or made more specific by causal beliefs about the object. If the general appetite to pleasure is a disposition, it is distinct from any felt craving for the object and from any other element of the set of phenomena to which, in having it, we are disposed. Insofar as we have a general desire for pleasure as a dispositional property, what is likely to be true is that when we come to believe an object has pleasure in store for us, we come to want it or feel an inclination to pursue it. But the disposition and the inclination are of different ontological kinds, so if we call them both "desires", that is merely an accident of language. Insofar as we have the disposition, we will feel this inclination given the right belief and circumstances; but the disposition does not *become* the inclination toward the object, nor is it made more specific or directed by the belief. The general desire for pleasure is a property of the mind, not an impulse or urge to be directed. Thus a dispositional analysis of this general desire will not permit us to explain Hume's account of the causation of action according to the "hydraulic" model so long associated with Hume. The crude image used for that model is of moving water in a pipe that changes direction as it reaches a new segment of pipe angled a different way. The general desire for pleasure before the arrival of the causal belief is represented by the water; the specific desire for the object is represented by the same water redirected by the new length of pipe. On a dispositional account of the general desire, this metaphor gets it quite wrong, because it depends on understanding the general desire for pleasure at an earlier time as identical with the specific desire that later causes action.

unmistakably dispositional (*T* 2.1.7.7 / SBN 297; *T* 2.1.8.2 / SBN 299). Is a dispositional account of this desire and this aversion compatible with Hume's overall outlook?

VII. DOES HUME RULE OUT DISPOSITIONAL PROPERTIES IN HIS ACCOUNT OF CAUSATION?

There are many controversies in metaphysics and the philosophy of science about the nature of dispositional properties, all of which we may safely ignore here. The question we must address, however, is how *Hume* would understand dispositional properties if he is to tolerate them at all. A reader of Hume might think that his philosophy in the *Treatise* rules out any role for dispositional properties. We will see that this is not so, but other, revealing consequences follow from his commitments in this regard, with consequences for the two models we have discussed.

If the general desire for pleasure were a conscious feeling, I would be aware of its existence in myself immediately, and in others by means of sympathy. But if it is not felt by anyone, but is instead a dispositional property, then Hume must explain how we can have any warranted belief that there is such a thing, or even any idea of it. The obvious place to seek his position on dispositional properties is his account of causal powers; for presumably a dispositional property such as magnetism is the *power* of a piece of metal to cause certain other metals to move. Does Hume think we can coherently attribute any powers to objects, including persons?

In Book 1 of the *Treatise* the term 'power' is used mainly as a synonym for causal efficacy or the necessary connection between cause and effect (*T*, *passim*, e.g., 1.3.14.4 / SBN 157 and 1.3.14.10 ff. / SBN 160). It is of power in this sense that Hume says in Book 1 that "the distinction, which we often make betwixt power and the exercise of it is . . . without foundation" (*T* 1.3.14.34 / SBN 171). It is slightly mysterious why he says we cannot distinguish between a power and its exercise, and some may think this shows that he denies the existence of powers. But what he seems to have in mind by the claim is this: to know about an object's (causal) power—given that 'power' is equivalent to 'productive quality' (*T* 1.3.14.4 / SBN 157)—is simply to know of its constant conjunction with its effect (*passim*, e.g., *T* 1.3.14.19 / SBN 164). The idea of something's having a power is simply the idea of its being a cause, which is either simply the idea of its constant conjunction with its effect, or that plus the transition of the mind when the mind is presented with the first object and expects the second. Thus we have no idea of an object's unexercised power, because our idea of a power just is or includes the idea of the conjunction of that object with its effect. If a particular A is not followed by a B on a single occasion, then according to *this* idea of power, A had no power to produce B on that occasion. And of course, only experience with past instances of the effect will give us this idea of power.

This understanding of power or ability is correct in "a . . . philosophical way of thinking" (*T* 2.1.10.4 / SBN 311), Hume says. It clearly is not an idea of an unexercised power, but rather of causal action—of cause being conjoined with effect. Even our idea of the transition of the mind is not an idea of a power present in the absence of its effect, but is rather the idea of our expectation of the effect. A power in this sense could not be a dispositional property, especially one that a being might have when not behaving in the ways to which it is disposed. Hume's focus on this concept of power in Book 1 thus suggests that he does not think we have any idea of a dispositional property at all.

However, in Book 2 Hume introduces a different concept of power or ability, one drawn from "common notions" and "our vulgar and popular ways of thinking" (*T* 2.1.10.5 / SBN 312); and this second idea of power allows us to think coherently and perhaps even truly of an unexercised power.[20] So understood, an object's power to cause another object consists in the probability that the one object will cause—that is, will be followed by—the other under suitable circumstances. To say that fire has the power to warm us in this sense would be to say that if we approach a fire we will probably grow warm. Sometimes he says that the power is the probability or *possibility* that the effect will ensue (*T* 2.1.10.6 / SBN 312–13; 2.2.3.7 / SBN 350).[21] Our idea of power in this sense still always refers to its exercise (ibid.); attributions of such powers are warranted only by observations of past regularities. But there is apparently no fiction or nonsense (though there may be some kind of philosophical error) involved in talking of power this way. The fact that A has the power to produce B, so understood, is the fact that A probably will produce B given certain conditions. On this account, A may well have the power to produce B during times when it does not produce B. Bread has the power to nourish us even though it will not nourish anyone until it is eaten.

This vulgar but still empirical notion of power as the probability of conjunction under suitable circumstances is developed in Book 2 to explain the way we attribute power to persons and to property even at times when they are not generating their effects. We do think of some other people as having the power to hurt or help us when they have not yet done so, and we think of money as having

---

[20] Like several other concepts that Hume introduces in Book 2, this new idea is explicated very much in the middle of the pursuit of other things. Here he is trying to explain how it is that people can derive pleasure or uneasiness from what they think of as the unexercised power of a person or object to benefit or harm them; all this is in the service of supporting his analysis of the origin of pride in a double relation of impressions and ideas. What he has to account for here is the pleasure that people derive from ownership of property and from money even at moments when they are not experiencing the "pleasures and conveniences of life" to which these things give them access.

[21] What we regard as a possible effect is an event of the same type as one we have at some point observed to follow on the type of event now observed, though perhaps not regularly conjoined with it (*T* 1.3.12.8 / SBN 133–4).

the power to bring us property, which yields the "pleasures and conveniences of life" (*T* 2.1.10.3 / SBN 311), though it has not yet done so. We think other persons lack the power to hurt us when either there is some physical impediment to their doing so or they have a strong motive not to (such as fear of the civil magistrate). When these obstacles are absent, and in particular when the person also has a motive to do what will prove harmful to us (e.g., he stands to gain from it), we say he *has* the power to harm us, even though he does not harm us. This attribution of power need not be retracted even if in the end he never harms us. Hume says this "power consists in the possibility or probability of any action, as discover'd by experience and the practice of the world" (*T* 2.1.10.6 / SBN 313). His reference to the "practice of the world" suggests that we may judge from our experience with other human beings as well as with the given individual.

Once Hume articulates the vulgar sense of 'power' by examining the unexercised powers we attribute to human beings, he finds powers all about us. He says that wit, beauty, and riches are powers.[22] We can even make correct and incorrect attributions of power in this popular sense. Correct attributions are based on experience and reflect actual probabilities, or at least possibilities. One unwarranted—indeed, false—attribution of power is based instead on a miser's "false sensation of liberty": he attributes to his money the power to provide him with pleasures, though in forty years his riches have never brought about any such result, and so in reality they have no such power, not even in the vulgar sense. (It is no more probable that this man, possessed of money, will acquire delicious wine or solicitous servants than it would be if he had no money.) The miser imagines that the money makes probable his acquisition of such enjoyments, because he imagines he can will to do anything, even spend his money (*T* 2.1.10.9 / SBN 314–15).

The general appetite to pleasure as such, of which we seek a dispositional analysis, might be understood as a power in this popular sense: as the probability that something A will bring after it B and C. To say that someone has this appetite, construed dispositionally, then, is to say that it is probable that some A will be conjoined with B and C.

Let us attempt such an analysis. We know what B and C are, roughly: feelings (such as longing or volition) and actions to get what is thought to be a source of pleasure. But what is A, the bearer of the power? What is it that probably will give rise to feelings of longing and attempts to obtain the pleasure-yielding object?

It seems that there are two perfectly correct possibilities. First, A could be the human mind. All human minds have the power to cause (or better, the tendency

---

[22] Wit and beauty are described as, in essence, the power to produce pleasure that belongs in the one case to a person's conversation, in the other to a body's appearance (*T* 2.1.7.7 / SBN 297 and *T* 2.1.8.2 / SBN 298–9). "[R]iches are to be consider'd as the power of acquiring the property of what pleases" (*T* 2.1.10.3 / SBN 311).

to undergo) certain characteristic feelings and actions when they possess a hedonic belief. Or, alternatively, A could be the hedonic belief itself; the claim about power could be that all hedonic beliefs have the power to cause (will probably be succeeded by) such feelings and actions in human beings. Humean powers of the popular sort, of course, always have reference to effects, and constitute probabilities. If we state the first alternative in the language of the popular idea of power, it says that, given a human mind, when a hedonic belief is present, certain feelings and actions will probably follow, given the right conditions. The second alternative says that hedonic beliefs, when present in a human mind, have the power to produce the specified feelings and actions, given the right conditions. But we can see that this is exactly equivalent to the first option: when a hedonic belief is present in a human mind, certain feelings and actions will probably follow. On Hume's account of causation, even using the popular idea of power, we have no way to distinguish which of these (mind or hedonic belief) has the power and which is a required background condition to the causal interaction. Both attributions of power are based on the same prior regularities and express the probability of the same occurrences.

Here is another way to think of it, in terms of a *reductio*. Suppose the general desire for pleasure is a disposition to have certain feelings or impulses when a hedonic belief is present; but suppose also that hedonic beliefs do *not* cause feelings or impulses in human minds. That would entail that in human minds, hedonic beliefs are *not* constantly conjoined with such feelings or impulses, and thus that it is not especially probable that someone who has a hedonic belief will have the relevant urges or feelings. If this is not probable, then it is not true that human minds have the power to generate longings and actions when faced with the belief that an object promises pleasure. And so human minds do not have the dispositional property that is the general desire for pleasure.[23]

We have seen that there is some sense to understanding our general appetite to good and aversion to evil as dispositions; Hume can consistently say that they are powers or capacities, if by saying this we refer to their probable exercise. If the desire for pleasure is a dispositional property in this sense, it can be present even at times when we have no felt urges or impulses to pursue pleasant objects. So

---

[23] This sketch of a Humean account of dispositional properties makes no assumption that Hume is not a realist about causal necessity, in the following sense: it is not assumed that Hume denies that causal necessities in objects exist. It does, however, assume what seems true: that on Hume's view we are never epistemically warranted in attributing such necessities to objects, and have no idea of them. There could be a secret power in the human mind to create cravings and motives to pursue pleasant objects, a power whose existence is independent of any observed causal relation between hedonic beliefs and such cravings and motives. But we can know nothing about such a secret power, and could not appeal to it in our theory of the causation of motives. If a general appetite to pleasure is thought to be that unknowable power, any claim about it would be at best a fantasy without foundation, and at worst a nonsensical utterance. The only sort of power we have grounds to attribute to anything is the one that describes a probability based on observed regularity. And that power—that dispositional property—depends for its existence on the observed regularity which is the causal relationship as we understand it.

a dispositional account of these two mental states is available to explain the fact that we don't consciously crave pleasure or feel revulsion toward the prospect of pain at every moment.

But the Humean account of dispositional properties, if we have understood it correctly, has a surprising consequence for the Background Impulse model of the causation of motivating passions. If the background desire and aversion are dispositional properties, this in fact shows that the Spontaneous Creation view is correct: impulses or inclinations to act to seek or avoid objects are directly caused by hedonic beliefs, provided those beliefs occur within a human mind. For we have seen that an object possesses a Humean disposition only if a specific causal relation is present, and only as a consequence of that relation. Only in this case are we entitled to think that human beings have the general desire for pleasure, understood as a dispositional property. We are entitled to attribute these dispositional properties to people because we already observe that hedonic beliefs cause feelings and volitions in human minds—that is, have regularly been conjoined with them in the past and render their next occurrence probable.

So even if Hume allows that there are dispositional properties, and even if it is his unofficial doctrine that the general appetite to pleasure is one of them, the thesis that hedonic beliefs cause new motivating passions is inseparable from his motivational psychology. The specific passions that cause us to pursue pleasant objects—these specific longings and urges—are caused by hedonic beliefs; indeed they must be if we are to have a disposition to experience and act on such passions, and so if the dispositional account of the general desire for pleasure is to be true. Consequently, the Spontaneous Creation model is not undermined, but is rather vindicated, by relaxing the occurrence assumption and introducing a dispositional (but still Humean) analysis of the background desire and aversion. On that dispositional account, the Background Impulse interpretation is right that each of us has a generic desire for pleasure and aversion to pain constantly present in the mind; but it goes wrong in saying that these combine with hedonic beliefs to become or to cause motivating passions. Rather, the causal relation holds between the hedonic belief and the motivating passion, within the context of a human mind; and it is only in virtue of this regularity that we can truly be said to have the general, dispositional desire and aversion.

We have seen that desire for pleasure (or aversion to pain) as a Humean dispositional property can be ascribed to human minds only on the presupposition that hedonic beliefs proximally cause motivating passions. It is tempting to object here that while that assumption is needed, a further assumption is not needed: that hedonic beliefs *alone* cause motivating passions. It might still be the case that hedonic beliefs need some further item or condition in the mind in order to produce such passions. If this were so, the *reductio* argument would not succeed. Here is why: if we assume that hedonic beliefs *alone* do not cause passions (if this is our assumption for the *reductio*, the negation of the thesis to be defended), we could still attribute to the human mind the dispositional property which is the general appetite to pleasure, provided hedonic beliefs plus something else did consistently cause motivating passions. It has not been shown that for Hume beliefs alone generate passions.[24]

However, this point is quite unfounded if understood in one way; but it can readily be granted if we understand it another way, since so understood it is no objection. Its significance turns on the meaning of 'alone'. If the objector means, in saying that hedonic beliefs alone do not cause motivating passions, that they cause them only with the help of the general appetite to pleasure and aversion to pain, understood as dispositional properties, clearly this has been ruled out by our argument. The point of interpreting this desire and this aversion as dispositional properties was to explain how they might be constantly present in the mind, so that they could be available to cause actions when directed by new beliefs about means. But once they are understood as Humean-style dispositions, we find that we can attribute them to persons only on the assumption that hedonic beliefs (with, perhaps, other help) *already* cause motivating passions. The dispositional properties therefore cannot play a causal role in the generation of motivating passions, the proximal causes of action. For us to have those dispositional properties at all, our hedonic beliefs must be causes of passion that operate without *their* help. Indeed, dispositional properties of this Humean kind are not the sorts of phenomena that could combine causally with a hedonic belief to generate a motivating passion—they are not causes.[25] So if 'alone' means "without the help of the general desire for pleasure or aversion to pain", then we have shown that hedonic beliefs alone cause motivating passions.

Alternatively, by 'alone' the objector might mean, not "without the help of the general appetite to pleasure or aversion to pain", but "without the help of any other causal factor whatsoever". And no doubt an objector in this vein is thinking that the other causal factor must be some sort of passion or affection, rather than a belief or even some neurological condition (though nothing in the objection itself requires that this should be so, and it is hard to see what passion other than the desire for pleasure or aversion to pain would be relevant). Our argument has not ruled out the possibility that the constant (or at least highly reliable) conjunction of hedonic beliefs with motivating passions in fact occurs only in the presence of some third factor. But there is no need to rule this out. Hume happily grants that there are many hidden causal factors; the possibility that they may be needed does not constrain us from calling one known item in a conjunction a cause and the other known item an effect. In this very strong sense of 'alone', there is almost nothing that alone causes anything else. Interpreters who think that

---

[24] Geoffrey Sayre-McCord raised this objection when I presented some of this material at the 31st Hume Society Conference in Tokyo, Japan, in August 2004.

[25] Ainslie points out (1999a) that for a dispositional property to be the cause of a feeling or bit of behavior, it would have to be constantly conjoined with it, but dispositional properties are not datable events but are always present, and so there are no grounds to think that they are causes of some feelings or behavior and not others.

Hume denies that beliefs alone cause motivating passions think him committed to the contrasting claim that passions alone *do* cause (other) motivating passions; but in this sense of alone, Hume could not say this either. For surely there are conditions that must be met even for a passion to be conjoined with a motivating passion. We have seen one of these already: no matter how much I desire money, I will not form a motivating passion to act to get some without the presence of a belief about means. Other factors are easy to think of as well: I must be alive and have a more or less normal human mind. I may even need not to be clinically depressed, since depression may break the link between desire and the impulse to act.

This is the outcome if the objection is taken to say that there could be something or other that plays a (so far hidden) role in the production of motivating passions from hedonic beliefs. If there is reason to suppose that there *must* be something specifically affective or passionate that makes possible the conjunction of hedonic belief with motivating passion, we have not seen it.

In the next chapter we will see that the common reading misunderstands what Hume means by 'alone' where he does use it. He means it in neither of the two senses just considered.

Dispositional properties are well worth having in one's ontology, and are particularly handy in accounts of the mind and of character. Indeed, it is natural to read Hume as treating virtues and vices as dispositional properties. So it is good that Hume can accommodate such properties in his philosophical system, even in a derivative form. But treating the general appetite for pleasure and aversion to pain as dispositional properties does not enable him to deny that hedonic beliefs cause passions. Indeed, such an understanding of them rules out the Background Impulse interpretation, requires Hume to treat hedonic beliefs as causes of motivating passions, and rules out a causal role for the general desire for pleasure and aversion to pain.

VIII. CONCLUSION SO FAR

We have seen strong textual and systematic reasons to read Hume as regarding hedonic beliefs as causes of motivating passions. Thus the common reading's claim that Hume regards all beliefs as inert is so far shown to be false. We have seen that his commitment to the power of beliefs to cause passions is not shaken but only reinforced by construing the general appetite to good and aversion to evil as dispositional properties.

To avoid triggering expectations that will be disappointed, I should say that I do not intend to go on to argue that moral evaluations are a species of hedonic beliefs and so, for that reason, are truth-evaluable, yet can cause motivating passions. That would be an interesting and tidy view, and one for which there is some limited textual support in Hume's discussion of the common point of view;

but I do not think it is what he thinks, for reasons that should become clear later. I have argued that Hume does not subscribe to the Inertia of Belief Thesis, but rather thinks that hedonic beliefs cause a great many of our motivating passions, because this is what makes the best sense of the textual evidence, even though this position about desire and action sounds quaint today. As we go on, this interpretation will also help to sweep away the common reading, in particular that of Argument M as a brief for noncognitivism.

In the next chapter we consider what reason is, and why and in what sense reason alone is not a motive to the will; and then we can turn to what Hume means in saying that morals are not derived from reason. We will interpret Argument M and Hume's other arguments against the moral rationalists to see where his most central disagreements with them lie.

3

Reason Alone and Moral Discrimination

In this chapter I explain why Hume thinks reason is not a motive to the will by clarifying his conception of reason, and then I use this conception to understand what he means when he says that moral distinctions are not derived from reason and to explicate his arguments in support of this.

I. WHY HUME THINKS THAT REASON IS NOT A MOTIVE TO THE WILL

In the last chapter we saw ample reasons to read Hume as saying that motivating passions are caused by hedonic beliefs. Most interpreters of Hume, however, make every effort to read these passages in some other way, so that Hume is *not* committed to that thesis. They interpret the passages, as does the Background Impulse view, to allow that the actual motivating passion in cases where we expect pain or pleasure from an object is causally independent of the hedonic belief, and is merely guided by it. They do so because they think that if Hume really were to say that hedonic beliefs create new motivating passions, he would contradict himself; for they think that Hume is committed to the impossibility of beliefs alone, whatever their content, influencing the will. And hedonic beliefs, even though their topic is the believer's pleasure or pain, are ordinary causal beliefs.[1]

Hume, of course, never says that beliefs alone cannot influence the will. What he says is that *reason* alone (or "of itself") cannot do so. But according to the common reading this claim implies that a belief cannot, for the following reason.

---

[1] In Ch. 1 I noted some of the important advocates of this interpretation (Harrison, Mackie, Snare). The thesis that for Hume beliefs alone cannot cause motivating passions is assumed in articles too numerous to list, especially in discussions of noncognitivism and expressivism. Radcliffe (1999) defends a version with a new twist. (This is a particularly searching paper; I deal with some issues that it raises below.) We saw in the last chapter that those who understand the hedonic belief as merely guiding an existing passion rather than generating it understand some key passages differently than I do, especially *T* 2.3.3.3 / SBN 414 and 1.3.10.2–3 / SBN 118–20. Their interpretation may be based on finding their reading of these passages the most natural. But in some cases the reading of the passages and the choice to discount certain turns of phrase as merely figurative seem to be based instead on the conviction that Hume simply cannot have meant to say that hedonic beliefs cause the formation of motivating passions because he says that no beliefs do so.

Beliefs are generated by reason, on that view. If a belief that is so generated could of itself cause a desire or aversion in me, then it simply follows—on this account—that my reason of itself would be the cause of my motivating passion, and hence would control my will.[2] The common reading not only finds this consequence obvious in itself, but thinks that Hume commits himself to it in Argument M. On the common reading, that argument says that because reason cannot cause passions or actions, while moral judgments can cause them, moral judgments are not caused by reason alone. But why should this follow? Even if reason alone could not cause a passion or action, it might give rise to a moral judgment, and that moral judgment might cause a passion or action. For it to follow that this cannot happen, and so for Argument M to be valid, Hume must assume that what cannot be the sole cause of passions or actions (reason) also cannot be the cause of their cause (in this case, moral judgments).[3] The contrapositive of this assumption is that the cause of the cause of a passion is also to be considered the (sole) cause of that passion. That is, remote causes of a passion are still its causes, and indeed its *sole* causes. Matter-of-fact or probable reason is the cause of hedonic beliefs; they are simply conclusions from past observations of objects that yielded pleasure or pain, applied to a present object. So if hedonic beliefs were to cause passions without assistance, then reason would be the (sole) cause of passions, which is ruled out. Therefore, according to the common reading, on Hume's account beliefs alone cannot cause motivating passions.[4]

It was argued in the last chapter that Hume says (and fully means) that hedonic beliefs themselves cause motivating passions, without the assistance of any causally independent passion such as the general appetite to pleasure or aversion to pain. Thus we must answer a pressing question. If it is true that causal reasoning produces hedonic beliefs, and hedonic beliefs produce motivating passions such as hope and fear, desire and aversion, then in what sense is reason alone not an influencing motive of the will, for Hume? Why does he deny that reason of itself can produce passions, volitions, and actions? What follows is an

---

[2] This seems to be taken for granted by Radcliffe (1999), esp. 104–5.

[3] Shaw, e.g., fails to see the need for this premise and thinks the argument valid once 'alone' is added to the conclusion (1998: 3). No doubt he finds the principle self-evident.

[4] Here we ignore the complexities of exactly how 'alone' figures in this argument and how the modals operate. My statement of the unstated assumption (that what cannot be the sole cause of a passion cannot be the cause of its cause) is not quite right; presumably it should say that what cannot be the sole cause of a passion cannot be the sole cause of its cause, or perhaps of its sole cause, or something of the sort. (For the common reading actually allows that a product of reason alone can be the *partial* cause of a passion or action, in conjunction with a desire or aversion.) And my restatement of this assumption to say that the cause of a cause of a passion is also to be considered the cause of that passion is not quite right either. Besides lacking the restriction to sole causation, it is not really the contrapositive of the modal thesis about what cannot cause a passion, but at most one of its consequences, since it is not a necessary thesis. For clarity and simplicity we may ignore these subtleties at present, since they have no effect on the argument to follow.

account of why motivating passions are never the products of reason alone, even though some of them are the products of hedonic beliefs.[5]

Neither advocates of the common reading nor their challengers have yet explained why Hume denies that reason alone can produce motivating passions. As many have remarked, his arguments for this by themselves are not satisfactory.[6] We need some account of Hume's conception of reason in order to see why it cannot do this, and to see what follows about beliefs (including hedonic beliefs). A thorough treatment of Hume's theory of reason is not possible here. But we can explain enough to illuminate this doctrine that reason of itself is inert—what we have called the Inertia of Reason Thesis. (This is a thesis Hume definitely espouses, unlike the Inertia of Belief Thesis, which we deny that he holds.)

Hume's conception of reason is not announced; it slips out here and there, beginning in Book 1 of the *Treatise*.

Reason in Book 1

In Book 1 it is evident that, given his empiricism, Hume does not think of the mind as antecedently divided into parts with definite characteristics to which one might appeal in explaining our thinking. The nature of the mind must be discovered entirely by observing what occurs in it. Thus he says:

> For to me it seems evident, that the essence of the mind being equally unknown to us with that of external bodies, it must be equally impossible to form any notion of its powers and qualities otherwise than from careful and exact experiments, and the observation of those particular effects, which result from its different circumstances and situation. . . . we cannot go beyond experience; and any hypothesis, that pretends to discover the ultimate original properties of human nature, ought at first to be rejected as presumptuous and chimerical. (*T*, Intro. 8 / SBN p. xvii)

And further: "We . . . glean up our experiments in this science from a cautious observation of human life" (*T*, Intro. 10 / SBN p. xix).

Although he uses the terminology of 'faculties', Hume identifies reason, imagination, and memory solely as particular mental activities. Imagination is just (putting it very crudely) the forming of images or (perhaps better) representations, in particular those that are fainter than memories and occur in an order or combination of ideas that may differ from that of the impressions

---

[5] Botros (2006) has recently argued that Hume not only says that reason alone or of itself cannot produce passions or actions, but also that reason (without qualification or disclaimer) cannot produce them—that is, that reason plays no causal role whatsoever in the generation of passions and actions, not even one of providing information that makes a difference to what action is performed. Her principle reason for attributing the latter "extreme" thesis to Hume is that he needs it to make Argument M valid. As we shall see, on my interpretation the argument is valid with the restricted premise.

[6] See, e.g., Stroud 1977; Mackie 1980; and Millgram 1995 for criticisms of his arguments (construed according to the common reading).

from which they were copied. Memory is the repeating of impressions as vivid ideas that retain the order of their originals (*T* 1.1.3 / SBN 8–10), for example in the pairing of perceptions we call causes and effects (*T* 1.3.6.2 / SBN 87). Reason is just the comparing of ideas to find relations between them. It would not be amiss to substitute the gerund 'reasoning' almost everywhere Hume says 'reason'. This conception of reasoning as forming chains of ideas that bear certain relations to one another has its roots in Locke. (Of course, Hume famously argues that causal inference is not an activity of reason, e.g., at *T* 1.3.6.12 / SBN 92 and *T* 1.3.7.6 / SBN 97; but almost in the same breath he goes on to talk of causal *reasonings* (*T* 1.3.6.14 / SBN 93; *T* 1.3.7.6 / SBN 97), and in Book 2 he explicitly subsumes causal or probable inference under the heading of reason and argues that it, too, does not influence the will.) In intuition we compare ideas without intermediary and necessarily recognize a relation between them (*passim*, e.g., *T* 1.3.1.2 / SBN 70). In demonstration we proceed step by step in linking related ideas in sequence, preserving our assent—or the degree to which the ideas are evident—at each step, so that in the end we find evident (indeed, we are necessarily determined to grasp) a relation between our starting and resulting ideas (*passim*, e.g., *T* 1.3.7.3 / SBN 95). In causal inference we proceed from a present impression or memory to an idea, with some of the vivacity of the former being transferred to the latter (*passim*, e.g., *T* 1.3.4 entire). These processes are just what Hume means by reason; there is no independent definition. And this is to be expected, given his empiricism. On his view we cannot find reason first and then discover what it does, for we have no separate impression of reason. All we have in experience is the activity. Reason(ing) is one of a number of mental activities that Hume discusses (imagination and memory are others), and each also has its characteristic outcome. The outcome of reasoning—its only possible outcome, given the nature of the process—is an enlivened idea. In reasoning we compare ideas and find them to be related, or not; so its only available upshot is the enlivening of some idea.[7]

Of course, once he has identified a certain characteristic activity of the mind that has many instances, Hume can attribute to the mind the power to perform this activity and call this the faculty of reason. But as we have seen in Chapter 2, a

---

[7] For detailed interpretations of Hume's conception of reason, see Owen 1999: chs. 5–8 and Garrett 1997: esp. ch. 1. My gloss is particularly influenced by Owen's book. Owen says, e.g., "At the basic level for Hume, there are ideas and impressions that can be classified in various ways. These perceptions of the mind interact in various ways; one set of such interactions we call 'reasonings', either demonstrative or probable" (1999: 76). Radcliffe (1999: 104 and n. 9) also points out that Hume's empiricism requires him to identify reason by its activities.

There may be one further feature that Hume attributes to reason: he seems to assume that when we are reasoning, we get things right, and when we err, we are not genuinely reasoning (though he does sometimes speak of false or sophistical reasoning). That is, he may on the whole treat 'reason' and 'reasoning' as success terms, like 'learning'.

As Owen notes (1999: ch. 3), Hume's conception of reason(ing) as the activity of linking ideas that bear relations to one another to form a chain of ideas has its origin in Locke's view of reason, and important features of it can be traced to Descartes (Owen 1999: ch. 2).

power is to be understood entirely by reference to its actual or probable exercise. To say that the human mind possesses the faculty (that is, power) of reason is just to say that the process of linking perceptions in this characteristic way does or probably will occur in the mind. It is not to postulate any reasoning organ that carries out these tasks. Even in speaking of the faculty of reason, then, Hume speaks only of the reasoning process.[8]

Hume's immediate rationalist predecessors (Clarke, Wollaston, Balguy) say very little about exactly what reason is, in spite of the substantial use they make of it in their ethical theories. What little they do say suggests that Hume's picture in the *Treatise* coincides with theirs in places but probably also diverges from theirs. John Balguy, for example, adopting and making more explicit some of Samuel Clarke's views (1991[1706]), defines reason as "a faculty enabling us to perceive, either immediately or mediately, the agreement or disagreement of ideas, whether natural or moral" (1991[1734]: 399). Since Clarke and Balguy are not empiricists, the ideas in question could be innate, though many of their examples are drawn from experience. Furthermore, although they do not say one way or the other, Balguy and Clarke may well think of the faculty of reason as something identifiable independent of its operation, an entity that performs the comparative operation and enables the thinker to grasp the agreement or disagreement of ideas. If so, their view differs from Hume's, and that difference (if it is real) is the result of Hume's empiricism. Hume would say that there is (so far as we know) no entity that compares, but only the process of comparing. But the root notion that reason in some way involves the comparing of ideas to discover their agreement or disagreement is found in both, as we will see even more plainly below in the language of *Treatise* Book 3.

Given Hume's picture of reason in Book 1, we may tentatively draw certain conclusions. First, reason for Hume is simply reason*ing*, a certain sort of process. Second, production of something by reason *alone* is generation solely by this process and no other. And third, what is produced by reason alone is also limited to the possible outcomes of this process. (Although there are really three processes grouped together under the heading of reasoning, we may speak of them in the singular, since they have a common structure—that of comparing perceptions to find relations among them—and they can be intermingled, steps of a demonstration being instances of intuition, for example.) Passions and actions, of course, are not generated by any process of comparing ideas (or linking present impressions with ideas) in a way that reveals relations between those ideas and preserves assent or evidentness. It is true that passions, being secondary impressions, are always preceded in the mind by some impression or idea which presumably is the passion's cause; but this antecedent perception does not give rise to the passion by participating in a process of comparison

---

[8] I am grateful to Ernesto V. Garcia for pointing out that on my interpretation the faculty of reason is a Humean power.

and assent. The generation of passions is not the discerning of relations between ideas directly, by intuition; nor is it the relation-discovering, stepwise linking of ideas to one another that occurs in either demonstrative or causal inference. Also, passions and actions are not the right sorts of items to be the outcome of a reasoning process, for they are not ideas.

That is why reason alone cannot produce motivating passions. Passion generation and reasoning are distinct activities. Likewise, the generation of volitions and actions is a distinct process from reasoning, and that is why reason alone cannot produce action.

Reason in Books 2 and 3

This much we can obtain from Book 1 of the *Treatise*. Hume's commitment to this conception of reason as reasoning is restated in Books 2 and 3. For example, in Book 3 he remarks that "Reason or science is nothing but the comparing of ideas, and the discovery of their relations" (*T* 3.1.1.24 / SBN 466). But the concept of reasoning is also further developed.

What we have called the Representation Argument, which appears in each of those two books, purports to show what the comparison of ideas in reasoning comes to, and how finding things true enters the picture. (We can leave aside questions about whether the discussion of reason and truth in Books 2 and 3 is compatible with the characterization of reason in Book 1.) The first version of the Representation Argument, in Book 2, claims that passions have no "representative quality, which renders [them] a copy of any other existence or modification [of existence]", and therefore it is impossible that they should be "oppos'd by . . . truth and reason" (*T* 2.3.3.5 / SBN 415), since such opposition can only consist in the disagreement of ideas with the objects they represent. Thus it is not only because passions are more vivid than mere ideas that they are not suitable outputs of a reasoning process, but because they are not Humean representations. For Hume a representation is a fainter copy of an original that is caused by that original and serves to represent it in thought. Representations can be outcomes of the reasoning process; passions, not being copies of some original that represent it in thought, cannot.[9]

---

[9] Persson (1997) raises the objection that since Hume's categories of perceptions (mere ideas, believed ideas, memories, impressions) are distinguished from one another solely by vivacity, and form a continuum of vivacity, his claim that reason can produce believed ideas but not impressions cannot bear the weight he gives it. Here I suggest a way in which Hume may overcome the difficulty. His official account of how X represents Y is simply X's being a copy of Y that was caused by it. (See Cohon and Owen 1997.) Perhaps that is all he means, and passions are not representations because they are not caused by more vivid passions that they exactly resemble. Or perhaps he tacitly assumes something further that characterizes representations: a functional role in thought that "original existences" lack, that of serving as material in reasoning. The idea of anger can serve in this role, but the anger itself cannot. Whether or not this is Hume's view, it seems true, and may be part of the reason why Hume insists that passions have no representative quality.

On its second appearance, in Book 3, the Representation Argument goes as follows:

1. "Reason is the discovery of truth and falsehood."
2. "Truth or falsehood consists in an agreement or disagreement either to the *real* relations of ideas, or to *real* existence and matter of fact."
3. "Whatever, therefore, is not susceptible of this agreement or disagreement, is incapable of being true or false, and can never be an object of our reason."
4. "[O]ur passions, volitions, and actions. . . [are] original facts and realities, compleat in themselves, and implying no reference to other passions, volitions and actions."
5. Thus, "[our passions, volitions, and actions] are not susceptible of any such agreement or disagreement."
6. " 'Tis impossible, therefore, they can be pronounced either true or false, and be either contrary or conformable to reason." (*T* 3.1.1.9 / SBN 458)

I long wondered why Hume says "Reason is the discovery of truth and falsehood" if he means that reason is *that faculty which discovers* truth and falsehood. Why does he express his thought so poorly? Let us propose that this is not what he means. This is not a remark about the faculty of reason or the part of the mind labeled "Reason". Hume really means that reason is the *discovery* of truth and falsehood—the process of discovering them. That is, *reasoning* is the *discovering* of truth and falsehood.

Hume uses somewhat similar language in the key paragraph examined in Chapter 2 (*T* 2.3.3.3 / SBN 414) when he says that "reason is nothing but the discovery of this connexion [of cause and effect]", also sounding as if he is making the category mistake of identifying a faculty of the mind with a discovery, and also naturally (but erroneously) interpreted as a sloppy way to say that reason is the faculty that makes the discovery. Here too I propose to read Hume as saying instead that (in this instance causal) reasoning is the discovering of cause and effect.

Another turn of phrase that seems to commit Hume to a peculiar conception of reason occurs in the "Dissertation of the Passions" (in a few words omitted when this passage was quoted in Chapter 2): "reason, in a strict sense, as meaning the judgment of truth and falsehood, can never, of itself, be any motive to the will." This wording strongly suggests an identification of reason with judgments or beliefs: it makes it seem that for Hume reason in a strict sense just is a set of judgments, so that the very judgments themselves—the beliefs—are identical with, or are parts of or instances of, reason. And some interpreters think that this is Hume's view, though if it were his whole conception of reason, it would be incompatible with his theory of belief, according to which there is no *intrinsic* difference between a belief with a certain content rationally acquired (and so part of reason, so construed) and one with the same content acquired in a non-rational way, for example by listening to moving rhetoric.[10] (Perhaps many of us who interpret Hume slide from thinking of causal and other inferentially derived beliefs as *products* of reason to regarding them as constituent parts of reason, thus disguising to ourselves the oddity of the identification of a belief with a bit of reason.) If reason consisted of a set of judgments, reason's inability to cause passions on its own would entail the motivational inertia of rational beliefs as well. Or, put another way, if a rationally derived belief were (a part of) reason, and it were to cause a motivating passion, then reason (alone) would cause a motivating passion. But this is a misreading of Hume's understanding of reason; a rationally derived belief is the outcome of reasoning, but is not a part of reason at all. We should read this passage as we read those from Book 2, as saying that *reasoning* is the discovery of truth and falsehood, where 'discovery' is the name of a process. That is, reasoning is the *discovering* of the truth or falsehood of our ideas. 'Reason' in a strict sense means not each and every belief about truth and falsehood, but *the judging* of truth and falsehood. 'Judgment' can mean *a* judgment, or the process of judgment, and here it means the latter. Read in this way, these remarks are actually much clearer and simpler.

We know from Book 1 that reasoning is the comparing and linking of ideas, and produces a lively idea as its outcome. This is reiterated in many passages in the first section of Book 3 (e.g., *T* 3.1.1.4 / SBN 456–7). In the Representation Argument, reason(ing) is also the process of discovering perceptions in the mind to be true or false. Truth and falsehood are understood as agreement or disagreement with real relations of ideas or real matters of fact. 'Agreement' in step 2 of the argument presumably means being a faithful copy and an accurate representation, given the reference to copies and representation in the first version of the argument at *T* 2.3.3. (Agreement cannot simply mean resemblance, for of course passions may resemble other passions and actions may resemble other actions, yet Hume denies in step 5 that passions and actions are susceptible of "such agreement or disagreement".) Thus it follows from steps 1 and 2 that reasoning is the process of discovering the accuracy or inaccuracy of an item as a representation of a real relation of ideas or a real matter of fact. Since (as Hume reiterates at the start of this very section) the mind has no direct access to reality, but only to its own perceptions, we do not discover truth by comparing items in the mind with the real matters of fact themselves. Presumably we discover truth by comparing items in the mind with our *perceptions* of real matters of fact—with other items in the mind. Thus reasoning is always a process of comparing perceptions, as it was in Book 1.

---

[10] Stroud (1977: 160–1), e.g., attributes to Hume the view that reason is a set of propositions, and criticizes this conception of reason. I suspect that many who think that Hume cannot consistently hold that any beliefs cause motivating passions without help from passions tacitly attribute to Hume this view of reason as a set of propositions.

What is the mental item whose accuracy as a representational copy (whose truth) is ascertained by such a process of comparison? Step 3 says that it cannot be an item that is "not susceptible of this agreement". For such an item cannot be true or false, and "can never be an object of our reason". Thus, objects of our reason(ing) are items that we can find to be true or false by the process of matching them with other perceptions of whose accuracy we are confident. Objects of our reason, then, are not things in the world *about* which we reason, as we might have supposed, but rather the perceptions in the mind *with* which we reason, and which may be assessed and made more lively (or less so) by the process of comparison.[11] Passions, volitions, and actions, not being representations or copies of anything else, cannot be found to be good or bad representations—not even of other passions, volitions, or actions.[12] They are not items in the mind with which we reason. Therefore they are neither conformable nor contrary to reason, in the sense that they cannot be found true or false by means of a reasoning process.[13]

Hume also concludes in step 6 that therefore passions, volitions, and actions cannot be either "contrary or conformable to reason". This may be an attempt on his part to parse the moral rationalists' position: perhaps when they say that immoral actions are contrary to reason, they mean that immoral actions are false—that they are inaccurate representations of reality. William Wollaston,

[11] This is, I believe, consistent with Sturgeon's account of what Hume means by an object of reason (2001: 10–11).

[12] There is a difficult issue here concerning how Hume can consistently claim that passions are not representations, given that his lengthy analysis of the indirect passions makes considerable use of ideas in various roles: ideas of the self and of other persons, of objects that evoke pleasure, and so on. Hume is also quite well aware that direct passions such as anger have intentional objects, and premise 4 of the Representation Argument is frequently read as denying this. These tensions lead Baier (1991: 160 ff.) to discount the Representation Argument entirely as a mere flight of exaggerated anti-rationalism. That strategy seems implausible in light of Hume's emphasis on this argument in the *Treatise* (where it occurs twice) and his use of it as a foundation for further (and quite pivotal) arguments; on this see my discussion (Cohon 1994). I propose there that we follow Árdal in construing all the passions as having characteristic causes and effects rather than containing representations (ideas) within them. Haruko Inoue suggests (in a talk at the 32nd Hume Society Conference in Toronto, Canada, 2005) that premise 4 applies only to the direct passions, those that can be motivating. On her view, indirect passions do represent other things (objects and persons), but direct passions contain no such representative elements. This preserves the Representation Argument, provided we do not understand premise 4 as a denial that direct passions have intentional objects in any sense at all. Inoue seems to assume that a passion such as anger can have a "direction" (as Hume puts it) without being a representation or containing one.

[13] Hume seems to have progressed from the view in Book 1 that reasoning discovers various relations among our ideas to the view that reason discovers only their resemblance and contrariety (whether they match or do not match each other). In Books 2 and 3, does he try to reduce the other relations (degrees in quality and number, contiguity in space and time, cause and effect) to these? Does he mean to say now that in discovering that six is greater than four the reasoning consists not in comparing the idea of six with the idea of four, but rather in comparing our idea that six is greater than four with the "real relation" of these ideas? The text of the Representation Argument in its two versions is quite clear in saying that reasoning is the process of assessing ideas for truth, but how this fits together with the view of Book 1 is not so clear.

whom Hume criticizes, argues that actions such as stealing are wrong because they express a kind of falsehood, such as that the property taken is one's own.[14] Actions cannot themselves be true or false, Hume points out, so if 'contrary to reason' just means false, they cannot be contrary to reason.[15] But Hume seems to mean a bit more than the denial of truth-aptness when he says that actions cannot be contrary or conformable to reason. What could he mean, given that he thinks of reason as reasoning, a process rather than a set of propositions to which something could conform? What can be "pronounced true" is conformable to reason in the sense that it is a potential object of reasoning (a representation) of the sort that is or would be found by a process of reasoning to match the original that it represents. What can be pronounced false is contrary to reason in the sense that it too is an object of reason (a representation of some other item) that is or would be found via reasoning to differ from the original that it purports to represent. Its poor match with its original becomes evident by reasoning.

Generations of students have argued that Hume has an inexplicably narrow conception of reason. Why does he limit its scope to demonstration and causal inference? He admits that we often talk of reason influencing or directing our feelings and decisions. Why reject this piece of ordinary talk? And why go to such pains to deny what philosophers since Plato have thought obvious, that reason can be practical? The move smacks of begging the question: Hume seems so intent to prove that morals are not derived from reason (perhaps in order to clear the ground for a sentiment-based account) that he narrows the scope of reason to insure himself this result. But to read him this way is to overlook the dominance of his empiricism. Guided by it, he identifies reason only as certain characteristic activities: mentally comparing perceptions and detecting the presence or absence of relations between them. That is surely what goes on in demonstration, and also what goes on in causal inference, with appropriate adjustments. But the generation of desires and aversions is a process too different to be grouped among the activities of the understanding. As we have seen, the generation of direct passions is a causal process typically involving an idea or impression of pleasure or pain that causes a new impression; the generation of indirect passions is more complex (involving a double relation of ideas and impressions) but also generates new impressions. They are not processes of linking related ideas and finding true. If reason were an organ of the mind that could be identified apart from what happens when reasoning activity is going on, then it would be open to speculation, and to observation, what other things it might do or what its products might be. But as a thoroughgoing empiricist Hume cannot use such a notion of reason. The question, instead, is whether the processes by which

---

[14] Wollaston 1991[1724]: 239–54.

[15] Hutcheson apparently makes a related but less charitable guess at the rationalists' meaning, speculating that in saying that an action is unreasonable they mean that there are false propositions about the action (*Illustrations on the Moral Sense*, sect. 1, 1971: 213–15). So while Hume at times sets up a straw Wollaston, he is less unfair than his predecessor.

motivating passions are produced are sufficiently similar to the processes we call reasoning to be classified with them as reasoning activities. And Hume does not find them to be so.

Reason, Hedonic Beliefs, and Motivating Passions

We have seen that according to the common reading, Hume makes the tacit assumption that if reason alone produced belief and belief (without assistance) caused passion, then reason would be the (sole) cause of passion. Here the common reading applies the idea of a causal chain in which the initial item in the chain is rightly considered a cause of every item that occurs later in the chain; so we may call this the Causal Chain Assumption. It is a principle of the transitivity of causation. That is how I long understood the logic of Argument M. I assumed that what lay behind it was the suppressed premise that whatever is a cause of some further cause is a cause of that further cause's effect. The lack of a horseshoe nail caused the loss of the horse, the loss of the horse caused the loss of the rider, and so on along the chain to the loss of the war; from these links and the Causal Chain Assumption we can infer that the lack of a horseshoe nail caused the loss of the war. That causation works this way is a plausible and familiar assumption.[16]

But this Causal Chain Assumption is in fact inapplicable to the case of reason, belief, and passion.

To invoke the notion of a causal chain, one must link items with causal efficacy—whether objects, as Hume tends to call them, or events—that can occupy nodes on the chain. To invoke the notion here, one must assume that reason is such an item. On that assumption, reason is some sort of causal agent or prospective agent. To know that reason is the cause of beliefs but not of passions, we would need first to identify reason and then observe whether or not it is repeatedly conjoined with beliefs or passions. But, as we have seen,

---

[16] Plausible and familiar, but possibly false. A headache caused me to lie down for a nap; lying down caused a depression in the bed; but did the headache therefore cause a depression in the bed? At best the principle needs some refinements.

On the common reading, the Causal Chain Assumption is apparently also thought to apply to causation alone, or of itself, so that if the lack of a nail of itself caused the loss of the horse, the loss of the horse of itself caused the loss of the rider, and so on, then the lack of a nail of itself caused the loss of the war. If we add "alone" or its equivalent at every stage the principle is actually more defensible, but the successive antecedents will very rarely be true; certainly that is not the case in the nursery song about the horseshoe nail. If we add "alone" only in the first stage (say, in a two-stage progression), then transitivity fails for "causation alone" (the property "being the sole cause of"). A virus alone caused the illness; the illness caused boredom; but it does not follow that the virus alone caused boredom. (See Cohon 1997c.) This makes it tempting, on the common reading, to construe the moral premise of Argument M to say that moral judgments *alone* produce passions and actions. The trouble with that reading is that Hume never says this at all; his arguments for that premise do not support this version of it; and in the case of action, at least, he is very clear that moral evaluations are sometimes insufficient to rouse us to act.

Hume's empiricism does not permit him to think of reason as an independently identifiable item. Rather, he identifies it solely as reasoning activity. Consequently, reason cannot in the same way occupy a node in the causal chain.[17] This means that the transitivity of cause and effect expressed in the Causal Chain Assumption does not apply here. If an item X results from one process, and X goes on to produce a second item Y by a different process, it does not follow that the second item also resulted from the initial process; the transitivity does not hold between processes as it perhaps does between causally efficacious objects or events. For example, if a statue is made by the lost wax process, and that statue goes on to create a scandal, it does not follow that the scandal is made by the lost wax process. Whereas if we think of the cause of the statue as an active object (such as the sculptor), then if he produced the statue and the statue caused a scandal, it at least seems correct to infer that the sculptor caused the scandal. With reason understood solely as a process (reasoning) and not (to our knowledge) an agent or even an object or state of affairs, no such inference is warranted. For Hume the empiricist, reason is the lost wax process, not the sculptor. A rationally derived belief is brought into being by a process of comparing and assenting to perceptions; the belief might in turn cause something else by a different process; but it does not follow that the new item was caused by a process of comparing and assenting to perceptions. Similarly, if a manuscript is produced by typing on a computer, and the manuscript makes a loud noise by falling off the desk, it does not follow that typing on a computer (that process) produced a loud noise. A crystal is produced by a chemical process involving heating a material and subjecting it to pressure, and the crystal causes a rainbow to appear on the wall, but it does not follow that the rainbow was caused by heating something and applying pressure to it; in fact, it was caused by a different process involving the refraction of light. This is a point of logic: there is no transitivity of process parallel to the transitivity of causes expressed in the Causal Chain Assumption. From the fact that an object or event X resulted from a process P and X caused Y, we cannot infer that Y was the result of process P.

There is in fact no evidence that Hume accepts the Causal Chain Principle even with regard to objects or events. It is not among his "Rules by which to judge of causes and effects", and appears to contradict the first rule ("The cause and effect must be contiguous in space and time" (*T* 1.3.15.3 / SBN 173)). So there is certainly no reason to think he would accept it with regard to processes. And

---

[17] Hume does say at one point in Book 1 that "Our reason must be considered as a kind of cause, of which truth is the natural effect" (*T* 1.4.1.1 / SBN 180). But in its context this claim makes a very different point: not that reason is an item that can be identified and linked in causal relations apart from the activity of reasoning, but that while the steps in a demonstration are all necessary and its conclusion is necessary, we must back off from this process of inference and treat the steps and their upshot as conjoined items so that we can (using cause-and-effect reasoning) assess the probability that we made a mistake in the inference. Thus this remark is compatible with understanding 'reason' to mean the reasoning process.

our counter-examples show that for processes, and even for sequences consisting of a process, an object, a second process, and a second object or outcome, the relation "being a cause of" is not transitive. So we should not assume that Hume took such transitivity for granted.[18]

Understanding Humean reason as a process or activity also changes how we understand production by reason *alone*, or of itself. This is extremely important, because many interpreters place great emphasis on the expressions 'alone' and 'of itself' in articulating what they take to be Hume's position. Hume himself sometimes includes these terms and sometimes omits them, as if they do not make a great deal of difference. For the common reading, however, they make all the difference. The common picture is one of reason as an object that in fact, we find, exerts force on nothing but ideas and cannot move the will. But it is the kind of entity that might have proven to have causal efficacy, in that we could have observed suitable constant conjunctions. If we think of reason as such an

---

[18] There are occasions when we seem to make a valid inference that applies the Causal Chain Assumption to processes. Since there are clear counter-examples to the principle, this can only be an appearance. I am not sure exactly how to explain it each time it occurs; but in general what happens in these cases is that we tacitly rely on something other than transitivity of causation with respect to processes. Here are two examples that work in this way (the first offered by Robert Shaver, the second by Ernesto Garcia):

E1.
A hurricane (a process) causes flooding.
The flooding (another process) causes property damage.
Therefore the hurricane causes property damage.

E2.
A process of cooking and combining ingredients (including pouring in a large amount of salt) causes the production of egg salad.
The egg salad causes a bad taste in the eater's mouth.
Therefore the preparing of the egg salad (or the over-salting) causes the bad taste.

In E1 (which looks very much as if it makes a sound transition between processes) I think the transition seems to work because we do not really distinguish between the hurricane and the flooding (the movement of water into places where it does not normally occur); we think of flooding as part of the (single) hurricane process. (When insurance companies after Hurricane Katrina objected to paying their customers' claims on the grounds that the policy-holders held hurricane insurance but not flood insurance and their houses were damaged only by flooding, this seemed sophistical because it was taken for granted that the process that is a hurricane involves the sea rising and the flooding of low-lying coastal areas.) If we rewrite E1 to say "High winds on the coast cause flooding, and flooding causes property damage, therefore high winds on the coast cause property damage," there now seems to be something inaccurate in the conclusion—an additional causal factor is not mentioned in it, but should be if the argument is to be valid. Of course the argument would be valid if the conclusion incorporated everything in both premises (if it said "Flooding caused by high winds on the coast caused the property damage"); but if it detaches the cause from the first premise and combines it with the (detached) effect from the second, it is not valid. In E2 we tacitly add further causal factors to the cause in the second premise. It would be an instance of transitivity only if the very item said to be the effect in the first premise was treated as the cause in the second premise; but this is not so. The salty egg salad in the first premise is thought of as an object, a bowl full of stuff. What causes the bad taste is not just this bowl full of stuff, but it together with a further process, that of eating.

Thanks to Bradley Armour-Garb for very helpful discussion of these examples and the failure of transitivity for causal processes.

object, then it is natural to think of reason *alone* as that object unassisted by any other causally efficacious object (such as a passion of independent origin).[19] Reason, on that account, is like a billiard cue that in principle could move the ball but in fact cannot without a push from something else. This is certainly what I previously thought Hume meant by 'reason alone' or 'of itself': reason without assistance from a passion not of its making. Whereas, given Hume's understanding of reason as reason*ing*, there is a different way to read 'reason alone'. It is not "reason without another causally efficacious item", but rather "the process of reasoning itself, without another process". (If it is meant this way, the qualification "alone" or "of itself" is often simply understood as a matter at least of conversational implicature. If I say "I made my fortune by selling cars", it is implicit that I did it that way alone, and not also by winning the lottery; otherwise I would say "*in part* by selling cars". This explains Hume's intermittent use of the qualifiers.) So an offspring of reason alone—what is made by reasoning and nothing else—is something generated by that process with no other process. Thus the Inertia of Reason Thesis says that no reasoning process can generate passions, volitions, or actions without the help of another kind of process. Once the reasoning process is completed and another kind of process begins, the ultimate result is *not* a product of reason alone. Should reasoning alone produce a belief which in some other way produces a motivating passion, that passion would be analogous to the loud noise made by the manuscript falling off the desk, which is not made by the typing of it.

To be sure, the process by which a hedonic belief (such as the belief in an imminent pain) produces aversion in us is not traced in detail by Hume. Perhaps all we know is that such beliefs are constantly conjoined with such aversions in virtue of the natural constitution of the mind. But as we saw in the previous chapter, he does say (in *T* 1.3.10.3 / SBN 119–20) that the lively idea of pain to come operates on the will and passions in the same way as does an occurrent sensation of pain, although not quite as forcefully. And *that* causal process (the feeling of pain causing aversion) is obviously not one of comparing evident ideas. When a burning sensation from touching a hot kettle gives me a powerful aversion to that pain, this is not a process either of intuition or inference. There is no comparing of ideas here and no sequence of transferring assent to them. Hume says that a similar process to that involving current pain generates an aversion in me in response to my hedonic belief that I *will* have pain *if* I touch the kettle. So that process, too, is not one of comparing perceptions and transmitting assent.

Consequently, on this account of production by reason alone, the *conclusion* of a piece of reasoning (an idea lively enough that it is believed) might perfectly

---

[19] Practically all commentators, including Harrison (1976), Mackie (1980), and Stroud (1977: ch. 7), assume that 'alone' or 'of itself' means "without another causal agent or force", and as Stroud points out, there is textual evidence that this is so. Snare (1991: 68) argues that it means (specifically) without another motivating passion.

well cause a passion to come into existence. The resulting passion need not, and indeed could not, be the product of reasoning alone, because its causation would not be a step in any piece of reasoning. A passion is not produced by the comparing of related ideas and is not found evident—it is not generated by a reasoning activity—even if it is caused by a belief that was so produced. It is generated by another process. And a passion (much less an action) could not be the outcome of reasoning alone because it is not an idea, as indicated in Book 1, and not a representation of something else, as specified in Books 2 and 3. On the present view, then, the thesis that a hedonic belief causes a motivating passion without any additional causal input from an independent passion is perfectly consistent with Hume's claim that reason of itself cannot produce passions or actions. There is no contradiction. For when Hume says that reason alone cannot produce a passion, what he means is that a passion is not the outcome of a reasoning process; he does not mean that a passion is not produced by a belief without the help of a prior passion. If the hedonic conclusion of my causal inference in turn generates a passion, that passion is not produced by reason alone in Hume's sense. It is irrelevant to Hume's point whether another passion is involved in the causation of the passion; what matters is whether the process is one of reasoning.

The process conception of reason shows why reason alone cannot produce passions, volitions, or actions—why reason is inert—by showing what sort of phenomenon reason is. It has the added advantage of removing what appeared to be a contradiction in the text between that thesis and Hume's claim that hedonic beliefs cause new motivating desires and aversions. Shortly we will see how this understanding of reason provides an interpretation of the argument that morals are not derived from reason.

An Argument for the Inertia of Belief, and a Reply

The understanding of "reason" as reasoning activity provides a reply to an argument that some interpreters make that Hume is committed to the causal inertia of belief, one we could not address until now. The argument goes as follows. Suppose a belief were to cause a motivating passion. Indeed, to tailor this objection to our view, suppose a hedonic belief were to cause such a passion. For Hume, a belief has only two aspects: its representational content and its force or vivacity. Surely it is not the force or vivacity of the hedonic belief by itself that causes a motivating passion, for all beliefs are forceful and vivid, yet beliefs about many subjects (including many causal beliefs) cause no passions. Therefore it must be the representational content of the belief that has this causal efficacy—the belief's being about available pleasure or pain. But if beliefs cause motivating passions in virtue of what they represent, then representation has an effect on the will. But (the argument goes on) representation is the special prerogative of reason. Therefore, for a believed idea to bring a passion into being in virtue of its subject matter—its representational content—just *is* for reason alone to generate a passion. But Hume denies that reason alone can produce passions or oppose passions. Therefore, if Hume allows that hedonic beliefs cause motivating passions, he is committed to a contradiction.[20]

The problematic premise is that representation as such is a manifestation of reason, so that if representational content causes passion, that is an instance of reason causing passion. This misconstrues Humean representation as well as Humean reason. We have seen that, given his empiricism, Hume defines reason as certain activities or processes. He is not always as clear as we might like about which activities these are—for example, at first he seems to exclude, but ultimately he includes, causal inference. But the function of representing is certainly not the province of reason. Our ideas (or mental representations) of pleasure and pain are not produced by reason or the understanding, but by the imagination taking copies of our impressions. And our impressions are certainly not products of our reason. Both memory and the imagination perform the function of representing things to us, and both are explicitly distinguished from reason (e.g., *T* 1.3.6.4 / SBN 88–9; *T* 1.3.9.19 n. 22 / SBN 117–18 n. 1). Reason makes use of many representations that it does not create; arguably, it does not create any of them.

We should also note that the representational content of ideas—what they are ideas *of*—plays a determinative role in forming new passions in other contexts where no one would attribute this role to reason. In sympathy, for example, it is because my idea of your passion is an idea of *grief* (rather than an idea of joy, or for that matter of a square) that by sympathizing with you I come to feel grief rather than joy, or indeed that I come to feel any passion at all (*T* 2.1.11.8 / SBN 319 and *T* 3.3.1.7 / SBN 576). The representational content of my idea of your grief determines that I shall come to have a passion in this situation, and which passion I shall come to have. There is no temptation to say that because my believed idea is a representation (of grief), therefore it is *reason* that causes me to feel a passion when I sympathize. Although the generation of motivating passions from hedonic beliefs is a different process from sympathy, it would be a similar mistake to treat representation as a manifestation of reason there. The fact that my believed idea is a representation of *pleasure* explains my coming to have a desire, but there should likewise be no temptation to say that because of this causal influence of the representational content of my belief, *reason* causes my desire. Representational content is the product not of reasoning but of other processes or faculties, and what causes my desire is not reasoning.

An objector might grant that reason does not create the idea (the representation) of pleasure, yet still object that on the present interpretation it is reason that gives the idea of pleasure its vivacity within a believed judgment. And only vivid and forceful ideas influence the will, according to *T* 1.3.10. So reason, as the source

---

[20] This is a loose reconstruction of an argument in Radcliffe 1999: 109–10.

of the vivacity, is still solely responsible for the idea's capacity to cause desire, and hence reason alone causes the passion. However, this objection is blocked by the process conception of reason. True, the vivacity of the idea depends upon the workings of inference, and its generation of passion depends upon its vivacity. But, first, the representational content also plays a role in causing passion, since it is specifically beliefs about forthcoming pleasures and pains that cause them. And second, the increase in vivacity is an *effect* of reasoning, not identical with reason(ing) itself. The objector slides back into thinking of the belief as itself a bit of reason rather than reasoning's outcome; or rather, slides into a similar thought that the vivacity of the belief is itself reason. The vivacity is produced by reasoning, but it is something distinct from reasoning that, together with the belief's content, goes on to cause other phenomena by other processes. So this is not an instance of a reasoning process alone causing a passion.

Having met this objection, we can go on to consider morals.

II. WHY HUME THINKS THAT MORALS ARE NOT DERIVED FROM REASON

The first section of Book 3 of the *Treatise* is entitled "Moral distinctions not deriv'd from reason", and its purpose is to prove that this is so. But what is this claim? First, what are "moral distinctions", or, as Hume often says (perhaps interchangeably, perhaps not), "morals"? Secondly, what is it for something to be "deriv'd" from reason, and why might it be impossible for something to be so derived?

According to the common reading, by 'morals' or 'moral distinctions' Hume means moral judgments ("one's moral judgments, moral opinions, moral beliefs", as Snare puts it[21]), and the claim that they are not derived from reason is or entails that moral judgments are non-propositional, and so do not represent any states of affairs and are not truth-evaluable. The grand conclusion of the section, on the common reading, is noncognitivism. But we saw in Chapter 1 some ways in which this interpretation leads to difficulties.

I will propose that Hume is doing something rather different in *T* 3.1.1. When he speaks of "morals", he is often talking about the moral properties themselves: good and evil, virtue and vice, right and wrong, merit and demerit. When he speaks of moral *distinctions*, he is not talking about moral sentences or propositions; rather, he is talking about either (a) moral differences—the differences between good people and actions and evil people and actions—or (b) our activities of moral discrimination. When we distinguish between vice and virtue, we are engaged in the process of distinction—that is to say,

---

[21] Snare 1991: 46.

distinguishing.[22] So in those places where 'moral distinctions' does not refer to moral differences, it too, like the terms 'reason' and 'the understanding', refers to an activity, though Hume concludes that moral distinction is a different activity from any that goes on in reasoning. To begin with, however, moral distinction is that process, whatever it is, by which we discriminate good from evil.

To support this reading of the section, it is necessary to interpret the arguments in it with care. Hume may not be absolutely consistent in what he claims throughout the section, but the main intent of the section is to prove a certain point about reasoning and moral discrimination: that these two mental activities are not identical processes; nor is the latter activity a form or instance of the former. Admittedly, Hume does not talk without exception of reason or the understanding as an activity rather than an entity. Nor is his notion of moral discrimination always sharply in view; in places he quite understandably slides into treating moral distinctions as outcomes rather than distinguishings, complicating (though not ultimately undermining) his logic. But both the conception of reasoning as a process and the conception of the *activity* of discerning good and evil and discriminating them one from the other are sufficiently marked to be treated as his primary understanding of the matter.

At the opening of *Treatise* 3.1.1 Hume recapitulates the basic theory of the mind's contents that he provided in Book 1. Here he makes a point of telling us that under the heading of *perceptions* we find many mental activities:

all the actions of seeing, hearing, judging, loving, hating, and thinking fall under this denomination. The mind can never exert itself in any action, which we may not comprehend under the term of perception; and consequently that term is no less applicable to those *judgments*, by which we distinguish moral good and evil, than to every other operation of the mind. To approve one character, to condemn another, are only so many different perceptions.   (*T* 3.1.1.2 / SBN 456; italics added)

Given the string of gerunds, it seems that by 'judgments' he means judgings—acts of judgment. We are not to forget that the perceptions of interest here are all dynamic, all instances of the mind "exerting itself".

The question that Hume poses for this section is strikingly epistemic as well as activity-focused. He asks "*Whether 'tis by means of our* ideas *or* impressions *we distinguish betwixt vice and virtue*" (*T* 3.1.1.3 / SBN 456). That is, he asks: by means of which perceptions (where perceptions may be mental activities) do we carry out this discrimination? The goal is to reveal how we recognize goodness and evil. Thus far there is no evidence that Hume is interested in the semantic

---

[22] The *Oxford English Dictionary* entry for 'distinction', definition 3, reads: "The action of distinguishing or discriminating; the perceiving, noting, or making a difference between things; discrimination. With *a* and *pl.*, the result of this action, a difference thus made or appreciated." Definition 4 says: "The condition or fact of being distinct or different; difference. With *a* and *pl.*, an instance of this, a difference." The *OED* notes occurrences from long before Hume's day of the expression "a distinction without a difference".

status of moral judgments thought of as propositions, sentences, or beliefs. He is interested in the activity of moral judging.

The same emphasis is clear in his depiction of the position of his moral rationalist opponents, "[t]hose who affirm that virtue is nothing but a conformity to reason" (*T* 3.1.1.4 / SBN 456). He continues:

All these systems concur in the opinion, that morality, like truth, is discern'd merely by ideas, and by their juxta-position and comparison. In order, therefore, to judge of these systems, we need only consider, whether it be possible, from reason alone, to distinguish betwixt moral good and evil, or whether there must concur some other principle to enable us to make that distinction.

Clearly, here, "reason alone" is the "juxta-position and comparison" of ideas, the process of reasoning. The rationalists think that we can discern the presence of good and evil by comparing our ideas. (In this Hume is not unfair, at least to his eighteenth-century rationalist predecessors. See, e.g., Clarke 1991[1706]: 192–4 and 198, and Balguy 1991[1734]: 398–400.) Hume will argue that another "principle" must concur with reason to "enable us to make that distinction". By 'principle' Hume frequently means a causal factor, origin, or foundation of something, and this is his meaning here.

The Introduction of Argument M

Recall that Argument M consists of two premises and a conclusion, stated, for example, thus:

1. "Morals . . . have an influence on the actions and affections."
2. "Reason alone . . . can never have any such influence."
3. "It follows, that [morals] cannot be deriv'd from reason." (*T* 3.1.1.6 / SBN 457)

Hume's first argument in the section defends what we may call the Influence Premise, the thesis that morality naturally influences "human passions and actions". His evidence for this is that it would otherwise be pointless to inculcate morality in people; that morality is included in the purview of practical rather than speculative philosophy; and finally, that in common experience "men are often govern'd by their duties, and are deter'd from some actions by the opinion of injustice, and impell'd to others by that of obligation" (*T* 3.1.1.5 / SBN 457). Since *morality* is that which is inculcated, and men are governed both by their duties and by the *opinion* of injustice and obligation, Hume seems to use the term 'morality' both for good and evil and duty themselves (that which is studied by practical philosophy) and for our awareness of or opinion about good and evil and duty, since it is not only their actual duties but also their opinion of what their duties are that influences men. Surely when morality influences our passions and actions, it does so through our awareness of it; it is not like gravity or magnetism, influencing us whether we are aware of it or not. (This is clear in *EPM* 1.7 / SBN 172 in a very similar context: "The end of all moral speculations is to teach us our duty; and, by proper representations of the deformity of vice and beauty of virtue, beget correspondent habits, and engage us to avoid the one, and embrace the other.") The Influence Premise asserts that our moral discriminations "naturally" produce motivating passions and actions. That is, it is to be expected that when someone discerns that an action of hers would be unjust, this evokes some sort of aversion to doing it.

Hume next introduces Argument M. The second statement of the argument (its repetition immediately after its initial introduction) is worded in a way that makes the common reading of it very natural, and the reading that I am about to present less so; but if I am right, this is only a quick gloss on an argument that he develops in more detail later, and the later statements strongly suggest the new reading. (He states the argument at least five times in the section.) The other premise (besides the Influence Premise) is the Inertia of Reason Thesis, that reason (alone) cannot produce actions or affections. As we saw, on the common reading the argument looked flawed. However, the process interpretation of Humean reason and the further interpretive claim about moral distinctions provide a new reading of this argument. According to the further claim, the Influence Premise is not about static judgments or opinions about good and evil; it is instead about a mental activity, that of discerning or discriminating good from evil. The premise asserts that that process—moral discrimination—is one that results in passions, and sometimes in actions. By its nature it is an affection-generating process. The argument's conclusion, on the new reading, is that the two mental processes, reasoning and moral discrimination, are distinct and do not overlap. Because our moral discriminations are the sorts of activities that yield passions and our reasonings are not, our moral discriminations are not reasonings or portions of reasonings. They are not performed *by* reasoning, but by some other goings-on in the mind. So this is the conclusion of the argument. This is the sense in which moral distinctions are not derived from reason. In numbered steps the argument says:

1. Reasoning processes alone (without another kind of process) cannot produce passions, volitions, or actions.
2. Moral discrimination (that process) can and does produce passions, volitions, and actions.
3. Therefore, our moral discriminations are not reasoning processes (alone), and are not performed by reasoning processes (alone).

The inference does not require any assumption of the transitivity of causation, because its conclusion is not a causal thesis (that reason or reasoning alone does not *cause* moral discriminations) but a non-identity claim about processes: the activity of moral discrimination is not identical with, and is not carried out by, any process of reasoning. One advantage of reading the argument this way is that the conclusion, so construed, is plausible. Another is that the argument is valid.

We can use this understanding of Argument M to make sense of a number of other things that Hume says in its immediate vicinity.

One cannot reject Argument M, Hume insists, unless one rejects its Inertia of Reason premise; and he reminds us that he gave many arguments to prove that thesis in *Treatise* 2.3.3. (Of course, on the present interpretation, in contrast to the common reading, what he proves there is simply that reasoning is not a process that causes passions or actions, not that beliefs do not do so.) The only one of those arguments he sees fit to repeat in *Treatise* 3.1.1 is the Representation Argument, which was quoted earlier in this chapter; he expands it to apply to volitions and actions as well as passions, and, as we saw, its conclusion is that passions, volitions, and actions cannot be "pronounced either true or false, and [cannot be] either contrary or conformable to reason" (*T* 3.1.1.9 / SBN 458). What is contrary to reason is what we see, by a process of reasoning, to be false to its putative original. Since passions, volitions, and actions are not representations, they cannot represent falsely, and no such dissimilarity to an original can be discovered by reasoning. If we are convinced by the Representation Argument, Hume thinks, we cannot help but be persuaded by his refutation of moral rationalism. Let us identify how this argument is intended to clinch his refutation.

The Representation Argument, Hume claims, proves directly that actions do not derive their moral merit from a conformity to reason, and also proves the "same truth" indirectly. In the compressed and somewhat repetitive paragraph (10) where he asserts this, he presents both the direct and the indirect arguments that he founds on (the conclusion of) the Representation Argument. Call the first the Direct Argument; the second is a fuller statement of Argument M itself.

The brief Direct Argument takes the conclusion of the Representation Argument to be simply that passions, volitions, and actions cannot be reasonable or unreasonable (synonyms for 'contrary or conformable to reason'), and uses it as a premise without modification. It goes as follows:

[1] "Actions may be laudable or blameable;
[2] but they cannot be reasonable or unreasonable;
[3] Laudable or blameable, therefore, are not the same with reasonable or unreasonable." (*T* 3.1.1.10 / SBN 458)

The argument is perfectly straightforward, and also valid. Actions may have either of the two properties of moral goodness and evil; but they are incapable of having the two properties reasonableness and unreasonableness; therefore goodness is not identical with reasonableness, nor evil with unreasonableness. The conclusion is the non-identity of these properties. We have seen that what is unreasonable is what can be found by reasoning to fail to represent its purported original (what is against the workings of reasoning in its discovery of truth;

what is shown or would be shown by the reasoning process to be false). So this Direct Argument indeed makes direct use of the conclusion of the Representation Argument. It establishes that for an action to be bad is not for it to be contrary to reason.[23] This is a tidy denial of one of the main theses that goes by the name 'moral rationalism', the thesis that wickedness in action consists in the action's inherent irrationality.[24]

Hume claims that the conclusion of the Direct Argument is the same as that of Argument M. He glosses both conclusions as the "same truth" that "actions do not derive their merit from a conformity to reason, nor their blame from a contrariety to it" (*T* 3.1.1.10 / SBN 458). But initially the two conclusions do not seem to be equivalent, as we saw in Chapter 1. The conclusion of the Direct Argument is the non-identity of properties. On the common reading, the conclusion of Argument M is that the moral judgments we make are not caused by reason (which may be a set of beliefs or propositions) and do not describe facts or possess truth or falsehood. These are, as far as I can tell, different and unrelated theses. The first could be true (that the virtue of an action is not the same as reasonableness), yet the second could be false (our judgments about virtue might be caused by reason or rational beliefs, or might even be logically entailed by them, and the moral judgments themselves might be true or false). Analogously, being spherical is not the same as being reasonable, but our beliefs about the spherical are sometimes the products of reason and can be true or false.

On my interpretation the two conclusions become much more closely related, although their connection needs to be explained. The conclusion of Argument M on my interpretation is that moral distinguishings are not instances of reasoning: that is, we do not discern virtue and vice by means of a reasoning process. This claim and the conclusion of the Direct Argument entail one another, given our understanding of reasoning. If virtue is not reasonableness (the conclusion of the Direct Argument), and reasonableness (truth, or correspondence with its original) is all that is discerned in the reasoning process, then virtue cannot be discovered in the reasoning process (conclusion of Argument M). And taking

---

[23] Among the otherwise very helpful notes in David Fate Norton and Mary J. Norton's student edition of the *Treatise* (2000) is one that misconstrues this Direct Argument as making a claim about the causal power of reason ("reason cannot be the proximate cause of the moral merit assigned to passions and actions because these are not ideas" (p. 535)). This is no doubt the result of trying to read the Direct Argument as proving the same point as Argument M as M is understood on the common reading, where it is treated as a causal argument invoking the Causal Chain Assumption. As we see by reading it (I use only Hume's own words in stating it here), the Direct Argument is not about what reason can cause but about the non-identity of the property reasonableness with the property laudableness or goodness.

[24] e.g., Clarke says: "He that refuses to deal with all men equitably, and with every man as he desires they should deal with him: is guilty of the very same unreasonableness and contradiction in one case; as he that in another case should affirm one number or quantity to be equal to another, and yet that other at the same time not to be equal to the first" (1991[1706]: 200). And recall Wollaston's view that immoral actions are unreasonable in the sense that they are (literally) false.

the inference in the other direction, if virtue cannot be discovered in the reasoning process, then virtue is not an instance of reasonableness (conformity to reason, truth), which can be so discovered. Thus they are very nearly equivalent.

Recall that there is a further mystery in this paragraph as interpreted through the lens of the common reading. The conclusion of the Representation Argument must serve as a premise not only of the Direct Argument but also of Argument M. Hume is quite explicit that this conclusion is all one needs: once one grants the soundness of the Representation Argument and the truth of the Influence Premise, one cannot duck the conclusion that morals are not derived from reason. But the conclusion of the Representation Argument is simply that passions, volitions, and actions cannot be conformable or contrary to reason. The Inertia of Reason premise in Argument M, however, according to the common reading, says that reason alone cannot cause passions or actions. As we noted in the first chapter, this is not equivalent to the conclusion of the Representation Argument and does not follow from it. Passions and actions might well have no properties of reasonableness or unreasonableness, as the Representation Argument shows, yet rationally derived beliefs might still cause us to come to have passions or to perform actions. So how can the conclusion of the Representation Argument serve as the Inertia of Reason premise in Argument M?

On our interpretation, the Inertia of Reason Thesis is that passions, volitions, and actions are not the outcomes of a reasoning process. Hume takes this to follow from the Representation Argument's conclusion that passions and actions can be neither contrary nor conformable to reason because he assumes (what is obvious on our interpretation) that if a reasoning process were to produce an action, it would do so by assessing that item and finding it a true copy. That is all a reasoning process *can* do, for that is all it is. (This is something one can know *a priori*, as distinct from an ordinary causal relation, which could only be known by experience.) Since reasoning cannot affirm or contradict any passion or action (since they are not representations), it follows that a reasoning process cannot produce any. As Hume puts it in explaining the transition from the conclusion of the Representation Argument to Argument M, "reason can never immediately prevent or produce any action *by contradicting or approving of it*" (*T* 3.1.1.10 / SBN 458; emphasis added). Of course, strictly speaking, reasoning, as an activity of comparing perceptions and discovering their relations, does not contradict or assert anything. But Hume talks of reason contradicting something as a shorthand for saying that when we juxtapose and compare a certain idea with another perception (when we engage in reasoning), we find them not to match, though one of them was initially thought to represent the other. To say that reason contradicts something is to say that a process of reasoning finds it to contradict real relations of ideas or real matters of fact—finds it false. Reason cannot do this with passions, volitions, or actions, and since this is the only activity of reason, it therefore cannot produce any passions, volitions, or actions—the Inertia of Reason Thesis is established.[25]

The Formulations of Argument M

We should look at the wording of the various statements of Argument M to see how well the present interpretation fits. It fits some better than others. The argument appears at least five times in *Treatise* 3.1.1, as follows:

A.
   1. "Morals . . . have an influence on the actions and affections."
   2. "Reason alone . . . can never have any such influence."
   3. "It follows, that [morals] cannot be deriv'd from reason" (*T* 3.1.1.6 / SBN 457)

B. In the same paragraph:
   1. "Morals excite passions, and produce or prevent actions."
   2. "Reason of itself is utterly impotent in this particular."
   3. "The rules of morality, therefore, are not conclusions of our reason."

C. Four paragraphs later, after the enhanced version of the Representation Argument (this is the "indirect" proof):
   1. "[R]eason can never immediately prevent or produce any action by contradicting or approving of it."
   2. "Moral good and evil . . . are found to have that influence."
   3. Therefore, reason "cannot be the source of the distinction betwixt moral good and evil".

D. Again in the same paragraph:
   1. "The merit and demerit of actions frequently contradict, and sometimes controul our natural propensities."
   2. "But reason has no such influence."
   3. "Moral distinctions, therefore, are not the offspring of reason."
   4. (reprise of conclusion) "Reason is wholly inactive, and can never be the source of so active a principle as conscience, or a sense of morals."

---

[25] I note the problem of the transition from the Representation Argument to Argument M (there called the Motivation Argument) in Cohon (1997*c*), and also emphasize the qualification "by contradicting or approving it". There I speculated about what the common reading might say to explain the transition, and argued that the best explanation led to the equivocal reading of Argument M mentioned in Ch. 1. (David Owen and I also touch on this in Cohon and Owen 1997.) At that time I did not yet see Argument M as addressing processes, but offered a different interpretation of it.

E. And a repetition a few pages later, after dealing with a possible rationalist objection about true or false non-moral judgments:

1. "[T]hat distinction [betwixt moral good and evil] has an influence upon our actions."

2. "of which reason alone is incapable . . ."

3. "Thus, upon the whole, 'tis impossible, that the distinction betwixt moral good and evil, can be made by reason." (*T* 3.1.1.16 / SBN 462)

Although the wording differs, it is clear that Hume intends these formulations to make the same argument.

It is worth noting that in none of these formulations does Hume mention moral judgments or moral sentences. This counts against the common reading, but on any interpretation it is puzzling. For four of these five formulations at some point speak only of "morals", and if they do not mean by this moral judgments, then what do they mean? The most literal reading would be that they mean actual moral properties. But if what Hume means is the properties goodness and evil, then he is making a rather different argument here than either that of the common reading or mine.[26]

I propose that the rationalist thesis that "morality . . . is discern'd merely by ideas, and by their juxta-position and comparison" is Hume's primary target in Argument M, and that by 'morals' in its various versions he mostly means moral properties grasped through acts of moral discrimination or distinguishing, but at times he means our grasp or awareness of moral properties itself. Combining these, 'morals' serves as a shorthand for "moral properties, when (or as) we distinguish them". So, for example, in C he means to say that "the merit and demerit of actions [, *insofar as we become aware of them*,] frequently contradict, and sometimes controul our natural propensities". It is not so surprising for this qualification not always to be made explicit; put this way, it is fairly obvious. As we have seen, this interpretation is based on Hume's expressed overall purpose in the section of determining whether it is by means of ideas or impressions that we

---

[26] There is a way to construe Argument M so that it is about moral properties rather than our discrimination of them, and actually parallels the Direct Argument even more than it does on the present interpretation. I proposed it in Cohon 1997c. Like the process interpretation advocated here, that reading solves some of the problems that trip up the common reading. It too explains how Hume can claim to know a priori that reason can produce some outcomes and not others, and it too avoids rendering the argument equivocal (and indeed makes it valid). It is compatible with the process conception of reason offered here, but makes no use of that notion. Very briefly, it reconstructs Argument M thus:

1. The reasonableness of passions and actions (that property) cannot cause us to have or perform them.
2. The moral goodness and evil of passions and actions do cause us to have and perform them.
3. Therefore the goodness of an action is not its reasonableness, nor is its evil its unreasonableness. (Cohon 1997c)

distinguish between vice and virtue, and also on both the dynamism of reason as he understands it and the use of the word 'distinction(s)' in versions C, D, and E, especially the conclusion in E that the distinction between moral good and evil cannot be *made* by reason.

So we understand the conclusion of Argument M to be that our grasp of morals is not achieved by reasoning.

One reason why the common reading of Argument M has been so seductive is that the conclusion of the argument, at least in some of its forms, does not seem to speak of a process but rather of its product. So we should look at the forms the conclusion takes.

Three of the five versions of the conclusion can easily be seen to lend support to my interpretation. The conclusion of version E ("'tis impossible, that the distinction betwixt moral good and evil, can be made by reason") is the best for this. If we think of Humean reasoning as a stepwise process, we can read this to say that our discernment of morality is not made up of inferential steps—it is not carried out by reasoning.[27] Reason(ing) is the discovery of the truth and falsehood of ideas, and this is done by means of the manipulation of ideas; but distinguishing between moral good and evil is not carried out by means of this process of manipulating ideas. It is not uncommon to say that one sort of process or activity is or is not carried out by means of another. A sculptor may sculpt by chipping stone or molding clay. We can earn our pay by pumping water. So this version of the conclusion may be read to say that it is impossible to make the distinction between moral good and evil by reasoning (without any other process). Similarly, the conclusion in version A, that morals cannot be derived from reason, says that we cannot derive moral awareness from a reasoning process alone. And in C, we can also understand the claim that reason "cannot be the source of the distinction betwixt moral good and evil" to say that reasoning cannot be what we use to distinguish them.

The other two statements of the conclusion require more explanation. Start with D. Its conclusion, that moral distinctions are not "the offspring of reason", is metaphorical, so we should not read too much into it. But 'offspring' suggests a causal product, and Hume thinks of parents as the causes of children; so one might understand this version of the conclusion as the common reading does, as denying a cause-and-effect relationship between two static items (reason and moral judgments), rather than as denying the identity or overlap of two processes. But it need not be read that way. It is hard to say exactly what the offspring of a process is; but one could say that the process of moral discrimination is not performed by or made by reasoning, and in that sense moral discrimination is not the offspring of reasoning. The restatement of the conclusion in step 4 suggests something similar, that reasoning cannot be what goes on when our

---

[27] I agree with Sturgeon (2001) that on Hume's view moral awareness or (to use this term in a present-day sense) knowledge is non-inferential.

sense of morals is engaged, since the sense of morals is, in itself, "active" (motive-generating), which reasoning is not. It does sound odd to say that reasoning, which I have been insisting is an activity, is "wholly inactive"; but it is clear that by this expression Hume means that it does not produce passions that activate the person, not that reason is a static item in the mind.

The most difficult version of Argument M to square with the present interpretation is B:

1. "Morals excite passions, and produce or prevent actions."
2. "Reason of itself is utterly impotent in this particular."
3. "The rules of morality, therefore, are not conclusions of our reason."

Premise 1 can be understood to say that moral discriminations (moral properties as grasped by us) excite passions and produce actions; that is, passions and actions are the outcomes of those processes. Premise 2 could be read to say that reasoning does not excite passions or produce actions, in that passions and actions are not the outcomes of reasoning processes (they are not "conclusions of our reason"). So far, so good for our interpretation. But the conclusion resists any plausible interpretation on which it expresses the non-identity of processes. A rule is not a process, much less a process of discrimination. In version B what is to be shown in the argument is that the rules of morality, the products of the one process, cannot be the products of the other process (reasoning) alone, because "morals" have an influence that the products of reasoning lack. Now if 'morals' in the first premise is supposed to be short for "the rules of morality", this is incompatible with our interpretation and nearly impossible not to construe in accordance with the common reading: moral rules are not the products of reason because they produce passion and action while reason does not. And all the difficulties come flooding back. But something quite different might well be going on here. 'Morals' in the first premise might mean not "the rules of morality", which are the outcome of moral discrimination, but rather the process of moral discrimination. It is this process that excites passions and produces or prevents actions. The processes of reasoning of themselves cannot do this. Therefore the two kinds of processes are distinct — this is an intermediate conclusion that is not made explicit. Now consider the rules of morality. They were generated by some process or other, and since they are the rules of *morality*, it must have been the process of moral discrimination. We have shown that this process is not identical with any reasoning process. Therefore it follows that the rules of morality are not conclusions of our reason. The anti-rationalist conclusion that moral evaluations or judgments are not the products of reasoning alone depends upon and follows from the non-identity of processes that Argument M establishes. The argument is enthymematic but perfectly valid.

Did the historical Hume clearly see the role of the non-identity of processes in all the formulations of Argument M? That is, of course, impossible to say. In version B he may have lost focus a bit, shifting to an understanding of the argument closer to the common reading and omitting the intermediate conclusion about processes. But the process interpretation makes possible a consistent and valid reading of all the versions of Argument M and explains the various transitions between it and its neighboring arguments, and so yields the most charitable interpretation.

We have seen in this chapter that Hume conceives of reason as reasoning, a process of a particular sort quite different from the process of passion generation, and consequently one that cannot give rise to new passions or actions. That is why reason of itself has no influence on the actions and affections. We have also seen why Hume thinks that moral distinctions are not derived from reason: moral discriminations are processes as well, ones that routinely give rise to passions and actions; and since reasoning processes do not, moral discriminations are distinct processes that cannot be carried out by reasoning. None of this requires Hume to commit himself to the claim that beliefs (or other cognitive states) cannot cause motivating passions without the help of a causally independent passion; so there is no contradiction between Argument M and Hume's claims earlier in the *Treatise* that hedonic beliefs cause our motivating desires and aversions. Furthermore, in reinterpreting Hume's moral psychology we have not found any commitment to noncognitivism, the thesis that moral evaluations or judgments do not represent anything and can be neither true nor false, for this is not what the conclusion of Argument M says. It is not about the semantic status of moral sentences, but about the process of moral discrimination.

How to Interpret the Long Concluding Argument of *Treatise* 3.1.1

The final eleven paragraphs of the section (*T* 3.1.1.17–27 / SBN 463–70) make one extended argument to prove that "those eternal immutable fitnesses and unfitnesses of things cannot be defended by sound philosophy" (*T* 3.1.1.17 / SBN 463). The argument is structured on the pattern of other such arguments about the activity of reasoning. "As the operations of human understanding divide themselves into two kinds, the comparing of ideas, and the inferring of matter of fact; were virtue discover'd by the understanding; it must be an object of one of these operations, nor is there any third operation which can discover it." (The language of mental activity is very explicit here.) So if the "understanding were alone capable of fixing the boundaries of right and wrong, the character of virtuous and vicious either must lie in some relations of objects, or must be a matter of fact, which is discover'd by our reasoning" (*T* 3.1.1.18 / SBN 463). The task, then, is to prove the negative ontological claim that "the character of virtuous and vicious" does not consist in any demonstrable relations or in any inferable matters of fact, in order to be in a position to prove the epistemic thesis that reasoning is not the activity by which we know the difference between virtue and vice. It has often been thought that Hume sets out to prove in the latter half of the argument (the part about causal inference) that there is no fact of the matter as to whether actions are virtuous or vicious, and so to prove that there is no truth to the matter; but to see it this way is to forget that the only matters of fact we discover by *inference* (that is, by reasoning) are causal relations, which gives Hume a narrower use of 'fact' than what we are commonly familiar with. The comma notwithstanding (after all, there are many more commas in eighteenth-century prose than we would use), the phrase "which is discover'd by our reasoning" is a qualification.[28] If reasoning could discern virtue and vice, then those properties would be abstract relations or matters of fact of a kind whose presence can be inferred by the operations of the understanding. This last chunk of the section, then, argues that virtue and vice are not relations of either kind: first, and at great length, that they are not demonstrable relations, and then very briefly that they are not causal relations. Whether they are other facts or not is mostly left open, but not entirely, as we will see in the next chapter. The argument ends with the observation that is now famous as the is–ought paragraph, and which, we shall see, is best read as a small corollary of this long argument itself, rather than as a separate argument for a grander thesis.

Hume argues in several stages that "moral qualities" are not relations of the sort whose presence can be demonstrated. They are manifestly not any of the relations he himself has argued are the sole ones "susceptible of certainty and demonstration"—resemblance, contrariety, degrees in quality, or proportions in quantity or number—for these are instantiated by irrational and even inanimate things, which are not "susceptible of merit or demerit" (*T* 3.1.1.19 / SBN 464). If moral rationalists wish to claim that "the sense of morality consists in the discovery of some relation, distinct from these" (*T* 3.1.1.20 / SBN 464), then they must specify the relation. Without knowing what it is supposed to be, all we can do is to state two requirements on any relation that is to constitute good or evil and consider whether they can be fulfilled. First, it must be a relation that is capable of being instantiated only between certain restricted types of relata: "actions of the mind", on the one hand ("our passions, volitions, and actions"), and "external objects", on the other. For if it could hold between items that are both in the mind, we could be "guilty of crimes in ourselves" regardless of "our situation with respect to the universe" (*T* 3.1.1.21 / SBN 465), which is absurd; and if the relation could hold between external objects, with no mental actions involved, then even inanimate objects could be morally good or evil, which is equally absurd. The second requirement on any relation that might constitute good or evil is that the relation be one that has a necessary "connexion . . . [with] the will" that takes place "in every well-dispos'd mind", even that of God. For advocates of an "abstract rational difference betwixt moral good and evil" suppose the effects of these relations, when grasped, to be of necessity the same for all rational beings (*T* 3.1.1.22 / SBN 465). These two criteria, however,

---

[28] On the punctuation of these sentences, see Sturgeon 2001: 60 n. 13.

cannot be fulfilled. It is very difficult to imagine any relation that could hold between the passions or actions of a rational being and external objects but could not also hold between two non-rational entities, and the best proposals for vice-constituting relations fail this first test. It is impossible for any relation to pass the second test, because a connection between a relation and the will would be a causal one, and "we cannot prove *a priori*, that these relations, if they really existed and were perceived, would be universally forcible and obligatory" (*T* 3.1.1.23 / SBN 466), since no causal relation can be discovered without experience. To reinforce the argument, Hume tenders the examples of parricide and incest, two acts universally acknowledged to be vicious whose vice seems to lie in the relations they exemplify; he argues that these identical relations also hold between trees or non-human animals, without there being any vice present in those cases.

The final stage of the argument, intending to show that virtue and vice do not consist in any causal relations (matters of fact discovered by reasoning), is extraordinarily terse, which is probably responsible for its frequent misinterpretation. Hume is in a hurry by this time to move on to his own positive account of what moral discrimination is and rushes through this last piece of his argument halfway through paragraph 26. After the tree and incest examples, he begins the paragraph thus: "Nor does *this reasoning* only prove, that morality consists not in any relations, that are the objects of science; but if examin'd, will prove with equal certainty, that it consists not in any matter of fact, which can be discover'd by the understanding" (*T* 3.1.1.26 / SBN 468; emphasis added). *Which* reasoning proves this? Presumably the reasoning that he has just completed above, but his application of prior reasoning is not explained; all he goes on to say is that if you examine a vicious act such as willful murder, you do not find the matter of fact (discovered by reasoning) that constitutes the vice, but only "certain passions, motives, volitions, and thoughts". A plausible conjecture is that Hume means the reader to apply his earlier point about abstract relations to causal relations. We make many causal inferences about the murder, such as that it was caused by particular "passions, motives, volitions, and thoughts" on the part of the murderer, that it caused various passions in the survivors, and so on. But none of these causal relations can constitute the vice of the murder, perhaps because similar causal relations can be found between the motives of animals and their violent actions, or perhaps because causal relations as such (A's causing B's) are found everywhere throughout the inanimate world without constituting vice. Just as with abstract relations, every causal relation we can find might equally well be present somewhere without vice.

This passage is often taken to assert noncognitivism, because Hume says that when we examine willful murder, "There is no matter of fact in the case. The vice entirely escapes you, as long as you consider the object." But here 'matter of fact' simply means "causal relation discovered by reasoning". He has already used the expression 'matter of fact' followed by the qualification "discovered by reasoning" (or its equivalent) twice in the preceding few sentences of the paragraph, so he sees no need to repeat it yet again here. How do we actually discern that the murder is vicious? By means of a "sentiment of disapprobation" in our "own breast". "Here is a matter of fact; but 'tis the object of feeling, not of reason." This particular matter of fact is not discovered by reasoning (inference) but by feeling; this is Hume's answer to his epistemic question. We become aware of vice and virtue by means of impressions, not by the comparing of ideas. (We consider other aspects of this paragraph in the next chapter.)

To apply what we have learned from this long argument showing that moral good and evil are not relations of either kind and so cannot be discerned solely by reasoning, Hume then urges us to consider what moralists do in writing their systems of morality. Each such author "proceeds for some time in the ordinary way of reasoning, and establishes the being of a God" (which is often done by means of demonstrative reasoning) "or makes observations concerning human affairs" (using probable or causal reasoning), "when of a sudden I am surpriz'd to find, that instead of the usual copulations of propositions, *is*, and *is not*, I meet with no proposition that is not connected with an *ought* or an *ought not*." The author Hume describes is *reasoning*, and trying to discover good and evil, ought and ought not, by this process alone, treating the moral properties as demonstrable or causal relations derivable from others. But 'ought' and 'ought not' (used to express the relations between sentences) articulate "some new relation or affirmation", which needs to be explained, and it seems impossible that such a new relation could be inferred from the completely different sorts of relations (demonstrable and causal) from which it is supposed to follow. We have in fact seen that moral qualities are not relations of either of these kinds, and consequently cannot be discovered or revealed for the first time by reasoning alone; a different process, one of feeling, is needed. Attending to these moralists' attempts to make inferential transitions to the new relation, then, would "subvert all the vulgar systems of morality, and let us see, that the distinction of vice and virtue is not founded on the relations of objects, nor is perceiv'd by reason" (*T* 3.1.1.27 / SBN 470). The "vulgar systems" are those in which authors attempt to discover what is good and evil, right and wrong, solely and originally by reasoning and identifying relations; and this strategy, as we have seen, is doomed.

Read this way, the famous paragraph follows from the long argument that precedes it and merely offers a concluding "observation", just as Hume describes it. On this interpretation the paragraph makes an epistemic point: the vulgar moralists cannot discover what people ought and ought not to do solely by reasoning about abstract or causal relations. Their transition from 'is' to 'ought' is illegitimate because they have misidentified the source of their knowledge of what one ought to do. It is not acquired by inferring the presence of a relation from the presence of other relations—at least not by that process alone. Hume's claim, then, is really not a point about the logic or semantics of moral expressions such as 'ought', 'good', or 'virtue'. Hume does not claim here that no assertion containing a moral word can be validly inferred from any assertion that does not contain a moral word. If a premise that contained no moral terms could allude to the "fact of feeling" in which moral good consists, then that premise might well entail or imply a conclusion that does contain a moral word. The real point is epistemic: our basic recognition of morality—our grasp of what vice and virtue fundamentally are—is not acquired by inferring. Those who create "systems" of morality claim to discover the essence of good and evil by doing just this, and they cannot do it; the inferences by which they mean to do it prove defective.

This interpretation avoids the difficulties that the paragraph presented on the common reading. As we now read it, there is no new argument or thesis presented in the paragraph, so there is no concern about dogmatism, question-begging, or lack of support. There is also no contradiction between what this paragraph asserts and Hume's extended arguments elsewhere in the *Treatise* that certain traits are virtues or vices on the grounds that they evoke human approval or disapproval on an unbiased examination. Since the "fact of feeling" is used to show the moral qualities of the traits, such arguments are not guilty of attempting to discover moral qualities by reasoning alone, or of treating moral qualities as either abstract or causal relations. We know by means of impressions that these traits are virtues and vices, and the arguments make use of this evidence.

Hume's understanding of reason and of moral discrimination as dynamic processes enables him to present a largely coherent moral psychology that has some appeal. Within the confines of his causal empiricism he is able to argue that reasoning is a process of a certain kind and, consequently, not the kind of process that results in passions. He also argues that the mental activity of discriminating moral good from evil is a different process, not one of comparing ideas or discerning relations among them. Given this position, he makes a reasonably good case that there are no eternal fitnesses of things that we discern by reasoning—this is neither the correct moral epistemology nor the correct moral ontology. While Hume's conception of reason as reasoning may not satisfy us today, it is not unwarranted or tendentiously narrow (though it may still be too narrow), and it raises what remains a very good question: If there is something more to reason than this process, what is it, and how is that further factor related to the activity of inference? This sort of question must have concerned Kant, who was at pains to demonstrate the unity of theoretical and practical reason. If the essence of immorality lies in an action or trait's unreasonableness, then we must be made to see why this is rightly called by the same name that is applied to the outcome of incorrect inference.

What is perhaps less defensible is Hume's rapid move from the conclusion that we do not discern morals by reasoning to the conclusion that we discern them by feeling. He seems simply to assume that this is the only viable alternative, and a rather obvious one, since moral discrimination is passion-producing. He could be right, but one wants some argument, and he gives us none.

In any case, we should note that in rereading Hume's moral psychology we have not found any commitment to ethical noncognitivism, or a commitment to a logical principle concerning moral and non-moral terms. We saw in the previous chapter that Hume also does not hold the core of the thesis generally called Humeanism in the philosophy of action: that beliefs or other cognitive states cannot cause motivating psychological states without the causal assistance of a causally independent desire. So Hume holds none of the three theses usually thought to compose his metaethics.

Moral good and evil are discovered by a process of feeling, Hume says. That leaves unanswered a pressing question: Do they have any existence independent of the feelings by which they are known? I take that up in the next chapter.

4

Feeling Virtue and the Reality of Moral Distinctions

Our next task is to identify Hume's positive theory of moral properties and moral evaluation. What are moral good and evil, for Hume? How do we acquire opinions or knowledge of them, if indeed there are such things? And what is Hume's analysis of a moral judgment?

In the course of answering these questions, we confront some interesting issues. First, we have seen no evidence so far that Hume is an ethical noncognitivist (though this could change as we sort out other matters). Now, noncognitivism has been closely associated with moral anti-realism; some authors even identify them.[1] That suggests to many readers that if Hume is not a noncognitivist, since (as they suppose) noncognitivism is logically linked with moral anti-realism, he is therefore some sort of moral realist. But a realist position appears to conflict with Hume's whole tone and with some of what he explicitly says. Is there a tension here? More generally, the issue of whether Hume is a moral realist should be addressed.

Secondly, while it is obvious that moral evaluation involves feeling for Hume, it is hard to figure out what exactly he thinks the content of a moral judgment is. Is it a description of our occurrent feelings? Is it a causal statement that a character trait or action provokes certain feelings? Or is the role of feeling in Hume's metaethics such that he must be construed as espousing a non-propositional or noncognitivist theory of moral judgment after all, or at least some inchoate version of one?

We need to tread carefully here. Issues about the meaning and linguistic role of moral sentences or propositions and about moral realism are notoriously present-day philosophical concerns. There is no antecedent guarantee that Hume addresses these issues in his writings. But he certainly *seems* to make commitments on some of them, and as long as we are careful to avoid anachronism, we are entitled to try to figure out whether he does, and if so what those commitments are. We will find Hume's views about the nature of our awareness of moral properties to have interesting consequences in these areas, offering a coherent if quirky position.

---

[1] McNaughton (1988) seems to identify them, or at least to treat them as logically very close, e.g., on p. 7.

I. CLARIFYING THE METAETHICAL ISSUES

"Those who have denied the reality of moral distinctions", Hume remarks at the start of his second *Enquiry*, "may be ranked among the disingenuous disputants" "who really do not believe the opinions they defend" (*EPM* 1.1–2 / SBN 169).[2] Surely Hume does not count himself among that lot. Presumably, then, *he* does not deny the reality of moral distinctions. But the passage is ambiguous. Does it show that Hume thinks the properties good and evil, virtuousness and viciousness, have some reality that is independent of our sentiments and provides grounds for them? That would make him, in one sense of the present-day philosophical label, a moral realist. It contributes to this impression that one meaning of 'distinction' in Hume's time is simply "difference", so the passage may say that no one sincerely denies the reality of the moral *differences* (between the good and the evil characters and actions). Hume's subsequent remark that different characters are "entitled" to different sorts of affection further suggests a realist reading. However, as we have seen, 'distinctions' can also mean our distinguishings, our acts of discrimination.[3] And Hume's main claim to support the assertion that no one sincerely denies the reality of moral distinctions is that everyone is "touched with the images of Right and Wrong". Thus he may only mean that we all experience moral reactions, not that they are grounded on anything independent of our feelings (*EPM* 1.1–2 / SNB 169–70). While most interpreters think that Hume is an ethical anti-realist, a few class him as a realist, and this and other passages give comfort to both.[4]

Then there is the vexed interpretive question whether Hume has a non-propositional (that is, noncognitivist) account of ethical judgment, or a cognitivist account, and if the latter, just what he thinks our ethical judgments affirm. (The term 'cognitivist' misleadingly names a thesis not about cognition but about the semantical status of moral evaluations. It is all we have for the view opposite to ethical noncognitivism.) A cognitivist theory of moral judgment says that our moral assessments are capable of truth and falsehood. As we have seen, a noncognitivist theory denies this of moral judgments—indeed denies

[2] The moral *Enquiry* and the *Treatise* differ greatly in emphasis and also on some substantial points, so one should not read them seamlessly. But on the main issues addressed in this chapter the position of the moral *Enquiry* proves compatible with that of the *Treatise*, as we will see.

[3] Recall the *OED* entries for 'distinction': definition 3: "The action of distinguishing or discriminating; the perceiving, noting, or making a difference between things; discrimination", and definition 4: "The condition or fact of being distinct or different; difference".

[4] Norton (1982 and 1985) argues that Hume is a moral realist. Although her concern is objectivity rather than realism, Swain (1992) takes a similar tack. Wright (1983: 21) cites this same passage from the moral *Enquiry* in the context of claiming that Hume is a straightforward scientific realist; but in fact Wright reads Hume's ethical theory as holding that "the real nature of things . . . excludes moral qualities" (p. 111), which depend upon a sentiment that nature has made universal in the human species (*passim*, e.g., p. 23).

that they possess any "cognitive content" in virtue of which they would be truth-evaluable—and also assigns to them a different linguistic function from that of assertion. The familiar emotivist version of noncognitivism says that moral judgments or utterances are mere ventings of emotion. More elaborate versions specify further functions. Noncognitivist interpretations of Hume are so numerous that I have treated this as part of the common reading. Some interpret him as an emotivist, some as holding one of the more elaborate noncognitivist theories.[5] But there are some who interpret Hume as a cognitivist.[6]

A limiting version of moral cognitivism, strictly construed, claims that while moral judgments are indeed truth-evaluable, they are all false. Someone might attribute such a view to Hume as well. So we should distinguish a particular version of cognitivism, *truth cognitivism*, according to which not only are moral judgments truth-evaluable, but some of them are actually true.[7]

As we saw, one might think initially that truth-cognitivist anti-realism is self-contradictory. But we will see both that in principle a truth-cognitivist theory of moral judgment can be consistent with the rejection of a realist metaphysic of value, and (eventually) that there are textual reasons to think Hume takes both these positions, and does so consistently. Of course, much depends on how we define moral realism and anti-realism. Were we to define moral realism as the view that moral judgments and utterances can be true or false and that some of them are true, and moral anti-realism as the denial of this,[8] then of course truth cognitivism and anti-realism would straightforwardly contradict each other. But this definition of moral realism does not capture the distinction that its investigators seem to have in mind. It treats moral realism as a thesis about judgments or utterances, rather than the metaphysical thesis that it is intended to be, and it fails to parallel now-familiar definitions of scientific realism and causal realism. Without delving into the definitional debates, let

---

[5] Among the great variety of noncognitivist interpreters are Flew (1963), Blackburn (1984: ch. 6 and 1993), and Snare (1991). Today perhaps some would wish to describe Hume as an expressivist, but the meaning of this term has shifted, so that views now called expressivist need no longer be committed to noncognitivism as I have defined it. As we shall see, Hume does not hold a deflationary (or disquotational) theory of truth of the sort that animates contemporary expressivism and enables its practitioners to say that moral judgments are in some sense true; nor (to my knowledge) do expressivists attribute such a semantic view to Hume. For contemporary expressivism, see Blackburn (1998) and Gibbard (1990, 2003).

[6] Among cognitivist interpreters of Hume are Hunter (1962), Capaldi (with qualifications) (1989: ch. 4), and Sturgeon (2001).

[7] Mackie (1980: 73–4) sees two different interpretations of Hume as most promising. The first, that moral judgments assert that an action is such as to arouse approval or disapproval in certain circumstances, is truth-cognitivist. The second, his Objectification view, certainly seems to have Hume construe all moral judgments as false. On that view moral judgments attribute moral properties to actions, and represent these properties as objective qualities analogous to primary qualities, though supervenient on other qualities and detected by a special sense. But the objective properties they describe are all fictitious. Hence, as Mackie acknowledges about his own very similar systematic view (1977: 35), all moral judgments are false.

[8] Sayre-McCord (1988: 5) so defines the terms.

us select a fairly natural and familiar pair of definitions that better capture what concerns writers on this subject. A realist theory of ethics says that ethical properties (such as good and evil, virtue and vice, or right and wrong) exist independently of human psychological reactions to the entities (such as people and actions) that are thought to bear these properties. An anti-realist theory denies this.[9] (So anti-realism can hold either that ethical properties exist but are reaction-dependent or that they do not exist at all.)

Clearly, moral anti-realism, so defined, is compatible with moral cognitivism of at least the limiting kind—the view that moral judgments are truth-evaluable yet all false. For one form of anti-realism is the denial that moral properties exist at all. Thus, these two views will be consistent if all moral judgments make tacit existence claims about the moral properties they predicate of their objects. But there is room for a broader and more interesting compatibility. Moral anti-realism is in fact compatible with *truth* cognitivism. For one version of moral anti-realism holds that moral properties (vice and virtue, for example) exist but are reaction-dependent properties. For this sort of anti-realist, as for the other, our psychological responses to people's characters and actions are not warranted by any independently existing moral properties. For this sort of anti-realist, however, human characters and actions do have moral properties—though only in virtue of our experiencing the psychological reactions we do. Given this, we might sometimes have true opinions about those reaction-dependent properties. There is nothing paradoxical about this. It is perfectly consistent.

Although this way of putting the issue between ethical realism and anti-realism reflects present-day philosophical concerns, the question whether moral properties are reaction-dependent arises in the eighteenth-century intellectual environment. It may be part of what troubled Hume in a famous letter to Hutcheson, for example, when he wrote "I wish from my Heart, I could avoid concluding, that since Morality, according to your Opinion as well as mine, is determin'd merely by Sentiment, it regards only human Nature & human Life."[10] If moral goodness depends for its existence on human psychological reactions, there is little reason to suppose that God, who does not have sentiments like ours, should take any interest in such a property; this is one reason why reaction dependence is controversial. And there is vehement disagreement about the issue of reaction dependence prior to Hutcheson and Hume, in debates about moral voluntarism of various kinds. Hobbes is explicit that 'good' and 'evil' in the state of nature are merely the names that people give to the objects of their individual

---

[9] Dancy, in his entry "moral realism" in the *Routledge Encyclopedia of Philosophy* (1998), includes reaction independence as item 2 in his three-item list of what a "full-blown" moral realist believes: "realists hold that moral facts are independent of any beliefs or thoughts we might have about them." Cf. entry "scientific realism and antirealism" by Arthur Fine (1998): " scientific realism asserts that the objects of scientific knowledge exist independently of the minds or acts of scientists and that scientific theories are true of that objective (mind-independent) world."

[10] *The Letters of David Hume*, letter 16 to Francis Hutcheson, 16 March 1740.

desires or aversions, and in the Commonwealth refer to what is commanded or forbidden by the sovereign's laws.[11] This reaction dependence (and decree dependence) inspires protest from critics who insist that morals must have an independent status. Both the Cambridge Platonist Ralph Cudworth and (later) Clarke reject Hobbes's position (that moral properties depend upon the desires of individuals or the commands of a sovereign) in favor of the view that moral properties are aspects of the immutable essences of things. Cudworth argues that the Hobbesian view, and also divine voluntarism, make moral good and evil (and other properties) arbitrary.[12] Balguy makes a similar criticism of Hutcheson's moral sense theory, claiming that because Hutcheson considers a certain "*natural affection* or *instinct* . . . as the true ground and foundation of [virtue]" and "makes virtue entirely to consist in it, or flow from it" (that is, because he analyzes moral good and evil as reaction-dependent properties), he understands virtue "to be of an arbitrary . . . nature".[13] So there was considerable interest in whether moral properties do or do not depend for their existence on either the choices or the passive experiences of human minds.

Here I will give an interpretation of Hume's account of moral judgment called *the moral sensing view*. It will prove to be truth-cognitivist. After setting out the moral sensing view and exhibiting the reasons to read Hume as a truth-cognitivist in light of it, I will enumerate the commitments that Hume makes about the nature of moral properties in his account of moral evaluation, to see whether he is a moral realist or anti-realist. We will find that in the *Treatise* Hume says only a little about what moral good and evil themselves are, and most of that is about what they are not. But one crucial passage shows him to believe that moral properties are essentially reaction-dependent properties: they depend for their existence on the emotional responses of sensitive beings. This makes him an ethical anti-realist in our sense. A similar moral anti-realism is evident in the *Enquiry concerning the Principles of Morals*, where the rhetoric is more explicit. But his anti-realist view is perfectly compatible with truth cognitivism.

Before interpreting the text, I should clarify a point obscured by an ambiguity in the words 'virtue' and 'vice'. Hume often talks of *a* virtue or vice as a quality of a person's mind that can be described in value-neutral terms. Speaking in this way, he lists such virtues as greatness of mind, benevolence, and chastity. Whether one *is* great, benevolent, or chaste is a fact whose obtaining does not depend upon the emotional reactions of observers, but rather on one's own psychological

---

[11] Hobbes, *Leviathan*, Part I, ch. 6 (1996: 39).

[12] Cudworth 1991[1731], *passim.*, e.g. 112; Clarke 1991[1706], *passim.*, e.g. 194–5. Cudworth may have other strong reasons for arguing against reaction dependence. For conflicting interpretations of his views, see Darwall 1995 and Gill 2006.

[13] Balguy 1991[1734]: 389–90. Here I oversimplify Balguy's position, which includes arguments to the effect that Hutcheson cannot avoid the charge with his claim that our moral sense is implanted by a benevolent God.

features.[14] Moral realist and anti-realist interpreters can agree about this. The thesis considered here, though, is not that Hume is an anti-realist about these properties, the virtues and vices. 'Virtue' is also the most graceful-sounding name for the property of being a virtue or being good, the property *virtuousness*, and 'vice' its analog. Hume often uses the terms this way as well. So used, they are synonyms for his terms 'merit' and 'demerit', which are features *of* qualities of mind. Thus he talks of 'the vice or virtue that lies in' various degrees of pride and humility (*T* 3.3.2.1 / SBN 592). When he asks us to scrutinize an "act of wilful murder" to try to find the "vice", since no one doubts that a cold-hearted act of violence has occurred, he plainly means that we cannot find in that set of facts the viciousness *of* the murder (*T* 3.1.1.26 / SBN 468–9).[15] Moral realists and anti-realists disagree about the reaction dependence of (and even the existence of) the property of virtuousness or viciousness—the virtue or vice *of* the trait, in this second sense of the terms. To say that Hume is a moral anti-realist is to say that he denies that virtuousness and viciousness (the "morality of" actions and persons) are independent of our psychological reactions.[16]

II. THE MORAL SENSING VIEW

A. "The impressions by which good and evil are known"

Treatise Book 3, Part 1, is best read as an epistemology of value: an account of how we become aware of the moral properties, rather than an account of the semantic

---

[14] e.g., the natural virtue of benevolence consists of the disposition to feel humanity (a concern for the happiness of others and for the relief of their misery) (*T* 3.2.1.5 / SBN 478, and also see the basic definition of the passion of benevolence as "the desire of happiness of the person belov'd", *T* 2.2.6.3 / SBN 367); a well-founded and well-concealed pride (this psychological feature) is a virtue, not a vice (as Christian readers might have supposed) (*T* 3.3.2.8–10 / SBN 596–7); and celibacy, humility, self-mortification, and the other "monkish virtues" are not virtues but vices (*EPM* 9.3 / SBN 270).

[15] The term 'morality' in the period has a similar sense among its meanings. See *OED*, "morality", definition 6: "The quality or fact of being moral . . . . c. The quality or fact of being a 'moral action' (see Moral *a*. 6a), i.e. of being morally either good or evil. *Obs*. . . . 1736 BUTLER *Anal.* I. iii. 72 The . . . advantage in this case is gained by the action itself, not by the morality, the virtuousness or viciousness of it."

[16] It seems that Norton (1982 and 1985) argues mainly for Hume's realism with respect to virtues and vices in the sense of the neutrally describable traits, not in the sense of the properties of virtuousness and viciousness. The former seem to be what he refers to as the objective correlates of our sentiments of approval and disapproval. Similarly, on Swain's view, the qualities we objectively judge to belong to people, those that "can be characterized without reference to their psychological effects" (1992: 485), are "mental qualities that are useful or agreeable to the person who possesses them or to others" (p. 486). If I am right, then Hume does not understand virtuousness to be the same property as being useful or agreeable (though we discover that the two are coextensive), and so this claim leaves unanswered the question whether the property of being virtuous is reaction-dependent. Note that these works were written prior to the recent flood of writing in ethical theory on the subject of moral realism and anti-realism, so could not have responded to the many distinctions made there.

status of moral judgments. The moral sensing view is an interpretation of this moral epistemology.[17] I hope to show that the moral sensing view is reasonable given the text, but I will not argue against all the alternative interpretations.[18] Once the view is before us, we can see what commitments Hume makes about the nature and status of moral properties, given this reasonable interpretation.

As always, of course, Hume begins with the contents of the mind and no supposition that our opinions or moral assessments are about anything "out there". Having reminded us of the theory of the mind that he developed in the first two books of the *Treatise*, Hume poses his first philosophical question about morals at the start of Book 3, which is worth reviewing.

Now as perceptions resolve themselves into two kinds, viz. *impressions* and *ideas*, this distinction gives rise to a question, with which we shall open up our present enquiry concerning morals, *Whether 'tis by means of our* ideas *or* impressions *we distinguish betwixt vice and virtue, and pronounce an action blameable or praise-worthy?* (*T* 3.1.1.3 / SBN 456)

Thus Hume's guiding question is: How do we become aware of, or discriminate between, vice and virtue? How do we "discover" or "discern" their difference? Do we do it by means of ideas, or do we require new impressions? If it were entirely the work of ideas that we already have, then reason alone would be responsible for bringing the contrast between good and evil to our attention. But, as we have seen, it is impossible to distinguish them by reasoning alone (*T* 3.1.1.4 / SBN 456–7).

Hume's answer to this epistemic question is well known: we do not discover vice and virtue merely by comparing ideas—we require the help of impressions. In the *Treatise* he draws this conclusion immediately after the end of 3.1.1: "Thus the course of the argument leads us to conclude, that since vice and virtue are not discoverable merely by reason, or the comparison of ideas, it must be by means of some impression or sentiment they occasion, that we are able to mark the difference betwixt them" (*T* 3.1.2.1 / SBN 470). Although he calls the impression in question a "sentiment" right at the start (assuming a bit quickly

---

[17] It has evident affinities with—and debts to—interpretations offered by others. See Capaldi 1975: ch. 7, pp. 154–72, and 1989: ch. 2; Sturgeon 2001; and Garrett 1997: ch. 9. With respect to Capaldi's latter work, I do not agree with the thesis that "Moral judgments are factual judgments about moral sentiments" (1989: 126), or with his parsing of the arguments of *Treatise* 3.1.1 in subsequent chapters. I agree with Sturgeon that Hume thinks that moral awareness is (fundamentally) non-inferential, but disagree with the thesis that Hume also—inconsistently—thinks that it is causal knowledge.

[18] In particular, I will give only a few abbreviated arguments against the noncognitivist interpretations. I do not mean to dismiss the noncognitivist Hume. He was not merely the product of early twentieth-century emotivists and prescriptivists using bits of the *Treatise* as their Rorschach test. In Ch. 1 we saw some traditional considerations in favor of this interpretation. I argue in Cohon 1997c both that there are tempting exegetical reasons to hold it, and that in the end it is mistaken. We saw in the previous chapter that the present interpretation of Hume's arguments in *Treatise* 3.1.1 does not support it.

that it is that sort of impression and not another), he soon claims empirical grounds for regarding "the impression arising from virtue, to be agreeable, and that proceeding from vice to be uneasy. Every moment's experience must convince us of this" (*T* 3.1.2.2 / SBN 470). Moral discrimination is carried out by the approbation and disapprobation we feel when we contemplate character traits or actions ("a satisfaction or uneasiness from the survey of any character") in a disinterested way, and (he says later) from a common point of view. "[T]he distinguishing impressions, by which moral good or evil is known, are nothing but *particular* pains or pleasures" (*T* 3.1.2.3 / SBN 471).

What I propose with the moral sensing interpretation is that for Hume our basic awareness of vice and virtue is *a direct apprehension by feeling*. In the standard case, we grasp good and evil directly, by experiencing the sentiments of approval and disapproval. In approving a trait we feel its virtue; in disapproving a trait we feel its vice. Thus, as he famously says, "To have a sense of virtue, is nothing but to *feel* a satisfaction of a particular kind from the contemplation of a character. The very *feeling* constitutes our praise or admiration" (*T* 3.1.2.3 / SBN 471). Experiencing such impressions is necessary in order to have moral concepts in the first place. And it is by means of these impressions that we discern virtuousness and viciousness routinely in daily life. Ordinarily, to realize that someone is vicious is not merely to have an idea, but to have an impression, an occurrent feeling. Hutcheson defines a *sense* as any faculty of the mind that conveys new impressions into it.[19] Intending 'sense' in approximately this way, though without accepting Hutcheson's treatment of the moral sense as something basic, Hume understands our capacity for moral sentiment (the "sense of virtue", as he often calls it) to be a sense: it generates new impressions. We feel a person's virtue or vice, an action's merit or demerit, in something like the way we feel the warmth of the sun on a hot day or see the redness of a ripe tomato.[20]

The moral sensing view relies on Hume's partial analogy between moral evaluation and sense perception. If you are to find the vice (viciousness) of a murder, it is not enough to examine the external matters of fact; you must feel "a sentiment of disapprobation, which arises in you, towards this action. Here is a matter of fact; but 'tis the object of feeling, not of reason". And just after this, "Vice and virtue, therefore, may be compar'd to sounds, colours, heat and cold" (*T* 3.1.1.26 / SBN 469). We will return to this important passage. For now note two things. First, Hume sees a similarity between moral sensing and the sensing of colors, sounds, heat, and cold. Second, when we feel disapprobation, what we discover is a matter of fact, and is not the object of reason but the object of

---

[19] Hutcheson, *An Essay on the Nature and Conduct of the Passions and Affections*, sect. I (1971: 4).

[20] Hutcheson does not give the various senses further explanation. But for Hume the "sense of virtue" consists in sentiments whose causes are discoverable by introspection, and he gives a detailed naturalistic account of their origin, as we will see in the next chapter.

feeling.[21] Given the analogy with the sensing of colors and heat and cold, the "object of feeling" here seems to be comparable to an object of the senses: it is the quality or property that we feel, that feeling detects. The senses feel heat and cold and colors; they notice these qualities. The moral sentiments similarly feel virtue and vice.

Note that the analogy is only partial: it has its force and its limits. Here is its force. When I look at a ripe tomato, my seeing red is a vivid and lively experience, an impression rather than an idea. It need not be a copy of something else (perhaps it never is), but is, as Hume later says of passions, "an original existence" (*T* 2.3.3.5 / SBN 415; similarly *T* 3.1.1.9 / SBN 458). As a result of the experience, though, under normal conditions I form the lively *idea* of a red tomato. This *is* a representation of something else, and undoubtedly can be true or false. If it is a sufficiently lively idea, then on Hume's view it is believed. Indeed, normally I obtain my beliefs about what colors things are in response to a sensory experience. In doing so, I do not engage in a process of inference, as Hume notes in 1.3.2 (*T* 1.3.2.2 / SBN 73). I do not infer from my visual experience that the tomato is red; rather, I see that it is red. Similarly, Hume says, "We do not infer a character to be virtuous, because it pleases: But in feeling that it pleases after such a particular manner, we in effect feel that it is virtuous. The case is the same in our judgments concerning all kinds of . . . sensations" (*T* 3.1.2.3 / SBN 471).

The analogy with sense perception is limited by the differences between Humean sensations and sentiments. One difference is that, unlike sense impressions, moral sentiments are impressions of *reflection*—they are caused by some other impression or some idea that precedes them in the mind. Sense impressions, on the other hand, arise in the soul "from unknown causes" (*T* 1.1.2.1 / SBN 7). One consequence of the status of moral sentiments as impressions of reflection is that, in order for them to occur, and so for us to feel someone's virtuousness or viciousness, we need far more than to look at the person or touch her, or see her action. We need the right triggering ideas or impressions. What we need, in fact, proves to be a whole set of beliefs about the surrounding "circumstances" and "relations". Hume gives this more emphasis in the second *Enquiry*: "If any material circumstance be yet unknown or doubtful, we . . . must suspend for a time all moral decision or sentiment" (*EPM* App. 1.11 / SBN 290). But the stance is also evident in the *Treatise*: for example, with the remark that when we learn that a person's motive was thwarted by some circumstance previously unknown to us, our moral sentiment changes (*T* 3.2.1.3 / SBN 477–8). The moral sentiments respond to our conception of a complete phenomenon composed of such things as motives, mitigating

---

[21] We find similar language in the *Enquiry concerning Human Understanding*, *EHU* 12.3.10 / SBN 165: "Morals and criticism are not so properly objects of the understanding as of taste and sentiment."

and excusing conditions, and expected consequences.[22] There is no analogous prerequisite for feeling the heat of fresh-brewed coffee; we need only put it to our lips.[23]

Moral impressions, then, are feelings partly analogous to sense impressions. And Hume is fairly explicit about what sorts of feelings they are. "[T]he impression arising from virtue [is] agreeable, and that proceeding from vice [is] uneasy" (*T* 3.1.2.2 / SBN 470). "[T]he distinguishing impressions, by which moral good or evil is known, are nothing but particular pleasures or pains" (*T* 3.1.2.3 / SBN 471). They differ from other pleasures and pains in their phenomenological quality (they are pleasures and pains of a "peculiar" kind, qualitatively different from the pleasures of wine and music), and also in virtue of two causal characteristics they have. First, they are those psychological pleasures and pains that are caused by the contemplation of a character or action "consider'd in general, without reference to our particular interest" (*T* 3.1.2.4 / SBN 472); Hume adds further restrictions on their generation later in the *Treatise* and in the moral *Enquiry*. Secondly, these particular pleasures and pains that arise from characters and actions in turn always themselves cause pride, humility, love, or hatred in the observer who experiences them, whereas the pleasures and pains derived from inanimate objects need not do so.

Next, how do we acquire *opinions* or *knowledge* about good and evil, virtue and vice? Is such a thing possible? And what is Hume's analysis of a moral judgment or belief?

Hume does not say a great deal about this matter, but if the moral sensing view is correct, the answer follows from his general account of impressions, ideas, and belief. We come to have moral ideas by first feeling the moral properties of persons, traits, and actions (having moral impressions), and then acquiring idea-copies of these impressions. All impressions are susceptible of such copying; Hume makes no exceptions for the moral impressions. Furthermore, like other ideas, some moral ideas attain great forcefulness and liveliness, which renders them beliefs. A moral opinion or belief represents a person, trait, or action as having a moral property (*T* 3.1.1.5 / SBN 457). This is its content. No doubt at least some of the copies of our moral sensings will be memories, just as the copies of sensations are. Our moral ideas and beliefs can figure in discussion and inference, just as other ideas do. The imagination, of course, has the power to separate complex ideas and recombine their simple components

---

[22] Falk (1976) is helpful on this point.

[23] Another way in which sense impressions differ from moral impressions is that insofar as the causes of sense impressions are "specifically different" from our perceptions, they cannot be distinctly conceived. All we can conceive are our perceptions. (See, e.g., *T* 1.2.6.7–9 / SBN 67–8 and *T* 1.4.2.56 / SBN 218). While there is legitimate controversy over how skeptical Hume is about objects external to the mind, it is clear that because of this impossibility of distinct conception, we cannot come to know the extra-mental causes of our sense impressions (if there are some). Impressions of reflection, by contrast, have causes that can be conceived clearly and discovered by causal reasoning, because they are themselves perceptions.

(*T* 1.1.3.4 / SBN 10). Thus we can at least entertain moral analogs of the golden mountain, such as a virtuous horse (*EHU* 2.5 / SBN 19). And some complex moral ideas will be false (for example, the monkish opinion that abject humility is a virtue). Moral opinions that agree with the moral impressions we experience under the right conditions, on the other hand, are true, just as color opinions that agree with our impressions of color in good light are true.

Some interpretations of Hume, notably the noncognitivist ones, construe him as recognizing only one type of moral perception, the moral sentiment.[24] Since Hume claims that this is not a copy of anything else, and given his understanding of truth as the faithful correspondence of a copy with its putative original, moral perceptions therefore are not truth-apt, and one cannot reason about virtue and vice. The error here is to suppose that moral impressions cannot be copied. They can be, and the resulting moral ideas (and moral beliefs, when the ideas are sufficiently vivid) are truth-apt and can be compared with other ideas and impressions in reasoning processes. Other interpretations recognize that moral beliefs are mental items distinct from moral feelings, but treat them as fundamentally causal beliefs (e.g., that a character causes approbation), rather than as attributions of the properties virtue and vice to characters. This creates an inconsistency in the text, as we shall see. On the moral sensing view we avoid both pitfalls. There are two species of moral perceptions: moral impressions, which are felt sentiments and incapable of truth or falsehood, and moral ideas, which may be believed, and which are potential truth-bearers, but are not originally causal in content. With respect to the moral *ideas* (in which category fall moral opinions and beliefs), on the moral sensing view Hume is a cognitivist.

As we have noted, some see noncognitivism expressed (perhaps even defended) in Hume's is–ought paragraph. We have already seen another way to read this paragraph. On the moral sensing view we have further grounds to correct the noncognitivist misreading. In that paragraph Hume targets moralists who begin with some basic non-moral ideas and claim to show, through a series of inferences, how our fundamental knowledge of moral duty is derived from them. Those moralists offer an inferential account of how we first come to grasp virtue and vice and distinguish the one from the other, Hume claims. They claim to extract moral relations from non-moral relations by reasoning alone. The last paragraph of *T* 3.1.1 says: any author who gives such an account has not looked closely enough at his inferences. He helps himself to ideas that are not available solely from the non-moral ideas with which he begins. The reader cannot acquire such ideas by reasoning, but only via impressions. For the person who is not yet acquainted with virtue and vice, the connection between things she already knows and a moral conclusion is not inferential but causal. Reflection on the

---

[24] See, e.g., Árdal's otherwise illuminating account of Hume's moral judgments (1977 and 1966).

non-moral facts of a situation will cause her to feel approval or disapproval—to discriminate virtue from vice.

Hume states that facts about our duties are not to be inferred from other kinds of facts—those described with 'is'. Note that this does not entail that moral propositions do not assert any facts, or do not assert anything at all, and lack truth and falsehood. Hume never draws such a conclusion, and it would be a *non sequitur*. Even if 'ought'-relations cannot be inferred from 'is'-relations, 'ought'-statements might nonetheless express facts—just different facts.[25]

B. More about Hume's Understanding of Truth

As we saw in the last chapter, in *Treatise* 2.3.3 Hume defines "contradiction to truth and reason" as "the disagreement of ideas, consider'd as copies, with those objects, which they represent" (*T* 2.3.3.5 / SBN 415). Thus *accordance* with truth (and reason) would be the *agreement* of ideas, considered as copies, with those objects they represent. What are these objects? It is difficult to pin down Hume's use of the term 'object' here. One possibility is that they are impressions.[26] If moral opinions are ideas considered as copies of moral impressions, then by this definition they can certainly be true. But Hume seems to mean more by 'truth' than correspondence of an idea with an impression.

In *Treatise* 3.3.1, in expanding the discussion of 2.3.3, Hume reformulates this "agreement" theory of truth: "Truth or falsehood consists in an agreement or disagreement either to the *real* relations of ideas, or to *real* existence and matter of fact" (*T* 3.1.1.9 / SBN 458). (He gave a similar account at *T* 2.3.10.2 / SBN 448: "Truth is of two kinds, consisting either in the discovery of the proportions of ideas, consider'd as such, or in the conformity of our ideas of objects to their real existence.") The item that agrees or disagrees is presumably still an idea. Does a moral belief ever agree or disagree with any real relation of ideas or with real existence and matter of fact? If it does not, then it cannot be true. Now, the mere use of the word 'real' in "real existence and matter of fact" does not bar Humean moral judgments from being true; it is a real matter of fact, for example, that people feel approval, and moral judgments might agree with this

---

[25] See Sturgeon 2001: 8–11, for an account of which facts are described by each type of statement.

[26] According to Waxman (1994: 51–7), only ideas and not impressions are capable of truth, for Hume (p. 56), because only ideas have the status of representations, a status established empirically. This suggests that truth consists in the agreement of ideas with the impressions they represent; but for Waxman the story is more complex. The truth of an idea of a matter of fact consists not in this relation itself, but in the "felt accord" of our mental operation delineating that idea with the operation involved in apprehending the corresponding sensation or passion.

Such a view presents a difficulty: how to account for the intentionality of impressions, including sense impressions. However, it seems in principle possible that sense impressions should have some sort of intentionality even if (as this type of view claims) they are not representations, which they cannot be if the only way to represent is to be a copy. But for present purposes we need not investigate the intentionality of impressions.

fact (though to do this they need not *describe* this fact, as we see later). But what text is there to settle whether moral judgments can be true, for Hume? Hume talks about errors in moral opinion and their correction, but it must be admitted that he does not explicitly say anywhere that "some moral opinions are true". However, it is significant that he never denies it; nor does he deny that a person's property of being vicious is a real existent or a real matter of fact. Much of *Treatise* Book 3 is devoted either to arguing for or explaining attributions of merit and demerit that he clearly takes to be true: for example, that justice is a virtue that depends on artifice, and that a well-founded and concealed pride is virtuous and not vicious. If he thought that this long book were filled with fictions and falsehoods, one might expect him to say so. He does, of course, deny that someone's being vicious is a matter of fact that can be *inferred by reason*, but that is a far narrower claim. Not all matters of fact are inferred by reason; with some we are acquainted non-inferentially, for example by sense impressions. Note that Hume's "agreement" theory of truth is introduced to make a minimal point: only perceptions that purport to represent (indeed, to be copies of) something else are potential truth-bearers. Such perceptions, to be true, must agree with reality. But he never says that ideas, to be true, must agree with continued and independent existence, or reality external to the mind. We can surely have true ideas of many mind-dependent facts, such as that steel can administer painful cuts and fire warms us pleasantly (*T* 1.4.2.12 / SBN 192). So if Hume turns out to be a moral anti-realist of the sort who claims that moral properties exist but are reaction-dependent, he can still consistently hold that some moral opinions are true.

For further insight on this subject, we may consider what Hume says about judgments of color, heat, and cold. One example is suggestive. We can discern a considerable difference in quality between two instances of "colour, taste, heat, and cold" by *intuition* (*T* 1.3.1.2 / SBN 70). For Hume, what we intuit is known with certainty. Thus, when we see and touch ice and freshly-brewed coffee at the same time and compare our sensations, we not only judge but *know* that the ice is colder and lighter in color than the coffee. What we *know* is, of course, true.[27] Therefore some of our beliefs about color, taste, heat, and cold are true. More generally, since for Hume resemblance is a philosophical relation capable of being known, we know some resemblances between sensible qualities such as colors (he mentions many such resemblances in Book 1), and hence our judgments about these are true.[28] Unfortunately, these are the only contexts in which Hume commits himself to the truth of a judgment of sensible quality.

---

[27] And intuition is not inference, since it involves no intermediate step. For Hume's understanding of intuition, and a novel and helpful account of his conception of inference, see Owen 1999: esp. ch. 5.

[28] E.g., "That idea of red, which we form in the dark, and that impression, which strikes our eyes in sun-shine, differ only in degree, not in nature" (*T* 1.1.1.5 / SBN 3). Thanks to Donald Ainslie for helping me to see the general point about resemblance.

Otherwise he does not address the topic of whether there are truths about color, taste, smell, heat, and cold. But the vulgar surely think it *true* that coffee is brown and fragrant and ice is cold. Had Hume thought otherwise, then, given the high priority he assigns to challenging our vulgar views where he thinks them wrong, he would probably have made a point of saying so. And if judgments about color and coldness can be true, presumably judgments about merit and demerit can be true as well, since they are analogous.[29] Even if it should turn out that moral properties are reaction-dependent, it would not follow that opinions about reaction-dependent properties cannot any of them be true.[30]

We should note that where Hume denies that merit and demerit are identical with truth and falsehood (*T* 3.1.1.15 and n. 1 / SBN 461–2), he is not denying that moral beliefs can be true. His arguments on this subject are intended to show that the property virtuousness (of, say, an action) is not itself identical with the truth of that action (that action's being true)—not that beliefs *about* virtuousness are not true. (Recall Wollaston's proposal that actions themselves were in a sense true or false, and that the virtue of good actions consisted in their truth, and the vice of bad actions in their falsehood.[31]) Using analogous arguments, Hume could make the same sort of case that extension is not identical with truth, but of course he would not deny that some beliefs about extension are true.[32]

---

[29] In "The Sceptic", published shortly after Book 3 of the *Treatise*, Hume says of the doctrine that tastes and colors, and also virtue and vice, "lie not in the bodies, but merely in the senses", that it "takes off no more from the reality of the latter qualities, than from that of the former" (*EMPL* 166). This is not decisive: maybe the doctrine "takes off" equally from the reality of both. But the gist seems to be that while both are dependent upon human psychological reactions, neither is unreal in any sense that precludes there being true judgments about them. For more about "The Sceptic", see below.

[30] At *T* 1.3.5.2 / SBN 84, Hume entertains the thought that sense impressions themselves (rather than our ideas of them) may be true or false. He says we can never know the causal origin of all our sense impressions; they may be produced by objects, by "the creative power of the mind", or by "the author of our being". But, he adds, this skeptical point makes no difference to the subject there at hand, the analysis of our causal reasoning, for "[w]e may draw inferences from the coherence of our perceptions, whether they be true or false; whether they represent nature justly, or be mere illusions of the senses". Here Hume seems to grant that all sense impressions (and presumably all ideas copied from them) would be false if there were no external world of independent bodies that produced them. However, this is incompatible with his later denial that sense impressions themselves represent objects as continuing existents external to the mind (*T* 1.4.2.11 / SBN 191). The feeling of heat, on Hume's view as explained later in the *Treatise*, does not itself contain a claim that its cause exists outside the mind; thus the feeling of heat would not be false simply on the grounds that it and all other sense impressions were caused merely by the "creative power of the mind". The prior remark at *T* 1.3.5.2 / SBN 84 is best construed, then, as merely preliminary. Hume's arguments that sense impressions themselves "give us no notion of continu'd existence" nor of "distinct existence" (*T* 1.4.1.11 / SBN 191) are yet to come.

[31] Wollaston (1991[1724]): 240.

[32] Hume also argues here that the merit or demerit of an action does not consist in its tendency to cause observers to form a true or a false non-moral judgment. The fact that a man's surreptitiously creeping into a window by a ladder leads observers to no false judgments about what he is doing (either they make no judgment because his stealth succeeds, or they see him and know he is burgling

We have seen that whether Hume understands truth as agreement between ideas and impressions, or agreement between ideas and real relations of ideas or real existence and matter of fact, he implicitly allows that judgments about both sensory and moral qualities may be true. A more complete reconstruction of Hume's conception of truth would need to incorporate a role for abstract ideas, since they often figure in predications. For Hume abstract ideas are not, of course, Lockean indeterminate representations. Rather, we notice a resemblance among various objects and mark this by using a general term for them; the term is directly associated with a determinate idea of an individual instance, but one that carries with it associations with the many other instances that appropriately resemble it. When we think of the general term, we habitually call to mind the set of ideas of all the other instances that resemble this one, and in this way the particular idea linked with the term acquires general signification (*T* 1.1.7.1–9 / SBN 17–22). Don Garrett proposes a Humean account of predicative judgments, including moral judgments: in attributing a property to an object, we place the object of predication in the "revival set" of our abstract idea of the property. (This is the set of ideas resembling the determinate idea associated with the general term—the set whose members are habitually called to mind by the term.) Our ideas of persons or traits having moral properties come originally from moral feelings, but after multiple experiences we form standard Humean abstract ideas of the moral properties (whose revival sets we adjust from the common point of view). Ultimately, when we make judgments such as "David is virtuous", or "David's gratitude is a virtue", we place David or his gratitude in the revival set of our abstract idea of virtue.[33] This permits a more complex analysis of truth as agreement with real matters of fact. The moral judgment is true provided it agrees with the fact that David, or his trait, appropriately resembles the other items in the revival set of the relevant term. Clearly, on this construal as well, moral judgments will sometimes be true.[34]

According to the moral sensing interpretation, the usual way to acquire a moral belief is to experience a moral impression and form a lively idea from it. But just as we can form beliefs about the colors of objects we have not seen on the basis of the trustworthy testimony of those who have seen them, so under special circumstances we can form beliefs about the merit or demerit of characters and actions without experiencing any moral sentiments in contemplation of

the house) does not render the action meritorious, Hume says. Clearly Hume does not here deny that the judgment "his action is wicked" is true; rather, he denies that the truth of observers' judgments about what the man is doing renders the action meritorious.

[33] Garrett 1997: 196–9. He explains abstract ideas at pp. 24–5.

[34] Garrett suggested the importance of abstract ideas to an account of Humean truth when I presented an earlier version of this chapter at the 28th Hume Society Conference in Victoria, British Columbia, in July 2001. On his view the revival set in question will be an idealized one: the set of items whose ideas the thinker would place in this term's revival set given complete experience and normal human nature.

them. If I know no history of England, I will feel no moral sentiment at all in contemplating Queen Elizabeth I. But if reliable historians tell me that she was vicious, I can form the belief that she was, making use of the idea of viciousness I already possess as a result of my prior emotional responses to other people.[35]

C. Attribution and Identity of Moral Properties

What property do I attribute to a trait (such as Rousseau's ingratitude) when I believe it is vicious?[36] Hume argues that moral good and evil are not discovered by probable reasoning—at least not originally. So it would be an error to construe my opinion "Rousseau's ingratitude is vicious" as a causal belief; for causal beliefs are ones I can form *only* on the basis of probable reasoning resulting from repeated observations. I should instead be able to feel the vice of this trait when I encounter it and form my belief directly from that, without inference. Thus the belief that Rousseau's ingratitude is a vice is not the belief that his ingratitude is the cause of (or is such as to cause) disapprobation in human beings who contemplate it from a particular perspective. The property I attribute to Rousseau's ingratitude—what I regard this trait as having—cannot initially be a causal property.[37] Here the moral sensing view again takes its cue from sense perception. In believing the tomato before me to be red, I do not believe (I need not believe) the surface properties of the tomato to be the cause of a sensation of redness in human observers under bright light. That is not what I think when I think that the tomato is red. I probably have no metaphysical or physical theory of what redness consists in, but even if I do, I do not invoke it when I think "There's a red tomato", but rather I think with the vulgar. I think that the tomato is *red*. The property I attribute is redness. This is the property I am familiar with from sense perception. I identify it, as it were, ostensively: it is the property that looks like *that*.[38] For Hume, in sense perception I do not form any impression of continued or independent existence (e.g., *T* 1.4.2.9–10 / SBN 190–1). So in the belief I form immediately, as a copy of my sensation of the red tomato, I do not attribute the redness to a continuing and independent body. (That will require a separate activity of the imagination.[39]) We can say the same about moral beliefs. In believing that Rousseau's ingratitude is vicious, the property we attribute to Rousseau's character trait is *viciousness*. This attribution

---

[35] This is a point Garrett makes (1997: ch. 9, pp. 197–8).

[36] See *The Letters of David Hume*, various letters about Rousseau's mistreatment of Hume, e.g., letter 334 to Richard Davenport, 26 June 1766.

[37] Here I depart from Capaldi (1989), and I resist the move by Sturgeon (2001) to grant that Hume is inconsistent on this point.

[38] Of course, I will also depend on others to confirm what looks like that and what does not. There need not be any problem here about a private object or a private language.

[39] Strictly speaking, as the vulgar, we think that the redness is in the object, the object exists unperceived, but the object is identical with our sensations; but none of this comes into the mind in the act of perceiving (*T* 1.4.2.36 / SBN 205).

is not a causal judgment; nor is it an attribution of a property to something we think of as independent of our perceptions. (Nor is it, of course, an attribution to something we think of as *de*pendent upon our perceptions.) My belief attributes to Rousseau's ingratitude the very property with which I am familiar because I have felt it—the property that feels like that.

On this interpretation the predication of a moral or sensory property of an object is simply that. It is the attribution of a property—whatever it may be—that one is aware of by sensation or feeling. For me to attribute redness or warmth to something is not itself, then, to believe that I am having a red or warm sensation now, though the two thoughts will often occur together. If I pick up a cup of coffee and feel warmth, I will assent to both propositions ("The coffee is warm" and "I feel warmth when I hold the cup of coffee"); but they are not equivalent. And I can certainly believe something to be warm without believing that I feel anything. Similarly, in thinking "Rousseau's ingratitude was a vice" I need not think "I feel disapproval when I contemplate Rousseau's ingratitude". Thus a sensory or moral predication is not a description of the thinker's present experience. It is sometimes thought that on Hume's view for me to think that something is a vice is to believe that were I to contemplate it in the right way I *would* feel disapproval, or that most people would, or that some similar counterfactual holds. But while I may well have these counterfactual beliefs when I judge some trait to be a vice, Hume would not identify the believed idea that a trait is a vice with the counterfactual thought. For that counterfactual thought, unlike a thought about my present sensations or sentiments, is a generalization from past experience and is the product of inference. It is, indeed, a causal prediction.

It may be that Hume thinks that the property viciousness is *in fact* identical to a causal, dispositional property: namely, the tendency a trait has to cause disapproval in the well-informed and imaginative human observer. He does not say this explicitly, but there are strong hints of it. This hypothesis, however, is compatible with the claim of the moral sensing view that in *believing* someone vicious we do not attribute to him a dispositional, causal property. To see a conflict here would be to substitute incorrectly into an opaque context. I attribute to someone's character that property, whatever it is, that I sense when I disapprove; but that property that I experience, unbeknownst to me, may *be* the tendency of the character to evoke disapproval in properly-situated observers. If it is, then this identity holds metaphysically, though it is a contingent matter whether we should know of it, as Kripke would say.[40] In attributing viciousness to a man, we need not *attribute* a causal property to him, even if the viciousness *consists in* a causal property. (Think of the Morning Star and Venus.) Hume does not make this point, of course; I mention it only to show that the positions

---

[40] Kripke 1972: lecture 2. Also see Putnam 1973 on identities that hold (necessarily) but are not entailed by a competent speaker's concepts.

are compatible. (In passing, note that if the identity holds, there will be many truths about the moral properties, since they will be real causal properties.)

III. COMMITMENTS IN *TREATISE* 3.1.1–2 ABOUT WHAT MORAL PROPERTIES ARE AND ARE NOT

So far the moral sensing view has made the Hume of the *Treatise* sound quite neutral with respect to what moral properties themselves are. He never says that virtuousness and viciousness are fictions or fallacies; so we are not entitled to conclude that they do not exist or that we have no reason to believe in them. As for their nature, that is not specified. We feel them and form beliefs about whatever properties feel that way, but what they are in themselves is not spelled out.

But this is too quick. We have already devoted attention to most of Hume's arguments in these sections of Part 1 and must not overlook their consequences. In order to argue that we do not discern good and evil by means of ideas alone, and so by means of reasoning alone, Hume has *inter alia* made commitments in places to *some* claims about the nature of good and evil. Below are the explicit commitments about moral properties in general that emerge from the arguments of *Treatise* 3.1.1 and 3.1.2. Since we have already looked at most of them in detail, we can be brief. The list prominently includes negative claims, statements of what the moral properties are *not*.

1. Virtuousness and viciousness influence the will (in a way that reasoning alone cannot), presumably through our sensing of them. Our grasp of moral properties yields passions that are often motivating.[41]

2. Moral merit and demerit are not identical with reasonableness and unreasonableness. Whatever the moral properties may be, they are not these. (Also, the good of an action does not consist in the action's being true and its evil does not consist in its being false, as vs. Wollaston.[42])

3. Moral good and evil do not consist in the truth or falsehood of (non-moral) judgments *about* actions, either those made by the agent or by others. (The wickedness of a man's consorting with his neighbor's wife does not consist in the falsehood of an observer's judgment that she is his own, for example (*T* 3.1.1.15 and n. 1 / SBN 461).) (This argument was not discussed in Chapter 3.)

4. "[V]ice and virtue" do not "consist in relations susceptible of certainty and demonstration," as they would have to do if morals were discerned

---

[41] This commitment is, of course, in Argument M and its precursors.
[42] The argument for this is, as we have seen, the Direct Argument (*T* 3.1.1.9 / SBN 458).

by demonstrative reasoning (*T* 3.1.1.19 / SBN 463). Specifically, merit and demerit do not consist in resemblance, contrariety, degrees in quality, or proportions in quantity and number. What this seems to mean is that the moral property of an action does not consist in the action's resembling or being contrary to something else, or being greater or less than something else. The evil of parricide does not lie in the contrariety between the act of taking life by the offspring and the giving of life by the parent, as the tree and sapling story shows (*T* 3.1.1.24 / SBN 467).

5. The "character of virtuous and vicious" is also not the kind of matter of fact inferred by our causal reasoning, the other operation of the understanding (*T* 3.1.1.18 / SBN 463). Probable reasoning against a background of prior experience enables us to infer the *causes* of the perceived act of willful murder ("passions, motives, volitions and thoughts" (*T* 3.1.1.26 / SBN 468)), but its viciousness is not one of these causes.[43]

6. Now for the crucial passage about colors and heat and cold, which I now quote more fully. You find the viciousness of willful murder when you

> turn your reflection into your own breast, and find a sentiment of disapprobation, which arises in you, towards this action. Here is a matter of fact; but 'tis the object of feeling, not of reason. It lies in yourself, not in the object. So that when you pronounce any action or character to be vicious, you mean nothing, but that from the constitution of your nature you have a feeling or sentiment of blame from the contemplation of it. Vice and virtue, therefore, may be compar'd to sounds, colours, heat and cold, which, according to modern philosophy, are not qualities in objects, but perceptions in the mind: And this discovery in morals, like that other in physics, is to be regarded as a considerable advancement of the speculative sciences; tho', like that too, it has little or no influence on practice.   (T 3.1.1.26 / SBN 468–9)

This passage, on which the moral sensing view has relied, in part, for its account of our awareness of moral properties, also asserts that these properties lie in us, not in the object. Like heat, cold, sounds, and colors as understood in "modern philosophy", moral properties are not qualities in objects but perceptions in the mind. And this is no vain speculation of the "fantastic sect of sceptics", but an advancement in the study of morals.

It is difficult to parse Hume's exact meaning when he says that vice and virtue, like colors and so on, are not qualities in the objects but perceptions in the mind. Presumably he does not mean that when I (a spectator) feel disapproval for someone's act of murder, *I* am vicious. Although the viciousness

---

[43] This is from *T* 3.1.1.26 / SBN 468, understanding it as we did in the previous chapter as paralleling the previous argument to show that viciousness is not a demonstrable relation by pointing out that it also does not consist in a causal relation between the action and any of its causes.

Some read this passage as claiming that the viciousness is not any fact at all. But as we have seen, Hume is usually careful to say "any matter of fact, whose existence we can infer by reason", and here too he seems to limit his point to *inferred* facts.

is not in the action, it is not a property of me, or my mind; it is still a property *of* the action. Now, relational properties can be properties of an action without being in the action. An action can have the property "being done before dinner", yet that property is not in the action (say, of murder). It is not intrinsic to the act of murder that it is done before dinner. So one thing Hume may mean here is that viciousness is a relational property, not a simple quality. But he is not merely saying this, of course; he is claiming that one term in this relation that constitutes viciousness is a human psychological reaction. (Like the sensation dependence of color, the reaction dependence of vice is something that philosophy reveals, of course, not something implicit in ordinary judgment.) The viciousness of an action or character is a property that depends for its existence on human beings' experiencing a feeling of disapproval when they contemplate it. And that is a version of moral anti-realism as we have defined it.[44]

So there is one (but only one) passage in the *Treatise* where Hume commits himself to moral anti-realism. (We will see that there are others in the moral *Enquiry*.) This passage, though, is likely to provoke some concerns about the viability of the moral sensing view and of the claim that Hume is a moral anti-realist.

IV. THE PUZZLE POSED BY THE MODERN PHILOSOPHY

In *Treatise* 1.4.4, "Of the modern philosophy", Hume, assuming (that his reader will assume) "there is both an external and an internal world" (*T* 1.4.2.57 / SBN 218), examines a philosophy that claims to *"*arise only from the solid, permanent, and consistent principles of the imagination" (*T* 1.4.4.2 / SBN 226), those we may trust, as distinct from those that may lead us into unfounded prejudices. This modern philosophy is based on one fundamental principle: that colors, sounds, tastes, smells, heat and cold are "nothing but impressions in the mind, deriv'd from the operation of external objects, and without any resemblance

---

[44] One sentence in the quoted passage is a stock piece of evidence for the noncognitivist interpretation: "when you pronounce any action or character to be vicious, you mean nothing, but that from the constitution of your nature you have a feeling or sentiment of blame from the contemplation of it". Flew (1963) says that here Hume is groping for the emotivist thesis but, not quite grasping that, maintains that in making a moral utterance the most you can mean to say is that you have a certain feeling. On the moral sensing interpretation this is of course incorrect. Since Hume uses "pronounce an action blameable" virtually as a synonym for "distinguish its vice" or "judge it vicious" (*T* 3.1.1.3 / SBN 456, and *T* 3.3.1.3 / SBN 575), and he says nothing else in this paragraph about utterances, there is little reason to think he is talking here about the meaning of linguistic expressions. Here apparently 'pronounce' means 'judge' or 'regard'. (To pronounce something thus-and-so is to judge or form an opinion that it is so.) Hume says here that when you find any action or character to be vicious, *all that happens* in your mind is that from the constitution of your nature you have a feeling or sentiment of blame from the contemplation of it.

to the qualities of the objects". Both the sole argument he gives for this fundamental thesis and the thesis itself he labels "satisfactory". Given this fundamental principle, he says, the other theses of modern philosophy follow: that the primary qualities (extension, solidity, motion, and figure) are the only ones that belong to continued existents themselves, "the only *real* ones, of which we have any adequate notion" (*T* 1.4.4.5 / SBN 227); and that all occurrences in nature (the movements of bodies, growth and decay of animals, and so on) are to be explained in terms of the primary qualities alone. But Hume famously argues next (following Berkeley) that we cannot form any distinct conceptions of the primary qualities that do not make use of one of the secondary qualities such as color.[45] The consequence of accepting the modern thesis about colors and their ilk is ultimately "that instead of explaining the operations of external objects by its means, we utterly annihilate all these objects, and reduce ourselves to the opinions of the most extravagant scepticism concerning them" (*T* 1.4.4.6 / SBN 227–8). And later, "upon the whole [we] must conclude, that after the exclusion of colours, sounds, heat and cold from the rank of external existences, there remains nothing, which can afford us a just and consistent idea of body" (*T* 1.4.4.10 / SBN 229). Thus the solid and consistent principles of the imagination lead us to conclude that nothing in the universe has a continued and independent existence (*T* 1.4.4.15 / SBN 231).

In light of this section, and also some remarks at 1.2.3.15–16 (SBN 38–9) that we can have no idea of extension without thinking of the extended object or its components as colored or tangible, we might interpret Hume as offering a *reductio* of the basic principle of the modern philosophy, and conclude that he rejects it. We might—until he says quite seriously in Book 3 that this very principle is "a considerable advancement in the speculative sciences". Since he is certainly sincere in calling his discovery of the reaction dependence of moral properties a comparable advancement, we cannot treat the admiring reference to the modern philosophy as ironic.[46]

This leaves an interpretive quandary. Hume says in *Treatise* 3.1.1 not only that moral properties are in part analogous to colors, heat and cold, but that they are like these qualities as they are understood by the moderns. This seems to direct us to *Treatise* 1.4.4 for illumination about the nature of moral properties. But, one might think, to look to 1.4.4 for help with morals is to seek light where there is great darkness. There has long been intense interpretive controversy over what stance Hume takes there toward the modern thesis and where it leaves him, given the contradictions and skeptical results he derives from it.

---

[45] For Berkeley's version of the argument, see, e.g., Berkeley 1998[1710]: 106 (*Principles* 1.10).

[46] Blackburn (1993) interprets Hume as rejecting the primary–secondary distinction. Blackburn argues that because Hume does reject it, and because he realizes that he can devise no tenable analysis of "the indicative nature of sensible qualities" (p. 282), Hume could not possibly intend to use color, heat, and cold to help explain the nature of moral properties. Obviously I disagree with this interpretation.

This is not the place to defend a particular interpretation of 1.4.4. However, regardless of all the complexities with which an interpreter must grapple, there are only a few possible conclusions one can draw. They fall into three mutually exclusive categories.

1. Hume holds that colors, heat, and cold—or properties resembling our sensations of these—are actually in bodies, as are the primary qualities.

2. He believes that no sensible qualities—neither colors and heat nor solidity and extension—resemble any properties in the external world, but all are merely "in the mind".

3. He agrees with the moderns that there are two kinds of sensible qualities: ones that do and ones that do not have external exemplars.

Hume may hold one of these views outright; or (more likely) he may consider one of these views the most eligible among plausible hypotheses, a supposition that cannot be established or even, perhaps, clearly conceived, but that has appeal and may be true.

It is not necessary here to determine which view Hume holds. All three of these options are consistent with the moral sensing view, and with Hume's being a moral anti-realist of the sort described.

Let us take the most difficult case first. Suppose Hume utterly rejects the basic thesis of the modern philosophy in the first way, and holds that there are properties in bodies resembling felt colors and heat.[47] If he held this view, he would no doubt do so for one of two reasons: either because he finds the skeptical consequences of modern philosophy unacceptable yet thinks them unavoidable if we grant the basic modern thesis (so he would opt to deny the skeptical argument its premise), or because he rejects the "satisfactory" modern argument that supports the basic thesis. Even if so, in 3.1.1 he makes a serious comparison between moral properties and colors, etc., *as understood in modern philosophy.* Thus we should construe the comparison in 3.1.1 as follows: moral properties really are as the modern philosophers take colors to be, although colors are not that way. Now if Hume finds unacceptable the skeptical result that extension and solidity too cannot be conceived as independent of the mind (since an extended or solid object can be conceived only as colored or tangible), and this leads him to reject the basic principle of modern philosophy, this does not mean that he sees anything objectionable about saying that virtue and vice cannot be conceived as independent of the mind. Indeed, that is just the point of putting his comparison

---

[47] I think this an unpromising interpretation, and do not know anyone who defends it. Garrett defends the more moderate interpretation that Hume never excludes this possibility. On Garrett's view, Hume regards the causal argument for the basic modern principle as an argument of a legitimate type that in fact fails, and Hume is in a position to regard the thesis that "at least some continued and distinct objects do have both secondary and primary qualities" as consistent and not undermined by any sound causal arguments (Garrett 1997: 219–20).

in these terms. Virtue and vice are not conceivable as existing independently of a sensitive observer. The skepticism that ostensibly worries Hume in 1.4.4 is doubt that we can form any conception of mind-independent reality. This need not worry him at all when it comes to moral good and evil. Alternatively, Hume might embrace (or not reject) the first view, that colors and heat or their exemplars are in bodies, not because he fears the skeptical consequence of the modern thesis, but for the alternative reason: he does not accept the causal argument offered to establish it. If the weakness of that causal argument is his reason to reject the modern thesis, it leaves him free to embrace the analogous view of virtue and vice, since he does not base that view on the same type of argument at all.

Next take the second option, that Hume rejects the modern view of primary qualities, and thinks we cannot understand any sensible qualities whatsoever (not even extension) as having external exemplars. What he says in 3.1.1, then, is that virtue and vice are just two more qualities that cannot be conceived as independent of our psychological reactions. They differ only in being dependent upon sentiments rather than sensations. So this option presents no difficulty.

Finally, take the third option, and suppose that Hume thinks the modern philosophers are more or less right, both that colors have no "external archetypes" and that external objects do have properties that resemble perceived extension, motion, and solidity.[48] On this view there is no difficulty in making an analogy between moral properties and colors as understood in modern philosophy. Both are reaction-dependent, and they differ only in the type of reaction on which they depend.

On all these interpretations, then, Hume makes a commitment in 3.1.1 to moral anti-realism as we have defined it, one that is compatible with his understanding of moral awareness as moral sensing, and his views in 1.4.4 pose no problem for it.

Hume's essay "The Sceptic" of 1742 (just two years after the publication of Book 3 of the *Treatise*) can be read the same way.[49] He says: "there is nothing, in itself, valuable or despicable, desirable or hateful, beautiful or deformed;

[48] It is unlikely that Hume embraces the modern position outright, since he argues so persuasively that it leads to contradiction between our causal conclusions and our belief in bodies. But a more moderate interpretation is plausible: Hume thinks the hypothesis that extension and so on are in bodies, but that color and its ilk are not, is for various reasons preferable to its alternatives, or cannot be ruled out, although he grants that it does not permit us to conceive of bodies clearly. Perhaps he thinks the modern theory, even if it is misconceived, is the most fruitful one for use in scientific investigation. For a subtly argued view of roughly this third sort, see the interpretation of this passage by Wright (1983: ch. 3). Wright has systematic reasons to argue that Hume opts for the causal conclusions.

[49] We cannot be sure that he speaks in his own voice in "The Sceptic", although he probably does. It is one of four essays in which Hume tries to enter into the thinking of "sects, that naturally form themselves in the world, and entertain different ideas of human life and happiness" (*EMPL* 138, "The Epicurean"). The topic is what sort of life we should try to lead in order to be happy.

but that these attributes arise from the particular constitution and fabric of human sentiment and affection" (*EMPL* 162). Initially he makes this point only about the value of pursuits that also incorporate the bodily appetites and about aesthetic properties ("natural beauty and deformity"). But eventually he says that when it comes to beauty either "natural or moral", the quality is *thought* to lie in the object, but in fact lies in the "feelings of mankind" (*EMPL* 166). The supporting discussion is entirely in terms of aesthetic examples (some of which, such as the circle, he repeats in the second *Enquiry*), but it is clear that he means the point to hold for moral properties. In footnote 3 Hume reminds the reader of the doctrine of the modern philosophy, " 'That tastes and colours, and all other sensible qualities, lie not in the bodies, but merely in the senses' ", and adds: "The case is the same with beauty and deformity, virtue and vice" (*EMPL* 166) Again he is cagey about his degree of support for the modern philosophy, but again his endorsement of reaction dependence for moral properties is clear.

It may be thought that there is a fourth possibility: that Hume refuses to take any of the three positions normally offered by the distinction between primary and secondary qualities, because he rejects the terms in which the question is asked. On this view Hume rejects the dichotomy between primary and secondary qualities not because he thinks all qualities are in bodies that are continuous through time and distinct from the mind, or that all qualities are merely in the mind and not distinct from it, but because he rejects as incoherent the whole notion of an external world distinct from the mind and independent of its perceptions. Thus Hume regards the question which properties exist in bodies that are independent of the mind and its perceptions as ill-formed; it does not even make sense to *deny* that there are such things. If all our conceptions are derived from our impressions, we have no ideas—no concepts—with which to think about whether anything is independent of the mind's perceptions. And to ask such a question about redness, warmth, extension, or motion simply makes no sense; we conceive these only as ideas or impressions, not as anything extra-mental. (The idea of body that we do have is an idea of perceptions that, through the workings of the principles of association, we come to think of—erroneously—as having continuous and distinct existence. But it is nonetheless an idea of perceptions, not of anything "specifically different" from those.) Hume, on this interpretation, cannot entertain any metaphysical questions; he repudiates metaphysics as talk without meaning. Call this the anti-metaphysical interpretation.[50] According to this reading, Hume could not embrace any kind of realism or anti-realism, whether moral or scientific or of another sort. It would be correct to say that he is not a moral realist, but not

---

[50] For a terse, clear characterization (and advocacy) of the anti-metaphysical interpretation, see Morris 2008. I am grateful to him and to Charlotte Brown for pressing this interpretation on me in discussion.

that he is a moral anti-realist of the particular kind we have focused on, one who claims that moral properties exist but depend for their existence on human psychological reactions. According to the anti-metaphysical interpretation, this is either incoherent or trivially true. As a trivial statement it simply says that we perceive moral properties; it is like saying that we perceive colors. If it goes beyond that, it must be contrasting moral properties with other properties that do not depend for their existence on psychological reactions, and no sense can be made of this.

This interpretation must explain various difficult passages in the *Treatise* and the two *Enquiries*, and it would take us too far afield to examine those textual issues in any detail. But one strategy that might be used by such an interpreter should be mentioned. Someone might say that although Hume talks in *Treatise* 3.1.1 of primary and secondary qualities, he has by this point co-opted that distinction. It is now a distinction within the set of purely impression-based properties (the only ones we can conceive).[51]

It is true that according to the anti-metaphysical interpretation, the question of realism versus anti-realism does not arise, and realism about anything is either incoherent or false. If this is Hume's position, then we should not say that he is a moral anti-realist, but rather that he is not a moral realist. Fair enough. In any case my points can still be made. He does not hold that there are moral properties that are independent of our reactions and serve to warrant them; he thinks we grasp moral good and evil by the process of feeling certain sentiments; and his position is compatible with a cognitivist understanding of moral opinions or beliefs. Thus the fourth possibility presents no difficulty for the moral sensing view.

V. THE REALITY OF MORAL DISTINCTIONS AND TRUTH IN THE SECOND *ENQUIRY*

Hume begins the second *Enquiry* with the ambiguous remark about the reality of moral distinctions quoted earlier in this chapter. In the next paragraph, the question of "the general foundation of morals, whether they be derived from reason or from sentiment", turns out to be just the epistemic question "whether we attain the knowledge of them by a chain of argument . . . or by an immediate feeling" (*EPM* 1.3 / SBN 170). So far, then, we do not know the metaphysical status of good and evil. For that we turn to Appendix I.

There Hume argues that reason plays a sizeable role in our "decisions of praise or censure". Nonetheless, when, after a great deal of rational investigation,

---

[51] This strategy will have a bit of difficulty with the moral *Enquiry* and "The Sceptic", where Hume addresses an uninitiated audience and makes no use of his theory of ideas and impressions; there no context makes it clear that when he says that tastes, colors, and moral qualities "lie not in the bodies, but merely in the senses" (*EMPL* 166), and invokes the modern philosophy, he does not have the ordinary primary–secondary distinction in mind.

the facts about the usefulness of a trait are at last known, we must *feel* the difference between virtuousness and viciousness. In the second *Enquiry* the relevant sentiment is "a feeling for the happiness of mankind, and a resentment of their misery". "Here therefore *reason* instructs us in the several tendencies of actions, and *humanity* makes a distinction in favour of those which are useful and beneficial" (*EPM* App. 1.3 / SBN 286). Hume goes on to develop an analogy with "natural beauty": The beauty of the circle and pillar are not particular qualities or parts of them, nor relations that obtain between their parts, considered in independence of "an intelligent mind, susceptible to [the] finer sensations. Till such a spectator appear, there is nothing but a figure of such particular dimensions and proportions: from his sentiments alone arise its elegance and beauty" (*EPM* App.1.14 / SBN 292). The beauty or virtuousness is a relational property that cannot be instantiated in the absence of sensitive minds, because one of the relata is the reaction of such minds. So far we have the view of the *Treatise*.[52]

There is a temptation to read Hume as a noncognitivist in the second *Enquiry* because of the first two sentences of the final paragraph of Appendix I: "Thus the distinct boundaries and offices of *reason* and of *taste* are easily ascertained. The former conveys the knowledge of truth and falsehood: the latter gives the sentiment of beauty and deformity, vice and virtue" (*EPM* App.1.21 / SBN 294). A present-day reader might construe this to say that reason conveys *truths* and *falsehoods* to us, whereas moral sentiment does not. In light of what we have seen, though, such a reading is anachronistic. What Hume literally says is not that reason conveys truths and falsehoods, but that reason conveys the *knowledge* of truth and falsehood. And this is indeed a special function of Humean reason, as distinct not only from taste but from other faculties of the mind. Hume could as easily assert the paraphrase "Reason conveys the knowledge of truth and falsehood: vision and touch give the sensations of color and heat and cold." Sight, touch, taste, and other faculties give impressions from which ideas are ultimately made, and those ideas may be true or false. Sight and touch themselves, however, do not discover *whether* the ideas drawn from their impressions are true or false; insofar as that task can be performed, it falls to reason(ing). Of course only reason can give us knowledge (which for Hume, strictly speaking, entails certainty) that a given proposition is true or false. To obtain such knowledge, we must compare our ideas with one another or with our impressions to determine whether they agree, which for Hume is an activity of reasoning alone. But what reason so assesses may well be ideas (including true ideas) we obtained from sensation or from taste.

---

[52] Hume says (*EPM* App.1.10 / SBN 289): "[The hypothesis we embrace] defines virtue to be *whatever mental action or quality gives to the spectator the pleasing sentiment of approbation*; and vice the contrary." I take this to be a definition of *a* virtue, rather than of virtuousness.

Much has been made of the sentence in which the different tasks of reason and taste are enumerated—where it is said that reason "discovers objects as they really stand in nature, without addition or diminution"; while taste "has a productive faculty, and gilding or staining all natural objects with the colours, borrowed from internal sentiment, raises in a manner a new creation . . . "(*EPM* App.1.21 / SBN 294). The metaphor of our taste having a "productive faculty" that "gilds" and "stains" is, it must be said, unhelpful. It is striking, but it does not actually mark a change, if we parse it correctly. The literal point that Hume intends to make is probably just this: the relational property that constitutes virtue or vice comes into being in the interaction between the observed character (a natural object) and the sensitive mind. Compare the way in which the public gilds and stains actors and athletes with the colors borrowed from its adulation, raising in a manner the new creation of celebrity. Celebrity is a property *of* the renowned athlete, but not a quality *in* him; it is, in a manner, the creation of the sentiments of his fans. To say that virtuousness and viciousness are like this is to reiterate the *Treatise* account.

The remark about gilding and staining is often cited in support of the interpretation that in moral evaluation we *project* our sentiments onto external objects (perhaps as a film projector projects images from a film within it onto a screen), a description of ethical evaluation as metaphorical as Hume's own.[53] This may or may not be a correct interpretation; its main disadvantage is that it is very difficult to state in non-metaphorical language to see whether Hume says anything of the sort. (What is it to shine reflections of our emotions on external objects? Do we mistake our emotions for characteristics of such objects—thinking external objects are pleased or uneasy?) The interpretation depends on an analogy with Hume's account of causal reasoning, in which he says that we tend to conjoin with external objects the internal impression we have of causal necessity or power (which is in fact nothing but the habitual movement of the mind), and that this is an instance of the mind's "great propensity to spread itself on external objects" (*T* 1.3.14.25 / SBN 167). Since the idea of necessary connection comes solely from the movement of the mind, this is an error of thinking: we mistake something internal for something external. This may or may not be a coherent thesis.[54] However, the textual evidence for the application of this accusation of error to morals is thin. Hume never compares moral evaluation with causal judgment (whereas he repeatedly compares moral discrimination with sense perception). In the *Treatise*, in particular, no error

[53] The term 'projection' and the interpretation come from Barry Stroud (1977; see also his 1993). Mackie (1980: 73–4) sees hints of a projectivist view in Hume's account of moral judgments (Mackie's "Objectification theory"). Blackburn (1984: 171) deems Hume a projectivist, but denies that the projectivism that both he and Hume embrace involves a mistake.

[54] Stroud (1993) argues that it is not. On his view Hume makes projectivist claims about causal necessity and aesthetic properties as well as moral ones, and all are vulnerable to the same criticism.

is attributed to the mind at all in moral evaluation. "The Sceptic" does make one claim of error (though not of projecting): it says we think of beauty (which is very similar to virtue) as being in objects, although really it is not (*EMPL* 165–6). But this is simply the mistake of thinking a relational property is an intrinsic quality (a quality "in objects"). And it does not say that we make a mistake in attributing beauty or moral goodness to objects at all, in the way that we make a mistake in attributing causal necessity to objects. In any case, in our passage in the second *Enquiry* reason and taste simply have their different roles; Hume does not say here that in gilding, staining, and raising a new creation we make any error. The fact that the colors are "borrowed from internal sentiment" has, I think, distracted commentators from the fact that they are used to produce a "new creation". We use sentiment to render certain natural objects moral, and once we do, they *are* moral—we are not mistaken about that.

As we saw earlier, there is no reason to think that because of the rejection of realism, moral opinions do not describe any property and are neither true nor false. Nor is there reason to think they are all false. They do not describe anything in nature; they describe, instead, the "new creation". But they can be true accounts of that new creation or false ones.[55]

CONCLUSION

We have seen that, if the moral sensing view is right, Hume is a cognitivist about moral beliefs; yet this is compatible with the sort of moral anti-realism (or at

[55] If the Hume of the *Treatise* himself thought that even our ideas of primary qualities depend upon our ideas of color and the like, then there is one subtle change in the second *Enquiry*. For there Hume says that reason discovers objects as they really stand in nature, while taste or sentiment adds to objects something not a part of nature. It is not certain exactly what Hume means by 'nature', but he seems to mean the world of objects external to and independent of our perceptions. (In the second *Enquiry* Hume does not introduce his theory of impressions and ideas and does not discuss skepticism with regard to the senses or criticize the modern philosophy. His intended audience is certainly not limited to those acquainted with his or others' work in this area. Given the context and the broad intended audience, it is likely that Hume expected his readers to understand "objects as they really stand in nature" as objects independent of the mind.) In the *Treatise* Hume is reluctant to commit himself to the claim that reason discovers objects as they stand in nature; especially if he is persuaded by the skeptical critique of the modern philosophy, he believes that the understanding has no distinct conception of objects as they exist apart from our perceptions. So all conceivable properties are dependent upon our psychological proclivities, and moral properties are no different from the others. Here in the second *Enquiry*, though, he sounds confident that we do have knowledge of objects external to the mind. This talk may be no more than a rhetorical flourish. But if it is more than that, then the moral anti-realism of the second *Enquiry*, compared to that of the *Treatise*, has more bite. The second *Enquiry* seems to assume that *some* features of objects external to the mind can be known as they really are, and claims that moral properties are not among these. So whereas the anti-realism of the *Treatise* did not treat moral properties as importantly different from all the understood properties of things in nature, the doctrine of the second *Enquiry* does.

least rejection of moral realism) to which he commits himself. And we have seen that Hume explicitly rejects moral realism at one important point in the *Treatise* and also in "The Sceptic" and the second *Enquiry*. To do so is not, of course, to argue that we have any less reason to lead a moral life—as Hume is anxious to insist. In both works, however, Hume's commitments regarding the nature of moral properties, or lack of them, are entirely compatible with cognitivism about moral judgments.

The upshot is that for Hume, it is in experiencing the moral sentiments of approval and disapproval that we discriminate between good and evil, virtue and vice—that we acquire moral awareness. In having these impressions we feel virtue and vice. We then form ideas that are copies of these impressions and that can be combined into various sorts of (believed) judgments, some of which are true because they are accurate copies of their originals. These judgments are facilitated by the formation of Humean abstract ideas; when we judge that someone's trait is a vice, we include the trait in the revival set of the idea of vice, and our judgment is false if the trait does not sufficiently resemble the other items in that set. But importantly, that of which we are aware in moral discrimination and about which we make true or false moral judgments is not independent of our feelings of approval and disapproval. Those feelings create good and evil, much as the sentiments of the public create celebrity. And the moral properties themselves (not as we conceive of them but as they really are, if it is possible to talk about that) may well simply be tendencies to cause approval and disapproval in human beings who contemplate an object in a sufficiently disinterested way.

Consequently Hume has an understanding of ethical evaluation that rejects moral realism and relies on sentiment, and is in that sense subjective (though not in another sense, as we will see in the next chapter); yet it is not burdened with the grave disadvantages of a non-propositional theory of moral judgment. Since its inception in the twentieth century, noncognitivism has been hard pressed to explain how it is that we use moral sentences, which do not express propositions and are not truth-apt, in all kinds of discourse, including (so it seems) valid arguments, and how it is that many of them seem perfectly decomposable into parts linked by truth-functional logical connectives.[56] Many theories have been devised to try to explain this, of course.[57] But regardless of the success or failure of such theories, the thought that our moral judgments are not really saying anything, that their close connection with the emotions deprives them of truth and falsehood and of the role in inference played by ordinary assertions, has turned many away from the noncognitivist position. Yet some of those very thinkers remain convinced that our emotions play an ineliminable role, even a constitutive role, in making good and evil what they are; and so they are not

---

[56] See Geach (1958, 1965), who attributes the point to Frege, and Searle (1962; 1969: 136–41).

[57] For a recent and sweeping example, see Gibbard 2003.

willing to accept moral realism. Hume's moral sensing view reconciles these positions. Moral properties are emotion-dependent, yet we can think and talk about them in a perfectly sensible way, the same way we talk about other things. For many this will be an attractive feature of the resulting theory, particularly in light of the refinements we consider in the next chapter.

5

The Common Point of View

We have seen that for Hume moral assessment has two aspects: a feeling, which provides non-rational cognition of moral properties, and an idea typically copied from such a feeling, that of an object with a moral property. The idea is capable of being true or false, and some such moral ideas are true, which makes Hume a truth-cognitivist. We have also seen significant evidence that Hume is the sort of moral anti-realist who thinks that virtuousness and viciousness, goodness and evil, exist but are properties that depend on human psychological responses for their being. More specifically, for Hume moral properties are relational properties one of whose relata is the human psychological reaction (approbation or disapprobation) experienced when we contemplate a quality of mind. Even if the anti-metaphysical interpretation is right, and we are entitled to say only that Hume rejects moral realism, he regards moral good and evil as relational properties involving particular characteristic emotional responses as relata, rather than other sorts of perceptions, which distinguishes him from his opponents.

But Hume significantly supplements his account of ethical assessment in order to resolve what he himself takes to be potential problems with it, and that addition both strengthens his theory and raises new difficulties.

According to common sense, morality is a stable and shared system of evaluation, one that transcends the individual and the moment. We do not regard just any idiosyncratic emotional reaction as a moral reaction, or as the appropriate one. We expect what we count as an individual's moral reactions to be fairly consistent over time, and we expect a certain amount of agreement among people in a community about what is good and what is evil, at least in broad outline. A philosophical theory of ethics like Hume's that understands moral assessment as essentially a matter of emotion will have to accommodate these expectations. Hume tries to do this. For Hume claims both that moral judgments are (in the relevant sense) products of our sentiments, and that people make moral evaluations in a way that keeps each individual's judgments fairly consistent over time and mostly coordinated with the moral judgments of nearly everyone else. He regards moral evaluation as inter-subjective. Although Hume's account of the coordination of our moral evaluations has features that a present-day ethical theorist is unlikely to accept, one who shares Hume's basic views about the nature of morality and moral judgment stands to learn something from the difficulties that confront Hume's theory when he adjusts it to explain moral inter-subjectivity.

In the *Treatise*, after some 125 pages about ethics, Hume adds a famous wrinkle to his account. He says that in making moral evaluations, we do not consider character traits and persons "only as they appear from [our] peculiar point of view", but rather, "we fix on some *steady* and *general* points of view; and always, in our thoughts, place ourselves in them, whatever may be our present situation" (*T* 3.3.1.15 / SBN 581–2). This addition appears to generate internal disorder, perhaps contradiction, within Hume's moral theory. We will focus on two apparent difficulties. First, on a natural reading of this addition, moral evaluations are now to be understood as inductively grounded, empirical beliefs about what one *would* feel if one occupied the common or general point of view; but this would contradict Hume's explicit claim that vice and virtue are not matters of fact that can be discovered by (empirical) reasoning. Secondly, Hume says here that we must use the common point of view to "correct" the sentiments we experience from our "peculiar station", which suggests that those latter sentiments are in error. But since Hume denies that any sentiments represent reality, he cannot say that the sentiments we feel from the common point of view better represent or more accurately match the character traits being judged. He would seem to have no reason, then, to reject the sentiments we feel from our peculiar point of view as needing correction, and no consistent explanation of why we should adopt the steady point of view and prefer it as the basis of moral judgments. Hume introduces the common point of view in order to account for the fact that our moral judgments tend to remain constant, to converge with those of other people, and not to vary as idiosyncratically as one might expect given that they are manifestations of our individual feelings. But can he add to his system the requirement of evaluating from the common point of view without taking back some of his fundamental claims about moral evaluation?

I shall develop an interpretation that resolves these two difficulties and represents Hume's theory of moral evaluation as self-consistent; and I shall trace some of the consequences of reading Hume this way. This extends and further elaborates the moral sensing interpretation of Hume's account of ethical evaluation.

This part of the investigation will focus on the *Treatise*, although it will look briefly at the second *Enquiry* as well. (Although the emphasis is very different there and we find some other differences, Hume's reasons for introducing the common point of view are much the same, and the device functions in similar ways.) To understand the problems for which the common point of view is intended to provide a solution, and the new problems posed by the common point of view itself once it is introduced, let us briefly consider the details of the *Treatise* account in their context.

I. THE CONTEXT: SYMPATHY AND SENTIMENT

We skip ahead to *Treatise* 3.3. Hume has already argued that our moral judgments predicating virtue and vice, good and evil, of character traits, persons, and actions are not the deliverances of reasoning, but are products of the sentiments of approbation (praise, esteem) and disapprobation (blame), feelings of pleasure or uneasiness that we have when we survey a person's overall character, specific trait, or action.[1] As we have seen, Hume makes a point of distinguishing the moral sentiments from more self-centered reactions to character traits, persons, and actions, both by their characteristic feeling (moral approval is a pleasure qualitatively distinct from other pleasures) and by the fact that we feel the moral sentiments only when we consider a character "in general, without reference to our particular interest" (*T* 3.1.2.4 / SBN 472)—that is, without regard to whether or not it serves our advantage. The *standard* judgment we make that manifests the moral sentiment is a judgment that a specific quality of mind of the person in question is a virtue or a vice, and to what degree it is; for example, a judgment that Jane's courage is a (great) virtue, or that John's laziness is a (minor) vice (suggested *passim*, e.g., *T* 3.3.1.21 / SBN 585 and *T* 3.3.1.24 / SBN 587). The "quality of mind" (character trait) which we evaluate is a psychological disposition in part consisting of an enduring sentiment or tendency to feel a sentiment, often one capable of causing action. This quality of mind can typically be described non-evaluatively, as we have seen, so that it is a matter for empirical discovery whether (what we all recognize as) pride is a virtue or a vice, and whether celibacy, self-denial, humility, and the rest of the "monkish virtues" belong in the column of the virtues or should be transferred to the catalogue of the vices (*EPM* 9.3 / SBN 270). By this point in the *Treatise* Hume has also presented his theory of the artificial virtues, according to which honesty with respect to property, fidelity to promises, allegiance to government, and female chastity and modesty are analyzed as virtues whose existence depends

---

[1] The problems we address in this chapter arise on pretty much any interpretation of Hume's view of the nature of moral judgments, including not only the moral sensing view but also noncognitivist readings (according to which moral judgments and utterances express or give vent to feelings but do not describe them), readings that identify the moral evaluation with the felt sentiment alone (allowing no room for a moral idea copied from it) and those according to which our moral opinions are descriptions or other representations of our own or everyone's (or a spectator's) emotional reactions to the trait or action in question (whether or not they allow, as Capaldi does, for both a moral feeling and a descriptive judgment). For a brief discussion of some of the interpretations available, see Ch. 4. The argument of this chapter is not intended to provide any further support for the cognitivist reading of Hume, but rather to deal with the separate issue of how Hume can consistently explain and give reasons for the regulated inter-subjectivity of moral judgments without abandoning his claim that they are not derived from reason. However, I draw on the cognitivist interpretation and of course seek consistency with it in articulating Hume's implicit response to these problems.

upon the social invention of rules for the common good, and the approval of which comes from sympathy with the public interest (*T* 3.2.2.24 / SBN 499–500). (Much more will be said about the artificial virtues in subsequent chapters.)

In keeping with his Newtonian project of hunting for the causal origins or "principles" of all things mental, Hume does not treat moral approbation and disapprobation as unanalyzable instincts implanted by God, but rather sets out to explain their causal origin. For this he uses the mechanism of sympathy, a process of communication of sentiments from one person to another first elaborated in Book 2 (2.1.11, summarized 2.2.7.2 / SBN 369). There he observes that human emotions are contagious: when we see and hear the outward signs of a sentiment in another, we frequently come to feel that very sentiment. He defines sympathy as the "propensity" we have "to receive by communication [the] inclinations and sentiments [of others], however different from, or even contrary to, our own" (*T* 2.1.11.2 / SBN 316). He explains its operation using the associationism so carefully articulated in Book 1. First, when I observe the outward expressions of a person's passion in his "countenance and conversation", this brings into my mind the idea of the passion he is feeling.[2] For example, seeing him smile and jump excitedly and hearing him crow with laughter cause me to believe that he is feeling joy. Observing the typical cause of a passion also conveys its idea into the mind: if we see the instruments laid out for someone's surgery, they evoke ideas in us of (the patient's) fear and pain. Next, Hume claims that at all times each of us possesses a maximally vivid and forceful impression of himself. According to his associationism, the liveliness of one perception will be automatically transferred to those other perceptions in the mind that are related to it by resemblance, contiguity, or cause and effect (the three vivacity-transferring relations). All human beings, regardless of our many differences, are similar in basic bodily features and functions, and in a parallel way are similar in our psychic features, including our passions. So any person whom I contemplate resembles me in having a human body and mind subject to the same characteristic responses as my own. And some persons may resemble me even more in some specific respect such as age or nationality. Because of the resemblance between us and my proximity to the observed person, some of the great liveliness of the impression of myself is transmitted to my idea of the other person's sentiment. The sole difference between an idea of a passion and an actual passion is the degree of liveliness or vivacity each possesses. So great is this newly acquired liveliness that the idea of his passion in my mind (the mere thought of it) becomes an impression, and I actually experience the passion—so in the examples, I actually feel joy or feel fear and pain. If the other person resembles me not only in being human but in some further respect, or is contiguous with me in space or time, or bears me any causal (that is, familial) relation, this will

---

[2] In this period, of course, 'passion' can refer to any emotion or psychological feeling.

enhance the enlivening process, making my passion livelier. Hume specifically invokes this process in Book 3:

When I see the *effects* of passion in the voice and gesture of any person, my mind immediately passes from these effects to their causes, and forms such a lively idea of the passion, as is presently converted into the passion itself. In like manner, when I perceive the *causes* of any emotion, my mind is convey'd to the effects, and is actuated with a like emotion.   (*T* 3.3.1.7 / SBN 576)[3]

At 3.3.1 Hume claims that sympathy is the cause of (almost all of) our moral sentiments, as follows. What we approve and disapprove are traits of character, and we approve actions only as signs of the quality of mind within. If we catalog the various virtues and consider what they have in common, we discover that we approve traits that produce some pleasure or advantage for other people (individuals, or all of society) or for their possessor himself, and disapprove traits that yield uneasiness or harm to the person who has them or others.[4] The cause of this is as follows. We observe the causal connection between a particular person's quality of mind such as benevolence (or malice) and the pleasure or advantage (or uneasiness or disadvantage) of its possessor or others. Those people receive pleasure or uneasiness from the quality of mind, either because the quality is itself a pleasant or unpleasant one to have or observe, or because that quality of mind moves its possessor to act in ways that produce pleasure or pain for himself or others. This pleasure or uneasiness that is brought about in those affected by the quality of mind is transferred to us, the surveyors, via sympathy. This new feeling of pleasure or uneasiness becomes our moral approbation or disapprobation of the trait. Of course, not every sympathetically acquired pleasure

---

[3] Hume's readers may well wonder how we know that other people have passions at all. In order for us even to acquire the idea of another person's passion (the first step in sympathy), we must somehow have already acquired causal beliefs of the form "external sign Z (e.g., smiling) is caused by passion Y (joy)" and "event-type X (the birth of a son) causes passion Y (joy)", and this may require that we have observed a constant conjunction between Z's and Y's and between X's and Y's, so that when we are presented with the one we can infer the existence of the other. But of course we cannot directly feel the passions of others in the first place. We reach such beliefs or mental habits, Hume seems to think, by making some sort of analogy between our own minds and the minds of others, or perhaps by making an analogy between two resemblances, that of our own bodies to other people's bodies—knowable by means of sense impressions—and that of our passions to other people's (supposed) passions (*T* 2.1.11.5 / SBN 318). I take no stand here on exactly how this happens, or on whether, given Hume's views, the belief that others have passions like ours is warranted. For a discussion of this issue, see Pitson 1996 and 2002: ch. 8.

[4] More accurately, we approve traits that are either advantageous (tend to produce pleasure) for their possessors or others, or are immediately agreeable to their possessors or others. Some of the virtues are not advantageous to their possessors or her associates, but are simply immediately agreeable upon contemplation. Our approbation for these does not depend entirely upon sympathy, since it arises spontaneously from "particular *original* principles of human nature, which cannot be accounted for" (*T* 3.3.1.27 / SBN 590). But "it has also a considerable dependence on the principle of *sympathy*", since this spontaneous appreciation of a trait (e.g., my associates' appreciation of my agreeable wit) is transferred by sympathy to others who are not exposed to the trait and so have not felt that immediate appreciation (*T* 3.3.1.29 / SBN 590).

or pain becomes or is a moral sentiment; we feel great sadness, for example, in contemplating a parent whose child has died of an untreatable disease, without feeling moral disapproval of anyone involved. Hume is not explicit on this point, but there seem to be two features that distinguish the causal origin of the moral sentiments from that of other sympathetically acquired pleasant and painful emotions: the moral sentiments are produced by the contemplation of an enduring character trait and its causal impact on those affected by it (rather than solely by awareness of people's feelings, and rather than by the contemplation of the ravages of disease or other causes of people's pain or pleasure), and the pleasure or pain acquired by sympathy with those affected is associated in the observer's mind with the trait of the person under evaluation. If the child had instead died as the result of someone's greed, negligence, or violence, and we (observers) knew this, we would associate our sympathetically acquired pain with the perpetrator's persistent character, and this would make our uneasiness an instance of moral disapprobation. For this association to occur, we must believe the harmful action to be the product of a character trait of the agent, a "durable principle of the mind" (*T* 3.3.1.4 / SBN 575; see also *T* 2.3.2.6–7 / SBN 411–12).[5]

It is in order to reply to two objections to this causal story, which we shall call the variability objection and the "virtue in rags" objection, that Hume introduces the stipulation that we make moral evaluations only from the common point of view.

First, Hume's objector reminds us that "this sympathy is very variable" (*T* 3.3.1.14 / SBN 581); it works more effectively between persons contiguous to one another than those far apart, between acquaintances than strangers, between countrymen than foreigners. If our moral evaluations proceed from sympathy with those benefited or harmed by a trait, presumably we will assess a trait in China as less virtuous (or less vicious) than the very same trait in England (assuming we are English and live in England), because sympathy will communicate to us a much weaker version of the pleasure or pain of those affected in China than of those affected in England, since the Chinese do not resemble us in nationality or language and are far away. And in our moral opinion or belief, which is copied from the moral feeling, we will likewise judge the trait in China less good or evil than the trait in England. But we do not judge in that way. Two identical traits "appear equally virtuous, and recommend themselves equally to the esteem of a judicious spectator" (ibid.). The sympathy theory is inconsistent with the phenomena to be explained: those of uniform moral feeling about and judgment of exactly similar traits wherever they are found.

---

[5] This specification of the moral sentiment raises many issues that cannot be addressed here, such as how a moral sentiment can have an intentional object (can be directed to, or be an evaluation of, a person or trait), and what the exact relationship is between the moral sentiments and the indirect passions of pride, humility, love, and hatred. I make a start on these issues in Cohon 2008.

Note that the variable operation of sympathy is not caused by the different affectionate attachments we have, as such. Love of friends, like self-interest, is to be distinguished from the moral sentiments (e.g., at *T* 3.3.1.17 / SBN 583; self-interest is already screened off at *T* 3.1.2.4 / SBN 472) and disregarded when we consider a trait "in general". The variability of sympathy results from differences in the three vivacity-transferring relations, and these differences remain even after the interests of self and friends are set aside. It is not because the English people who are affected by someone's quality of mind are my friends or loved ones that I feel a more intense pleasure or uneasiness toward the trait that affects them; this increased effectiveness of sympathy occurs even when the English people are strangers or people I dislike, simply because they resemble me and are close at hand.

Before responding to the variability objection, Hume says that on any non-rationalist, sentiment-based theory the same objection would apply: "if the variation of the sentiment, without a variation of the esteem, be an objection, it must have equal force against every other system, as against that of sympathy" (*T* 3.3.1.15 / SBN 581). Consequently, Hume addresses himself to the same problem in the moral *Enquiry*, even though in that work he leaves out his own analysis of sympathy as a mechanism for enlivening our ideas of (other people's) sentiments so that they become impressions. He handles the variability objection in much the same way, by introducing the common point of view.[6] One can see why a sentiment-based theory of moral evaluation would be vulnerable to such an objection. Resemblance and proximity do influence our feelings in a largely unconscious way; yet ordinarily we think these factors irrelevant to the moral evaluations we make. The objector has a point.

Hume says this first objection is easily answered, however:

> Our situation, with regard both to persons and things, is in continual fluctuation; and a man, that lies at a distance from us, may, in a little time, become a familiar acquaintance. Besides, every particular man has a peculiar position with regard to others; and 'tis impossible we cou'd ever converse together on any reasonable terms, were each of us to consider characters and persons, only as they appear from his peculiar point of view. In order, therefore, to prevent those continual *contradictions*, and arrive at a more *stable* judgment of things, we fix on some *steady* and *general* points of view; and always, in our thoughts, place ourselves in them. . . .   (*T* 3.3.1.15 / SBN 581–2)

Consequently, we blame or praise a person on the basis of the influence of his qualities of mind "upon those who have an intercourse with" him, without regard to whether those in his group of associates are close

---

[6] The expression "common point of view" comes from the moral *Enquiry*. I prefer it to the term "general point of view", more widely used in the secondary literature, because it better captures what Hume has in mind, which is not some sort of generalization or abstraction but rather a commonly accessible but intimate perspective. Also, Hume himself never uses the term "general point of view" in the singular.

to or far from us, our countrymen or foreigners. We sympathize with those individuals, and it is sympathy with them that becomes or gives rise to our moral sentiments. Our sentiments are not always fully corrected by this method, however. Where they prove resistant, we at least correct our language. In these cases we *say* that reason requires such impartiality but passion cannot follow our judgment. However, by 'reason' here we mean only "a general calm determination of the passions, founded on some distant view or reflexion" (*T* 3.3.1.18 / SBN 583).

The "virtue in rags" objection says that if the sympathy theory were correct, we would approve only those traits that actually bring about people's good, since sympathy would only bring us the actual pleasure of the beneficiaries of the trait. Where a character trait would otherwise provide people with pleasure or benefit, but is prevented from being beneficial merely by some external circumstances, there is no actual pleasure to be observed and transferred, and so we cannot feel approbation toward the trait via sympathy.[7] But in fact, we approve not only the traits that do generate public advantage, but also those that *would* do so if they had the chance. "Virtue in rags is still virtue; and the love, which it procures, attends a man into a dungeon or desart, where the virtue can no longer be exerted in action, and is lost to all the world" (*T* 3.3.1.19 / SBN 584). Here again, our actual moral judgments do not follow the pattern that they would follow if the sympathy theory were true.[8]

---

[7] Our perceptions of the outward signs of other people's pleasure or uneasiness (our sense impressions of these) convey to our mind the lively idea of these passions, which becomes an impression. For this to happen, obviously we must observe real people experiencing actual pleasure or uneasiness. Hume also says that our perception of a cause of pleasure (in this case, a trait of character) immediately conveys our mind to its effect, and our idea of the effect can be enlivened to become an impression; this may seem to avoid the "virtue in rags" objection at the start. But in describing this operation of sympathy (*T* 3.3.1.8 / SBN 576, quoted above), Hume is talking about actual causes, not merely potential causes, or at any rate not merely usual causes which we know have no effect in the case at hand. The instruments for surgery (in this era before anesthetics) are expected actually to cause the anticipated fear and pain. If we perceive a trait that *might* have caused pleasure under other circumstances, but in fact is in no position to do so and does not, the idea we form of the effect will not be a belief, and we will not feel pleasure via sympathy. At least, this is what Hume has given us reason to think up to this point. Thus if approbation consists of the pleasure we obtain via sympathy, we would not approve virtue in rags.

[8] The sympathy theory tells us that once we perceive and come to share the happy effect, we associate that pleasure with its cause—with the trait that has a tendency to produce the happiness. It does not tell us how we can get pleasure from something that does not cause a happy effect. It may seem, however, that Hume has already solved the "virtue in rags" problem. Hume's word 'tendency' is misleading in this passage. Sometimes he seems to mean by it simply causation; but he says "natural tendency" (*T* 3.3.1.19 / SBN 584), to indicate the effect that the trait would otherwise have, although it does not cause this result here. If we read 'tendency' as "cause", then we might think that he could say that we approve virtue in rags because of its *tendency* to give pleasure, just as we approve virtue when it causes actual pleasure. But this would run together his two different uses of 'tendency'. In fact Hume is right to think he has not yet answered this objection when he brings it up. We approve a trait because it is the *cause* of the pleasure of society in general—because of its tendency, in this sense. But what if it does not cause the pleasure? Somehow we approve it anyway. That is the problem.

Hume replies that "[w]here a character is, in every respect, fitted to be beneficial to society, the imagination passes easily from the cause to the effect, without considering that there are still some circumstances wanting to render the cause a compleat one" (*T* 3.3.1.20 / SBN 585). Sympathy can enliven *imagined* pleasure or uneasiness as well as believed pleasure or uneasiness. The impression of pleasure we get from sympathy with real beneficiaries of a virtue is, indeed, more lively than what we get from imagined beneficiaries, "and yet we do not say that [the trait] is more virtuous" (*T* 3.3.1.21 / SBN 585). We know that the trait succeeds in benefiting people only because of good fortune, and this fortune might change. Consequently, "we separate, as much as possible, the fortune from the disposition" (ibid.). We correct our sentiments, just as we correct for the differential workings of sympathy over different distances. We evaluate character traits from a steady point of view, rather than from the vantage point of the traits' actual effects.

II. THE PROBLEMS, AGAIN

We now turn to the two problems for Hume's moral theory that the common point of view seems to introduce.

First, the requirement of the common point of view raises the question whether Hume's account of moral evaluation is a genuinely anti-rationalist, sentimentalist one. The resulting account seems to treat moral judgments as beliefs (frequently counterfactual ones) about what someone or anyone would feel if she occupied a point of view close to the person being evaluated. This would make moral evaluations into inductive, empirical beliefs, presumably based on repeated past experiences of the effects of people's character traits on oneself and one's closest associates. Such beliefs are, for Hume, the deliverances of (causal) reasoning. This way of understanding moral beliefs contradicts Hume's explicit claims that to make a moral evaluation is not to infer or conclude but to *feel* a certain way, and that the making of a moral evaluation is an activity not of causal reasoning but of sentiment.[9] (Note that according to the moral sensing interpretation, while

---

[9] *T* 3.1.1 and 3.1.2, *passim*, as we saw in previous chapters. Some familiar passages can serve as a reminder. *T* 3.1.1.26 / SBN 468: "morality . . . consists not in any *matter of fact*, which can be discover'd by the understanding." *T* 3.1.1.26 / SBN 468, again: "But can there be any difficulty in proving, that vice and virtue are not matters of fact, whose existence we can infer by reason?" *T* 3.1.2.1 / SBN 470: "Morality, therefore, is more properly felt than judged of". *T* 3.1.2.3 / SBN 471: "To have a sense of virtue, is nothing but to *feel* a satisfaction of a particular kind from the contemplation of a character. The very *feeling* constitutes our praise or admiration . . . We do not infer a character to be virtuous, because it pleases."

This is a potential problem even for an interpretation such as Capaldi's, in which a moral distinction or sense of virtue is a sentiment, while the moral judgment is a belief about what sentiments people have. What is it, on such a view, to think or say that a trait is virtuous? It may seem that it is simply to report on one's own sentiment, and so not to infer anything. Given the fact

a moral belief is truth-evaluable and represents something, namely a felt moral property, we have not understood the moral belief to be the product of any gathering and comparing of instances—of any inference at all, demonstrative or causal.)

The second difficulty is related to the first. Hume claims that we feel sentiments upon contemplating the characters of persons from our ordinary, individual perspectives (call these our "situated sentiments"); but we may also feel a different sentiment and/or make a different judgment if we imagine ourselves to occupy a different point of view. Why should we, in our thoughts, always place ourselves in that other point of view and make our moral judgments from there? One might claim, of course, that we must do so in order to judge *correctly*. But if moral sensings are feelings and not deliverances of reasoning, and moral beliefs are representations of that which we feel, then there is no reason to think one sentiment or one representation of a felt property more correct than another. Given Hume's claim that vice "lies in yourself, not in the object" (*T* 3.1.1.26 / SBN 469)—that is, that it is the sentiment aroused in us by a trait that makes a trait a vice rather than some non-relational feature intrinsic to the trait—his grounds for giving precedence to some feelings that a trait arouses in ourselves over others cannot be that those feelings better match what is in the object. And since he says that sentiments do not represent or stand for anything else (*T* 2.3.3.5 / SBN 415 and *T* 3.1.1.9 / SBN 458), his grounds for preferring the sentiments triggered by the common point of view and regarding only those as the basis of moral evaluation cannot be that these sentiments more accurately represent the trait being evaluated.

Hume says, of course, that if we judge from our particular points of view, we will encounter uncertainty and contradictions and be unable to communicate. But why should we have any such problems? There is no uncertainty about what our situated feelings *are*. There is no logical contradiction between statements that describe or express different feelings. And in other contexts we have no difficulty communicating our diverse felt reactions. If I say "Espresso is delicious" and you say "Espresso is vile", we have no trouble understanding that what we are doing is revealing divergent felt reactions: namely, that I derive pleasure from

---

that we make moral judgments (and especially, moral utterances) from the common point of view, however, it is not merely to think that I have a feeling of pleasure when I contemplate the trait, for apparently I regularly make a true moral judgment or utterance without having the feeling. A virtue judgment is rather some sort of causal claim, that a certain trait or action tends to cause pleasure in those who contemplate it under the proper conditions. But causal relations are matters of fact, and causal judgments (and so virtue judgments, on this account) are produced by causal inference from many instances; yet vice and virtue are not matters of fact whose existence we can infer by reason.

This sort of difficulty leads Loeb (1977: 401 n. 18) to the following observation about Hume's introduction of the common point of view: "Sometimes our interested sentiments are 'stubborn and inalterable,' in which case they are not correctable, and we correct 'our language' . . . instead (*T* 582). At this point, Hume's attempt to explain all moral distinctions in terms of sentiment collapses."

it while you derive uneasiness. We have no need to adopt a common point of view in order to communicate about this, so there is no apparent reason to expect such a difficulty in communicating our varying moral reactions either. Now, the interpretation offered in the last chapter reveals *some* communication difficulties. On that reading, what we communicate is an attribution of a moral property to an object; we make no claim about the metaphysical nature of the property, but merely attribute to the object the property that "feels like this". Our attribution is analogous to attributions of heat or color. Now if I say "The coffee is brown" and you deny this, we do contradict one another; so, similarly, if I say "David's kindness is a virtue" and you deny this, we contradict one another regarding whether David's kindness has the feature of virtuousness. But there is only a little inconvenience in communicating about color, and there need be no more difficulty in the moral case than in that one. You do contradict me, but we typically resolve it with ease by both looking at the coffee. If we continue to disagree, then we simply understand one another to have different sensitivities to color or dispositions to make fine or coarse color distinctions (you call the creamy coffee brown while I think it light enough to count as beige), but we still communicate without difficulty. If this is what would go on were we to make moral evaluations using our situated sentiments, then, when faced with different sentiments, we could retry our feelings, and if they still diverged, we would shrug and say "Well, that's not how it feels to me". No grave difficulties of communication threaten us. It does not seem "impossible we could ever converse together on any reasonable terms, were each of us to consider characters, and persons, only as they appear from his peculiar point of view" (*T* 3.3.1.15 / SBN 581–2). So why bother with the common point of view, or base our moral judgments on it alone?

Let us turn to the interpretive task of eliminating these internal conflicts.

Given the interpretation developed in earlier chapters, it might seem that the solution is obvious. We have already argued that for Hume there are two mental phenomena relevant to moral evaluation: the impression and the idea—the feeling and the belief. So it is natural to propose an interpretation based on this dichotomy: that the occurrent sentiment is the only item that must *not* be analyzed as a product of inference, and that the common point of view is introduced only to correct the believed idea, whose corrected version will indeed be reached by causal reasoning about what a spectator would feel from the common point of view. The simple ideas of virtuousness and viciousness of course originate in the experience of moral sentiment, and cannot be generated by reasoning from non-moral ideas alone. But once we have these ideas of good and evil, one might argue, we can alter our attributions of them to indicate something other than what we feel at any moment, and a good deal of causal reasoning might be involved in refining our moral opinions beyond anything that we actually feel. On this interpretation, the moral impression is the situated sentiment, and the moral judgment is ultimately a causal judgment about what an observer would feel from the common point of view.

This position might have independent merit, and it looks at first glance like a tidy solution to Hume's problem, but there are strong reasons to think that it is not his view. It incorporates the view that for Hume moral beliefs are causal judgments resulting from matter-of-fact inference, and this thesis will not support the sort of anti-rationalism that Hume actually espouses. The thesis does allow Hume to make one important point against the moral rationalists: he can say that only a being possessed of sentiments has moral concepts at all. This is something that at least some of his rationalist opponents vehemently deny; so it makes him an anti-rationalist of a sort.[10] But in fact it treats Hume's anti-rationalism as only skin deep, contrary to both the letter and the spirit of his moral philosophy. First, if all he meant by the claim that reason alone cannot yield moral discriminations were that the simple ideas contained in a moral belief do not originate in reason, then on the same grounds reason alone could not yield any of the conclusions of our inferences, whether demonstrative or causal; for of course on Hume's view reason does not generate any new simple ideas, but only compares ideas drawn from experience. Moral beliefs, then, would be no less the product of reason alone than beliefs about congruent triangles or the effect of one billiard ball on another. But Hume clearly thinks they are. Furthermore, Hume makes claims that imply that not only the sensing of virtue but also beliefs about it are not typically the result of inference at all, even if in a few parasitic cases the beliefs might be acquired inferentially. To understand things otherwise is to set too great a gulf between the moral feeling and the attribution of a moral property. If the moral sensing view is right thus far, then an interpretation that treats the moral opinion (*per se*) as a causal judgment about what would happen if one were to occupy the common point of view gives the wrong account of the moral opinion's epistemic origin. Moral beliefs are analogous to perceptual beliefs about colors, hot and cold. I do not ordinarily acquire beliefs about the colors or warmth of objects by estimating how they would appear or feel under ideal perceptual circumstances. I *can* acquire perceptual beliefs this way, but it is not the standard way. (To find out whether any of the folders in the box are blue, normally I just look in the box. I don't consider how the folders would look to me, or to an observer with better vision than mine, in good light.) As

[10] To state the thesis more fully: Only beings with past experience of moral sentiments have the simple ideas of these sentiments, and so only such beings can make causal generalizations about what would be felt from the common point of view; therefore, even if moral judgments are in fact causal predictions about what would be felt from the common point of view, reasoning alone is not sufficient to generate such judgments, and only feeling creatures can make them. This is very close to the interpretation of 'reason alone' offered in Cohon and Owen 1997. It was partly dissatisfaction with this interpretation that spurred me to develop the understanding of reason alone in Ch. 3 of this book as a reasoning process without any other sort of process. I am grateful to an anonymous reader for Oxford University Press for bringing it up in connection with the issues about the common point of view raised in this chapter.

the moral sensing view construes it, Hume's position is that ordinarily I acquire moral beliefs as the result of feeling a trait's goodness or evil—sensing the moral property directly—and then forming an idea-copy of my moral sentiment (and, perhaps, classifying the trait just observed in the revival set of the moral property). My own moral sentiments are not merely a source of simple ideas as raw material to be deployed later in various moral judgments, but actual guides to the moral properties of things in daily life. Furthermore, as should be apparent from the passages quoted above, such a reading does not fit the text in which Hume introduces the common point of view, where he talks a good deal of the feelings we acquire when we imagine ourselves to occupy that perspective, their difference in felt quality from those of our situated perspective, and their effect in changing our initial sentiments.

An important further worry arises for any interpretation according to which Hume thinks we routinely and typically form moral beliefs that do not reflect any actual sentiments we experience at the time we make them. One main reason why Hume rejects moral rationalism is that he thinks that it cannot account for morality's influence on the will. An account of moral judgments or opinions that claims we make them by calculating what sentiments we or others would feel in circumstances other than our real ones introduces some grave difficulties for any subsequent explanation of how morals influence the will. The moral feeling itself may still be or cause a motivating passion, of course. But that feeling could on some occasions be one of approval of a trait when the moral opinion (which results from thinking how people would feel if they adopted the common point of view) attributes vice to the trait. In such a case, it seems, the moral sentiment might cause action, but exactly the wrong sort of action—not action in accordance with our opinion of our duty, but action contrary to it. And there is no reason to suppose that the moral *opinion* would cause any action at all, since it is merely a causal judgment, and not one about any pleasure or pain in store for the agent. Hume does not redeem the paper draft he provides in *Treatise* 3.1.1 when he says that morality is an active principle; he never explains *how* the moral sentiment influences the will. But he does make it plain that mere causal beliefs that do not pertain to the believer's prospective pleasure or pain cannot do so.

So alas, the obvious interpretation will not work; we need a more nuanced one to solve the problems introduced by the common point of view.

III. SOLVING THE FIRST PROBLEM

We could solve the first difficulty with which we began, the apparent rationalism or inferentialism introduced into the theory by the addition of the common point of view, if we could interpret Hume as claiming that when we take up the common point of view we always (or anyway normally) have *actual* feelings, and do not merely infer what feelings we would have if we were differently situated. Then our moral feelings could be, and our moral beliefs could correspond with, these actual (although often calm and faint) feelings, rather than our moral beliefs being conclusions of causal reasoning. And in fact this is what I think he does say.

Unfortunately, however, Hume certainly seems to say that this is not always the case. "Experience soon teaches us this method of correcting our sentiments, or at least, of correcting our language, where the sentiments are more stubborn and inalterable" (*T* 3.3.1.16 / SBN 582). "But however the general principle of our blame or praise may be corrected by those other principles, 'tis certain, they are not altogether efficacious, nor do our passions often correspond entirely to the present theory" (*T* 3.3.1.18 / SBN 583). "The passions do not always follow our corrections; but these corrections serve sufficiently to regulate our abstract notions, and are alone regarded, when we pronounce in general concerning the degrees of vice and virtue" (*T* 3.3.1.21 / SBN 585). Finally, "And tho' the heart does not always take part with those general notions, or regulate its love and hatred by them, yet are they sufficient for discourse, and serve all our purposes in company, in the pulpit, on the theatre, and in the schools" (*T* 3.3.3.2 / SBN 603).[11] If there are regular occasions on which we make use of the common and steady point of view to adjust our abstract notions and our utterances, but our passions are inalterable, then what do we acquire by imagining ourselves to occupy that point of view? Presumably not a passion, but some sort of belief about what we would feel if we really were to occupy that point of view. How do we know what we would feel? Presumably, by induction from past experience.

Hume is always thought to be saying in these passages that at many times, when we imagine ourselves occupying the common or steady point of view, the imaginative act does not produce any moral sentiment at all; it simply fails to stimulate the moral sentiments. Thus on these occasions we are left to judge on the basis of how we would feel if we were really under those conditions, and so to judge in conflict with the only passions we actually do feel. But does Hume say this? These passages do not say that there are times when we adopt or attempt to adopt the common point of view but we feel *nothing* as a result. All they say is that when we imagine ourselves in the common point of view, we sometimes fail to *change* our initial sentiments to match the sentiments of that station. We can, with perfect faithfulness to the text, understand the process as follows: we feel certain passions from our particular vantage point, and whenever we contemplate the same character from the common point of view, we feel *another*, weaker sentiment. That is, we feel two sentiments toward that same character trait.

---

[11] As far as I can tell, these are *all* the passages in the *Treatise* in which Hume discusses the possibility that the passions may resist such correction. The analogous passages in the *Enquiry concerning the Principles of Morals* are EPM 5.41 and 5.42 / SBN 227 and 229.

Often we can use the new, calm sentiment (stimulated by imagining ourselves in the common point of view) to correct or adjust the original one, making the situated sentiment exactly like the new one and merging the two sentiments into one; but sometimes we cannot. The recalcitrance or stubbornness of the passions occurs when we cannot change our situated sentiments, and so persist in having two sentiments toward the trait that differ in intensity or perhaps even in kind (one of approval, the other disapproval). However, in these circumstances the sentiment of the steady point of view is "alone regarded when we pronounce in general concerning the degrees of vice and virtue": whether or not we succeed in changing our situated passion, when we form a moral *belief*, we attend only to the calm sentiment we feel when we imaginatively project ourselves into this special vantage point, and disregard the other sentiments we may be feeling at the same time. The sentiment we feel from the common point of view is the original from which the moral belief is copied. Thus, in the instances where the passions are inalterable, there are two emotions of like species that differ in their "feeling", so much so that even their contrary versions can coexist without destroying each other, something that Hume explicitly allows (*T* 3.3.1.23 / SBN 586–7). The one that arises from imagining oneself to occupy the common point of view is the source of moral judgment.[12]

If we *always* have a calm sentiment when we adopt the common point of view (providing everything is working normally), then moral sensing can be identical with, and moral opinion can represent, the feeling we have when we imagine ourselves into this point of view, and we preserve Hume's thesis that moral evaluations are not conclusions of reasoning.[13]

On this interpretation we read Hume as describing a familiar experience, that of a situated sentiment being strengthened or weakened by an imaginative effort. I may feel outrage over some misdeed initially, because it harms people I know and with whom I easily sympathize. If I think about the painful situation of the man who acted this way and of the pressures on his family, however, and of the difficult choices he had to make, I may find my outrage shrinking to become a

---

[12] The two-sentiment interpretation is also consistent with the relevant passages of the second *Enquiry*, e.g., "General language . . . must affix the epithets of praise or blame, in conformity to sentiments, which arise from the general interests of the community" (*EPM* 5.42 / SBN 228). That is, we feel some sentiments from (considering) the general interests of the community, and our language conforms to those.

[13] This reading also fits well with Hume's account of how the origin of the moral sentiments in sympathy can be squared with the limited generosity of mankind. He says that because of our "extensive sympathy" we feel the sentiment of taste, which is enough for judgment, but often is not enough to cause us to act (*T* 3.3.1.23 / SBN 586). This is consistent with the view that the sentiment of taste is universally felt by all who take up the common point of view.

Although I have not considered whether Hume gives us any account of *how* moral judgments can produce action (as he says they can in *T* 3.1.1), those who read Hume as a moral judgment internalist should find this interpretation of the common point of view to their liking. Since a sentiment is always present, at least the right sorts of materials are available, although they may often be insufficient to the task.

milder form of disapproval—still disapproval, but "put in perspective", as we say, calm rather than violent. This particular instance of theft (or neglect, or mistreatment) is no worse than others like it, I think; and when I do, my outrage loses its edge. Similarly, I may be rather blasé about some misdeed, because its victims are distant foreigners. But if I imagine its impact on those victims vividly enough, my disapproval becomes more pronounced, and remains so. We do experience some such adjustment of emotion as the result of the sympathetic use of imagination. And at times we find that the adjustment fails to occur, and we feel two ways about a person. So, a parent of a rambunctious young child may find his high-spiritedness both annoying (from the point of view of others who have direct dealings with him) and endearing (from his own perspective as a doting parent).[14] In more serious cases where the moral assessment of a grown person's character is at issue, while we might be both amused by, for example, someone's manipulativeness or cruel sarcasm from our situated perspective and also distressed by it once we enter into the viewpoint of its victims, we regulate our moral judgment by the latter feeling. While we ourselves chuckle at the trait ("there he goes again, exploiting people's fears to make them act against their better judgment"), because we do also feel for those affected, we think it a vice.

If the sentiment we feel when we take up the common point of view is *the* moral sentiment, though, then why does Hume write of correcting "the general principle of our blame or praise" (*T* 3.3.1.18 / SBN 583)? I have argued that there are two sentiments: the situated sentiment, which may need correcting, and the sentiment generated by the imagination, which ultimately is the moral sentiment, the one from which the moral opinion is copied. But in this passage it sounds as if it is the situated sentiment—the one that needs correcting—that is the moral one, since he calls it the general principle of blame or praise. Furthermore, Hume says that even if his sympathy theory is not the correct account of the causation of moral sentiment, such sentiment or "moral taste . . . whence-ever [it is] deriv'd, must vary according to the distance or contiguity of the objects" (*T* 3.3.1.15 / SBN 581). So it may look as if the *moral* sentiments are the variable ones, not the steady ones.

This presents no problem, however, if we consider one of the ways in which Hume categorizes passions in Book 2. Near the end of *T* 2.3.3, "Of the influencing motives of the will", just after he claims that the promptings of the calm passions are confused with the operation of reason, he identifies pairs of passions "of the same kind", one calm and one violent (*T* 2.3.3.9 / SBN 417–18). There is calm, instinctive resentment and also a violent passion of resentment; there is the calm, instinctive, general aversion to "evil as such" and also the violent emotion of aversion to immediately threatened, grievous ills. Whether a person experiences a calm or a violent passion of a given kind depends

---

[14] Thanks to Mary Clayton Coleman for this lovely example.

upon "the situation of the object"; furthermore, "a variation in this particular will be able to change the calm and the violent passions into each other" (*T* 2.3.4.1 / SBN 419). "The same good, when near, will cause a violent passion, which, when remote, produces only a calm one" (ibid.). Thus, there are pairs of conspecific passions available to us, one (typically) calm and one (typically) violent, the calm one issuing from consideration of a remote object, the violent one from consideration of a near object.

Hume uses this part of his theory of the passions in his answer to the "virtue in rags" objection in *Treatise* 3.3.1, where he is explicitly talking about our aesthetic and moral feelings. Recall his reply: our moral sentiments can be triggered merely by imagining the effects that a trait *would* produce if external conditions permitted, and we imagine these effects when we adopt the common point of view. "The imagination has a set of passions belonging to it, upon which our sentiments of beauty much depend. These passions are mov'd by degrees of liveliness and strength, which are inferior to *belief*, and independent of the real existence of their objects" (*T* 3.3.1.20 / SBN 585). And then (*T* 3.3.1.23 / SBN 586–7): "The *seeming tendencies* of objects affect the mind: And the emotions they excite are of a like species with those, which proceed from the *real consequences* of objects, but their feeling is different. . . . The imagination adheres to the *general* views of things, and distinguishes betwixt the feelings they produce, and those which arise from our particular and momentary situation." So the ideas of the imagination, even though they are of things *so* remote that they are merely hypothetical and not real (even though the ideas are not beliefs), elicit a calm sentiment which can differ from and conflict with the violent passions of the same kind caused by what is near. Here the two sentiments are much in evidence. General views of things produce the calm sentiment, whereas, presumably, particular views may produce a violent one of the same kind and a contrary direction. The kind in question is approbation or disapprobation. Hume makes the connection with the earlier section (*T* 2.3.3) explicitly at *T* 3.3.1.18 / SBN 583: "Here we are contented with saying, that reason requires such an impartial conduct, but . . . that our passions do not readily follow. . . . This language will be easily understood, if we consider what we formerly said concerning that *reason*, which is able to oppose our passion; and which we have found to be nothing but a general calm determination of the passions, founded on some distant view or reflexion." Although we talk as if this is an instance of conflict between reason and a passion, in fact it is a calm passion acquired by contemplating matters from the common point of view that opposes our situated passion.

Our claim, then, is that the violent passion of our actual situation, with all its fluctuations resulting from variations in the three relations, and the calm and steady sentiment we feel on every occasion when we imagine ourselves in a general point of view, are sentiments of the same species that differ in their "feeling". Sometimes the two sentiments may be contrary to one another, or if not contrary, they may differ in degree. On many such occasions, the steady sentiment will actually alter the situated one, so that "the general principle of our blame or praise" is corrected by this "other principle", another sentiment of the same kind. The situated sentiment is the *general* principle of our praise or blame in the sense that it is the general *origin* or source of what later *becomes* our praise or blame (the word 'principle' here again being used for a causal origin). Even when the situated sentiment is not made to conform to the steady one, the steady approbation or disapprobation is present, and is what is manifested in the moral judgment we make. So *it* is the moral sentiment, properly so-called, although under the best conditions, in which the steady sentiment converts the situated one, there is really no issue of which is the moral sentiment properly so-called.

IV. SOLVING THE SECOND PROBLEM

This two-feeling interpretation explains how moral evaluation can be a matter of sentiment and not reasoning, even though moral judgments are made from the common point of view. But it does not answer the second question, why we should take up steady and general points of view at all. Indeed, it makes it more puzzling that we should. If our situated passion is already of the same species as the moral sentiment, what need do we have to adopt another viewpoint and feel (and judge by) something else? Why should the sentiment stimulated by the imagination be of special interest, even to the point of usually transforming the situated sentiment? Indeed, why should such a change be called a "correction"? Hume suggests that "instability" and "contradiction" of moral judgments are undesirable and prevent communication, requiring us to adopt a means of making all moral judgments match each other; but so far we have not seen why this is so.

Hume believes that, as a matter of empirical fact, we expect everyone else to concur with us in their moral judgments, and that most of the time they do. It is possible that Hume introduces the common point of view just *ad hoc*, to make sure there is room in his theory for these observed facts. But Hume's theory owes us some explanation of them. And he is surely saying something further, that we each try to *make* our moral evaluations coincide, both with other moral evaluations we make of the same person at other times and with those made by other people. Why do we do that?

Our moral evaluations need to be uniform, not because it matters in itself that we should all have the same feelings or make unanimous moral judgments, and not because the true or correct moral judgment about a given, unchanged character is fixed in some way independent of our reactions, but because our moral evaluations always carry with them certain *other* judgments that *are* about matters of fact discovered by reasoning. These are causal judgments (indeed, often predictions) about the effects of the traits in question on those who have them and on others with whom the judged persons interact, and they play a major role in our social lives. When we evaluate someone from the common point of view, "'Tis . . . from the influence of characters and qualities upon those who have an intercourse with any person, that we blame or praise him" (*T* 3.3.1.17 / SBN 582). And, "in judging of characters, the only interest or pleasure which appears the same to every spectator, is that of the person himself, whose character is examined, or that of persons who have a connexion with him" (*T* 3.3.1.30 / SBN 591). The common point of view is not a detached perspective, but the vantage point of the person being evaluated and the particular individuals with whom he has direct dealings. It gives us not a wide panorama, but an intimate glimpse. The common point of view is distant from us only in the sense that our presence there is imaginary rather than actual. It is general or common not in the sense of being a broad view, but rather in the sense that it is a view available to every reflective person and the same for all who adopt it. This intimate glimpse yields *two* products, which are necessarily related to one another: a *sentiment* of approbation or disapprobation, discussed already and produced by sympathy with the pleasure and uneasiness of those directly affected by a trait, and a *causal judgment* about what impact the trait or person being judged is likely to have on his near associates—typically a judgment about the power of the trait in question to cause pride or love, humility or hatred. These latter are the judgments that need to remain constant within an individual over time if he is to avoid uncertainty and instability in his thoughts about persons as he moves about, and these are the judgments that need to be consistent between people if we are ever to "converse on reasonable terms" (*T* 3.3.1.15 / SBN 581).[15]

Just after he introduces the moral sentiments for the first time at *T* 3.1.2.5 (SBN 473), Hume says that the moral sentiments (in distinguishing virtue and vice) "must give rise" to pride or humility, love or hatred. He goes further in *T* 3.3.1, a few pages before he introduces the common point of view:

[W]hatever mental quality in ourselves or others gives us a satisfaction, by the survey or reflexion, is of course virtuous; as every thing of this nature, that gives uneasiness, is vicious. Now since every quality in ourselves or others, which gives pleasure, always

---

[15] In some of the passages quoted above where Hume says that when we adopt the common point of view, the passions, or "the heart", are not entirely regulated thereby, he is referring not to the moral sentiments but (explicitly) to the passions of love and hatred (*T* 3.3.3.2 / SBN 603). That is, when we enter into the common point of view and actually feel approval or disapproval, we may not actually feel the love or hatred that usually attends virtue and vice, even though we judge that the quality being evaluated is likely to cause love or hatred in those who (unlike ourselves) really have direct dealings with the person. But note the qualification that Hume makes explicit in the moral *Enquiry*: "And though the heart takes not part *entirely* with those general notions, nor regulates *all* its love and hatred, by the universal abstract differences of vice and virtue, without regard to self, or the persons with whom we are more intimately connected" (*EPM* 5.42 / SBN 229; emphasis added); so perhaps we feel just a little bit of the love or hatred that we predict for the person's real associates.

causes pride or love; as every one, that produces uneasiness, excites humility or hatred: It follows, that these two particulars are to be consider'd as equivalent, with regard to our mental qualities, *virtue* and the power of producing love or pride, *vice* and the power of producing humility or hatred. In every case, therefore, we must judge of the one by the other; and may pronounce any *quality* of the mind virtuous, which causes love or pride; and any one vicious, which causes hatred or humility.   (*T* 3.3.1.3 / SBN 574–5)

If we always judge of the one by the other—if in judging a quality of the mind to be a virtue we thereby also judge it to have the power to produce pride and love, or if (vice versa) in judging a quality of the mind to have the power to produce pride and love we thereby also judge it to be a virtue—then in making moral judgments we always simultaneously make *objective, causal* judgments about the traits we evaluate. We are never *merely* having feelings or representing objects as endowed with feeling-dependent properties, but always also judging that the trait in question has the power to cause pride or love, humility or hatred.[16] Such causal judgments entail more specific empirical predictions, such as the prediction that were I to become acquainted with the man who is now at a distance from me and to reflect on his traits I would grow to love (or hate) him.

Consider the perceptual analogy Hume makes in introducing the common point of view. If I were to convert my raw visual experiences into perceptual judgments without compensating for the fluctuations of perspective, I would judge that the Rocky Mountains are shorter than I am when I see them from a great distance, for example from an airplane. This would entitle me to make certain empirical predictions, such as that, were I to come close to them, I could easily step over them. Once I change my position, of course, I make a contradictory judgment. In this way I "meet with contradictions" whenever I convert how things seem to me (my sense impressions) directly into perceptual judgments about objects without making "corrections". I have to reject and revise my beliefs about material objects almost constantly. I also tend to bump into things and to be otherwise inconvenienced, because some of my predictions are false: I spend days trying to reach the point in the distance where the sides of the road converge, I am run over by what I took (a short while ago)

---

[16] I take Hume to mean, here, that when we "judge of the one by other", what we do is make the one judgment whenever we make the other. Whether we take the one judgment to be sufficient grounds for the other, or see any tighter logical relation between them (mutual implication, or indeed literal equivalence), is left open; but there need not be an inference involved. It is possible that in some cases it works as follows: to evaluate whether a woman's generosity is a virtue or a vice, I imagine myself in the place of those directly affected by it. Given what I know of her, I imagine that they experience joy and relief when she alleviates their suffering (not, e.g., embarrassment), and this pleasure of theirs, transmitted to me by sympathy, becomes my moral approval of her trait. At the same time I recognize that a trait that produces joy in others as this one does probably also produces love, since there is a well-known causal relation between these things, and so I predict that anyone who enters into similar close contact with her will love her. But of course it can be more complicated than this, since not only the joy of being rescued from want but also the love one feels for one's benefactor can be transmitted to the imaginative spectator via sympathy.

to be a miniature wagon, and the like. In determining what effects to expect from material objects, I need to imagine perceiving them from a steady point of view.[17] Human discourse also fails in certain ways. People viewing an object from different angles cannot tell each other what object they are referring to. In order to have a public language in which to discuss objects, we have to do more than simply convert our subjective sensory experiences into assertions about objects. In imagination at least, we have to make our assertions from a common and steady point of view close to the object if anyone is to know what we are talking about.[18] We also need a steady point of view from which to inform others about objects if they are to benefit from the information. For when we describe objects to other people, *they* make causal judgments. If I tell you about the row of tiny bumps that runs down the North American continent, *you* are likely to come to grief trying to step over it.

I take Hume to be saying something exactly analogous about virtue and vice, as he claims (*T* 3.3.1.16 / SBN 582; *T* 3.3.3.2 / SBN 603; *EPM* 5.41 / SBN 227–8). Whenever I judge a trait to be a virtue, I simultaneously judge it to have the power to produce pride and love. If I based my virtue judgments entirely on my present situation, I would presumably make the accompanying causal judgments from that perspective as well. If I judge my servant more virtuous than Marcus Brutus, I will also judge that my servant's traits have the power to produce more pride and more love than Brutus's traits. So I predict that if I could join Brutus's intimate circle, I would not love him as much as I now love my servant. But this prediction is false. "We know, that were we to approach equally near to that renown'd patriot, he wou'd command a much higher degree of affection and admiration" (*T* 3.3.1.16 / SBN 582). Without recourse to a stable point of view, as we change our distance from living people we would often discover the falsehood of our predictions, and would have to revise our causal judgments about people's characters almost constantly. We would also get into trouble. We depend upon causal knowledge about people's traits when we decide whom to trust, whom to avoid, whose friendship to cultivate. If our causal judgments about love and hatred were to change with each change in our position relative to other people, we could not make any reliable predictions of who is likely to

---

[17] "The same object, at a double distance, really throws on the eye a picture of but half the bulk; yet we imagine that it *appears* of the same size in both situations; because we know that on our approach to it, its image would expand on the eye" (*EPM* 5.41 / SBN 227–8; emphasis mine). This is explicitly compared to the correction of moral evaluations. It is possible that Hume means here that even our sense impression of the perceived object is altered by our knowledge of how it would look if we were close to it, so that once we know that the object *is* large, it begins to *look* large.

[18] For example, if I ask you to fetch the elliptical penny from the table in the other room, you will go looking for an elliptical penny, see a round one, and return to tell me there is no such item there.

I do not see in Hume's thought here any precursor to the private language argument; for all I know, Hume thought a private sensation language perfectly possible. Whether or not he thought it possible is irrelevant here. This is a claim about a public language for referring to objects.

cause hatred or love and how much. We would make unfortunate choices of employers, spouses, patrons, or political leaders. Hume says at T 2.3.1.15–16 (SBN 404–6), in his discussion of moral evidence, that we are all implicitly committed to the belief that traits of character cause intentional actions, and that our beliefs about the causal properties of character traits determine what we expect from others when we levy a tax, lead an army, hire a commercial agent, or give orders to a servant. The "obstinacy of the gaoler" leads the prisoner to attempt to burrow through the prison walls rather than try to persuade the guard to let him escape; so such predictions influence our decisions. Presumably predictions to the effect that people's character traits will cause love or hatred, pride or humility, influence our decisions as well. We also need to predict which traits we would be proud or ashamed of in ourselves were we to cultivate them, or else we might cultivate the wrong ones, to our regret. Love and pride are, after all, pleasures, and humility and hatred are pains.

Without correcting our judgments from the common point of view, we would also "bump into things" in the human realm. If I judge the captain of another vessel less cruel than the captain of my own just because his suffering subordinates are farther away from me, I might choose to ship out with him next time; but when I am under his command, I may find that I hate him much more. And it would be unfortunate to be mistaken in my judgment that my prospective spouse (say, in a marriage arranged after limited acquaintance) has traits with the power to produce love in me, or to be mistaken in my judgment that the young nobleman whose tutor I am invited to become has traits that could elicit my esteem. Take Hume's example of Marcus Brutus (which may be a piece of wicked sarcasm). We feel a situated sentiment toward Brutus from the distant perspective of history. This might lead us seriously to miscalculate what we could expect from Brutus were we to have direct dealings with him. If we imagine ourselves in the steady point of view of those who were intimate with him, we will more accurately gauge what love or hatred a close friend would feel toward Brutus on surveying his character.

We have only canvassed the difficulties caused by fluctuations in one's own judgments about pride and humility, love and hatred—not yet the problems of communication with others. But it is clear how that will go. The character judgments made by *others* often tell me whom to trust, whose help to enlist, whose wrath to avoid. While some others are known to be poor judges of character, for the most part I can and do rely on the character assessments of others in forming the expectation that I will like or esteem someone or dislike or "contemn" her. And this is an expectation of (often significant) pleasure or uneasiness. But interpersonal discourse about character would be a shambles if it arose solely from each participant's peculiar point of view. Our reliance on it would be completely undermined if others could not compensate for the differences in their situated feelings. It would have been a terrible problem in Hume's day, where letters of introduction were needed to gain admittance into most new social or professional relationships, and where personal patronage was necessary for so many endeavors. But it would be equally devastating in our own day. Every character assessment we received from others, whether in person, in writing, or in court testimony, would be like those letters of recommendation that certain professional colleagues are rumored to write, in which each year the candidate recommended is his "best student in thirty years", not because he has better students every year, but because he has no perspective on the bright star of the moment or the more distant stars of the past. We would make literally contradictory predictions about what effects other people will have on us. We might even have difficulty identifying the same person in our conversations. If we wish to choose a plumber, an auto mechanic, a physician, or a babysitter, we depend on the fact that the character assessments given by others are made from a commonly accessible point of view, and so can be the basis of reliable predictions.

We have considered why people find it necessary to adopt a common point of view at all, rather than simply making all evaluations from their situated perspective. We need a single perspective from which to make causal predictions, and if those predictions are to be accurate, it must be that of people who make regular observations of the individual in question and so possess a basis for causal generalization.[19] Merely having divergent feelings about character traits, like our differing tastes with regard to espresso, may cause neither confusion nor harm; but it matters a great deal that we get these causal predictions about character traits right.

One of the difficulties with adopting the common point of view with which Hume does not explicitly deal is what happens when the person's qualities of mind have very different effects on different members of her narrow circle, or she reveals very different qualities to different people. The person we evaluate may be a cooperative colleague and a faithful friend, but an insensitive, self-centered spouse or parent; or she may be a patient friend to some and an impatient antagonist to others; or she may have "parts and capacity", but be indolent (*T* 3.3.1.24 / SBN 587). The closest Hume comes to addressing this issue is at the end of *T* 3.3.3, where he argues that we always regard a trait that causes harm or displeasure to those "who live and converse with" the person as a defect, and a trait which makes him "a safe companion, an easy friend, a gentle master, an agreeable husband, or an indulgent father" as a virtue. "[I]f there be no relation of life, in which I cou'd not stand to a particular person, his character must so far be allow'd to be perfect. If he be as little wanting to himself as to others,

---

[19] Christine Korsgaard (2001) takes this a step further, arguing that for Hume a person's character (which, according to her interpretation, Hume understands as a form of causality) *exists* only in the eyes of the members of that person's circle of near associates, for only they observe her regularly enough to regard her as a cause of anything. Character must be evaluated from the common point of view, then, because only from that point of view does one have a character at all. While the view proposed here is not committed to this claim, it is compatible with it.

his character is entirely perfect. This is the ultimate test of merit and virtue" (*T* 3.3.3.9 / SBN 606). Something of this sort goes on in Hume's presentation of Cleanthes, the perfect son-in-law, in the moral *Enquiry* (*EPM* 9.2 / SBN 269–70). His aim there is primarily to show that the qualities of mind we praise are useful or agreeable to self or others; but he has the discussants consider Cleanthes in each of his roles (student, businessman, parlor conversationalist, private sufferer of misfortune), and describe the effects of his traits on himself and on those toward whom he fulfills his various roles. The ideal person will evoke our approval from the perspective of everyone who has direct dealings with him, in every social role he occupies. What of the person of mixed character? Hume does not say. On any interpretation, this is a lacuna to be filled in by the reader. Where the different associates in the narrow circle call forth distinct qualities of the person's mind, we will feel approval for the virtues and disapproval for the vices; so in this kind of case the different reactions can simply be conjoined in our overall evaluation, should we make one. Hume is quite content to describe some individuals as possessing a mixture of virtues and vices; he does not subscribe to the unity of the virtues. In the cases where the person judged is variable in his exercise of one and the same trait (loyal to Cassius, disloyal to Caesar), it is not clear what we should say. Perhaps we are to imagine ourselves in each of his associates' positions in turn, coming to feel what we imagine each to feel, until a resultant feeling, or a proportionately mixed feeling, emerges within us. Perhaps to reach this point we must actually sympathize with all his associates at once.

In the second *Enquiry*, Hume talks about the common point of view as being that of the community, which seems to undermine the present claim that the common point of view is an intimate glimpse of the person herself and her nearest associates. However, this shift is really an artifact of the different organization of that work. In Book 3 of the *Treatise* Hume first writes about the artificial virtues, and argues that our approval of them (once their rules are established) ultimately comes from sympathy with the whole of society, whose pleasure they increase in the long run (*T* 3.2.2.24 / SBN 499–500). Since acts of justice can fail to benefit any person in an individual case, only this sort of sympathy can account for our universal approval of just acts. This account of the origin of the approval of justice is further explained and developed in *T* 3.3.1. Consequently, in evaluating the artificial virtues and vices, we already take up a point of view that is the same for all evaluators. There is no differential working of sympathy for which we must compensate. It is only when he comes to analyze the natural virtues that Hume confronts discrepancies between feelings and judgments that result from the differential workings of sympathy. In the second *Enquiry*, however, the artificial and natural virtues are not divided into separate groups for separate examination (indeed, the distinction is barely present in that work), and the "social" virtues of benevolence and justice are handled together. Consequently, Hume has to include the proper perspective from which to evaluate justice and injustice (that of the whole community), as well as the proper perspective from which to evaluate benevolence (that of the benevolent person and his direct associates) in his discussion of the common point of view. And his detailed account of the enlivening of ideas as a result of their relations to self is left out of the second *Enquiry*. So Hume's emphasis there is simply on finding a point of view that will be the same for all evaluators and will apply to all persons as potential evaluees. What he says on this topic, though, is perfectly consistent with his holding the view that with respect to the natural virtues, the common point of view is that of the person evaluated and those who have direct dealings with him.

V. THE RESULTING THEORY

In sum, our interpretation of the common point of view has two parts. First, each and every time we reflect upon someone's character from the common point of view, we feel a (typically calm) sentiment of approbation or disapprobation, even though that sentiment may be too weak to transform our situated passions. Secondly, whenever we make moral evaluations, we also make inferential, causal judgments about the love and hatred, pride and humility, that the trait in question will produce. Because of the way we depend on this information, it is very inconvenient to have false judgments of this kind and for different people to make mutually contradictory ones. So it is important to us to insure that these judgments be true and consistent. If we adopt the common point of view when we make our moral judgments, the accompanying causal judgments tend to be true, and tend to be consistent over time and between persons, whereas if we make those causal judgments without adopting the common point of view, they are often false and mutually contradictory. Perhaps adopting the common point of view is itself part of a reliable process of making causal predictions about pride, humility, love, and hatred. Once we do adopt the common point of view, our moral sentiments respond to what we imagine: we feel pleasure or uneasiness in contemplating the trait in question. Indeed, this moral approbation or disapprobation in part reveals whether the person herself or her intimates will feel pride or humility, love or hatred, on account of the trait; for it reveals whether the person has virtues or vices, and virtuous qualities always elicit love or pride, vicious ones humility or hatred. The common point of view is the position from which to make moral evaluations because it is a privileged position from which to make causal judgments about pride, humility, love and hatred, and moral evaluations are inseparable from these.[20]

---

[20] For some other views on why, according to Hume, people adopt and judge from the common point of view, rather than their peculiar points of view, see, e.g., Jensen (1977), who says that Hume regards this as a requirement of the correct use of moral language; Mackie (1980: ch. 7),

To see this more clearly, consider an observer of characters. Suppose she makes assessments of traits not (of course) from the perspective of her own interests (this would be the wrong kind of sentiment altogether), but from the situated sentiments she feels when she contemplates character traits in general from her peculiar point of view, rather than from the common point of view; and suppose she regards these as moral judgments. She will attribute to the person's quality of mind one property she knows by feeling (say, virtue, or exalted virtue), rather than a different property (say, slight virtue, or even vice) that she would know by feeling if she imaginatively placed herself in the common point of view so as to experience a different feeling. Her situated judgments will turn out to be inconvenient, since they will be accompanied by inaccurate causal predictions. Over time she will learn not to rely on them, but instead to take up an imagined perspective close to those who interact with the person she is judging, and to form her causal opinions on the basis of the other, shareable sentiments that this imaginary situation stimulates in her. Because of the usefulness of adopting this perspective and finding what feelings it evokes, and especially what causal judgments accompany them, she will develop a habit of performing this imaginative exercise. This habit will be strengthened by conversation with others who have made the same discovery and so regularly feel this same calm sentiment. (Hume gives a bigger role to interpersonal discussion in fixing the habit in the second *Enquiry* than in the *Treatise*. See *EPM* 5.42 / SBN 228.[21])

There are other important practical results of the common point of view as well. Once we have the useful habit of considering people's character traits from the common point of view, we can deploy it to overcome the difficulties we face in distinguishing our moral sentiment from our more selfish reactions to qualities of mind. In the *Treatise*, Hume initially says that the moral sentiment is caused by a special sort of act of contemplation of the trait or person, a contemplative act in which we do not attend to the person's impact on our interested affections but only consider his trait "in general" (*T* 3.1.2.4 / SBN

Baier (1991: 179), and Sayre-McCord (1994), all of whom give versions of the account that people form a convention (rather like those involved in the artificial virtues) to make moral judgments from the common point of view, for the common good; and Loeb (2002: ch. 4), who argues that we seek a steady standard of moral judgment because the knowledge that one's situated sentiments would be different if one were differently situated tends to undermine moral beliefs based on them. In "Morality without Metaphysics", a talk given at the Canadian Philosophical Association meetings in Winnipeg, Manitoba, in October 2005, Charlotte Brown argues that people adopt the common point of view because (as a result of sympathy) they feel pressure from the conflicting moral attitudes of others to come to have the same feelings those others do.

[21] On the importance of discussion to moral evaluation, see Taylor 2002: 57–8. I agree with her that Hume gives a greater role to public discussion in the moral *Enquiry* than in the *Treatise*, both in establishing in us the habit of imagining the effects of traits on those concerned and in further adjusting our sympathetic responses. But I am not persuaded by Taylor's argument that in the moral *Enquiry* Hume significantly changes his characterization of the common point of view and hence offers a different (and superior) standard of virtue from that of the *Treatise*.

472). It is difficult to "separate" the feeling so produced from the pleasure or uneasiness we feel because the person is a friend or an enemy, but a "man of temper and judgment" can do so. By *Treatise* 3.3 Hume can offer the common point of view as a ready way for even an ordinary person to distinguish his moral sentiments from his interested reactions. What we feel from the common point of view is always a moral sentiment alone, not an interested affection, because in genuinely envisioning ourselves there rather than here, we leave our actual interests behind. A further distinguishing feature is that interested reactions will be different for different individuals, but the sentiment felt from the common point of view will be the same for all who adopt it.

In the second *Enquiry* (*EPM* 9.9 / SBN 275–6), Hume further proposes something he only hints at in the *Treatise*. The calm and faint moral sentiment, albeit originally weak (little able to trigger action), is reinforced by sympathy with others all around one who have the same sentiment, until finally its force can exceed that of our interested affections, to which sympathy with others brings opposition more often than reinforcement. The device of making the moral sentiment originate in the common point of view thus provides Hume with some resources for explaining how we are ever caused to act by the moral sentiment. That faint inkling of sentiment that arises from the imaginative act becomes very strong when echoed by all those around us, for their feelings become our own through sympathy.

Notice that all we have offered here is an account of how people acquire the habit of entering into the common point of view, what happens to them when they do, and how their use of this point of view to make moral judgments is compatible with those judgments not being the products of empirical reasoning. The present interpretation is not an account of which qualities of mind we approve from the common point of view (which traits are virtues), or of how one comes to have those qualities. Hume goes on to make his case for particular traits as well, and we will explore some of what he says in later chapters.

But a further question presses. Does Hume also think that we *should* make moral evaluations solely from the common point of view? So far we have seen a causal explanation of our doing so, but not a justification.

There are, I believe, at least two issues embedded in this question, and they are best considered separately. The first is whether the common point of view partly insures the truth of moral evaluations, in that moral evaluations made from someone's situated perspective are for that reason more likely to be false. If this is the case, then we should make our moral judgments from the common point of view in one sense of 'should', since we are more likely to form true beliefs if we do. (We will not explore here why one should seek true rather than false beliefs, but most would agree that we should.) The second issue is why we should care about having the traits judged virtuous, and doing the actions judged meritorious, from the common point of view. This asks whether we should make moral evaluations from the common point of view in the following sense: are these the evaluations that matter, and if so, why?

In addressing the first issue, whether moral evaluations made from the common point of view are more likely to be true, it may seem that the answer is no. Given the experiences of the moral judge, it is difficult to see how we could say that her moral opinions formed from the common point of view (once she has developed this habit) are more often true than those she used to form on the basis of her situated sentiments before she developed the habit. Her accompanying causal predictions will more often be true; but the moral beliefs themselves, as we saw in the last chapter, represent a felt property, and so far there is no standard by which to judge that it is not the right felt property, or not the moral one. It is just a different felt property, the one that feels like *this* to me when I consider it from where I in fact am, as distinct from the one that feels like *that* when I reflect on it from the common point of view. Why should one of these give rise to a false and the other to a true judgment? It seems that in each case the opinion is true if it corresponds to the felt property that it purports to represent.

But in fact it follows from some of Hume's positions that forming moral opinions from the common point of view is a better way to obtain true moral beliefs than forming them on the basis of situated sentiments, though it takes a little work to see why, and also to gauge what follows from this (which might be less than one thinks).

The language of "correcting" the situated sentiments certainly suggests a place for truth here, or at least for error, not merely in the accompanying causal judgments but specifically in the moral opinions. Since moral opinions are truth-apt, as we saw in the last chapter, it seems that their truth might consist in correspondence with (the complex state of affairs that includes) the sentiment that observers feel from the common point of view, and that those moral opinions that do not match this feeling would be false.

There is certainly room for the error of misidentifying our feelings. That was present even before the common point of view was introduced. We can confuse a self-interested feeling with a feeling of moral approval, and as a result form a moral opinion that does not match our approbation or disapprobation. And without having any actual feelings on the matter, we can accept the testimony of those who say that a certain trait (say, a monkish one) is a virtue when it is not, and in this way form false moral beliefs. So there are various sources of false moral opinions.

It is also reasonable to think that Hume regards moral judgments not made from the common point of view as likely to be false just for that reason. This is because it is open to Hume to say that it is not correct to use the term 'moral' for our situated feelings or the beliefs that represent them, nor to use the ethical terms ('virtue', 'vice', 'merit', 'duty', and so forth) in framing those beliefs. This position is not explicit in the *Treatise*, but it may be part of his view there, particularly where he talks about the difficulty of conversing together about characters without adopting a common point of view. He makes it explicit in the moral *Enquiry*:

When a man denominates another his *enemy*, his *rival*, his *antagonist*, his *adversary*, he is understood to speak the language of self-love, and to express sentiments, peculiar to himself, and arising from his particular circumstances and situation. But when he bestows on any man the epithets of *vicious* or *odious* or *depraved*, he then speaks another language, and expresses sentiments in which he expects all his audience are to concur with him.   (*EPM* 9.6 / SBN 272)

And again: "language must . . . invent a peculiar set of terms, in order to express those universal sentiments of censure or approbation, which arise from humanity, or from views of general usefulness and its contrary" (*EPM* 9.7 / SBN 274). Both these passages contrast *moral* feelings (those felt from the common point of view, available to all) with *self-interested* feelings, rather than with what we have been talking about, a sentiment felt when contemplating a trait "in general" (apart from self-interest) but without adopting the common point of view. But the point holds for both self-interested and situated though not self-interested sentiments, since the situated sentiments, like the self-interested ones, also fail to be universal. Neither can be expressed in the special terms that are reserved to indicate a feeling that is capable of being felt by all—the moral terms.

While Hume does not offer a theory of truth, in the last chapter we saw two ways in which he characterizes it. We also considered Garrett's interpretation of Hume's account of predication in terms of abstract ideas, from which a third, more detailed, characterization of truth (true predication) will easily follow. For Hume a believed idea (or any idea), moral or otherwise, is true when (a) it is an accurate copy of the impression it is purported to represent, or (b) it matches or corresponds to real relations of ideas or real matters of fact, a correspondence we determine by comparing the believed idea with impressions or ideas in the mind which we find evident. In light of Garrett's interpretation we can give an account of Hume's conception of true predication which is not set out in the text but is a reasonable extrapolation from what Hume says.[22] In predicating a property of an object, we place the idea of that object in the revival set of the abstract idea of that property. So in judging this apple to be red or David's kindness to be a virtue, we place the idea of this apple in the revival set of our abstract idea of redness, or the idea of David's kindness in the revival set of our abstract idea of virtue. We do so on the basis of the idea's resemblance to other ideas in the revival set. The items in the revival set of red resemble one another in that they look a certain way, and the items in the revival set of virtue resemble one another in that they feel a certain way. We can thus characterize a true predication as one that correctly places an item in the revival set of the predicate-idea, where correctness consists in the item suitably resembling the other items in that set.

---

[22] I do not know whether Don Garrett would approve this use of his interpretation.

(This is not the place to try to determine how these different characterizations of truth are supposed to fit together, or whether they do so. We have enough here to enable us to address the question at hand.)

Given these understandings of truth, are moral judgments false or more likely to be false when they are not made from the common point of view, but only from someone's situated feelings? A spectator could form an idea-copy of a situated sentiment and call that a moral judgment. Would it be likely to be a false one?

Take the first characterization of truth. If the resulting believed idea is an accurate copy of her situated sentiment, by hypothesis it is not false to its original. It is a true attribution to an object of *a* property that feels like that. But saying this leaves open the question whether it is incorrect to call it a *moral* judgment, and for the spectator to call the property a virtue, a vice, or the like. We have seen that at least by the time he writes the moral *Enquiry* Hume thinks that it is indeed incorrect: when we speak the language of morality we expect all to share our feelings, and it is to those universally accessible felt properties (those we feel from the common point of view) that we apply the moral terms. If the spectator uses the concepts of moral good and evil, virtue and vice, or duty in this case, but the feeling in question is not one that can be shared in common with every observer, then her judgment is false. That is, if the situated sentiment differs from the one a spectator would experience from the common point of view, the moral judgment, because it is thought of as a *moral* judgment, is false. Now on a particular occasion a spectator's situated sentiment might happen to coincide with what she and others would feel from the common point of view, because, for example, in that case sympathy does not happen to introduce any distortions. In that case her moral judgment will happen to be true. (Whether she is epistemically warranted in making it is another question, which we leave aside here.) But this will not always be so. Thus it is clear that each spectator can best insure forming true rather than false moral beliefs by forming them from the common point of view. On the conception of truth as being an accurate copy, it matters what the idea in question purports to be a copy of. Since in this case the spectator's language shows that it purports to be a copy of a sentiment all can share, it will not be an accurate copy if the sentiment is not of that kind.

Much the same point holds on the second understanding of truth, as correspondence to a real matter of fact. (Since in the case of moral judgments we are talking about facts of feeling, we can leave aside relations of ideas.) Similarly here, if the moral belief corresponds accurately to (the idea of) the matter of fact in question, it is true. The question is which is the relevant matter of fact with which a moral idea must correspond. This depends on whether the spectator thinks of the felt property as a moral one and of the judgment as a moral assessment. Suppose she does, but her believed idea corresponds to her situated feeling and not to the generally accessible feeling that she would have from the common point of view (a feeling of the same species that in this case differs from it). Then, given the restriction on moral language and concepts, her belief is false, because her assessment is not a moral one.

The same point can be made about false predication on the Garrett model. If we place a trait such as David's kindness in the revival set of the abstract idea of virtue, this predication will be true provided the idea of David's kindness bears the right resemblance to the other ideas in that revival set. The right resemblance is one of feeling, but for virtue it is not just any feeling: all the items in the set feel a similar way when contemplated from the common point of view. Suppose a trait, say John's brazenness, evokes the same sort of feeling in a spectator from her situated perspective at some distance from John that David's kindness does from the common point of view, though if the spectator were to consider John's brazenness from the common point of view, she would feel quite differently about it. (A brazen person might garner admiration from a distance but be very trying to his associates.) If she predicates virtue of this trait (brazenness), she places it in the wrong revival set. It does not resemble the other items in that set in the appropriate way. It belongs in a different revival set. Thus the predication is false.

So much for the first issue, whether moral beliefs are more likely to be true if made from the common point of view. So let us turn to another question that can take the form, 'Should we adopt the common point of view in making moral evaluations?' Let us grant that in navigating through the human realm we catch on to the convenience of making moral evaluations from the common point of view, and learn to do it routinely. This gives us a causal account of the origin of the imaginative exercise that is in fact involved in moral judgment, and one reason to think that it is a good idea to develop the habit. But we think of moral judgments as having an importance that goes beyond convenience, and it would be nice to know whether making them from the common point of view provides them with this importance. We have seen that on Hume's view evaluating people and their traits from the common point of view is more likely to give us true moral judgments than other methods of evaluation we have considered, including accessing our self-interested passions or our situated "general" sentiments. But that is largely because he thinks that only judgments formed from the common point of view can rightly be *called* "moral"; if we call other judgments "moral", we misuse language. This definitional stop is insufficient to answer our further question. If we call one type of belief "moral" and the other type "schmoral", the question remains: why is one required instead of, or why is one preferable to or more important than, the other? And our only answer from Hume so far is that if we rely on "schmoral" (situated) feelings and beliefs, we incorrectly predict the effects of people's traits on ourselves and our friends, and get ourselves and others into trouble that way. We may still wonder what gives the moral judgments any authority over us, or any claim to be heeded—any claim to guide our actions, our self-development, and the rearing of our children. Why, for example, should we set out to raise children whose qualities of mind will elicit approval (and true attributions of virtue) from the common point of view, rather than children of some other sort?

The present account of what happens when we adopt the common point of view, and how we come to adopt it, is not intended to answer these questions by itself. However, Hume can use other resources of his theory, in addition to the common point of view, to give an answer of a sort. If the interpretation offered here is right, we have an actual feeling of approval of these traits when we enter into the common point of view, so we *do* care about them, by hypothesis, in the sense that they give us pleasure. This concern might well be lacking in violence or strength, but as we saw above, it can be greatly strengthened via sympathy, because it is echoed by everyone we meet. And because we project ourselves into the common point of view to make our moral judgments, we come to believe that the qualities we approve from that perspective are ones we would be proud of if we had them ourselves, and ones for which we would love other people who possessed them. This gives us an added incentive to acquire or maintain them if we can, and to link ourselves with those who have them (or induce the formation of them in those with whom we are linked), so as to live intimately with people we love rather than people we hate or hold in contempt. If the sort of guidance one hopes for from moral judgments is some kind of incentive to promote the good qualities and discourage the evil ones, then moral judgments that are brought about in the way I have described can provide it readily.

A further question may remain. These are indeed incentives to seek to acquire or keep virtue, to seek it in our friends, and foster it in our offspring; but are these the incentives we *should* have and act on? Why *should* we care about the virtues? This question remains, because for Hume so-called motivation is simply causation; to say that we have motives to promote the good traits and discourage the evil ones is simply to say that there are in us potential psychological causes of such behavior. But as deliberators we may wonder whether these particular causes have anything special to be said for them, to distinguish them from the other psychological causes that can operate on us, such as selfishness, hatred, and revenge. From the point of view of deliberation, what we seek is not merely to be moved but to be guided, not merely to have motives but to have grounds for action. All Hume can say to this is that in general, the virtues bring greater pleasure, the vices greater pain. Hume's view may be that we not only have motives to pursue the virtues, but we endorse those motives, or that we not only approve the virtues, but endorse that very approval.[23] Hume does say that the moral sentiment approves itself as well as its origin in sympathy

---

[23] We consider these suggestions in Ch. 9. The self-endorsement of the moral sentiment is proposed as Hume's test of the perfection of virtue by Baier (1991: 196–7, 277). Korsgaard (1996: 61–3), argues that for Hume, the normativity of the moral sentiment (and so of the virtues of which it approves) is provided by the moral sentiment's endorsing itself and also being endorsed by self-interest.

(*T* 3.3.6.3 / SBN 619). But for Hume, what this comes to is that on the contemplation of our motives to pursue virtue, or on the contemplation of our approval of virtue, we feel a further pleasure. Hume is a hedonist, in the sense that he takes the good in life to be pleasure and the evil to be pain or uneasiness; and in the end, the only warrant for any motivating passion, any reaction, and any quality of mind we have is its role in the generation of pleasure and the avoidance of pain.

PART II

FABRICATING VIRTUE

6

The Difficulty with the Virtue of Honesty

I. TRANSITION: ARTIFICIAL AND NATURAL VIRTUES

After a long journey into Hume's metaethics, it is time to move beyond that part of his moral philosophy to consider which traits Hume characterizes as virtues and which as vices. In *Treatise* 3.1.2 he offers a simple method for discovering "the origin of [any action's or sentiment's] moral rectitude or depravity": we ascertain why that item "upon the general view or survey, gives a certain satisfaction or uneasiness" (*T* 3.1.2.11 / SBN 475). Since feelings of approval are how we, as observers, know that a character is laudable, uncovering whatever it is that causes a trait to evoke these sentiments both proves that the trait is laudable and explains why it is. So Hume proceeds to explicate how various qualities of mind give such satisfaction or uneasiness, and so why they are virtues or vices; and occasionally, by such an examination, he challenges our prior assumptions as to whether a trait is a vice or a virtue. Thus Hume is apparently in a position to give an argument that is both causal and normative for each of the virtues and vices. He can show that a trait has particular features that cause approval from the common point of view, and in this way he both explains the mechanism by which it is rendered virtuous and also demonstrates that—since we approve it—it is indeed a virtue.

Hume expresses a preference for the style of moral philosophy of the ancient moralists with its emphasis on traits of character over that of the "moderns" with its focus on duty and obligation. And by present-day standards as well, insofar as we have them, Hume is a virtue ethicist. For example, he endorses a version of the view that the primary object of moral evaluation is a trait of character, and he identifies a good action derivatively as what the virtuous agent (one with this trait) would do, both marks of virtue ethics according to present-day theorists.[1] But there is a striking difference between Hume's virtue theory and the virtue theories of Aristotle and present-day neo-Aristotelians. Aristotelians old and new define the virtues as those character traits that play a constitutive role in the flourishing human life of those who possess them; this is their criterion of virtue. Hume, by contrast, defines a virtue as any

---

[1] See, e.g., Hursthouse 1999: ch. 1. Gary Watson (1990) calls this the doctrine of the primacy of character over action.

quality of the mind that evokes approval in an observer when it is contemplated in an unbiased way (*T* 3.1.2.3–4 / SBN 471–2; *T* 3.3.1.3 / SBN 574–5; *T* 3.3.1.15–17 / SBN 581–3). Hume gives no explicit account of the good or flourishing human life, and whatever implicit account he may have (e.g., at *T* 3.3.6.6 / SBN 620–1) does not serve as a criterion for identifying the virtues. The question whether the virtuous person is happy is, for him, a matter for empirical investigation.

For a virtue ethicist Hume says surprisingly little about what he thinks a virtue or a vice is, or even a "character" (trait) in general. We have seen that the virtues and vices are qualities of mind, and he gives many examples of virtues (among them benevolence, justice, gratitude, lenity, industry, compassion) and some, but far fewer, of vice (among them knavery, treachery, indolence, inhumanity, and cruelty). He seems on the whole to identify a virtue with a particular motive, and a vice with the absence or disregard of that motive (*T* 3.2.1.2–3 / SBN 477–8), or perhaps with an opposite motive. What he calls a "motive" in such cases is a motivating passion. But he also argues that self-esteem (a form of pride) is a virtue when properly concealed and regulated (*T* 3.3.2.11 / SBN 598), and the passion of pride is not in his view a motivating sentiment, although it can enhance the ability of certain direct passions to cause action when it arises from the same objects or situations they do (*T* 2.3.9.4 / SBN 439). Thus Hume's conception of a trait of character, while not well developed in his writings, seems to be roughly this: a character trait is either a passion or a disposition to experience a passion of a characteristic sort in certain circumstances, together with the tendency to be caused to act by it or by its associated passions. He is quite explicit that *actions* are evaluated derivatively: when we observe someone's action, we take it as a sign of the inner quality that must have produced it, and derive our moral evaluation of the action from our assessment of that inner quality (*T* 3.2.1.2 / SBN 477; also *T* 3.3.1.4 / SBN 575). Thus a man who loves his children so little or is so little moved by his love that he neglects them has a vicious quality of mind in light of which we judge his actions also to be vicious.

Hume's catalog of the virtues and vices is not wildly original overall, but it does have some singular features. Perhaps the most striking one in the *Treatise* is the distinction between the traits he calls artificial virtues and those he calls natural virtues, with his different explanations of why they each evoke the approval they do. In this Hume takes a new position on a question about which his predecessors disagree: whether morality is natural or conventional ("artificial", in the sense of being the product of human craftsmanship). To say that a virtue or duty is *natural* is usually to say two things: that the character trait or action itself is not something socially invented but is a (perhaps refined) manifestation of a familiar feature of human nature, and that the trait or action's goodness (its being a virtue or a duty) is not the result of inculcated social custom, but rather is solely a consequence of something in the nature of things (whether in the rational order of the universe, the divine will, or human nature). Hobbes and Mandeville see morals as conventional, while Hutcheson and Locke see them as natural.[2] Hume is the only one to take an intermediate position: some important virtues are natural, but others, equally important, are socially invented. He mocks Mandeville's contention that the very concepts of vice and virtue are foisted on the public by scheming politicians for the purpose of managing us more easily. If there were nothing in our affective experience to give rise to the concept of virtue, Hume says, no lavish praise of heroes could generate it (*T* 3.2.2.25 / SBN 500). But while natural features of the human mind account for some of the traits we have and for their classification as virtues, they cannot account entirely for others.

In the *Treatise* this distinction between artificial and natural virtues is prominent, and the very next task that Hume undertakes after arguing that moral distinctions are "not deriv'd from reason" but are "deriv'd from a moral sense" is to prove that "our sense of every kind of virtue is not natural; but that there are some virtues, that produce pleasure and approbation by means of an artifice or contrivance" (*T* 3.2.1.1 / SBN 477). The distinction is almost entirely suppressed in the moral *Enquiry*. Yet that text presents us with no reasons to think that Hume abandoned the distinction; indeed, there he uses some of the same arguments to establish the utility of justice and its dependence on circumstance that he used in the *Treatise* in talking about its artificiality.[3] Since the two accounts are compatible but the *Treatise* account is richer, we will follow the *Treatise* account here.

The virtues that Hume classifies as artificial are equity or honesty with respect to property (sometimes called justice), fidelity to promises and contracts (at times also lumped under "justice"), the less stringent sort of honesty and fidelity appropriate to heads of state in their official roles, allegiance to government or law-abidingness, chastity and modesty (disinclination toward non-marital sexual relations) in women and girls, and good manners (introduced later, in the midst of his discussion of the natural virtues). To these he gives rigorous scrutiny, and one naturally wonders on what grounds he identifies them as artificial rather than natural and so separates them from the rest. The natural virtues are apparently very, very numerous, on Hume's view, but fall into three main categories: the virtues of greatness of mind, the virtues of goodness or benevolence, and the natural abilities.

In this and the next two chapters we consider why Hume thinks certain virtues are artificial rather than natural, and we attempt to resolve some puzzles

---

[2] Hobbes 1996[1651]; Mandeville 1988[1723]: esp. 41–57; Locke 1986[1690]: Hutcheson 1971, e.g. ii. 205–333.

[3] One can only speculate as to why Hume suppressed this distinction, so central to Book 3 of the *Treatise*, when he wrote the moral *Enquiry*. One possibility: after facing the charge (that he himself notes, 1967/1745) that his position with regard to the conventionality of justice in the *Treatise* "destroy[s] all the Foundations of Morality", Hume may have seen self-interested reasons not to describe justice in the same terms ("artificial", "contrived") in the later work.

in his accounts of each of the three artificial virtues to which he gives the most attention: honesty concerning property, fidelity to promises, and allegiance.

First we can make some general observations about Hume's distinction between the natural and artificial virtues and indicate the overall pattern that emerges in his treatment of the artificial ones. In the more detailed analysis that follows we will see how this pattern is instantiated in his discussion of particular artificial virtues.

Hume seems to suppose that there are certain characteristic sentiments, including motivating passions and capacities for love and hatred, that are simply part of human nature, just as it is in the nature of various species of nonhuman animals to be timid or ferocious, loyal or indifferent, according to their kinds. The natural virtues are more refined and completed forms of these natural human sentiments. Any sentiments that are not part of this natural stock must have been induced in us by some process of invention and socialization (as we would say today). However, Hume does not claim to know a priori which sentiments are natural and which socially induced; that requires argument. We will try to establish that Hume does indeed provide arguments to show that some of the sentiments familiar to us that may seem part of our species' original equipment could not be so, because the assumption that they are entails paradoxes (*T* 3.2.1.9 / SBN 470–80; *T* 3.2.5.2–5 / SBN 516–18; *T* 3.2.6.9 / SBN 531–3). One of our goals in what follows is to understand these paradoxes and demonstrate that in each case where Hume finds a paradox in our commonsense thought about a trait, he sees it as the consequence of thinking the trait natural when it is not.

Hume observes that the natural virtues, as manifestations of natural human sentiments, include the virtues of attachment and devotion to particular individuals, and so tend to exhibit partiality (*T* 3.2.2.8 / SBN 488–9). It is a virtue, for example, to be devoted to one's own child; it is no virtue to be indifferent as between one's own child and all other children. Indeed, thoroughgoing impartiality as between different persons is contrary to virtues such as friendship and parental devotion. Hume finds this fact salient.

The artificial virtues have a couple of features that distinguish them right at the surface from the natural ones. First, they are traits we need for successful *impersonal* cooperation. Our natural sentiments enable us to cooperate reasonably well with those we love—or at least, they do when refined into natural virtues. But, Hume argues, our natural sentiments are too partial to give rise to traits that would allow us to cooperate with those with whom we have no intimate bond—or rather, they cannot do so on their own, without intervention. The virtues that Hume categorizes as artificial exhibit, at least to some extent, a kind of evenhandedness or impartiality. Secondly, Hume observes that the particular actions manifesting the virtues he calls natural directly benefit someone on each occasion when they are performed, whereas a particular action manifesting one of the artificial ones may not benefit anyone, although it contributes to a systematic practice that is highly beneficial to all. Each generous act, for example, benefits its recipient; but a particular act of repaying a loan (an act of honesty) might impoverish the debtor while restoring to a miser wealth he will never enjoy. Hume thinks that nonetheless we need people who are disposed to adhere strictly and without exception to the rules of property and promise if we are to maintain any sort of society; and without society, life would be precarious and dreary.

Hume's analysis of each of the artificial virtues has the same basic structure. He first shows that a particular familiar virtue is artificial and not natural. In two important cases this requires an argument, because it is controversial to view these virtues as artificial; in other cases he needs only to point out how obvious it is that the virtue is artificial, since this thesis is widely believed or has been well defended by others. Next he gives an account of why human beings would want to invent the virtue in question. Each artificial virtue is devised in order to solve a problem inherent in human life—some practical difficulty to which we are all vulnerable and which our natural sentiments are not equipped to remedy. Finally, Hume offers a speculative account of how the relevant convention might have come into being.

The two virtues of honesty with regard to property and fidelity to promises have only rarely been thought artificial. (Even Hobbes, who regarded property and nearly all the rest of morality as dependent upon the contract by which a commonwealth is formed, and so as conventional, gave credence to the idea that in the state of nature human beings have a duty to keep their covenants.[4]) Consequently, Hume argues in some detail that these two virtues are artificial, not natural. By contrast, he thinks it too obvious to require defense that the feminine tendency to recoil from illicit sexual advances is not a naturally occurring trait. Hume argues for the artificiality of honesty and fidelity by means of a *reductio* in each case, showing that when we suppose that the virtue is independent of any collaborative social arrangement (when we suppose that the character trait could exist and win our approval without one), insoluble paradoxes arise; hence we must conclude that the supposition is false, and although we did not previously suspect it, that some sort of social engineering has occurred. He then goes on to explain the human problem or natural disability that we solve by entering into conventions of ownership and promising, and to sketch a plausible tale of how each convention might have formed.

We should note that each sketch of the genesis of an artificial virtue is an account of how free, unsubordinated, uncoerced individuals could, in principle, develop the psychological characteristics that he describes: a sense of honor with respect to property and promise-keeping, respect for international conventions such as boundaries and treaties, a disposition to chastity, deferential manners. Even in the invention of government, as we will see in Chapter 8, although

---

[4] Hobbes 1996[1651]: e.g. 102–3.

subordination of some people to the authority of others is the result, the process is carried out by individuals who act freely and initially have no masters—indeed, among whom civil authority is unknown. (This is true of the adults involved. The children seem to be subordinated to their parents at least while young, and are trained to conform to the new conventions both physically and emotionally without being given a choice.) Hume does not argue that there is never any coercion involved in the development of the artificial virtues; perhaps on various historical occasions there was. He simply describes entirely non-coercive mechanisms that could in principle produce these results: voluntary steps people might take that ultimately work profound changes in the members of the societies so formed.

To appreciate the strategy in action, we take up Hume's detailed accounts of three of the artificial virtues: honesty, fidelity, and allegiance. Each presents some puzzling features that I hope to interpret and explain. The remainder of this chapter is about honesty; the next two are about fidelity and allegiance, respectively. At the end of the chapter about allegiance (Chapter 8) we consider how the general strategy might be extended.

II. A PUZZLE ABOUT THE VIRTUE OF HONESTY WITH RESPECT TO PROPERTY ("JUSTICE")

In Book 3, Part 2, of the *Treatise* Hume makes the following three claims. The first is a point about all virtue; the other two are specifically about the virtue of equity, or honesty with respect to property:

[I]t may be establish'd as an undoubted maxim, *that no action can be virtuous, or morally good, unless there be in human nature some motive to produce it, distinct from the sense of its morality.* (*T* 3.2.1.7 / SBN 479)

'Tis requisite, then, to find some motive to acts of justice and honesty, distinct from our regard to the honesty; and in this lies the great difficulty. (*T* 3.2.1.10 / SBN 480)

[W]e have no real or universal motive[5] for observing the laws of equity, but the very equity and merit of that observance; and as no action can be equitable or meritorious, where it cannot arise from some separate motive, there is here an evident sophistry and reasoning in a circle. Unless, therefore, we will allow, that nature has establish'd a sophistry, and render'd it necessary and unavoidable, we must allow, that the sense of justice and injustice is not deriv'd from nature, but arises artificially, tho' necessarily from education, and human conventions. (*T* 3.2.1.17 / SBN 483)

---

[5] This wording is from p. 483 of the first Selby-Bigge edition, Oxford University Press, 1888, repr. 1975, *not* the (second) Selby-Bigge–Nidditch or the Norton and Norton edition. Norton and Norton, following Nidditch, interpolate the word 'naturally': "we have naturally no real or universal motive for observing the laws of equity", following revisions made in Hume's hand in the printed first edition of the *Treatise*. (I am grateful to V. C. Chappell for drawing this difference to my attention.)

Although our topic in this chapter is honesty, we should note that later Hume offers an intentionally parallel claim about the virtue of fidelity to promises:

Now 'tis evident we have no motive leading us to the performance of promises, distinct from a sense of duty. If we thought, that promises had no moral obligation, we never shou'd feel any inclination to observe them . . . it follows, that fidelity is no natural virtue, and that promises have no force, antecedent to human conventions.   (*T* 3.2.5.6 / SBN 518–19)[6]

A. The Difficulty

What we seem to see here is a set of contradictory claims:

1. Honesty is a virtue. (This is implicit, since Hume's intent in discussing honesty at all is to show that "some virtues . . . produce pleasure and approbation by means of an artifice" (*T* 3.2.1.1 / SBN 477).)

2. For every virtue there is in human nature some non-moral motive—some motivating passion distinct from moral approval and disapproval (distinct from the "sense of virtue" or the "sense of duty")—that characteristically produces actions expressive of that virtue, and that, by eliciting our approval, renders virtuous the actions that are so motivated.

3. There is no morally approved, virtue-imparting, non-moral motive of honest action. The only approved, reliable motive of honest action that we can find is a moral one, the sense of virtue or "regard to the honesty" of the actions.

(2) and (3) together imply the negation of (1). As Hume points out, the three propositions also jointly generate a vicious definitional circle, discussed below. But Hume does not conclude from this that (1) is false—that honesty is not a virtue. Instead, he somehow infers from these claims that honesty is artificial (the product of human invention) rather than natural.

Since Hume asserts (2) and (3) in close proximity, one might well ask how he ultimately reconciles these incompatible claims. Since Hume introduces them in the course of providing "a short, and, I hope, convincing argument" that honesty is one of the "virtues that produce pleasure and approbation by means of an artifice or contrivance, which arises from the circumstances and necessities of mankind" (*T* 3.2.1.1 / SBN 477), one might ask how the artificiality of honesty is supposed to follow from these mutually inconsistent claims. And since Hume himself draws dramatic attention to the circle or "sophistry", one might expect him to tell us how this may be avoided. The answers to these questions do not

---

6 A comparable claim occurs in Hume's essay "Of the Original Contract" (*EMPL* 480): "The second kind of moral duties [which includes those of honesty] are such as are not supported by any original instinct of nature, but are performed entirely from a sense of obligation."

leap easily from the text. How does Hume solve his "great difficulty" with the virtue of honesty?

In what follows I offer an interpretation that answers these questions. According to it, the circle and the contradiction result, on Hume's view, from a misapplication of some of our ordinary moral concepts; and the moral sentiment itself plays a motivating role in the virtue of honesty. Then I distinguish my interpretation from a family of interpretations that see a much more prominent role in the virtue of honesty for redirected (self-)interest, and argue that mine has important interpretive and philosophical advantages.

Hume seems right to assume (1). Honesty with respect to property (the only kind of honesty that concerns him here, oddly enough) is an ethically good character trait—a virtue.

Hume's considerations in favor of (2) are fairly persuasive. (2) follows from Hume's understanding of what a virtue is. A virtue is some sort of admirable "quality of mind": a psychological state or disposition that motivates action. So, an analysis of a particular virtue, such as benevolence or justice, must tell us what the relevant psychological feature or disposition is that wholly or partly constitutes the virtue. For example, for benevolence it is a concern (or the disposition to feel concern) for the well-being of others. Now on Hume's sentiment-based metaethics, a virtue is a trait of character which, when contemplated impartially and from a commonly accessible perspective, gives to the observer the particular kind of pleasure called approbation; a vice gives the observer the uneasiness called disapprobation. What principally elicits approval and disapproval, Hume says, is the motivating sentiment of the person under evaluation, and actions only derivatively (*T* 3.2.1.3 / SBN 477–8). Consequently, there must be some motivating sentiment distinct from moral approval or disapproval to serve as the object of approval when a trait is designated a virtue. We may call this the non-moral, approved motive. According to (2), every virtue consists, at least in part, of a characteristic non-moral, approved motive. In the case of benevolence (a natural virtue), it is a virtue because, when we reflect on someone's concern for the well-being of others, we approve it. Clearly the approval is distinct from this concern that is the motive of benevolent actions.

I should clarify Hume's confusing uses of the term 'natural'. On the one hand, he contrasts the natural with the artificial (the product of human invention). But he uses the term in two other ways as well. "In the following discourse *natural* is also opposed sometimes to *civil*, sometimes to *moral*" (*T* 3.1.2.9 n. 70; SBN 475 n.). On topics where Hume is evidently using 'natural' to mark what is not moral, as in his discussion of the different kinds of motivating sentiments, we will say non-moral.[7]

"But may not the sense of morality or duty produce an action, without any other motive?" (*T* 3.2.1.8 / SBN 479). Hume considers whether the production

---

[7] Gauthier 1992 is helpful on the meanings of 'natural'.

of a virtuous action solely by the sense of duty, which is a *moral* rather than a non-moral motive, would be a counter-example to (2). To see his response requires some explanation of duty and the sense of duty. First, Hume says that it is my duty to have a certain motivating sentiment just in case my having it would elicit approval and my failure to have it or deficiency of it would elicit disapproval. Thus my duty is, first, to have certain sentiments. Next, an *action* is my duty if it is the sort of action that would be brought about by one of those obligatory motivating sentiments. Thus, for example, it is my duty to love my children. (This is because we disapprove the absence or a miniscule amount of what is "normal and natural" in human beings, which love of offspring is.) Because it is my duty to love my children, it is my duty to give my children the care and education that such love would prompt. So actions can be duties as well, but again, derivatively. Actions are identified as duties in light of the fact that they are the standard products of such sentiments. We condemn the failure to perform these actions (such as caring for one's children) solely because we understand the omission as evidence that the agent lacks the requisite motivating sentiment. My duties are actions that would be prompted by virtuous motives in me if I had such motives; if I fail to perform them, this indicates a regrettable deficiency in me of the motivating sentiment that constitutes the virtue in question (and perhaps even the presence of vice). Now, if I lack a virtuous motive which I know it would be better to have, I might feel ashamed, and be moved to do the deeds that it typically produces anyway, for another reason: a desire either to correct in myself, or to conceal from myself, my own deficiency of sentiment. This, for Hume, is action produced by the sense of duty alone (*T* 3.2.1.8 / SBN 479). Clearly, in the case of honesty (or any particular virtue), there must be an approved motive definitive of honest action that is present in (at least some) human beings in the first place, before someone who lacks that motive can identify what she is missing that an honest person has and consequently regret her lack of it. Furthermore, there would need to be an approved motive in honest people in order for the deficient individual to determine what action an honest person would be moved to do (what her duty is), before she can do it solely from a sense of duty. The existence of the sense of duty, on Hume's theory, depends upon the existence of some approved motive of honest action in the generality of honest people, and so the sense of duty cannot *be* that approved motive. Thus the existence of the motive of duty is no threat to (2), but actually supports it.

Hume also has plausible things to say in favor of (3), that there is no approved, non-moral motive of honest actions. He canvasses the non-moral motives that people might have for repaying a loan in various circumstances in which this would be the honest thing to do, such as when the loan is to be kept secret, or when it is owed to a "miser", or a "profligate debauchee", attempting to find some morally approved motive in light of which each such action would be shown to manifest the virtue of honesty (*T* 3.2.1.9–16 / SBN 479–83). Virtue theorist that he is, Hume expects to find some single type of sentiment that constitutes the character trait of honesty and reliably produces honest action, and, given (2), the sentiment should be distinct from moral approval and disapproval. The only candidates available seem to be the debtor's private interest, the public interest, the love of mankind as such, and private benevolence (the desire for the good of the creditor). Each of these fails to produce the approved action under some circumstances in which we would deem the action honest, and so none could be the motive constitutive of the virtue of honesty. (The love of mankind as such causes no action under any circumstances, since there is no such sentiment (T 3.2.1.12 / SBN 481).) For example, private benevolence will not move me to repay a fortune I borrowed from a profligate debauchee, who will only use the wealth for self-destructive dissipation; yet insofar as I am honest, I will be moved to repay it nonetheless, and we would count it honest to do so. Furthermore, sometimes these proposed motives simply do not fit the virtue as we find it. Thus, "men, in the ordinary conduct of life, look not so far as the public interest, when they pay their creditors . . . and abstain from theft, and robbery, and injustice of every kind. That is a motive too remote and too sublime" (T 3.2.1.11 / SBN 481). Indeed, in practice we find that the reason or motive that people cite for repaying a loan and other honest acts is simply their "regard to justice, and abhorrence of villainy and knavery" (T 3.2.1.9 / SBN 479)—that is, their sense of morality. Thus Hume offers good empirical evidence in support of (3).

The circle arises quite directly from (2) and (3). Moral approval of an action is elicited by the presence of a virtue-imparting motive; this is what makes actions of this type virtuous at all. So, the approval cannot *be* the virtue-imparting motive. Yet, in the case of honest action, it is. The person who has the virtue of honesty repays loans and refrains from theft out of approval of honest behavior and disapproval of dishonest behavior. Thus, to behave honestly is to do certain sorts of outward acts (those we recognize as required by honesty) from an honest motive, a motive definitive of the virtue and productive of approval; but the only honest motive has turned out to be approval of honest action. So, an honest action is an action produced by approval of honest action. And that is *all* it in fact is. This is a viciously circular definition, since it defines honest action in terms of honest action and gives us no other way to identify it. (What is honest action? Actions performed from approval of honest action.) The motive of honest action is also identified only circularly: the motive of honest action is approval of honest action, which in turn is approval of action produced by the motive of honest action. We can never say what the approval is approval *of.* We have useless definitions both of honest action and of the motive of honest action, but useless definitions that seem to be the only correct ones. This is seriously paradoxical.

It is noteworthy that it does not resolve the paradox to say that honesty is a social invention. It makes no more sense that a product of human convention should be capable only of a viciously circular definition than that a product of nature should be so. A product of human ingenuity cannot be such that its only correct definition is one that is no definition at all.

B. Main Features of the Solution

Here is my interpretation. Hume himself accepts (1), that honesty is a virtue. (2), the requirement that virtue consist of an approved non-moral motive, is something that on Hume's view we commonly presuppose, but not something that Hume himself endorses, on reflection, with respect to all the virtues. Instead, he holds a weaker thesis, that there must be an *approved motive* constituting any virtue, but it need not be a *non-moral* one; and he also holds that, in the right social conditions, actions themselves can be approved without regard to how they were produced. At the same time Hume accepts and defends (3), that there is no non-moral motive of honest action of which we approve. That is how Hume avoids the contradiction. In the end Hume's view is that our *ordinary conception of a virtue* requires the existence of a non-moral motive of which we approve and which makes virtuous the actions so motivated. (2) is a thesis of common sense. Honesty is not a virtue in this sense. But honesty is a virtue in the sense that matters for Hume: it is a trait of which we approve when we contemplate it in general and from the common point of view. And honesty is a trait of character, not merely a pattern of behavior, for there is an approved and characteristic motive of honest action as well; it simply is not a non-moral one. The difficulties arise in part because we mistake honesty for a natural virtue, and (2) *does* hold for the natural virtues (such as benevolence, gratitude, and parental attentiveness). Thus, for Hume, honesty is a virtue in roughly the sense in which an artificial leg is a leg. It is a virtue because it functions as a virtue. But if we take it for a natural virtue, we are mistaken, just as we are mistaken if we take a well-functioning artificial leg for a natural leg. It is because we *take* honesty to be a virtue of the commonsensical sort, a natural virtue, that the contradiction and the circle arise. They are the consequence of conjoining our over-generalized concept of a virtue with our actual motives for and reactions to honesty. Indeed, the presence of a "sophistry" buried just below the surface of our network of concepts and sentiments is a revealing clue that our natural conception of virtue has been grafted intentionally onto a set of facts and sentiments which it does not fit. The contradiction and vicious circle show that our presuppositions could not all have arisen from experience, but must somewhere include supposed ideas that represent no impression, and so are nothing. It further suggests that human social inventiveness has been at work to obfuscate matters, albeit (as it turns out) for a good purpose. Thus the illogical relations of these concepts lead Hume to classify material honesty as artificial in the first place. The artifice does not remove the logical difficulties, but rather is posited to explain why they are there. The contradiction and the circle, however, are not actually instantiated in the world, even though in our concepts we may unknowingly be committed to them. So as philosophers we can free ourselves from them.[8]

C. The First Stage: Redirected Interest

Hume thinks that honesty is an artificial virtue and that property is a human social invention. On the interpretation that I propose, here is what this inventing comes to. Human beings are physically weak and lacking in bodily defenses, in need of forms of nourishment and protection from the elements that can be generated only by considerable labor, vulnerable to "fortune and accidents", and individually limited in their ability to develop useful skills. Consequently, we need to associate with one another for cooperative production, for mutual aid, and for division of labor (call these economic advantages), as well as for companionship and the other benefits of a social life (*T* 3.2.2.2–3 / SBN 484–5, and suggested at *EPM* 3.13 / SBN 188). However, basic selfishness coupled with "confined generosity", under conditions of moderate scarcity, lead to conflict over material goods, which are easily transferred from one person to another (*T* 3.2.2.5–7 / SBN 486–8). If we do work together or otherwise interact with one another, it is not only my selfishness which will lead me to use force or stealth to make off with the fruits of your labor or the whole of our joint product. My partiality to my own friends and family will lead me do the same kinds of things. If this sort of behavior goes unchecked, our cooperative arrangements will soon disintegrate, leaving every individual much the worse off for lack of the economic and emotional advantages of society. So our interests dictate that we restrain our greed and partiality in some way, so as to be better served in the long run. We need to attach material goods to persons in such a way that each person can count on controlling certain goods undisturbed. Then it will be profitable to have regular social interactions with others, such as cooperative production (often involving division of labor) and exchange of goods; and a network of informal social relations can then achieve stability (*T* 3.2.2.9 / SBN 489), bringing about greater material wealth and individual safety for all involved. Hence, greed (specifically) and self-interest (more broadly) move us to make declarations of the following form: I will refrain from taking or using the goods now in your possession, provided you will refrain from taking or using the goods in my possession (*T* 3.2.2.10 / SBN 490). Individuals announce

---

[8] For the different view that Hume introduces artifice to *remove* the circle, see Harrison 1981: 8; Mackie 1980: 79–80; and Snare 1991: ch. 7. Harrison and Mackie think that Hume does eliminate the circle; Snare thinks that he confuses two distinct circles and has the materials to eliminate one but not the other, which is in fact intractable. Penelhum (1975: 154–5) does not address the issue of the circle directly, but thinks that Hume's account of the origins of honesty in the convention of ownership eliminates the puzzle of how we can regard honesty as a virtue even though we lack natural inclinations to such actions.

such conditional intentions to one another, and each abstains from the designated goods on condition that the others behave similarly. This is the invention of property. Such practices gradually catch on among larger numbers of people, in a way similar to that in which "languages [are] gradually establish'd by human convention" and gold and silver become media of exchange (ibid.). Similarly, and at the same time, individuals propose and accept rules for acquisition of property and for the transfer of ownership by consent (*T* 3.2.3–4). All this is done from "a sense of common interest", and without making or accepting any promises, just as "[t]wo men, who pull the oars of a boat, do it by agreement or convention, tho' they have never given promises to each other" (*T* 3.2.2.10 / SBN 490). Practices of respecting property are kept in a fragile balance entirely by voluntary compliance, as the only penalty or bad consequence of taking possession of the goods reserved to another is the collapse of the practice and the return to a "free for all" condition, or perhaps ostracism of the violator from the community of cooperators. Participants learn by trial and error that if they are so short-sighted as to violate the rule of "mine and thine", others will soon disregard the rule as well, and the society will disintegrate, quickly bringing to an end the security and prosperity provided by it. Such purely voluntary cooperative arrangements easily fall apart when anyone realizes that some others are not abiding by the arrangement. Since these conventions take shape at first in small, face-to-face groups of rather low material productivity, it is fairly obvious when anyone violates the rules. This gives us the first temporal stage: greed and broader self-interest induce us to invent rules attaching goods to individuals, and experience with the fragility of small societies teaches us that it is in our interest to conform to these rules. Thus "the *natural* obligation to justice, *viz.* interest, has been fully explain'd" (*T* 3.2.2.23 / SBN 498).[9] This much is fairly uncontroversial.

To the imposition, then, and observance of these rules, both in general, and in every particular instance, they are at first mov'd only by a regard to interest; and this motive, on the first formation of society, is sufficiently strong and forcible. But when society has become numerous, and has increas'd to a tribe or nation, this interest is more remote. (*T* 3.2.2.24 / SBN 499)

Successful cooperative groups grow larger and more prosperous, using the economic advantages of such an informal society to improve their material productivity. In more stable and more anonymous groups of this kind, where there are more goods available to tempt people, self-interest alone will not always reliably induce individuals to conform to the rules of property; some people are likely to be drawn by greed to violate the rules from time to time (ibid.). This

---

[9] What Hume means by obligation is much discussed. It includes, at least, being disposed to act by a motivating passion; but presumably obligation is this disposition with some special status. In this passage Hume distinguishes natural from moral obligation, and calls the moral obligation "the sentiment of right and wrong".

is likely to happen whether or not it actually *is* in anyone's long-term interest to violate them, because at times some people will find the attractions of such behavior stronger than any calm promptings of long-term self-interest, and in a more complex society it is harder to see what ill effects one's own dishonest act might have. This is a vulnerable stage in human social development. What is needed is a further motive for people to comply with the rules of ownership.

D. The Second Stage: The Motive of Augmented Moral Sentiment

Adults living in such a society (which might well lack any formal government), especially parents, leaders, and anyone else with special influence over the feelings of others, have various incentives to attempt to create some further motive in others to follow the rules of property. It is in the interest of each person that others be disposed to conform quite strictly to the rules of property. Such compliance is what gives stability to society and insures that its shared advantages come into being. This consideration alone will move parents and politicians to instruct other people to follow the rules very strictly (whether or not they are disposed to adhere to them strictly themselves), in the hope of making those others useful to themselves. Furthermore, parents naturally love their children and want them to fare well, and only those individuals known to be disposed to honor property rights will be welcomed into society and commerce; so parents will wish to train their children to be scrupulous about property.

In addition, members of the society have a number of raw materials in the natural sentiments from which they can fashion a further motive in their neighbors to comply with the rules of material justice. Everyone, even the very young (once it is pointed out to them), can recognize that conformity to the rules of property is what makes possible the persistence of the social arrangement that benefits all. The mechanism of sympathy will thus naturally lead every member of society to feel approval for rule-following behavior within the system of property that is in place, given the happiness which that system yields and the misery it prevents. So moral approval will take hold. The initial moral evaluation—approval of acting in accordance with the rules of property, or of the (bare) disposition to do so—is an evaluation made naturally by all who reflect on society and on the preserving role played by behavior that conforms to the rules of property. This is an evaluation of actions (or bare dispositions to act), not yet of any character trait consisting of a motivating sentiment.[10]

---

[10] In this I agree with Mackie that Hume countenances approval of mere rule-following action. But Mackie thinks that the story can stop here. "For single acts of justice taken on their own", he says, "there is often *no* intelligible motive; they can be understood only as parts of a general scheme" (1980: 81). However, since according to Hume's moral psychology there must be some passion

Thus Hume says:

...when the injustice is so distant from us, as no way to affect our interest, it still displeases us; because we consider it as prejudicial to human society, and pernicious to every one that approaches the person guilty of it. We partake of their uneasiness by *sympathy*; . . . this is the reason why the sense of moral good and evil follows upon justice and injustice. And tho' this sense . . . be derived only from contemplating the actions of others, yet we fail not to extend it to our own actions. . . . *Thus self-interest is the original motive to the* establishment *of justice*; but a *sympathy with the public interest is the source of the* moral approbation *which attends that virtue.*   (*T* 3.2.2.24 / SBN 499)

Acts of conformity to the rules of material justice evoke moral approval. But notice also the further suggestion of this paragraph that while the original motive of complying with property rules is interest, when that wanes, the moral sentiment provides a further motive to fill the breach. This impression is reinforced in the next paragraph:

Tho' this progress of sentiments be *natural* . . . it is here forwarded by the artifice of politicians, who, in order to govern men more easily, and preserve peace in society, have endeavour'd to produce an esteem for justice, and an abhorrence of injustice. This, no doubt, must have its effect.   (*T* 3.2.2.25 / SBN 500)

If men are governed more easily by increasing their esteem for justice and abhorrence of injustice, then clearly those moral sentiments *move* people to conform to property rules where they might otherwise not. The moral sentiment provides a disposition to *behave* justly—indeed, one that is in some settings more reliable than interest.

What occurs to bring about this "progress of sentiments" is that parents and politicians engage in a further "artifice" which "extend[s] the natural sentiments beyond their original bounds" (*T* 3.2.2.25 / SBN 500): they convert their charges' approval of rule-following acts, which arose naturally upon reflection about the convention of property, into a motivating sentiment. Through "custom and education" (ibid.) they turn the moral disapproval of violations of the rules into a deeply rooted abhorrence of violation, a horror of "villainy and knavery" too strong and too visceral to be readily overcome in any particular instance by greed or general self-interest. The children are taught "to regard the observance of those rules, by which society is maintain'd, as worthy and honourable, and their violation as base and infamous. By this means the sentiments of honour may take root in their tender minds" (*T* 3.2.2.26 / SBN 500–1). This enhanced moral sentiment has the power to produce action. And once moral approval of material honesty is widespread, this sense of obligation

---

prompting actions that accord with that general scheme, Mackie adds that "the artifice consists in the cultivation of a sentiment in favour of every act that honesty requires, including those that are not beneficial" to anyone (ibid.). What this sentiment might be, and how it can be specified non-circularly, is not explained. We also need to know how an enduring character trait is to be engineered, since honesty must turn out to be a virtue.

or sentiment of honor will be strengthened by concern for one's reputation. Here is how Hume summarizes people's psychological development from the initial self-interested motive to create the rules of property and to conform to them, through the approval of just acts and of the bare disposition to perform them, and finally to the "sense of honour and duty", the moral motive that eventually inspires a strict conformity to every honest act in a person of probity:

> Upon the whole, then, we are to consider this distinction betwixt justice and injustice, as having two different foundations, *viz.* that of *self-interest* . . . and that of *morality* . . . 'Tis the voluntary convention and artifice of men, which makes the first interest take place; and therefore those laws of justice are so far to be consider'd as *artificial*. After that interest is once establish'd and acknowledg'd, the sense of morality in the observance of these rules follows *naturally*, and of itself; tho' 'tis certain, that it is also augmented by a new *artifice*, and that the public instructions of politicians, and the private education of parents, contribute to the giving us a sense of honour and duty in the strict regulation of our actions with regard to the properties of others. (*T* 3.2.6.11 / 533–4)

Thus a *second* artifice is employed to give us a motive to adhere strictly to the rules of property.[11]

This change occurs within the constraints of Hume's system of the passions, which we can draw upon to reconstruct its progression. As we saw in Chapter 2, the motivating passions fall into two classes: those that arise from natural impulses or instincts, which are incapable of further analysis (*T* 2.3.9.8 / SBN 439), and those that arise from good and evil (pain and pleasure) either present or in prospect (*T* 2.3.9.2 / SBN 438). We saw that the instincts include "the desire of punishment to our enemies, and of happiness to our friends; hunger, lust, and a few other bodily appetites" (*T* 2.3.9.8 / SBN 439), and perhaps also "the love of life, and kindness to children" (*T* 2.3.3.8 / SBN 417). Certainly no motive to acts of loan repayment and the like is instinctual. The passions that arise from (immediate or predicted) good and evil include the direct passions of desire, aversion, hope, fear, joy, and sorrow, and the indirect passions of pride, humility, love, and hatred (and various blends and imitations of these). Pride and humility do not directly move us to act, but they enhance our desire for or aversion to the objects of which we are proud or ashamed (and our hope or fear of acquiring them, joy or sorrow in having them), and so increase the motivational power of these direct passions (*T* 2.3.9.4 / SBN 439). An actual or prospective pleasure or pain of any sort, including those of moral approval or disapproval, can, under the right circumstances, give rise to one of these

---

[11] Michael Gill, in an illuminating discussion contrasting Hume's progressive view of human nature with the static view of human motives held by his predecessors, comes to a parallel conclusion that in these passages Hume describes a psychological transformation. He and I have taken turns making such points in print, approaching them from different angles; see Cohon 1997*b* (on which this chapter is based), Gill 2000 and 2006: ch. 18.

motivating direct passions. So the prospect of sympathetic acquisition of the pleasure of others, or of moral self-approval, can generate a desire or hope of obtaining it. Now, the prospect of moral approval by itself is sometimes too weak to cause a desire in us sufficiently strong to move us to act in a way that will give us that pleasure, especially when there are personal costs to the behavior.[12] But desires, aversions, and other motivating passions can be strengthened in various ways. Two occurrent passions in the mind "readily mingle and unite", and "[t]he predominant passion converts [the inferior] into itself" (*T* 4.3.4.2 / SBN 420). We have seen that pride and humility in particular strengthen the motivating direct passions. Because they are approved or disapproved, actions conforming to or violating the rules of property are an independent source of pleasure and pain related to the agent by cause and effect; consequently, according to Hume's account of how pride and humility are generated, people will naturally be proud of their conforming actions and ashamed of their violations (*T* 2.1.5.8 / SBN 288; *T* 2.1.9.1 / SBN 303), which strengthens the desire to do the one and the aversion to doing the other. In addition, through sympathy the "opinion of another . . . will cause an idea of good or evil to have an influence upon us, which wou'd otherwise have been entirely neglected" (*T* 2.3.6.8 / SBN 427). Specifically in the context of property, in "contemplating the [unjust] actions of others" even toward victims who are distant from us, "we partake of [the victims'] uneasiness by *sympathy*", and so disapprove the actions. Because we are addicted to general rules, and because we also share by sympathy in the attitudes of others toward ourselves, we come to disapprove "our own actions" in violation of the rules of property as well (*T* 3.2.2.24 / SBN 499). Also, custom imparts a "tendency or inclination" toward an object (*T* 2.3.5.1 / SBN 422) and "bends [the spirits] more strongly to [habitual] action" (*T* 2.3.5.5 / SBN 424); while eloquence can stimulate the imagination, giving motivational force to ideas that otherwise "may have but a feeble influence either on the will or the affections" (*T* 2.3.6.7 / SBN 427). Politicians add their eloquence in "publick praise and blame", and parents add the force of "custom and education" (*T* 3.2.2.26 / SBN 500). ("Education" for Hume is often a process of rote drill and indoctrination.) So pride and humility, custom, and eloquence strengthen our desire for and hope of the approval, and aversion to and fear of the disapproval, we will feel in keeping or violating the rules of property, making these direct passions into sentiments that have a powerful influence on our behavior.

---

[12] Nidditch provides a relevant manuscript amendment just before the artifice of parents and politicians is discussed at *T* 3.2.2.24 / SBN 499 which suggests one reason why the new artifice is needed: "Thus *Self–interest* is the original motive to the Establishment of justice: but a Sympathy with *public* Interest is the Source of the *moral* Approbation, which attends that Virtue. This latter Principle of Sympathy is too weak to controul our Passions; but has sufficient Force to influence our Taste, and give us the Sentiments of Approbation or Blame" (Textual Notes, SBN 670). Mere sympathy does not itself control our behavior, so the moral approval or blame it gives us must be enhanced.

This alteration of the psychology of the young is paralleled in the indoctrination of young girls that occurs after the invention of the artificial virtues of feminine chastity and modesty, described later in 3.2. Indeed, at the start of *Treatise* 3.2.12 Hume says that he introduces the topic of feminine chastity and modesty in order further to explain and defend one aspect of his system of the artificial virtues as a whole, "the universal approbation or blame, which follows their observance or transgression, and which some may not think sufficiently explain'd from the general interests of society" (*T* 3.2.12.1 / SBN 570). The problem in human nature that requires an artificial solution in the invention of chastity and modesty is that rearing children requires the efforts of both parents, but parents must believe that certain children are their offspring before they will love them and work to provide for them. For purely biological reasons, women always know which children are their own, but men do not. Marriage makes it clear which children are the offspring of which man, provided husbands can be confident that their wives' children are their own; for this, though, husbands must be extremely confident that their wives are perfectly faithful. How can this be arranged? Sexual temptation, like the temptation to take the property of others, can be very difficult to resist. Informal penalties are available in the form of "bad fame", and to this end people "attach a peculiar degree of shame" to women's unchaste acts and "bestow proportionable praises" on chastity, and this is influential; but even this is not sufficient to insure the exceptionless chastity of wives. Those persons who have an interest in the chastity of women of course disapprove any violation of conjugal duty, and others "are carried along with the stream", including, presumably, women and girls themselves. And then, "[e]ducation takes possession of the ductile minds of the fair sex in their infancy." It takes what begins as young girls' mere disapproval of actions that contravene a socially useful practice, and strengthens that feeling of uneasiness to make it a motivating passion: a deep-seated "backwardness and dread" at the prospect of a sexual liaison (*T* 3.2.12.5 / SBN 572) and a tendency (shared with everyone else) to be shocked by any feminine "lewdness". Although Hume gives little description of this feeling, the modest woman's "repugnance to all expressions, and postures, and liberties, that have an immediate relation to that enjoyment" (ibid.) seems to involve finding (improper, or perhaps all) sexual advances demeaning and regarding (non-marital) sex as shameful. This feeling is strong enough that the very great temptations to pleasure cannot normally overcome it, and it persists even past the childbearing years, when the connection to social utility is lost. Indeed, it is directed toward each and every unchaste act, without exception, regardless of the act's social utility or risk to reputation. This psychological change is necessary if society is to reap the hoped-for rewards, Hume seems to think. If wives merely regard extramarital affairs as generally socially harmful, this attitude will not give their husbands sufficient confidence of paternity. For that, the wife must have a stable character trait, preferably in the form of a visceral motivating attitude. Such a thing cannot evaporate once the woman passes childbearing age. Similarly with honesty: it will not be enough for the people to think that violation of the rules of property is generally socially harmful. For of course it will not be so in every instance, and even when it is, it may sometimes not seem so because its ill effects are so indirect. To secure the stability of our social arrangements and the rewards to be had therefrom, we need people who are strict and scrupulous in following the rules of property whether or not they see the social utility of doing so on each occasion, and even in the face of personal disadvantage. So we need a character trait—for Hume a separate feeling or disposition to feel—that governs action consistently and without significant agitation in the soul, in part as the result of custom (*T* 2.3.4.1 / SBN 418–19). This is why parents teach their children "to regard the observance of those rules, by which society is maintain'd, as worthy and honourable, and their violation as base and infamous. By this means the sentiments of honour may take root in their tender minds, and acquire such firmness and solidity, that they may fall little short of those principles, which are the most essential to our natures, and the most deeply radicated in our internal constitution" (*T* 3.2.2.26 / SBN 500–1). (Note the similarity to the shaping of the "ductile minds of the fair sex in their infancy.") This early manipulation of us, plus the subsequent powerful concern we develop for our reputation, enables each person to "fix an inviolable law to himself, never, by any temptation, to be induc'd to violate those principles, which are essential to a man of probity and honor" (*T* 3.2.2.27 / SBN 501). It provides a *motive* to perform each and every honest act, and to refrain from each and every dishonest one.[13]

E. Sophistry: The Natural Ideas of Virtue Meet the Actual Workings of Moral Sentiment

If this is the process that generates the motive characteristic of a person of probity and honor, then it is not a natural motive, in the sense of being non-moral. It is, instead, a moral sentiment, strengthened to become a motive. Furthermore, artifice has some hand in fashioning it, although artifice can only work on naturally arising materials (*T* 3.2.2.25 / SBN 500). However, in spite of these facts, we continue to accept and not question the "undoubted maxim" that there is a non-moral motive of each type of virtuous action—hence the circularity problem. But it is a problem in our concepts, not in the world. So long as the moral sentiment approves the motive of honest action, whatever that motive is (whether moral or non-moral), honesty is in fact a virtue: it is a quality of mind that elicits approval from the common point of view. If we grant that not only non-moral motives can win approval, but also moral motives and (at an early stage) even mere actions conforming to socially necessary practices, then the

---

[13] While no general account is offered here of how the moral sentiment provides motives, we have now seen one way in which it does so within the context of the artificial virtues.

circle disappears. (Since we have not actually granted this in our ordinary moral thinking, however, common sense retains the circle.)

This analysis requires that Hume relax his claim (2) that for every virtue there is a non-moral motive that we approve and that imparts moral merit to the actions it motivates. Or rather, on this reading it is not Hume's considered view that this claim is universal; he restricts it to the natural virtues, and thinks that when it comes to the artificial virtues, we expect (2) to hold, but it does not. On his view the circle about the motive of honesty is an effect of our conjoining our pre-reflective concept of a virtue with the psychological facts. Now if we are right that in his own voice Hume espouses only this weaker claim, this is downplayed in the text. But the signs are there. Hume draws attention to what he calls "our ideas of vice and virtue" which mirror "the natural, and usual force" of our passions (*T* 3.2.2.8 / SBN 488), or again "our common measures of duty" which follow the "common and natural course of our passions" (*T* 3.2.1.18 / SBN 484), especially their partiality. For example, in the absence of conventions of property we could not regard the taking of material goods for ourselves or our loved ones as immoral, because "our natural uncultivated ideas of morality, instead of providing a remedy for the partiality of our affections, do rather conform themselves to that partiality, and give it an additional force and influence" (*T* 3.2.2.8 / SBN 489). So we begin by thinking of all virtue as natural virtue. After the artifices are in place, it seems, we do not update our understanding of virtue. "[T]he vulgar definition of justice" assumes there is such a thing as ownership independent of the virtue of honesty (*T* 3.2.6.2 / SBN 526–7). It is the supposition that ownership is natural that leads us to a circular definition of justice or honesty, a sophistry. "This deceitful method of reasoning is a plain proof, that there are contain'd in the subject some obscurities and difficulties, which we are not able to surmount, and which we desire to evade by this artifice" (*T* 3.2.6.5 / SBN 528). The presence of circular thinking shows that there is an error, a misconception which we attempt to paper over.[14]

Hume uses the word 'artifice' and its cognates in various ways in the *Treatise*. Sometimes it has no connotations of disguise or misrepresentation

---

[14] This passage may identify a circle distinct from the one which Hume introduces at *T* 3.2.1.17 (SBN 483), but there is an interpretation on which he is talking about the same or nearly the same circle. The "vulgar definition of justice [is] . . . *a constant and perpetual will of giving every one his due*" (*T* 3.2.6.2 / SBN 526). We must read "a constant and perpetual will of giving every one his due" as the motivational disposition that is definitive of the virtue of honesty. The circle referred to at *T* 3.2.6.5 (SBN 528) is then this: the character trait of honesty is a motivational disposition to give to everyone his property, and property is (defined as) what someone who is honest is motivated to give to everyone. From this it follows that the motive of honest action is the motive to give to everyone what the motive of honest action moves an agent to give to everyone. This becomes the motivational circle of *T* 3.2.1.17 (SBN 483) if we substitute "do" for "give to everyone": the motive of honest action is the motive to do what the motive of honest action moves an agent to do.

(e.g., *T* 1.3.1.3 / SBN 70). But in places it indicates something counterfeit or unreal, a connotation that the term already could have in Hume's day.[15] Thus, he uses 'artifice' for our misrepresentations of our own characters to ourselves and others (*T* 1.4.3.1 / SBN 219), and for what mathematicians and philosophers do when they misrepresent their absurd ideas as rational ones that are purely intellectual and very obscure (*T* 1.3.1.7 / SBN 72). At 1.4.6 he uses 'artifice' to indicate a device we employ to preserve the pretense or illusion that one of our concepts is instantiated when it does not and cannot fit reality (we apply the concept of one and the same object over time—the same ship—when what is really present is a series of related objects (*T* 1.4.6.11 / SBN 257)). He seems to draw on this connotation in his discussion of the artificiality of material honesty. Our artifice not only creates the practice and its moral motive, but it preserves for us the illusion that our ordinary concept of a virtue is instantiated where it is not and cannot be. Our human social intervention in the affections is concealed.

When Hume comes to discuss fidelity to promises, he supposes that we think of this too as a natural virtue; and that thought leads us not only to an analogous definitional circle about fidelity but to an additional problem of having to "feign" a "peculiar act of the mind" (*T* 3.2.5.1–6 / SBN 516–19; *T* 3.2.5.12 / SBN 523), as we will see in the next chapter. Fortunately, the natural conception of vice and virtue—this bit of commonsense proto-theory that gives rise to the circle—is not in fact accurate, and can be ignored in practice. Once we invent rules of property, we can in fact develop a new motive, a moral one, that is impartial and that elicits our approval. This approval is sufficient to make the having of this motive a virtue on what Hume takes to be the right conception of virtue, which differs slightly from the commonsensical conception with which we are fitted at the outset. So there is no impossibility in having the actual, artificial virtue. The natural virtues have non-moral motives which generate approval, just as we expect from our acceptance of claim (2). The artificial virtues do not; they depend upon the sense of virtue or the sense of duty, which in them is generated in a different way. For the artificial virtues, we do not need a non-moral motive to identify the object of approval as we do for the natural virtues. Socially beneficial conventions specify types of actions by their outward form, and our approval is then directed toward these. If all goes well, this approval is then strengthened to become a motivating sentiment. So our approval of honest action, instead of depending upon the motive of honest action, ultimately provides it.

Thus for Hume, the honest *person* is someone whose approval of honesty has been both strengthened to become a motivating sentiment and directed toward each and every act required by the rules of property. Those who have such a

---

[15] *The Compact Edition of the Oxford English Dictionary*, i (Oxford: Oxford University Press, 1971, repr. 1979), 'artifice,' 'artificial'.

sentiment evoke our approval of their character. The having of this motive of honest action—the motive of duty—is the virtue of honesty. Mere rule-following is not enough for this virtue; one needs morally motivated rule-following.

One may wonder whether philosophical reflection is likely to undermine this virtue. From the point of view of psychology, Hume seems to think that the distaste for theft and fraud (the sense of honor) is too thoroughly ingrained to be eroded by the knowledge that our honesty is only a contrivance to serve society, just as the modest woman's "backwardness and dread" is too much a part of her to disappear in old age. It may seem, however, that even if the motivating feelings are permanent, and intrinsically aim at the pleasures of self-approval rather than at the goal of the social good, reflection shows us that the *justification* for these feelings lies solely in the good to society, and that this good does not in fact depend upon every individual act of honesty. In cases where no threat to society is at hand from an act of fraud, for example, while the feeling of disapproval remains, it may on reflection strike the philosopher as groundless, and so the disposition to exceptionless honesty may seem unjustified.[16]

Whether this is a real difficulty for Hume depends upon what he takes to be the basis of normativity or justification. One possibility is that he follows Hutcheson in reducing all justifying reasons to considerations that evoke approval:

When we ask the reason of an action, we sometimes mean, 'What truth shows a quality in the action, exciting the agent to do it?' . . . Sometimes for a reason of actions we show the truth expressing a quality, engaging our approbation. . . . The former sort of reasons we will call exciting, and the latter justifying. Now we shall find that . . . the justifying [reasons] presuppose a moral sense.   (Hutcheson 1971: ii. 215–16)

On this view there is no justification of moral judgment to be found outside human sentiments—not even in the public good. Approval and disapproval *are* our justifications, and our only justifications. This remains so even if the approval and disapproval of some actions is socially manufactured, originally for the purpose of serving the public good, as some of it is for Hume, though not for Hutcheson. The thought that our approval of some trait is unjustified because the trait lacks a certain connection with public good is then an incoherent one. Whether or not this is a satisfactory general theory of justification, if this is Hume's theory (which is a matter for debate), it leaves our approval of honest action no less justified than our approval of anything else.

Alternatively, we may adopt a less extreme reading of Hume on justification. An approved disposition and its resulting actions are justified, and our approval of them is warranted, according to this new view, provided the disposition has some systematic causal connection to the social good, although that connection need not be a direct or simple one. Thus approval of benevolence is warranted by

---

[16] An objection of this type is made by Christine Korsgaard (1996: 86–7) in her discussion of the knavish lawyer.

the tendency of that character trait to cause pleasure directly; approval of honesty is warranted by its tendency to cause pleasure obliquely (through its role in a practice); but approval of fasting, penance, and mortification is not warranted because these produce no good at all (*EPM* 9.3 / SBN 270), either individually or as needed features of any institution. If this is the Humean view of justification, there are no reasons, on reflection, to regard our disapproval of a seemingly (or really) harmless act of fraud as ungrounded. The disapproval of one dishonest act is sufficiently warranted by the oblique connection between the disposition to perform acts of this kind and social harm. Hume may be wrong, though, about whether approval of feminine chastity and modesty is similarly warranted by a suitable connection of these dispositions to the social good through the practice they make possible. The general issue of whether Hume could consistently give such an account of the justification of our moral approvals and disapprovals will be considered in Chapter 9.

As an aside, we can see how the less extreme view of justification, unlike the Hutchesonian one, might reveal that Hume is wrong about female chastity and modesty in his own terms. That justification of our approval of an artificial trait turns on its having a suitable connection to the social good. And empirical investigation might consequently show that both the modest woman's sexual reticence and people's approval of it are unjustified. Whether these dispositions actually are necessary for the persistence of the institution of parental marriage and father support of children, whether this institution really is indispensable for successful child-rearing, and whether the various features of feminine modesty that Hume enumerates really serve the social good in any way or are instead, perhaps, mere instruments of harmful male power, are empirical questions open to answers different from Hume's but consistent with his underlying theory. Hume is of course right that children must be provided for, but he may be wrong about how this can be done effectively. He may also be wrong to think that a man is likely to love only his own biological offspring. He is surely wrong to think that in the context of marriage and father support of known children, a loose standard for men poses no significant threat to the well-being of children. (The children whom men father with a few courtesans or prostitutes will also need, and will not receive, support.) If marriage is to be the artifice with which to solve the child-rearing problem inherent in the human condition, Hume might more consistently argue for chastity and modesty of both sexes. Other arrangements besides parental marriage and father support are also possible and might work adequately. Then again, technological innovations such as contraception and paternity testing might enlist fathers' support yet obviate the need for anyone's chastity or modesty, though the loss of these traits might introduce other practical difficulties. It is a matter for empirical investigation which psychological dispositions would be needed successfully to implement different arrangements, and how readily human beings can be molded to acquire them.

F. A Different Role for Redirected Interest?

The role of redirected greed or interest in this story, then, is largely preliminary. It enables us to create the convention of property and to keep it going for a while. And it gives parents and leaders one motive (among others) to magnify the moral sentiments of their charges into a distinct motive to do all conforming acts, which Hume sometimes calls the sentiment of honor. But redirected interest itself need not be a persisting motive of honest action, and it is not that in virtue of which we approve honest people and so classify them as virtuous.

Some readers of Hume think that he is doing something simpler and more straightforward. There *is* a non-moral motive of honest action, they claim: namely, enlightened or redirected interest. It is not a natural motive in one sense, for it is somewhat artificial; but it is natural in the sense of non-moral.[17] It is a non-moral, artificial motive. What is meant may be the specific passion of greed or avidity (the "love of gain"), but enlightened or reoriented to a new means. Or it may be general self-interest, the appetite to good and aversion to evil (pleasure and pain) as such, that is redirected.[18] Now, self-interest and greed are both natural rather than artificial motives, but adherence to rules of property is not their natural means of fulfillment. Without the invention of a practice of ownership, these motives would cause us to take whatever we could get. Only in the context of the artifice of property can they be directed to this different activity of conforming to the rules of property, for only in that context will such actions preserve society, which serves our interests. We then come to feel approval for this character trait of redirected interest, this special motive, since it serves to preserve society, which is so beneficial to all. Consequently, on this interpretation, redirected interest is a virtue, the virtue of honesty.[19]

There are two main difficulties with this interpretation. First, it identifies the virtue of honesty with the virtue of prudence as it takes shape in a social context, a bad move for a virtue theorist and a hard one to find in Hume. Hume the virtue theorist has things to say about the natural ability or natural virtue of prudence, the calm and informed pursuit of one's long-term interest (*T* 3.3.4.5 / SBN 610),

---

[17] Again, recall the three distinctions: natural versus artificial, natural (i.e, non-moral) versus moral, and natural versus civil. (The third does not concern us here.)

[18] Baier (1991: 220–1) is right that it is not self-interest in general that threatens the destruction of society, but rather "avidity" or "the interested affection"—i.e., material greed specifically. However, self-interest in general could well motivate compliance with the society-preserving rules of property, since the preservation of society not only gratifies people's greed but also fulfills desires and needs for security, mutual assistance, and companionship.

[19] Interpretations along these lines were proposed by Sayre-McCord in his comments on my "Why Are Some Virtues Artificial?", an address to the Hume Society in Chicago, April 1993, and by Don Garrett, in personal communication. Gauthier (1992) attributes this position to the Hume of the *Treatise*; I discuss his more complex interpretation briefly below, and at greater length in the next chapter in connection with the virtue of fidelity to promises.

but he shows no signs of identifying honesty with prudence, or with prudence in a certain context. If conformity to the rules of property in a social life serves my interest, then my prudence will move me to conform, just as it moves me to follow hygienic practices if I live in close proximity to other people. But the person who is thus prudent under social conditions does not fit the picture Hume draws of the "man of probity and honour". Hume is careful to distinguish honesty from benevolence, pointing out that if all we had was benevolence, "a man wou'd not be oblig'd to leave others in the possession of more than he is oblig'd [by benevolence] to give them" (*T* 3.2.1.14 / SBN 482). It seems that had he realized it was necessary, Hume would have distinguished honesty from prudence as well. Hume would not think it psychologically realistic to say that ordinary honest acts really are motivated by the desire to preserve society for my own good. If the public good is too remote to move me to repay a loan (*T* 3.2.1.11 / SBN 481), surely the preservation of society is as well. And there is no textual evidence that Hume thinks that our approval of the virtue of honesty or justice is aroused by the motivating sentiment of interest. Furthermore, that would be an implausible claim to make. We do not judge a person honest because of her lively and realistic sense of self-interest, and a reasonable virtue theorist is quite unlikely to claim that we do.

Secondly, as Hume himself notes both in the *Treatise* and in the second *Enquiry*, individual honest actions do not always serve our interests. They do not even always help to preserve society. In the *Treatise* Hume mentions returning a fortune to a seditious bigot (*T* 3.2.2.22 / SBN 497), an honest action that might well *reduce* social stability. In the moral *Enquiry* he introduces the sensible knave, who realizes that he stands to profit from dishonest actions that happen not to harm the social fabric, since not all violations of the rules of property or contract do in fact threaten to bring society down. If redirected self-interest is still self-interest (or redirected greed is still greed), and it moves us to conform to the rules of property in order to preserve society, then it seems that it will fail us in those cases where we realize that such conformity does not in fact help to preserve society (repaying the debt to the seditious bigot), or where we see that violation would not in the least endanger society (reneging on the secret loan at *Treatise* 3.2.1.11 / SBN 481, and acting as a sensible knave). Both general self-interest and the specific passion of greed are goal-directed motives, and they are motives founded on pleasure and pain. In Chapter 2 we saw how these work in Hume's psychology: one has the expectation of pain or pleasure from a certain object, which triggers desire or aversion for that object (or some other one of the direct passions); in the presence of beliefs about cause and effect, one consequently comes to desire or be averse to the object's causes. When we are inclined to act because we believe that a certain object will yield pleasure or allow us to avoid pain, once we see that this causal belief is false, "our passions yield to our reason without any opposition" (*T* 2.3.3.7 / SBN 416), and we are no longer inclined to act. Thus, any time we see that conformity to the rules of property is not needed to preserve society (and is personally costly) or does not in any way help to preserve it—any time we see that the causal belief is false—we will not be moved by interest to conform to the rules of property. Thus, redirected interest does not yield the kind of reliable conformity to the rules of property that we would expect of an honest person.

This has led some interpreters to attribute to Hume a "noble lie" or "error theory" of honesty. It has two main versions. In one, redirected interest is indeed the non-moral motive of honest action, and we simply don't know that our requisite causal belief is sometimes false. We believe that every act in conformity with the rules of ownership contributes to the preservation of society and so is beneficial to the agent. Thus redirected interest is an example of a passion founded on a false judgment (of the sort Hume discusses in general at T 2.3.3.7 / SBN 416), but a salutary false judgment that is perpetuated by parents and politicians in the form of a noble lie.[20]

In the other version, we do not find within ourselves any non-moral motive to honest action which we approve, either because we see all the exceptions and loopholes, so that redirected interest does not reliably generate honest actions in us, or because redirected interest is not a motive we approve. But we approve people who are disposed *always* to follow the rules of property, since such people are of great social benefit, and we suppose that such people actually are actuated by some non-moral motive to behave this way, even though we realize that we ourselves are not. We thus imagine a nonexistent or (in fact) ineffectual non-moral motive to be an obligatory motive, one we hate ourselves for lacking. And in so hating ourselves, we come to have a motive of *duty* to follow the rules of property on all occasions, either in the hopes of acquiring the (in fact unavailable) motive or in the hopes of concealing from ourselves our lack of it (T 3.2.1.8 / SBN 479).[21] The error pointed out in this type of error theory is our belief that there is a non-moral motive of honest action that we ought to have. Because this is an error, we are also in error to believe claim (1), that honesty is a virtue. So on this interpretation, Hume does not think that honesty is really a virtue at all, although he does not draw attention to his skeptical conclusion.

An intermediate position between these two versions says that in the *Treatise* Hume himself is taken in by the "noble lie" that compliance always preserves society and so in every case serves our (redirected) interest; *he* actually fails to

---

[20] This is the position of Baron in an important article (2001[1982]).

[21] The view of Haakonssen (1981: ch. 2, esp. part 8) is that interest is not a morally approved motive, and so we imagine another motive, the willing of an obligation, which we hate ourselves for lacking. Gauthier (1992) proposes that "the initial self-interested motive fails to survive critical reflection" (p. 420), but our approval of conformity to the rules of property persists, so we then imagine another non-moral motive, the willing of an obligation. Both writers apply this analysis to the virtue of fidelity to promises as well as to honesty. The idea that we "feign" a special motive, the willing of an obligation, comes from Hume's discussion of promising in *Treatise* 3.2.5.

notice that at times it does not. But in the moral *Enquiry* he realizes, with the introduction of the sensible knave, that compliance is not invariably necessary to preserve society, and so that redirected interest is not a reliable motive of compliance. Thus Hume sees in the end that there is no reliable non-moral motive; and hence all Hume can give us is the error theory that we falsely believe in a nonexistent non-moral motive. This is the interpretation of David Gauthier (1992). He points out that this leaves Hume with a defective view. Once we realize that redirected interest cannot move informed people to strict, constant compliance, we will cease to approve redirected interest. But there is no other non-moral motive of reliable compliance of which we can approve instead. Since, according to claim (2), which Gauthier construes as part of Hume's considered view, there must be a non-moral motive first if moral approval is to take hold, we will not be able to approve, and so we will be left without any *moral* motive for compliance either.

We return to Gauthier's interpretation in the next chapter, since there is more to say about it in connection with fidelity to promises. Here I note one further point of departure from this article. Gauthier also thinks that on Hume's account we cannot approve of the motive of honesty in the end, whatever that motive may be, because honest actions, while they benefit others, harm oneself. But this misunderstands the way moral approval works in Hume. Hume can certainly account for our approval of things that are a net loss to ourselves. In occupying the common point of view we take account of the responses of all persons affected by the trait, and so come to approve of what generates more pleasure than pain on the whole. In the case of honesty, in coming to feel moral approval or disapproval we imaginatively take the viewpoint of the whole of society. The impact of the trait on ourselves is encompassed in that already. So we will approve, even though we may not be moved, since mere approval is often weaker than interest in generating action. (On my interpretation, by contrast, we will also be moved, but for reasons not consonant with Gauthier's interpretation.)

These interpretations have some central points in common. They take (2), the "undoubted maxim" requiring a non-moral motive of every virtuous type of action, quite literally, as Hume's considered view, a claim I reject in my interpretation. The simple redirected-interest theories do not take literally Hume's claim (3) that there is *no* non-moral motive for honesty; they think he means that there is no non-artificial non-moral motive of honesty, but there *is* a non-moral motive—an artificial one. The noble lie and error theories grant (3) but deny that it is known to ordinary moral consciousness. Consequently, they treat (1), that honesty is a virtue, as something that common sense believes but Hume himself is committed to rejecting. And all these readings interpret the formation of the convention and the creation of an incentive to compliance as a process with a single stage, rather than the two stages that I have identified (one at which redirected interest suffices, and a later stage at which it does not and a new motive comes into being). Thus, since redirected interest surely *is* the operative motive when the rules of property are first in place, these interpreters find in redirected interest the only possible virtue-imparting motive of honest action. (So if it proves inadequate, there is no other motive to fall back upon.) But the result is that they attribute to Hume an account of the virtue of honesty that is implausible, both psychologically and from the point of view of virtue ethics, and in some versions an account that fails in its own terms. These interpretations also overlook an important bit of text: Hume's first response to the sensible knave. The knave suggests that "he conducts himself with the most wisdom, who observes the general rule [that honesty is the best policy], and takes advantage of all the exceptions". Hume first says:

[I]f a man think that this reasoning much requires an answer, it would be a little difficult to find any which will to him appear satisfactory and convincing. If his heart rebel not against such pernicious maxims, if he feel no reluctance to the thoughts of villainy or baseness, he has indeed lost a considerable motive to virtue. . . . But in all ingenuous natures, the antipathy to treachery and roguery is too strong to be counterbalanced by any views of profit or pecuniary advantage.   (*EPM* 9.23 / SBN 283)[22]

Here Hume appeals to the moral motive, the deeply ingrained "antipathy to treachery and roguery", for which he apparently sees no adequate substitute. The sense of duty is the typical motive to honest action.

On the reading offered here, redirected interest plays a smaller role than in the above interpretations. Redirected interest is the motive that gets the convention started and preserves and stabilizes it in a small subsistence-level community. But it is not the motive that makes honesty a virtue. The motive that makes honesty a virtue is a moral motive, approval of conforming acts and disapproval of violations, which has been strengthened and reinforced by habituation and association with pride and shame so as to become a motivating sentiment. Since it is not a form of greed or self-interest (or concern for others, for that matter), it can offer an opposing incentive in the face of the temptation to violate the rules for one's own profit or even for society's good. The motive will not collapse in those cases where we realize that redirected interest is not served by compliance. The person who complies with the rules even in the face of this realization is the truly meritorious person, the person with the virtue of honesty. This rings true to the virtue of honesty as we find it.

This may explain why in some places Hume seems to say that conformity to the rules of property in a cooperative community can be *genuinely* disadvantageous to the individual, and even disadvantageous or at least without advantage to the community (*T* 3.2.1.11 / SBN 481; *T* 3.2.1.13 / SBN 482; *T* 3.2.2.22 / SBN 497 ("the public is a real sufferer")), while in other places he seems to think

---

[22] Of course, Hume goes on to describe other unattractive features of the life of a sensible knave.

that conformity only *seems* disadvantageous because the person loses sight of the (net) long-term advantages (*T* 3.2.2.22 / SBN 497–8; *T* 3.2.2.23 / SBN 499; *T* 3.2.7.3 / SBN 535). Hume is not very concerned about whether the individual is right to think that dishonesty is sometimes profitable, since on his view people sometimes *will* think so, rightly or not, and his focus is on the behavioral consequences of their thinking so. Since they will, we cannot rely solely on the motive of interest to guarantee widespread conformity to the rules of property; but fortunately, another motive can be devised that is immune to this weakness.

Stephen Darwall agrees with Gauthier that in the *Treatise* Hume thinks that compliance with the rules of property is in fact in the (long-term) interest of every agent on every occasion, while in later writings he recognizes that on occasion it is contrary to that interest. For Darwall, however, Hume's ultimate position is no error theory. Instead, on his reading the motivating disposition which constitutes the virtue of honesty is the acceptance of the rules of property as authoritative in guiding one's actions, a "disposition to engage in a form of practical reasoning substantially different from any countenanced by [Hume's] official theory of the will".[23] The idea that an honest person engages in a form of practical reasoning and has an incentive to act which is not goal-directed in the way in which Hume thinks all motivating passions are is appealing on its own. But since there is no room for such a phenomenon in Hume's theory, I read him not as contradicting his hedonism and general theory of the will and motivating passions (which my account preserves), but instead as waiving a less fundamental requirement of his science of human nature, his requirement of a non-moral motive as the sole primary ground of approval.

We have seen how Hume's account of the virtue of honesty (equity, probity) construes it as a fabricated quality of mind, one that remedies an inherent disability in human nature, and so makes possible a kind of social life for which we are otherwise suited by nature but from which we are initially held back by natural obstacles. We discover that this trait is the product of artifice by finding that the contrary assumption saddles us with a sophistry. The artifice has been hidden from us, but it is all to the good. However, this fabrication of a motive to conform scrupulously to rules for the acquisition and transfer of material goods does not achieve much by itself. "The invention of the law of nature", as Hume ironically labels this artifice, "concerning the stability of possession, has . . . render'd men tolerable to each other; that of the transference of property and possession by consent has begun to render them mutually advantageous: But still these laws, however strictly observ'd, are not sufficient to render them so serviceable to each other, as by nature they are fitted to become" (*T* 3.2.5.8 / SBN 520). A further fabrication is needed, and with it we encounter further difficulties.

---

[23] Darwall 1995: ch. 10; the quote is from p. 317.

7

Fidelity to Promises and the Peculiar Act
of the Mind

I. HUME'S TWO CLAIMS ABOUT FIDELITY
TO PROMISES

Promising—with its more formal manifestation, contract—is a vital part of social life. Most forms of long-term cooperation, including commerce, depend in some way on the fact that people can bind themselves to others now to perform actions later. One philosophically intriguing question about promises is how this self-binding is possible. Furthermore, there is a special character trait associated with the honoring of promises that calls out for analysis. Intuitively speaking, being a person of your word, someone who is trustworthy about promises, is an admirable trait, one we inculcate in our children and long for in our public figures—a virtue.

In *Treatise* 3.2.5 Hume attempts to analyze and explain the virtue of fidelity (being a person of one's word), and also to give an account of how promising generates obligation. He seeks an explanation of the character trait as we find it in experience. Of course, it is to be an analysis in terms of the moral theory that he has developed up to this point; so fidelity to promises is to be treated as a quality of mind that evokes approval when considered from the common point of view; and part of Hume's task is to explain the source of this approval. In the course of his explanation of fidelity, Hume makes two very puzzling claims. In this chapter I offer an interpretation of Hume's account of fidelity that makes good sense of these claims. As a coda I offer a few cautious conclusions about virtue and duty based on Hume's insights.

What Hume says about fidelity to promises is laconic, and interpreters have struggled to make sense of it. We need a bit of background to set out the two specific puzzling claims on which we shall focus.

The first claim is that a particular conception of the virtue of fidelity to promises is vulnerable to a *reductio ad absurdum*. The vulnerable view is the view that fidelity is a natural virtue, and the obligation of promises a natural duty, as distinct from an artificial one. We have already seen that for Hume some virtues, and the moral obligations associated with them, depend for their existence upon the prior presence of a special social custom or convention and could not occur without it. Hume argues that fidelity is one of these. The conception of fidelity that he attacks, then, is that fidelity is a natural—that is, a non-conventional—virtue. On that view the virtue of fidelity and the phenomenon of promise-based obligation could occur even in the absence of any jointly made social rules. What is puzzling is Hume's diagnosis of what is wrong with non-conventionalism about fidelity. He does think that non-conventionalism is committed to a vicious definitional circle regarding motives to fulfill promises, just as non-conventionalism about honesty was committed to such a circle regarding motives to refrain from theft. But he also claims that non-conventionalists are committed to supposing that there is a "peculiar act of the mind" involved in promising—specifically, as it turns out, an act of *willing to be obligated*—that creates obligation when each promise is made, and that serves as the motive of virtue-manifesting compliance with the promise. The act in question, Hume argues, is an impossible one. Therefore, he concludes, non-conventionalism about fidelity to promises is false. Thus he says:

> If anyone dissent from this [that fidelity is no natural virtue], he must give a regular proof of these two propositions, viz. *that there is a peculiar act of the mind, annext to promises;* and *that consequent to this act of the mind, there arises an inclination to perform, distinct from a sense of duty.* I presume, that it is impossible to prove either of these two points; and therefore I venture to conclude, that promises are human inventions, founded on the necessities and interests of society. (*T* 3.2.5.7 / SBN 519)

We have already seen that (and why) Hume thinks that the natural conception of a virtue requires a "motive to perform, distinct from the sense of duty". If the virtue were simply a refined version of a naturally occurring human sentiment, then before moral approval could occur, there would need to be some non-moral motivating sentiment present to serve as the object of our approval. As we saw in the last chapter, if there is no such non-moral motive, this assumption about natural virtue results in a vicious definitional circle. Hume does not explain, however, why the non-conventionalist about fidelity must rely on a special act of the mind to support his position. This appears to be something unique to the particular virtue of fidelity that does not arise from non-conventionalism about the other artificial virtues.

The second claim we will discuss is even more cryptic. Hume says that even though the obligation of promises and the virtue of fidelity in fact depend upon social convention, and there *is* no peculiar act of the mind, we nonetheless pretend or imagine that whenever someone promises she wills a new obligation into existence. Our commonsense thought about promising "feigns" the occurrence of the peculiar act of the mind, and apparently can't avoid doing so. Thus he says:

> After [the invention of promises] a sentiment of morals concurs with interest, and becomes a new obligation upon mankind. . . . The difficulties, that occur to us, in supposing a

moral obligation to attend promises, we either surmount or elude. . . . Here, therefore, we *feign* a new act of the mind, which we call the *willing* an obligation; and on this we suppose the morality to depend.   (*T* 3.2.5.12 / SBN 523)

Many who explicate Hume's theory of the artificial virtues do not touch on these two claims about the peculiar mental act.[1] Commentators who do try to account for them have so far been able to do so only by postulating various sorts of errors or weaknesses in Hume's theory. The hope of the present chapter is to do better on Hume's behalf.

First I will explain why Hume thinks that the non-conventionalist about promises is committed to the impossible mental act of willing to be obligated, and also elucidate how Hume constructs his *reductio* of that supposition. I will argue that Hume has before his mind two general questions about promises: (1) What is the virtuous motive at work when a faithful person keeps a promise? And (2) How do we obligate ourselves merely by speaking? Hume determines that only certain answers to these questions are compatible with our experience of this virtue. If we start with those answers that are compatible with experience, combine them with Hume's general theory about virtue and duty and with his doctrine of the motivating passions, and suppose the absence of social convention, the peculiar mental act view more or less follows. So Hume has fairly good reasons to think that a non-conventionalist who stays close to the phenomena must postulate a special mental act associated with each promise. I will also explain why Hume thinks that even though non-conventionalism is false and conventionalism is true, we (all) still accept a fiction that there is such a peculiar act of the mind involved in promising. We do this, if the present interpretation of Hume is right, because at some level we are all non-conventionalists: our ordinary intuitions about virtue and vice are compatible only with non-conventionalism, not with conventionalism. We expect all virtues to have the same structure as benevolence and friendship, which are non-conventional, and we accept a fiction in order to make fidelity look as if it has this structure as well.

II. THE TWO QUESTIONS ABOUT PROMISES

At the outset I noted two interesting broad questions about promises, questions of general philosophical interest apart from Hume's writings. Since I shall argue that these are the questions that lie behind and animate Hume's analysis of fidelity, let me elaborate on them a little.

One is a special question that arises for a moral theory focusing on the virtues and vices, whether Hume's or another. Its general features will be familiar from

---

[1] e.g., there is no discussion of the peculiar act of mind in the otherwise illuminating account of Hume's theory of promise given by Baier (1991: ch. 10). I have learned a great deal, however, from Baier's detailed and perceptive interpretation.

the previous chapter, but in explaining how it arises for fidelity, we can also place it in a broader philosophical context. Fidelity to promises, or trustworthiness with respect to one's word, is a character trait we recognize as a virtue. For almost any virtue theorist, a character trait is (at least) a fairly settled disposition to have certain feelings and desires which induce one to act in characteristic ways in a range of circumstances. It is not just a behavioral disposition; it is an emotional and volitional one as well. (For some, though not for Hume, it also involves certain cognitions or dispositions to notice facts.) To behave virtuous*ly* (in a virtuous manner), one's action must be brought about by one or more of these suitable feelings or desires. This is because to act virtuously or well, it is not enough to do the right thing; one must do it for the right reasons. I don't manifest my benevolence in helping a homeless person if I help her only out of the desire to improve my reputation. What I do is right, but not benevolent. An action that manifests the virtue of benevolence is brought about, at least in part, by concern for the other person's welfare. That is the right reason. Now, what is the right reason for keeping a promise? What leads a trustworthy person, a person of his word, to fulfill a promise when he does so in a way that manifests his virtue? It should presumably be whichever feelings or desires (or thoughts or cognitions, according to some virtue ethicists) comprise this good character trait. But the appropriate—the virtuous—motive for keeping a promise is not self-interest. If I keep my promise only out of self-interest, I may manifest the virtue of prudence, but not of trustworthiness. A trustworthy person will keep her promise even when it is contrary to her interest; that is often the point of exacting a promise from her in the first place. But interestingly enough, the characteristic, virtuous motive for keeping a promise is also not concern for the other person's welfare. A trustworthy person will of course keep promises made to those she hopes to help. But she will also keep promises to people she has no reason to care about at all, and to those who receive little benefit or even receive harm from her fulfillment of her promise. She will be disposed to fulfill contracts with mortgage banks and credit card companies, though she has no reason to be concerned for their well-being, or, in many cases, to fear that her failure to comply would do them significant harm. She will be inclined to fulfill her promise to repay a large loan to Hume's "profligate debauchee" (*T* 3.2.1.13 / SBN 482), who will only use the money to harm himself. Nor is it a manifestation of trustworthiness about promises to fulfill them out of public spirit. If I keep my promise solely out of public spirit—because it will help my family, my community, or my country—I show my loyalty to the group in question but not my trustworthiness. (Keeping some promises will not help the group, but a trustworthy person will see reason to keep them nonetheless.) I might perform a public-spirited action anyway, without having promised, out of concern for my group; but if I am a person of my word, then when I promise, this act should add an additional and different reason to do it. And as Hume similarly remarks in the context of acts of material honesty, when I keep a simple promise, such as a promise to meet a colleague for lunch, I am not actually moved to keep it by any thought of the public good.

What really shows that someone is a person of his word is that he keeps his promise because it is a *promise*, because it is right to keep one's promises and wrong to break them, and he wants to be a keeper of promises and not a breaker of them. But what kind of feeling or desire *is* this? If we think of a different virtue, such as benevolence, we can understand the motivating feeling there without any recourse to explicitly moral concepts. The motive that manifests the virtue of benevolence—the desire for the happiness of another person—can be understood entirely apart from the moral concepts of virtue and vice and right and wrong. But the analogous motivating attitude for fidelity to promises, the desire to keep one's promises because it is right to do so and wrong not to, cannot be so understood. It draws upon a prior understanding of right and wrong action, at the very least, and perhaps also on a prior understanding of the virtue of being a trustworthy or honorable person. For some theories of virtue ethics, including Hume's but not limited to his, this is problematic. It runs afoul of the doctrine of the primacy of character over action. This doctrine is the one that says that right or good action is to be defined with reference to a prior notion of good character: a right action is whatever action the person who possesses the feelings and desires that compose the virtue would be moved by them to do.[2] For Hume, who understands virtues and indeed all character traits as motivating feelings and dispositions to feel, this doctrine says that a right action is whatever action someone with the feelings and desires that compose the virtue in question would be prompted by them to do. Furthermore, the desire to keep one's promises because it is obligatory to do so appears to be identical with the motive of duty. This causes some trouble for those virtue theories, both Hume's and others, that deny that genuinely good action, or the best action, can be produced by the sense of duty.

The second general question about promises that I mentioned arises more or less regardless of what moral theory one holds. In promising, I say certain words, in a certain sort of context, and perhaps with a certain sort of intention, and by doing so I make it morally obligatory for me to do A and morally wrong for me to fail to do A, *ceteris paribus*. How can I obligate myself to act in a certain way just by saying some words, perhaps in a special context and with special intentions? After all, I cannot obligate myself, for example, to touch my ear, just by standing in my office alone and saying "I hereby obligate myself to touch my ear". I can *say* this, but it does not in fact generate obligation. I can, however, obligate myself to pay someone $10 by saying to him "I hereby promise to pay you $10". Other moral obligations are not formed in this way or based on such an episode. I have general obligations—to tell the truth, to help those in need, not to kill or maim others—but these are not created by me at a stroke; they are always there. And I can incur obligation by some *action* of mine, as I do if I

---

[2] The term comes from Watson 1990.

injure you or damage your property and incur a duty to compensate you, or as I typically do if I bring a child into the world. But in promising it seems that I incur obligation just by saying that I do. This power of creating moral obligation just by speaking has struck some philosophers as so singular that they think that it can be explained only by a special social rule, something over and above whatever general moral obligations we have, and something over and above the ordinary conventions of language. These are the conventionalists, and not only Hume but Rawls and Anscombe are among them.[3] Most of Hume's predecessors, on the other hand, were non-conventionalists; and the non-conventional view has been espoused recently as well, most famously by Scanlon.[4]

To some extent, I claim, Hume's puzzling remarks about fidelity are to be explained by his own attempt to answer these two questions, of the motive characteristic of fidelity and the creation of obligation by fiat, in a way faithful to our experience of the virtue. The problem of motive, of course, is a further instance of the type of difficulty Hume encounters with the virtue of honesty, which was the subject of the last chapter, though I have tried above to put it in a broader context as well as to indicate how it arises for fidelity. The problem of the creation of obligation by fiat is unique to the virtue of fidelity.

III. HUME'S SENTIMENTALISM AND HIS VIRTUE ETHICS

Of course, the features of Hume's overall moral theory provide important pieces of the puzzle, just as they did in explaining the circle in the virtue of honesty. When Hume takes up the virtue of fidelity to promises in the *Treatise*, he has most of the main planks of his moral theory in place, including his account of honesty. We do not need to review them here, but a couple of points should be emphasized. Because of the nature of the human psyche as well as the homogenizing effect of the common point of view, people who possess the same factual knowledge and the same imaginative abilities and who contemplate traits from a common point of view will feel approval and disapproval in response to the same traits, and so will on the whole agree in their moral assessments. Furthermore, as we have seen, Hume is explicitly committed to virtue ethics, including the primacy of character. On his official view, traits of character are the primary objects of moral assessment.

---

[3] Rawls 1971: 344–50; Anscombe 1981*a*, 1981*b*. N.B.: Anscombe does not exactly think that the obligation of promises depends upon a rule distinct from the rules of language. She thinks that it depends upon a special rule, but that it is (roughly speaking) a rule of moral language.

[4] So Locke, e.g., sees the moral force of promises as coming from God; hence atheists cannot regard themselves as bound by them, and so ought not to be granted religious toleration (Locke 1955[1689]: 52). Scanlon's arguments for non-conventionalism are in Scanlon 1990 and 1998: ch. 7. Another recent author who takes a non-conventionalist view of promising is Robins (1984).

Hume takes as his paradigmatic virtues the natural virtues, such as benevolence, parental attentiveness, and gratitude. Although his explanation of why we approve them comes later (not until *Treatise*, Book 3, Part 3), he uses them as a standard of comparison throughout Book 3, Part 2. He thinks that people could have these natural virtues even if there were no organized society, even of an informal sort, that united individuals not bound by ties of affection. And again, Hume does not *assume* that such virtues as honesty and fidelity are different from these and artificial, on the present interpretation; he *concludes* it from the peculiarities of these virtues. Hume's *reductio* argument against the non-conventionalist view of promises is, of course, his second salvo in the struggle to show that some virtues are artificial.

In the preceding chapter we saw evidence that Hume thinks that we have a commonsense *conception* of a virtue as having a particular structure (*T* 3.2.1.2–7 / SBN 477–9; *T* 3.2.1.18 / SBN 483–4; *T* 3.2.2.8 / SBN 488–9). I have called this the natural conception of virtue, since it coincides with the actual structure of the natural virtues, which we should briefly review. Human beings are prone to feel love of their offspring, compassion for the suffering, and gratitude to their benefactors, at least to some extent. When these potentially motivating passions are strong and enduring enough in a certain person, we approve them when we contemplate them in the way appropriate for moral assessment. If we contemplate the degree of gratitude a person feels toward her benefactor in light of the facts and in a disinterested way, and find we approve it, then this motivating sentiment is a virtue. We may also contemplate someone's weak, inadequate, or missing grateful feeling, and disapprove the deficiency. The deficiency we thus disapprove is consequently a vice. (Hume may also think that there are vices of excess of a motivating sentiment; there again, what makes the trait a vice is that on reflection in the right frame of mind we disapprove it.) We approve or disapprove *actions* derivatively, because of the sentiments we take to have motivated them. An action is bad because its motive was bad. If our guess as to what sentiment caused an action proves incorrect, we revise our assessment of the action. So, if we take a man's neglect of his benefactor to be the result of his lacking gratitude, we disapprove the action. If we find out instead that he had a powerful motive of gratitude but failed to help for some other, good reason, we cease to blame him and may instead think his action a good one. Hume says, "The outward performance has no merit. We must look within to find the moral quality" (*T* 3.2.1.2 / SBN 477). So according to the natural conception of virtue and vice, our assessment of the action—our approval or disapproval of it, which is the only sort of moral assessment that Hume allows for—depends entirely on our assessment of its motive. Thus, the natural conception of virtue incorporates the doctrine of the primacy of character over action.

As we saw in the last chapter, it follows from the natural conception of virtue that the motivating sentiment or motive of a virtuous action must be something distinct from the moral sentiment. The moral sentiment, or sense of virtue, is of course approval and disapproval, and according to the natural conception of virtue, this is activated only in response to some existing motive, such as gratitude. So the sentiment of gratitude, or whatever the key motivating sentiment is in the virtue in question, cannot be identical to the moral sentiment, Hume says (*T* 3.2.1.2–7 / SBN 477–9; *T* 3.2.5.6 / SBN 518). There must be a prior, non-moral motive of action which we can in turn approve, if any approval is to occur at all, and so if the action is to qualify as virtuous. Approval cannot itself be the motive of which we approve. Or so it would seem.

Recall Hume's brief account of duty that we discussed in the last chapter (*T* 3.2.1.8 / SBN 479; *T* 3.2.5.6 / SBN 518). As we saw, according to Hume's theory our duties are the actions typically prompted by virtuous motivating sentiments which are common in human nature, motives the absence of which we disapprove. If someone is deficient in love of offspring, an approved motive, anyone will feel moral disapproval. If I am the deficient one, I will disapprove my own temperament and the actions to which it gives rise. This self-disapproval is my *sense* of duty. This moral sentiment, the sense of duty, may be unpleasant enough to move me to try to develop the missing parental affection, and I might try to do this *by* looking after my children. Or alternatively, this self-disapproval may move me to look after my children in order to disguise to myself my lack of love for them. So in this indirect way, the sense of duty can be a motive. But it has two important features, at least as it first appears in Hume's ethical theory. First, it can only exist if there is first some non-moral motive common in human nature—that is, some motive distinct from the moral sentiment—the absence or deficiency of which we disapprove. Second, the motive of duty is at most a second-best motive. A parent who tends to her children out of love has the virtue of parental devotion; a parent who does so from the motive of duty is deficient, not genuinely virtuous. She executes the "outward performance" for at most a second-best reason.

We can now see that the problem Hume encountered with regard to the virtue of honesty is a general problem about all the virtues he labels artificial. (Indeed, he classifies them as artificial largely because he finds them problematic in this way.) Although he elucidates the problem mainly in his discussion of honesty with respect to property, he says that the same thing occurs with fidelity to promises. When we try to specify the approved motive of an act of promise-keeping—the motive because of which the action exhibits the virtue of fidelity—we find that it can only be a *moral* motive, the moral sentiment itself. There is no non-moral motive of promise-keeping that manifests the virtue of fidelity. Consider the possibilities we briefly considered before, which are all taken up and rejected by Hume. The faithful person is not the one who keeps promises out of self-interest, or from benevolence. For these do not specifically induce us to keep promises; indeed, these sentiments can move us to break promises just as well. The faithful person is not even one who keeps promises out of concern for the public good, for, as Hume says, "men, in the ordinary conduct of life, look not so far as the

public interest, when they . . . perform their promises" (*T* 3.2.1.11 / SBN 481).
The motive that really exhibits a person's status as a person of his word, the
one that elicits our approval of his promise-keeping action when we contemplate
it appropriately, is his desire to keep the promise because he thinks he *should*
keep it and not break it. For Hume this is just his desire to keep it because he
approves of keeping promises and disapproves of breaking them. Hume says,
"If we thought, that promises had no moral obligation, we never shou'd feel
any inclination to observe them" (*T* 3.2.5.6 / SBN 518). But if the natural
conception of virtuous motives and virtuous action that Hume attributes to us
is correct, such a motive is impossible. In the absence of a *non*-moral virtuous
motive of promise-keeping that can stimulate our approval, we can *have* no
approval of acts of promise-keeping. The outward performance alone has no
merit or demerit; the approval of the acts must be derived from approval of a
non-moral motive. There is no non-moral motive. So we have no approval of
the acts. If approval is what produces the acts, then we have nothing that can
produce such acts. That's the general circularity problem. It is already familiar
to us from our discussion of it with regard to property, but Hume makes it even
plainer with regard to promises.

IV. HUME'S SPECIAL PROBLEMS WITH FIDELITY TO PROMISES

I have proposed that this is not the only problem with fidelity to promises that
concerns Hume. This problem, which plagues the other artificial virtues as well,
does not lead him to expect any peculiar act of the mind associated with the
others. There is nothing in his discussion of honesty, for example, about such an
act of the mind. We shall see that the "peculiar act" accusation arises because he
is also concerned with the problem unique to fidelity that promising creates a
new moral obligation. Of course it is possible to promise to do something that
is already obligatory for other reasons, but a great many of the actions I promise
to perform are not obligatory until I promise to do them, and become so only
because I promise (for example, to read the work of thirty undergraduates or
send money to a certain mortgage company). It is not some intrinsic property of
the actions that makes them obligatory. Somehow either my saying "I promise"
in the right way or the right place creates the new duty, or something else that
comes into being simultaneously with that utterance creates the new duty. It
cannot be something that was present before the utterance, or I would have been
obligated before, which I was not.

    If we reflect on what counts and what does not count as a promise in daily life,
we cannot help but notice that it is not merely my saying the words that creates
the duty, or even my saying them to someone who hears them. For if I do not

understand the words I utter (because, for example, I am a young child, or I am attempting to speak an unfamiliar foreign language), or I say them as an obvious joke, they create no obligation. As Hume observes, "one who shou'd make use of any expression [of promise], of which he knows not the meaning, and which he uses without any intention of binding himself, wou'd not certainly be bound by it" (*T* 3.2.5.13 / SBN 523). So merely saying the words is not sufficient to obligate. (Note that "the intention of binding himself" that Hume mentions here is not the intention to *keep* the promise. Hume is well aware that we can make binding promises we do not intend to keep, and acknowledges that this forms a part of our commonsense view (*T* 3.2.5.13 / SBN 523–4). It is not the intention to keep a promise, not *that* mental item, that distinguishes a genuine promise from a mere joke or a mere misuse of terms that one does not understand. Rather, Hume's thought is that there must be something else that distinguishes genuine promises from those utterances of 'I promise . . .' that do not bind.) Now, nothing occurs in the world outside me in the course of my making a promise, apart from my speaking and being heard, or so it certainly seems. And my understanding of what I say and/or intention to bind myself (as distinct from my intention to do what I promise to do) indeed seems relevant to whether I have bound myself. So presumably what differentiates binding promising from merely saying the words without incurring obligation is something that happens *in my mind*. There must be something specially suited to promising that occurs in my mind whenever I make a binding (that is, an actual) promise, in virtue of which I am obligated—something peculiar to the creation of promissory obligation. It might only be the awareness as I speak that I am creating a duty by saying these words—that this is what the words *mean*. But awareness of meaning is also something in the mind, for Hume. Whether the requisite state is awareness of meaning or something else, given what we know about when genuine promises occur and when they fail to occur, it is natural to think that the distinguishing item is mental.

Now we have the materials at hand to explain Hume's claim about the peculiar mental act and the *reductio* of the non-conventionalist view of promises based on it. He assumes that the non-conventionalist will be committed to the natural conceptions of virtue and duty. On these conceptions, in order for an action to be my duty, there must be some motive for it that is found in human nature, and this motive must be distinct from the moral sentiment, and so distinct from the sense of duty. The non-conventionalist must find this sort of motive for fulfilling promises. Here we should notice something about natural motivating sentiments and the actions they motivate. The natural sentiment of "humanity" (concern for the well-being of other people), for example, conduces to actions that all share a certain feature: they are actions that aim to relieve human suffering or otherwise contribute to human happiness. Similarly, love of offspring yields motives to actions that all serve a single goal toward which that passion prompts us: benefit to our own children.[5] In general, natural motivating sentiments all prompt us to actions that serve the object of that sentiment. But a huge variety of actions can be made obligatory by promising, and these actions need not have any characteristic in common that makes them means to the object of a single non-moral motivating sentiment. In particular, promised acts do not all tend to fulfill any particular goal of agents. Some of them aid the agent; some aid the agent's business partners, customers, students, or political constituents; some do not aid anyone, such as actions promised to those now dead, or promised acts of restoring a fortune to a profligate debauchee. Now for Hume, all motivating passions are goal-directed. Thus the non-conventionalist about promises must answer this question: What motive could there be that could in practice move us to any sort of action whatever, just in virtue of an event that occurs in the agent's mind at the time she says "I promise"? We need a *generic* motive, one not directed at any inherent features or expected outcomes of the actions it motivates, so that it could prompt just about any action, since one can promise to do so many different kinds of things. A reasonable candidate for this is a motive whose object is not some outcome or goal but the action itself. And we need a *new* motive, one that was not present ahead of time, before the promise was made.

For these reasons, Hume proposes that there are only four candidates available to the non-conventionalist for the right sort of motive: the resolution to perform the action itself, the desire to do so, the willing of the action, and the willing of the (promise-based) obligation to perform the action (T 3.2.5.3 / SBN 516). Although Hume does not spell this out, the other sorts of desires and aversions that he acknowledges in his moral psychology do not satisfy the prerequisites for a non-moral motive of fidelity. Hume's other motivating passions either are not motives that are generated anew at the moment of promising, and/or are only capable of provoking us to an action that will serve a particular end, not to actions of a wide variety of types. Recall that so far, for Hume, the only motives we have in life are (1) the instincts and (2) the desires, aversions, hopes, and related direct passions that arise in response to the agent's actual or prospective pleasure or pain. He also mentions volitions in Book 2, although their causal status there is unclear. Now he seems to add to the possible motives of action (3) resolutions and volitions—and perhaps also desires—to perform particular actions. The instincts are not suitable to move us to fulfill promises because they always reside in the mind, and so are not called into being by making a promise. (Of course they require beliefs about available means before they can cause action, so they are activated on specific occasions; but in general an act of promising does not create a belief about the means to fulfill our hunger, lust, or vengefulness, for example.)

---

[5] Strictly speaking, for Hume it is not the love of one's children that causes acts of caring for them, but the benevolence toward them that invariably accompanies such love (T 2.2.6 / SBN 366–8). Nonetheless, insofar as love of one's children generates motives, they are motives aimed at benefiting one's children.

The direct passions that depend upon pleasure and pain are not sufficiently generic, since they are caused by the expectation of pleasure or pain for the agent and prompt action to seek or avoid those outcomes or to express the passion itself (as when we jump for joy). However, Hume loosens these constraints to allow the possibility of a desire simply to do a certain action. This leaves him with the four candidates he mentions: the desire to do the promised act, the resolution to do it, the willing of the promised act, and the willing to be obligated to do the promised act. He has not demonstrated that there are absolutely no other possibilities; but we can see that the vast majority of Hume's motivating passions are ruled out by the requirement that the motive be both new and generic. In addition, the motive must be some mental phenomenon whose presence we have regularly experienced in conjunction with promising, and it is hard to think of any that are nearly as frequently conjoined with promising as these four are.

It is easy to miss the link between the peculiar act which creates the obligation of promises and the motive to fulfill the promise. But Hume says that non-conventionalists, to establish their position, must prove "*that there is a peculiar act of the mind, annext to promises* and *that consequent to this act of the mind, there arises an inclination to perform, distinct from a sense of duty*" (*T* 3.2.5.7 / SBN 519). So the motive to fulfill the promise must result from the peculiar act of the mind itself. This is so because the motive alone is the object of approval, on the non-conventional view. The approval of performance and disapproval of non-performance—the duty to perform—is merely derived from the obligatoriness of the motive to do so. Since the special mental act creates the duty to perform the promised action (which was not a duty before the promise was made), that act of the mind must either be or produce the motive to do what is promised as well.

Hume points out that consideration of the actual conditions under which binding promises are made quickly eliminates three of his four candidates. First, a resolution to act is not sufficient to obligate me. I can resolve or decide to do A (say, attend a film), change my mind and resolve not to do A, refrain from A'ing, and violate no duty. The resolution to A, then, is not what is peculiar to promising. A desire to do the thing is not necessary for making a binding promise; we can make perfectly binding promises to do things we have no desire to do and even feel averse to doing. And willing to do the thing does not actually occur at the time we make the promise, Hume thinks, since we promise now to perform later, and Hume apparently supposes that a volition occurs only at the time of action (*T* 1.1.4.5 / SBN 12; *T* 2.3.1.2 / SBN 399). (Even without this doctrine, there are other reasons to reject the volition to act as a necessary condition for promise-based obligation. It would make lying promises (where one has no intention whatsoever to act) non-binding.) This leaves only "the *willing* of that *obligation*, which arises from the promise" (*T* 3.2.5.3 / SBN 516), a mental act we can indeed perform at the moment when we promise. And this is indeed what we commonly think: that in promising we choose or consent to be obligated, and that is why we are. We are bound by our own will.

It is, however, according to Hume, a "manifest absurdity" (*T* 3.2.5.3 / SBN 517) that there should be such a special act of the mind, the willing of an obligation to A which would make it the case that I am obligated to A. On Hume's sentiment-based moral theory, for someone to have a moral obligation to perform some action is for his non-performance of that action to elicit our disapproval. Thus, to create a new obligation to act in a way not formerly obligatory, as promising does, is to change our sentiments: to cause a new sentiment of disapproval to arise in anyone who contemplates the omission in a disinterested way. But we cannot change people's sentiments, making something disapproved that was formerly approved, simply by willing that it be disapproved. Of course, we can make an action disagreeable that was formerly agreeable by performing some other action. If I ordinarily enjoy playing the piano, I can will to make it unpleasant, and carry out my volition by pouring a disgusting liquid on the keys. Hume is not denying this. Rather, he is denying that I can make a formerly approved or neutral action disapproved merely by willing that it be disapproved. To will to be obligated would be, according to Hume's metaethics, to will that a formerly approved or neutral action shall be disapproved by anyone who contemplates it from the common point of view. To obligate oneself by so willing would be *successfully* to cause the action to be disapproved in this manner solely by willing it to be so. And this is impossible. It is impossible actually to create a new obligation by willing it, and it would be absurd to try. In a footnote Hume adds an argument to show that even if morality consisted in relations of objects discoverable by reason, it would be impossible to obligate oneself by the act of willing oneself to be under an obligation, for this would require creating a new relation of objects simply by willing that the objects shall stand in this new relation, which is also impossible. So not only sentimentalists such as Hume, but also moral rationalists, must give up the peculiar act of the mind. "A promise, therefore, is *naturally* something altogether unintelligible," he concludes; "nor is there any act of the mind belonging to it" (*T* 3.2.5.4 / SBN 517.).[6]

---

[6] Hume's argument that even the rationalist cannot appeal to the willing of an obligation claims that such a volition would involve a vicious circularity. Suppose an obligation is a relation discoverable by reason, and suppose a new (promissory) obligation is created by a volition to create a new obligation. Therefore a new relation is created by a (mere) volition to create a new relation. Either this is absurd, because willing to create a relation does not create one, or willing does create a new relation, in that the volition itself is one of the relata. Suppose the latter: that the new relation is created by a volition V which is a volition to create a relation one of whose relata is V itself. Therefore V is (in part) a willing of V. But a volition must have an object: one wills something, or else one is not willing at all. (The object of one volition could presumably be *another* volition, but this must be individuated from the first by having a distinct object.) If the object of V is V itself (that very volition), then V has no object. Therefore V (the volition to create a promise-based obligation) is impossible. This circle may not really be vicious, but we will not investigate that here.

But, Hume says, "suppos[e] the mind could fall into the absurdity of willing [an] obligation" (*T* 3.2.5.5 / SBN 518). I suppose he means here that I could *try* to generate obligation by willing, just as I could try to move a matchbox on the other side of the room by willing if I thought I had telekinetic powers. Such an act of willing to be obligated could not naturally *produce* any obligation, for the reasons already given. A new obligation involves the development of new sentiments, and one cannot create new sentiments of approval and disapproval simply by willing them to occur.

Thus, Hume claims, the non-conventionalist view of promising is refuted.

V. THE TRUE ORIGINS OF THE OBLIGATION OF PROMISES AND THE VIRTUE OF FIDELITY

The truth, according to Hume, is that "promises are human inventions, founded on the necessities and interests of society" (*T* 3.2.5.7 / SBN 519). He gives a genetic account of the act of promising, the motive to conform, and the virtue of fidelity, which is supposed to explain the virtue as we find it. First we must notice the problem that human beings need to solve. Prior to forming a convention of promising, our selfishness, confined generosity, and imperfect gratitude impose limits on our usefulness to one another; promises help us overcome these limits. Without the institution of promise, human beings could invent ownership of property, Hume thinks, and by doing so stabilize possession and make possible very limited transfer of material goods by consent. But note how limited these provisions are in generating the hoped-for economic advantages. Given property as already fabricated by the process described in *T* 3.2.2–4, people who have reached this stage could simultaneously swap concrete goods that were within their view. But they would be unable to exchange services performed at different times (such as one neighbor exchanging his labor today for his neighbor's labor tomorrow (*T* 3.2.5.8 / SBN 520)), or goods at a distance (a house in one location for, perhaps, a grove of trees in another), or goods described generically ("ten bushels of corn, or five hogsheads of wine" (ibid.)); so they could not profit from a personal surplus or overcome a personal shortage of many goods on many occasions. Without promises, such exchanges would depend upon one party performing first (for example, the first neighbor laboring today, or one party handing over the house here and now) and the second performing in his turn (the second neighbor laboring tomorrow, or the second party relinquishing the grove after the two have journeyed there next) out of gratitude alone. But gratitude cannot generally be counted on in self-interested transactions or those between people who bear one another no affection. So people would rarely enter into arrangements of these kinds in which one party performs first and must hope that the other performs later, and the benefits of those forms of cooperation would be unavailable. Moralists and politicians cannot alter human selfishness and ingratitude, but they can teach us better to satisfy our appetites "in an oblique and artificial manner" (*T* 3.2.5.9 / SBN 521). This happens in two stages. First, people can easily recognize that additional kinds of mutual exchanges would serve their interests. All they have to do is express this interest to one another in order to give everyone an incentive to invent and to keep such agreements. They create a form of words to distinguish these exchanges from the generous reciprocal acts of friendship and gratitude. When someone utters this new form of words, he is understood to express a resolution to do the action in question, and he "subjects himself to the penalty of never being trusted again in case of failure" (*T* 3.2.5.10 / SBN 522), Hume says. This "concert or convention" (*T* 3.2.5.11 / SBN 522.) creates a new motive to act. One is led by self-interest to give the promising sign (in order to obtain the other party's cooperation), and once one has given it, *self-interest* demands that one do what one promised to do so as to insure that people will exchange promises with one in the future. In making a promise, then, one in effect leaves one's eligibility to be trusted as a security deposit that one forfeits on failure to perform.

Is a somewhat enlightened self-interest, then, the only motive for keeping one's promise, once the practice of promising has been created? Some interpreters say that this is Hume's view, just as they say this about conforming to the rules of property.[7] But here too, a careful look at the text shows otherwise. This is indeed how things work in the early days of the practice, in small, face-to-face communities that offer few temptations or opportunities to be a free-rider. But, Hume says, the sentiment of morals comes to play the same role in promise-keeping that it does in the development of honesty with respect to property (*T* 3.2.5.12 / SBN 523). In that account, self-interested compliance with the conventional rules can be expected to break down in larger societies where there are more anonymous transactions (making cheaters harder to catch) and where the effects of any one violation of trust on the social fabric are more diluted and distant (*T* 3.2.2.24 / SBN 499). So we need a second stage. We need to cultivate a *virtue* of fidelity in people, to insure that the benefits of cooperation persist even when people know that they can sometimes break a promise and still find others naïve enough to trade with them.

The next stage is that "a sentiment of morals concurs with interest and becomes a new obligation" (*T* 3.2.5.12 / SBN 523). This sentiment of approval and disapproval arises in response to public interest, education, and the artifices of politicians, just as the like sentiment arises toward honesty with respect to

---

[7] See Baier 1991. Haakonssen and Gauthier, discussed in detail below, consider enlightened self-interest the principal motive of promise-keeping, at least in the *Treatise*, but acknowledge that a motive of duty (understood as self-hatred or guilt for failing to have an imagined but nonexistent further motive) serves as an auxiliary motive when self-interest fails, just as they think it does for honesty with respect to property.

property.[8] Presumably, then, it works this way in the case of fidelity to promises: sympathy with the (actual or prospective) beneficiaries of fulfilled promises and victims of broken promises, which may amount to everyone in society, generates approval for rules of promise and for general compliance with them, and disapproval for violations. Parents, politicians, and others with influence over people's feelings then make use of this approval and disapproval. In a "second artifice", they use psychological manipulation (for good purposes) to produce a strong feeling of moral approval for every act of promise-keeping, and a strong feeling of moral disapproval for every act of promise-breaking, especially the agent's own, by associating the moral approval and disapproval with feelings of pride and shame.

As a result, these feelings become strong enough to become *motives* for promise-keeping for adults and children, at least some of the time, regardless of whether the agents see advantage in it or not.[9] Recall that Hume says about the virtue of honesty that though approval of honest action is natural, it is augmented when "politicians. . . in order to govern men more easily,. . . have endeavour'd to produce an esteem for justice, and an abhorrence of injustice" (*T* 3.2.2.25 / SBN 500–1). And this "must have its effect": the increased

---

[8] Recall Hume's account of that process for honesty from the last chapter (*T* 3.2.2.23–8 / SBN 498–501; *T* 3.2.6.11 / SBN 533–4, with some elaboration at *T* 3.3.1.9 / SBN 577). We come to approve of a system of rules of ownership by spontaneous sympathy with the beneficiaries of honesty and the victims of dishonesty, perhaps with society as a whole. This general approval is reshaped by a new artifice of politicians and parents who manipulate the public and children from their earliest infancy to feel that every instance of honest behavior is honorable and worthy, and every instance of dishonesty is "base and infamous" (*T* 3.2.2.26 / SBN 500–1). Thus these moral attitudes become well entrenched and come to be directed to each and every relevant action. The approval and disapproval are so greatly strengthened by being linked with pride and humility, love and hatred, that they can generate action.

[9] Hume is explicit that sympathy is the source of our moral *approval* of promise-keeping and *disapproval* of promise-breaking, so most interpreters would agree with the previous paragraph. I diverge from several of them in my further claim that the approval and disapproval so generated themselves become *motives* to keep promises distinct from self-interest, and, as I go on to argue, the sole virtuous motives at that. For Baier, for example (1991: 242), the motive of compliance with promises is "enlightened self-interest, awareness of her own share" in the public goods of order and safe commerce that the cooperative scheme makes possible; "but when it comes to approving such motivated acts, her own and others', it is the public interest as such that becomes the relevant concern, not just any one person's share in it". Only here does sympathy come into play. The text does not make it completely obvious that Hume thinks that moral approval itself becomes a motive of promise-keeping, although I argue that the pieces fit together to entail this.

One interpreter who reads this text as I do, as saying that moral approval and disapproval strengthened by "propaganda" provide a principal motive of just action, is Árdal (1966: 186–7), who sees the resultant problem of circularity as basically insoluble. His "Convention and Value" (1977*b*) also mentions the motive of duty, enhanced by education, as one of the motives of the just man (p. 64).

Mackie (1980: 100–1) thinks that moral sentiment plays *some* role in producing action. Self-interest is the principal motive, and we fulfill the occasional disadvantageous promise because the human psyche is inflexible: "[d]ispositions. . . cannot be quickly switched on and off." But the development of the full disposition to keep promises also depends upon moral feeling.

esteem and abhorrence they produce change people's motives, giving to the moral approval and disapproval that arose from sympathy the power to cause conforming behavior. The same effect occurs when "parents. . . inculcate on their children, from their earliest infancy, the principles of probity, and teach them to regard the observance of those rules. . . as worthy and honorable, and their violation as base and infamous" (*T* 3.2.2.26 / SBN 501). The same transformation is brought about with regard to fidelity to promises.

This *moral motivating sentiment* is itself a quality of mind—a "character". Thus it is available for observers to approve in its turn, through the workings of the psychological mechanisms involved in the generation of Humean approval. We consider those who have this quality of mind (the motivating moral sentiment toward promise-keeping and against promise-breaking), and observe or imagine its effects on those individuals on whom it has an impact for good or ill, in this case nearly everyone in society. Sympathy transfers to us as observers the pleasure or pain of those affected, and we associate that pleasure or pain with the quality of mind in question. The resulting feeling on our part is our moral sentiment of approval or disapproval of the trait. Since the motivating moral sentiment in the faithful person has a beneficial impact on others in society (or at least can be expected to have one), observers will come to approve that sentiment as a matter of course. So moral approval and disapproval have become motives which in their turn are subject to moral approval. A motivating sentiment that we approve is a virtue, according to Hume's account of what qualifies as a virtue. Thus we create, by means of two artifices, the virtue of fidelity.

VI. WHY WE STILL "FEIGN" THAT A PROMISOR WILLS AN OBLIGATION

Given this account of the fabrication of the virtue of fidelity and the obligation of promises, there seems to be no further reason to appeal to any special act of the mind. Yet Hume cautions that there remain difficulties "in supposing a moral obligation to attend promises" (*T* 3.2.5.12 / SBN 523). To elude these difficulties, "we *feign* a new act of the mind, which we call the willing an obligation" (ibid.), and we take the moral obligation to depend upon this act of mind; but of course it has been shown that no act of the sort is possible. He says that our practice of promising, seen as imposing a new obligation on ourselves by an act of will, resembles transubstantiation and the giving of holy orders, "mysterious and incomprehensible operations" (*T* 3.2.5.14 / SBN 524) in which a certain form of words together with a certain intention change a thing's very nature. Hume clearly means that in our practice of promising, as we ordinarily understand it, we invoke a fictitious mental power as part of a social scheme of deception. Our practice of promising, however, involves even more "contradictions" than do the two religious procedures, because unlike transubstantiation and ordination, which (Hume thinks) are useless, the practice of promising has been warped in various ways to serve the good of society.

But why do we have a social scheme of deception that invokes a fictitious mental act? Why do we not simply recognize that the moral obligation of promises arises from an extremely useful social convention, and dispense with any pretense that we obligate ourselves by a special act of the mind?

Other interpreters have offered answers that shed light but do not fully fit the text. For example, Knud Haakonssen says that we feign a special mental act to conceal from ourselves the fact that the only available motive for fulfilling promises is self-interest. We do not approve this real but morally neutral motive, and so fidelity is in fact no virtue. However, the promise-keeping acts done from this motive are obviously highly beneficial. As a result, we imagine that there must be a motive in others directing them toward these good consequences (although we never find it in ourselves), and we naturally come to approve the imaginary motive, creating the illusion that the actions are the products of a virtue. We consequently come to hate ourselves for lacking this approved (though imaginary) motive; and this self-hatred becomes a motive of duty for keeping our promises. We are indeed moved by this to keep promises, but since there is no natural sentiment on which duty may be based, it is not in fact our duty to do so.[10]

There are three textual difficulties with this. First, Hume is adamant that fidelity is no less a virtue for being artificial, and that the obligation of promise is genuine. Second, self-interest is not the sole motive to promise-keeping, and not the one characteristic of the virtue; there is another (albeit moral) motive that *is* approved, and Hume acknowledges the presence of this motive. Third, the problem of motive arises for the artificial virtues of justice (honesty with respect to property) and allegiance to government, as well as for fidelity—arguably even for chastity and modesty in women. To make the interpretation coherent, then, Haakonssen applies it to all the artificial virtues, postulating a feigned virtuous motive in each case. But it is only with respect to fidelity that Hume himself ever mentions any feigned mental act.

We now have the tools for a better answer. As I interpret him, Hume thinks that the *commonsense concept* of a virtue, any virtue, is the concept of a trait of character consisting of a particular laudable, non-moral, motivational disposition. That is, he thinks that what we ordinarily have in mind when we think of a virtue is the natural conception of virtue. We all have this, and we apply it (mistakenly) to all the virtues that we recognize. We have this conception because of the way our psyches function, and it is helpful to look more closely at what Hume says about this. We judge "immorality or vice" "from some defect or unsoundness of the passions, and . . . this defect must be judg'd of . . . from the ordinary course of

---

[10] Haakonssen 1981: ch. 2, esp. part 8. Haakonssen's is the most perceptive effort to account for the peculiar mental act that I have seen to date.

nature in the constitution of the mind" (*T* 3.2.2.8 / SBN 488). First, we see from
that ordinary course of nature that we are not naturally impartial creatures; we
have a natural bias in favor of ourselves and those near and dear to us. Partiality
to ourselves and those dear to us is part of "the original frame of our mind".
Secondly, this partiality has been taken up into our conception of virtue and vice.
We don't think we *should* have impartial sentiments. "This partiality . . . must
not only have an influence on our behaviour and conduct in society, but even on
our *ideas of vice and virtue*; so as to make us regard any remarkable transgression
of such a degree of partiality, either by too great an enlargement, or contraction
of the affections, as vicious and immoral. . . . [O]ur *natural uncultivated ideas of
morality*, instead of providing a remedy for the partiality of our affections, do
rather conform themselves to that partiality" (*T* 3.2.2.8 / SBN 488–9; emphasis
mine). The naturally virtuous sentiments such as compassion and love of one's
children exhibit a partiality which we approve, and which is plainly natural and
suitable to such creatures as we are. Consequently, this shapes our very concept
of a virtue. In order that we may cooperate for mutual gain with those outside
our circle of friends, our "judgment and understanding" supplies a remedy for
what is "irregular and incommodious in the affections" (*T* 3.2.2.9 / SBN 489),
in the form of a trait whose operation is *im*partial. We need that impartiality
in promise-keeping if a mere party to a contract is to have any security that
I will do my share in the face of the countervailing interests of my intimates
and myself. But we still think it virtuous in me to *care* more about my
intimates than my trading partner, to feel more compassion for them and be
more readily influenced to act by the feelings they communicate to me. The
partiality of sentiment continues to elicit our approval. A thoroughly impartial
temperament would never look as attractive. This shows that we retain the natural
conception of virtue. Thus we must employ a small fantasy in order to squeeze
fidelity under it.

According to the natural conception of virtue, which is the one we have, fidelity
to promises is not a virtue, and the obligation of promises is not a duty. For
fidelity is not a non-moral motivating sentiment whose deficiency we disapprove.
But we think of fidelity as a virtue anyway. The situation is similar with the other
artificial virtues, which also lack non-moral motivating sentiments. In their case
we do not notice the mismatch between our natural conception of virtue and the
traits we actually approve. It is easy enough to fail to notice that honesty does
not fit the natural conception of virtue, as we have seen. It takes some digging
to discover the definitional circle. However, each act of promising draws our
attention to the formation of a new obligation, and so presents a challenge to
the natural conception of virtue and of obligation based on it. The obligation
of promise is not like the steady obligations to refrain from the property of
others or to obey our rulers, which puzzle us only upon philosophical reflection.
It comes into conflict with our assumptions about virtue in daily practice, as
we make promises and enter into contracts and so create new obligations in

ways not consonant with our assumptions about virtue and obligation. Thus we must hit upon a way, within the framework of our preconceived notions of virtue and duty, to think about this sudden appearance of obligation. We do this by accepting a fiction and not noticing the contradictions to which it gives rise. We pretend that the obligation of a promise is created by a peculiar act of the mind, the willing of an obligation, and that *that* is the approved motive of promise-keeping. This keeps all the features of the natural conceptions of virtue and duty in place. There is thought to be a non-moral motive to keep each promise, and we can think of that motive as the object of our approval when we regard fidelity as a virtue. But it leaves us burdened with a fiction.

We found in the last chapter that Hume thinks the artificial virtues are virtues in the sense in which an artificial leg is a leg; and we see this with fidelity as we did with honesty. On the natural conception of virtue, they are not virtues, just as an artificial leg is not a natural leg. But, according to Hume's *own* account of virtue, any motivating sentiment that elicits approval is a virtue. He does not limit this official description of virtue to the motivating sentiments that are non-moral. And in the case of fidelity, there is eventually a motivating sentiment that elicits our approval of the promise-keeping acts it engenders: namely, the enhanced moral sentiment. Hence fidelity *is* a virtue on Hume's definition. It is functionally a virtue, and that is what counts for Hume.

Do we have to retain our pre-reflective, natural conception of virtue, for Hume? He does not say, but the answer seems to be no. We can be faithful to promises without it, since our actual motive to fulfill promises does not depend for its genesis on a belief in the peculiar act of the mind. We can become more philosophically consistent on this subject without undermining our fidelity. But I believe Hume would say it is a strain to give up this way of thinking of virtue, since it fits so comfortably with our emotional makeup. Giving it up may be uncomfortable for another reason. In relinquishing it, we make it clearer than ever that fidelity is a virtue; but we have to acknowledge that it is a prosthetic one. We see that our natural affections have left us with a universal disability, unable to solve the problems that promises can solve. But we are resourceful. We cooperate to construct an artificial substitute that functions much as a natural virtue would, and generates approval from the same source, sympathy.

VII. LESS SANGUINE INTERPRETATIONS

This interpretation allows us to explain Hume's remarks about the peculiar act of the mind without postulating that one or both claims are symptoms of Hume's confusion or even of general failure in Hume's theory of promises, as other interpretations do. Mackie and Snare, for example, each offer instructive explanations of why a mental-act account of promise-based obligation might be a natural alternative to a conventional explanation. Both, however, take

Hume to be confused or mistaken in seeing reason to claim that, even given the convention, we nonetheless always feign such an act when we promise.[11] On my view Hume is not mistaken on his own terms in saying that commonsense feigns a special mental act; it indeed follows from the natural conceptions of virtue and obligation he has identified.

Gauthier's finely honed analysis offers a more complex but even more dire diagnosis.[12] As we saw in the last chapter, he construes Hume's treatment of fidelity and the other artificial virtues differently in the *Treatise* and in the *Enquiry concerning the Principles of Morals*, but in each interpretation he leaves Hume with error or failure.

For Gauthier, as for Haakonssen, interest is the actual motive of conformity to the rules of promise; but on Gauthier's view this enlightened self-interest, redirected by the convention so as to cause promise-keeping acts instead of acts of selfish acquisition, *is* a virtuous motive, one of which we approve. It is artificial, in that it takes the form it does only in response to convention, but natural in that it is non-moral. This motive is in principle sufficient to account for the virtue of fidelity, and only needs to be reinforced by moral motives because in practice, in complex societies, we too easily overlook our own interest. Gauthier claims that in the *Treatise* Hume does not doubt that under conventional circumstances all individual acts of promise-keeping really are to the agent's advantage. Agents who recognize this, then, will be reliably moved; and the resulting benefits to society will cause this motive to be approved.[13]

This leaves Hume with no reason to say that after the moralization of the conventional practice of fidelity, we find ourselves having "difficulties . . . in supposing a moral obligation to attend promises", and so we feign the willing of an obligation (*T* 3.2.5.12 / SBN 523). And indeed Gauthier thinks that Hume "has no need to burden his own account with such an act";[14] it is just an error on his part. Gauthier allows that given his *Treatise* position, Hume might reasonably think the peculiar act of the mind is mistakenly postulated by non-conventionalists, or that an illusion of it resides in the popular imagination; but he does not say why anyone would postulate the willing of an obligation rather than just some non-moral motive or other, and there is no reason why a

---

[11] Mackie 1980: 96–104, esp. 103; Snare 1991: part II, esp. chs. 7 and 9 (see, e.g., pp. 265–9).

[12] Gauthier (1992).

[13] So for Gauthier, in the *Treatise* Hume successfully finds the requisite non-moral motive of promise-keeping that he seeks, which makes this reading attractive. However, just as he does with regard to honesty, he extrapolates from what Hume actually says about fidelity, since Hume never says that interest, even redirected by the convention of promises, is a motive of which the moral sentiment approves, and he explicitly denies that we are moved either by interest or concern for society when we conform to the requirements of the artificial virtues (*T* 3.2.1.11–14 / SBN 480–2). Hume does of course say that we approve of *justice* and *fidelity*. Gauthier construes this as approval of redirected interest by claiming that Hume identifies redirected interest with the sense of justice, so that to approve of one is to approve of the other. But it strains the text to understand the "sense of justice" to be a non-moral motive.   [14] Gauthier 1992: 416.

philosopher should insist that people in general cling to such a fiction. Perhaps Gauthier regards Hume's remarks to this effect as a slip. Given Hume's analogy with transubstantiation and ordination, though, the inclusion of the claim that we feign a peculiar act of the mind seems quite carefully thought out.

This reading depends upon the claim that throughout the *Treatise* Hume holds the naïve belief that all *individual* acts of promise-keeping (within society) redound to the net advantage of the agent, and furthermore, that this enables Hume to identify a reliable motive of promise-keeping in human nature, one that can genuinely bring about the advantages of the convention and evoke universal approval. The textual evidence that Hume holds that every individual act of justice yields a net advantage to the agent (call this the naïve belief) is equivocal.[15] But even if he holds the naïve belief in the *Treatise*, Hume explicitly recognizes that human nature is such that (rightly or wrongly) we will not be able to foresee such long-range net benefit in every case, and even when we do, we will not always be moved by it, because we are short-sighted, as Gauthier notes.[16] Thus, given human nature, in large societies we can be expected to lack a reliable non-moral motive to keep promises. Whatever Hume thought about the true wages of virtue, he saw the problem of being moved to promise-keeping as theoretical as well as practical, since rooted in human nature itself. And so this interpretation makes the *Treatise* position quite weak.

In the *Enquiry concerning the Principles of Morals*, according to Gauthier, Hume first confronts the fact that some acts of promise-keeping do not serve the agent's interest (even including her interest in preserving the practice), because in some situations breaking a promise would be highly profitable without posing any significant threat to the social confederacy. In people such as the sensible knave who reflect on this, "the initial self-interested motive fails to survive critical reflection"[17] Here Gauthier proposes that Hume's only available response is a developmental version of the error theory that Haakonssen finds in the *Treatise*. Redirected interest cannot move us to keep promises under some circumstances; therefore, in those cases we have no natural motive of fidelity after all. We continue to approve of general conformity to the rules of promise even so, because of its social benefits. So we then imagine a different non-moral motive on the part of others, the (nonexistent) willing of an obligation. We direct our approval to that and hate ourselves for lacking it, and this self-hatred becomes a sense of duty that causes compliance. This motive of duty can come into being only if we accept the fiction that there is such a motive in other people. However,

---

[15] e.g., *T* 3.2.22 / SBN 497 can be read either way.

[16] Gauthier draws support from Hume's later discussion of the need to create government, where Hume sounds as if he blames most common violations of the laws of justice (here including the rules of promise-keeping) on the irresistible temptation to choose near rewards at the cost of greater future benefits. Gauthier quotes *T* 3.2.7.3 / SBN 535 in this connection. But it does not seem to help his case for a reliable non-moral motive of fidelity. We will look more closely at the preference for the near in the next chapter. [17] Gauthier 1992: 420.

this Humean strategy cannot succeed, Gauthier argues. The fiction does not stand up to reflection, for it is impossible to will an obligation. When we realize this, Gauthier says, we will see that fidelity and the other artificial virtues are not our duty, and therefore "human society, which depends on these dispositions, lacks any moral foundation".[18] Hume's theory of promise collapses under this pressure.[19]

My interpretation leaves Hume in a far stronger position. It does not depend on the general, enduring efficacy of a self-interested motive to promise-keeping. It identifies a persistent (though moral) motive for promise-keeping even where the faithful person does not see such behavior as advantageous. It locates a morally approved and real motive, so human society does not lack moral foundation. It leaves Hume with explanations of the obligation of promises and of the motive for promise-keeping that are not undermined when people realize that it is not to their net advantage to fulfill certain promises and that there is no mental act of willing an obligation. And it finds a coherent reason within Hume's understanding of our commonsense conception of virtue for us still to feign a special mental act after the convention is in place. We do not feign the peculiar act in order to preserve our motive to fulfill promises, but rather in order to preserve our pre-reflective assumptions about the structure of virtue, in particular our view that there must be some non-moral motive of compliance that is created anew each time we make a promise.

VIII. TWO QUICK LESSONS FOR PRESENT-DAY VIRTUE ETHICS

It does not follow from Hume's discussion of fidelity that present-day virtue theorists must regard fidelity as conventional rather than natural, for they need not take on board all of Hume's premises. That is an issue for another occasion. The lessons we shall draw are more subtle than this, but follow more directly from Hume's observations about fidelity.

Some present-day virtue theorists are committed to the primacy of character over action. This apparently entails that we must have a prior, independent concept of what it is to have a certain virtue (an admirable set of psychological dispositions), and then use that to determine which actions are required of us.[20] The Humean version of this was the pivotal thesis in the natural conception of virtue that made fidelity (and the rest of the artificial virtues) impossible. If I have interpreted him correctly, Hume ultimately treats this thesis as an

---

[18] Gauthier 1992: 422.

[19] Also note that, on Gauthier's reading, feigning an obligation is introduced in the *Treatise* to solve a problem that Hume is unaware of until the moral *Enquiry*.

[20] In addition to Watson, McDowell says things like this (1979, pp. 331–350).

over-general commonsense assumption. On his own considered, philosophical view he weakens it in order to account for the actual approved motive of promise-keeping, which is moral. He allows that morally required actions are not all defined by their motivating sentiments; acts of promise-keeping are initially defined by a social convention, and only later become the object of a characteristic motive, a moral one. This may offer a general lesson for present-day virtue theorists, even those with different conceptions of a character trait from Hume's. The person of her word in fact fulfills promises because it is (on her view) obligatory to fulfill promises. Hume seems to be right about this. An accurate account of the character of the person of her word, then, makes essential reference to obligatory action. Hence the motivational and affective dispositions and other psychological features that make up that character trait cannot be our sole criterion for obligatoriness of actions. When it comes to fidelity and the other virtues that Hume calls artificial, character cannot determine *what* we should do; that must be settled in another way. It does not follow, of course, that it must be settled by conventional rules. But it must be settled by something other than agents' attitudes and psychological dispositions, at least initially. This runs counter to the doctrine of the primacy of character.[21]

The second lesson for virtue ethics is the *nature* of the true motive of trustworthy actions. Present-day virtue theorists tend to denigrate the motive of duty, to some extent understandably. If I visit a friend in the hospital, in Michael Stocker's famous example, for this to manifest the virtue of friendship I must do it out of affection for my friend and a desire to cheer him up.[22] If a husband rescues his wife from mortal danger in preference to a stranger (in Bernard Williams's famous example), for this to be a good action, one that manifests the husband's virtue of love, it should be engendered not by the motive of duty but solely by his love of his wife and sensitivity to what she means to him.[23] If I visit my hospitalized friend merely because it is my duty, I am not a thoroughly good friend. If the husband rescues his wife in preference to a stranger in part because it is permissible (not contrary to duty) for husbands to rescue their wives first, this is "one thought too many", in Williams's phrase, and the wife will have grounds for disappointment. These actions fail to manifest the relevant virtues because they are not done solely from love or concern, but rather (in whole or in part) from duty, revealing a deficiency in the agent's attachment. Many virtue theorists, then, like Hume in his preliminary discussion of this notion, regard the motive of duty as second-best, as a kind of fallback motive in case one's

---

[21] Some virtue theorists will be perfectly happy with this result. See Hursthouse 1995: 57–75. But note important differences in her later view (1999, *passim*).   [22] Stocker 1976.
[23] Williams (1981*b*), p. 18. Williams's actual example is more complex than this, and is aimed to make a subtler point, in criticism of Kantian ethics. He thinks that should the man reason that saving his wife in preference to a stranger is permissible and not unfair to the stranger, and save her on those grounds, this would be incompatible with genuine love, which would move him to save her solely because it is she who needs saving.

virtue fails. Stocker says, "Duty seems relevant in our relations with our loved ones and friends, only when our love, friendship, and affection lapse."[24] But if I am a person with the virtue of fidelity, what moves me to fulfill an inconvenient promise is my feeling or thought that I should do it, that it would be wrong (indeed, a betrayal) not to, that it is bad or shameful to betray my word. That is the motive of duty, and here it is the right motive. For fidelity to promises, love is not enough. But neither is self-interest or desire for the public good. We need the motive of duty, or we do not get the virtue of fidelity. Consequently, we had better not be too dismissive of the motive of duty; it requires an important place in any virtue ethics, as Hume has ultimately shown us.

[24] Stocker 1976: n. 8.

8

The Shackles of Virtue: Allegiance to Government

Virtue theorists today are beginning to deploy their ethical theories to address issues in political philosophy. Any good ethical theory is expected to provide some foundation for, or at least to be compatible with, an acceptable theory of just government. Virtue ethics, however, normally eschews talk of rights, liberties, and duties, and gives conceptual priority to individuals' motivational and emotional dispositions. Thus it seems difficult to develop a virtue-theoretic approach to the just state and the obligations of citizens, especially for heirs of the early modern tradition in political philosophy, with its focus on rights and duties. Hume is an interesting figure from this point of view. He at least attempts to combine a virtue-theoretic approach to ethics with developed positions on the crucial issues in the political philosophy of his day, such as the origin and justification of governmental power, the legitimacy of particular rulers, and the putative right to revolution. One may wonder how well he joins these two aspects of his moral philosophy, particularly given his sentiment-based ethical theory.

This chapter reveals connections between Hume's virtue ethics and his political philosophy by investigating two specific questions. First, is allegiance to government, as Hume understands it, a virtue of character like other virtues that Hume recognizes (such as honesty and fidelity to promises)? Is his account of allegiance in this way continuous with his account of the other artificial virtues? Second, can Hume account for the power or motivational influence of governments to engender obedience? The connection of the second question with Hume's virtue-theoretic approach will emerge in what follows. An objector might answer no to both questions, so let us regard these as two objections to Hume's account of allegiance to government, at least as it takes shape in the *Treatise*, and perhaps beyond that.

I. PRELIMINARIES: THE STAGES OF SOCIETAL DEVELOPMENT

As we have already seen, in order to illuminate the origins of justice and the rules of property, Hume first imagines human life without any general social structure.

This is not only a device for explaining the genesis of virtues; it is, of course, a familiar move in arguments in political philosophy, and we should compare Hume's imaginative exercise and type of argument with those of some of his predecessors. Unlike Hobbes and Locke, Hume believes that the transition from an unstructured condition to a governed society occurs in two distinct stages. The human race gets its start in a possible state in which relations with persons outside the family are not ordered by any rules at all. First a group of people develops into a society regulated by the informal and wholly voluntary customs of what Hume calls "justice" (the rules of property and the requirement of fidelity to promises); after that it *may* proceed to a further condition, that of being governed by magistrates and rulers. Readers who come to Hume from Hobbes or Locke may fail to notice that for Hume there are thus two separate developments: the development of society without government (call this pre-civil society) and the development of government. Pre-civil society is needed by all human beings, Hume argues, but only some societies need government. According to Hume, to create pre-civil society, people gradually but voluntarily adopt the conventions of ownership, transfer of goods by consent, and promise (contract) that we have already examined. Hume invokes the initial, entirely unstructured state of the human race only in order to explain the formation of these *informal* conventions of property and promise, not to explain or justify the formation of government.

So there is reason not to read Hume as invoking the "state of nature" in the sense found in Hobbes, for example. Hobbes sees the state of nature as the only alternative to *civil* society (society that includes government). By contrast, Hume thinks human beings could develop a primitive but moderately stable society without granting anyone dominion or authority over anyone else. Yet Hume's conception of the pregovernmental condition of human life also differs from Locke's. Locke indeed sees human life prior to the invention of government as laced with complex commercial interactions; but for Locke these interactions are regulated not by norms created by social convention, but by the laws of nature. (Hence for Locke this condition is still the state of *nature*.) For Hume there are no comparable laws of nature. Rather, such activities as cooperative work among mere acquaintances, buying, selling, and labor for hire, are made possible only by conventions of property and promise. (He calls the rules of stability of possession, transfer by consent, and keeping promises "the laws of nature", but he obviously does not mean this in Locke's sense, as antecedent to human convention. He is probably indulging in a bit of irony, but he also uses the phrase to distinguish the conventions of property and promise from the laws imposed by governors with coercive enforcement powers.) The conventions of ownership and promise-keeping need to be invented jointly by groups of people all of whom reach a shared understanding. When Hume considers the invention of government, then, he is not talking about a transition from a state entirely lacking in humanly contrived social organization. Furthermore, while Hume explicitly declares that the *state of nature* envisioned by philosophers is a mere theoretical construct, he maintains that pre-civil societies involving commerce and contract are and have been historically real (*T* 3.2.8.1–3 / SBN 539–41). He even claims that this is the actual condition "in the *American* tribes", except for temporary periods of war (*T* 3.2.8.2 / SBN 540). Clearly, then, Hume does not identify pre-civil society with a state of nature.

Thinking of Hume as a state-of-nature theorist is also unwise, because it may instead mislead the reader into thinking that Hume identifies the state of nature (that mere theoretical construct) with the imagined time before the formation of pre-civil society. In fact, he does not. The state of nature, as Hume uses the term, would be a state in which all people were solitary individuals without any emotional attachments—or rules—to regulate *any* of their interactions. This condition never existed, because "men are necessarily born in a family-society" (*EPM* 3.16 / SBN 190). Family members are joined in cooperative activities by ties of affection. They are also governed by simple rules of proto-ownership.

But if it be found, that nothing can be more simple and obvious than [the rule for the stability of possession]; that every parent, in order to preserve peace among his children, must establish it. . . . If all this appear evident, as it certainly must, we may conclude, that 'tis utterly impossible for men to remain any considerable time in that savage condition, which precedes society; but that his very first state and situation may justly be esteem'd social. (*T* 3.2.2.14 / SBN 493.)

Hume's own imagined condition of unstructured human life (human life without impartial rules of property and promise) is one in which economic activity takes place only within small family groups. This is not the (entirely fictitious) state of nature of the philosophers. Instead, it is probably a real though very brief stage in human prehistory. The transition to a pre-civil society with rules of justice occurs when *strangers* enter into conventions with one another to create and abide by such rules, and when moral approval is then extended to all adherence and moral disapproval to all violation of them, eventually building up a new virtue of character.

It may also seem that when Hume talks about human life without rules for transactions with strangers, he is making a hypothetical, normative argument. He seems to follow a pattern, now familiar in political philosophy, of arguing thus: if we were in the state of nature, which of course we never were and never will be, then we would have pressing reasons to form a society and follow its rules; therefore, as we actually are (or would be in a more nearly ideal society), we are obligated to conform to the rules of society. One might think that Hume gives such a hypothetical foundation of the obligation to obey the laws; but this interpretation would be in error. Hume's purpose in imagining the genesis of justice is not to give a hypothetical contract type of argument to the effect that rules of justice are warranted, or to the effect that we are obligated to obey the laws. His purpose is both to trace the natural (including psychological) history of justice and to explain its status as a virtue of character. Hume does, of course, make a normative argument about justice, but one quite different from a hypothetical contract argument. He argues that just characters generate approval. He has already established to his satisfaction that all mental qualities that generate approval are virtues; hence the character trait of justice is a virtue. As we have seen, just characters generate the approval they do as a causal consequence of the fact that they make possible smoothly operating conventions of property and promise, which produce happiness in society.

II. THE ORIGIN OF GOVERNMENT AND THE SOURCE OF ALLEGIANCE

In the *Treatise*, after explaining the formation of pre-civil society, which we have traced in the last two chapters, Hume proceeds with the sections called "Of the origin of government" and "Of the source of allegiance" (*T* 3.2.7–8).[1] Let us examine this account to see how our two objections arise.

Hume must tackle a special problem. Why do we need government, given that we can form a community of peaceful property-owners and traders without it, and obtain compliance with the rules of justice by means of informal convention and its voluntary sanctions? Submission to rulers reduces our individual liberty (*EPM* 4.1 / SBN 205), and so, *prima facie*, we must be shown why it is worthwhile. What might move people to create governments, and why is this a good idea? These are questions we must address before tackling our two objections (that allegiance is not a Humean virtue and that a government created by previously unruled people cannot acquire enforcement power).

Note that Hume is not giving the (pre)history of actual governments. He does this separately, acknowledging that many governments throughout history were the product of conquest or usurpation. He does not think the formation of actual governments from pre-civil societies followed a single pattern. Here he addresses a different consideration: we have governments, which we acquired one way or another. What good are they? Would we be better or worse off without them?

Human beings, Hume remarks, are in great measure governed by their own interest and that of their family and friends. The best way to serve this interest is to adhere inflexibly to the rules of justice already devised: rules of refraining from the property of others, transferring property only by consent, and abiding

---

[1] Hume's sole discussion of government in the second *Enquiry* occurs in a single paragraph at *EPM* 4.1 / SBN 205. His account there, that the "allurements of present pleasure and advantage" overcome our strength of mind and thus precipitate the need for government, is entirely consistent with the *Treatise* account, but leaves out all the details. So we follow the *Treatise* account here.

by promises and contracts. Only by so doing can people preserve society, which is indispensable to their interest. What is more, everyone knows that this is so. But human beings *cannot* always regulate their conduct by their judgments of interest.

Now as every thing, that is contiguous to us, either in space or time, strikes upon us with [a strong and lively] idea, it has a proportional effect on the will and passions, and commonly operates with more force than any object, that lies in a more distant and obscure light. Tho' we may be fully convinc'd, that the latter object excels the former, we are not able to regulate our actions by this judgment; but yield to the sollicitations of our passions, which always plead in favour of whatever is near and contiguous.   (*T* 3.2.7.2 / SBN 535)

He claims here that although we make an unimpaired *judgment* of which of two results would be better, this cannot reliably cause us to pursue the better result when the better is more distant than the worse, because the passions and the will are drawn to what is vivid and lively, and so move toward what is near. The harms to come from a breach of justice are (or seem) remote, whereas the profit of injustice is near at hand. So even though everyone in a pre-civil society acknowledges that the long-term disadvantages of a breach of justice actually outweigh its short-term advantages, at least some of the time people will not be able to control the urge to seek the near-term advantage.

It is clear from this passage that Hume thinks our judgment of the goodness of an outcome is distinct from our motive to pursue it. It is likely that to judge one outcome better than another, for Hume, is to predict that it will involve or provide more pleasure. If that is his view, and if he also thinks (as I argued in Chapter 2) that the expectation of pleasure causes motivating passions, he must allow that the motivational influence of such expectations is not directly proportioned to the quantity of pleasure expected. But there is no reason this should not be so. The vividness of an idea of prospective pleasure (its being a belief) enables it to cause a motivating passion in the first place, so it stands to reason that some additional vividness resulting from the prospective pleasure's proximity in time should increase the action-generating power of the motivating passion it causes. Thus the vivacity of the belief in prospective pleasure could be one factor in determining the strength of one's motive, and the quantity of pleasure expected could be another, at times competing, factor.

Because distance in time is especially what tends to distort the emotional and volitional influence of the near at the expense of the remote, let us call this psychological feature of human beings *temporal myopia*. This label fits, because Hume uses the analogy of perspective in vision to model the differential responses of the sentiments. The prospects of pleasure and pain cause motivating passions, but their influence becomes fainter with temporal distance, as a visual image becomes blurry with physical distance or short-sightedness. (We even call a person or action short-sighted when he or it aims for a present advantage at too great a long-term cost.)[2]

The strong and lively ideas of near-term advantages have a disproportionately strong influence on human passions, and so induce people to violate the rules of justice in spite of the greater long-term costs of such actions. But this will not occur while the people of a pre-civil society are eking out a bare subsistence. It will happen only when the pre-civil society eventually produces wealth, which may include disparities of wealth, for then the near-term gains become very tempting to passion (*T* 3.2.8.1 / SBN 539) and can make individuals "forget . . . the interest they have in the preservation of . . . justice" (*T* 3.2.8.2 / SBN 540). Over time injustices will occur more and more often. The perpetrators encourage others by their bad example, and after a while the frequency of injustice grows great enough that people fear they will be "the cully of [their] integrity" by conforming alone when all others violate (*T* 3.2.7.3 / SBN 535). At this point people lose confidence in the conditional intentions of property and promise ("I intend to conform if others will"), and the bond that preserves pre-civil society is broken.

One expects a solution that involves the consent of the people. However, it is not so easy to find such a solution, for the people will not consent to immediate sacrifices for the sake of long-term gain, because of their temporal myopia. Fortunately, a further feature of temporal myopia helps them consent to *future* constraints for the sake of gain in the more distant future. Because of their general "negligence about remote objects", they do not react to the intervals between separate events when both events are far enough in the future; they attend only to the relative magnitude of the goods to be produced (*T* 3.2.7.5 / SBN 536). If, for example, I must write a grant proposal now in order to travel next year, the present pain will influence my will much more than the future, and greater, good; and so temporal myopia will keep me from writing the proposal. But if I must *commit* myself now to write a grant proposal next year in order to travel the following year, the fact that I will bear the burden a year before I enjoy the advantage has no influence on my passions. (Thus it is misleading to call temporal myopia a preference for short- over long-term gains. It is only the *immediate* gains, which are in the myopic's clear focus, that have a disproportionate influence on action.) I will gladly commit myself to write the proposal next year, since the travel grant is well worth the trouble. Similarly, the people will gladly commit themselves now to more distant adherence to justice for the sake of the still more distant benefits of preserving society.

---

[2] Arthur Kuflik points out (in conversation) that a better label might be "temporal emotional (or motivational) distortion", since distance does not distort our *recognition* of which option is better for us, but rather distorts our sentimental and motivational *reactions* to the two options. We still "see" (i.e., believe) that the remote outcome is better, but we feel more drawn to the near outcome. However, if we keep in mind that it is the attraction that becomes faint, the short label 'temporal myopia' will serve.

However, it is evident at the outset that when the time comes to *fulfill* the commitment, temporal myopia will once again get in the way. So, at the time the people make the commitment, they need to adopt some expedient to change that circumstance in the future. "[T]he utmost we can do is to change our circumstances and situation, and render the observance of the laws of justice our nearest interest, and their violation our most remote" (*T* 3.2.7.6 / SBN 537). But we cannot insure at one stroke that when the time comes to conform, every person will have a powerful immediate inducement; that is too large an undertaking. What we can do is give to just a few individuals an immediate interest in the execution of justice, and leave those few to generate motives in the rest. (By an *execution* of justice Hume probably means an act of *enforcement* of the rules of justice, rather than an act of mere conformity to them. "These persons . . . are not only induc'd to observe those rules in their own conduct, but also to constrain others to a like regularity, and inforce the dictates of equity thro' the whole society" (ibid.).) These individuals whom we interest in enforcing the rules thus become civil magistrates, kings, governors, and other sorts of rulers. Apparently, we make the execution of justice their immediate interest by creating for these few people a preferred position in society, one they will take care to protect. This makes the preservation of society especially precious to them; and since "every execution of justice" is necessary to that preservation, they acquire an especially strong interest in every execution of justice. At the same time, most acts of injustice in society occur between people who are strangers to the magistrates and yield no immediate (or long-term) advantage to the magistrates, so the magistrates have no incentive to tolerate injustices (ibid.). Their near*est*-term interest is to preserve society and secure their position by stopping violations; they have none nearer. Once magistrates have their status and accompanying motives, they will naturally extend their activities from merely enforcing the rules of justice to deciding disputes concerning what those rules require (*T* 3.2.7.7 / SBN 538).

Hume thinks that pre-civil societies with a subsistence economy can endure for generations without need of government, even though their people are as temporally myopic as any. Increased productivity is what makes people need government. Even so, the idea for such a social innovation must arise somehow. Hume suggests that the idea probably comes from war. The purely voluntary cooperation of pre-civil society disintegrates under foreign attack, and internal chaos threatens. To save themselves not only from the enemy but also from each other, the people select and submit to a military leader for the duration of the war. Once they have experienced such authority, they can resort to it again when the social order is threatened by increased wealth (*T* 3.2.8.2 / SBN 541).

The first rulers, in a given pre-civil society, must be identified by some special joint action. A likely such action is this: the people assemble, select magistrates, decide what their powers will be, and all promise to obey them. (Apparently Hume sees this as one available option.) If this is the method used, then the resulting promissory obligation is the first obligation to obey the magistrates. Since promissory obligation was already extant in pre-civil society, it provides a lever to start government in motion. However, even if it is used, "the duty of allegiance . . . quickly takes root of itself, and has an original obligation and authority, independent of all contracts" (*T* 3.2.8.3 / SBN 542). This is because continued obedience to the magistrates, with or without a promise, proves highly beneficial to all. Indeed, allegiance to magistrates is invented to remedy "inconveniences" very similar to those for the remedy of which property and promise were invented. "On whichever side we turn this subject, we shall find, that these two kinds of duty are exactly on the same footing, and have the same source both of their *first invention* and *moral obligation*. They . . . acquire their moral sanction in the same manner, from their remedying those inconveniences" (*T* 3.2.8.4 / SBN 543). So an initial social contract is at most a launching device for a duty of submission which acquires independent moral force, force that is not derived from an original contract.

That independent obligation arises in the same way as other artificial duties arise. Interest induces us to invent a way of acting (in this case, obedience to magistrates). A great temptation can lead us to overlook the long-term advantage of conformity to the convention in our own case; but when others violate it, we see the defection (here, disobedience to governors) as "highly prejudicial to public interest, and to our own in particular. This naturally gives us an uneasiness, in considering such seditious and disloyal actions, and makes us attach to them the idea of vice and moral deformity" (*T* 3.2.8.7 / SBN 545). The uneasiness comes from sympathy and is an instance of moral disapprobation. "*Education, and the artifice of politicians*, concur in bestowing a farther morality on loyalty, and branding all rebellion with a greater degree of guilt and infamy" (*T* 3.2.8.7 / SBN 546). As Hume points out, this process exactly parallels the development of moral disapproval of property violations and infidelity to promises. Sympathy gives rise to the moral sentiment of disapproval of disloyal actions, and a second artifice is employed to raise this sentiment to the strength of a sense of honor, which may have an influence on action. Once this is accomplished, there is no further need for subjects to make a promise of obedience in order to be bound to obey both by interest and by duty. (Recall that to show that obedience to our governors is our duty, it is sufficient to show that disobedience is disapproved in the requisite way.)

This is fortunate, since, as Hume notes repeatedly, the subjects of most governments throughout history never promised their allegiance, explicitly or tacitly.[3]

---

[3] Much of Hume's work in this portion of the *Treatise* is aimed at refuting, first, the contractarians and, secondly, the advocates of passive obedience. I omit the parts of these attempts that have no bearing on the issues at hand.

III. THE TWO OBJECTIONS

A. Power and the Motive to Conform

The initial formation of government thus has the structure of a Ulysses contract, a contract in which we obtain a commitment now, from certain other people, to force us to act later as we now prefer that we shall act then, because we expect that then we will be unwilling to do so. Our temporal myopia is incurable; so we appoint magistrates who will be poised to enforce justice later, when the irresistible temptation to violate it will come upon us. We do this in order to get the greater benefit of social stability.

How is the magistrate to enforce conformity? He does not look as if he would have the power to induce the populace to obey the rules of justice. This is our first objection. The ruler is just one person, or at most a few persons; how are they to control the behavior of the many? Ulysses' sailors, after all, outnumbered Ulysses, and they tied him to the mast with strong ropes that held him in place. Even if the handful of magistrates had some armed minions, what use would they be against the myopic multitude? Hume himself has this concern in mind as early as 1741 (just after the publication of Book 3 of the *Treatise*), in his essay "Of the first principles of government" (*EMPL* 32–6). His opening sentences make it very clear that force is not sufficient:

Nothing appears more surprising to those, who consider human affairs with a philosophical eye, than the easiness with which the many are governed by the few. . . . When we enquire by what means this wonder is effected, we shall find, that, . . . FORCE is always on the side of the governed.

But if justice is not to be executed by force, then how? If, by virtue of his status, the ruler has a larger share of property than the people, he could induce obedience by reward; but given the universality of temporal myopia, he would soon deplete his fortune paying his subjects not to commit injustices. Long before that happened, he would cease to find it worthwhile to execute the rules of justice. Obedience to the magistrate is, of course, in everyone's *long-term* interest, if the magistrate is indeed enforcing the rules of justice. However, this is just the sort of interest whose motivational efficacy is defeated by temporal myopia. People who could not conform to the rules of property and contract for the sake of long-term interest will not be able to obey the magistrate from long-term interest either. It seems that the Ulysses contract cannot be carried out.

A related objection is considered by Hume himself in an essay written much later, also called "Of the origin of government".[4] Perhaps by causing the human

---

[4] According to Eugene Miller (*EMPL*, p. xiv), this was first published posthumously in 1777.

psyche to develop the feeling that we have a moral duty of allegiance (a duty
to obey the magistrate's commands), we may provide the motivating passion we
need to fulfill the Ulysses contract. (Perhaps the sense of duty is not subject to
the distortions of temporal myopia.) In that case, when the self-interested motive
to conform to justice is thwarted by temporal myopia, the duty of obedience to
the magistrate takes over, and provides the impetus for just action. "But still",
Hume worries in this essay, "it may be thought that nothing is gained by this
alliance, and that the . . . duty of obedience, from its very nature, lays as feeble a
hold of the human mind, as the . . . duty of justice. Peculiar interests and present
temptations may overcome the one as well as the other. . . . And the man, who
is inclined to be a bad neighbour, must be led by the same motives, well or ill
understood, to be a bad citizen and subject" (*EMPL* 38). That is, if the sense of
justice or equity was insufficient to cause a person to adhere regularly to justice,
the sense of allegiance or law-abidingness will be similarly insufficient to cause
obedience to the magistrate.

Thus it seems that government lacks the influence, whether interested or
moral, to bring about the results for which it is invented.

B. Is Allegiance a Virtue?

Our second objection, the more important one for Hume's general theory
of morals, is that his account of the origin of government does not seem
to analyze allegiance as a *virtue*. In examining Book 3, Part 2, of Hume's
Treatise ("Of justice and injustice") we have found a series of analyses of those
virtues he labels artificial. With respect to three of them (honesty, fidelity, and
chastity), he not only explains how and why the rules regarding the relevant
sorts of activities are cooperatively invented, but he depicts the artificial virtue in
question as a genuine state of character, defined in part by its characteristic, and
approved, motivating sentiment. There is plenty of interpretive disagreement
about the exact structure of these virtues; I have developed one interpretation
in the last two chapters. But that they are virtues, and that in coming to
possess them a person must undergo some change in her passions, is usually
acknowledged by present-day interpreters. Allegiance to government, while it is
also classified as an artificial virtue, seems to be given no comparable analysis.
Hume does not seem to say anything about the development of new or changed
motivating sentiments on the part of those who become law-abiding, or about
the general approval of their motives. Thus it may seem that Hume's virtue-
based approach to ethics fades from the picture when he turns to matters of
government.

This problem, that allegiance to government is not a genuine Humean virtue,
appears most acute if we interpret Hume as not merely expecting that every
virtue will have its own characteristic motive (as he seems to do, for example,
at *T* 3.2.1.10–14 / SBN 480–2), but as specifying *moral* motives for each of

the other artificial virtues. I have argued that he indeed does this for justice and fidelity to promises, and there is evidence that he does it for feminine chastity and modesty as well, which is another instance in which temporal myopia must be overcome somehow (*T* 3.2.12.5–7 / SBN 571–2). Let us look back briefly at his account of the development of the virtuous motive in the virtue of (property-related) justice or probity to see how this causes difficulty for his account of allegiance to government.

In describing the transition from the condition of small family groups to pre-civil society by means of the introduction of rules of ownership back in *Treatise* 3.2.2, "Of the origin of justice and property", Hume says that people are moved to impose the rules on themselves and to observe them at the outset by their own interest, which "on the first formation of society, is sufficiently strong and forcible"; but in a larger, more prosperous group, interest will not reliably move people to comply, and there will be danger that the convention will disintegrate (*T* 3.2.2.24 / SBN 499). However, "sympathy with public interest" (ibid.) results in moral approval of just acts and disapproval of unjust ones, even in one's own case, and there is considerable incentive for everyone with influence over the motives of others to make use of this moral sentiment to fashion a further motive of compliance. They do this by associating honest behavior with pride and dishonest behavior with shame, so that the moral approval and disapproval become "an esteem for justice, and an abhorrence of injustice" in every case, one that disposes people to *behave* justly—indeed, one that is in some settings more reliable than interest (*T* 3.2.3.25 / SBN 500).

Immediately before turning to the origin of government, Hume again refers to the "sense of honor and duty in the strict regulation of our actions with regard to the property of others", a moral sentiment "augmented" by the teachings of parents and politicians (*T* 3.2.6.11 / SBN 534). This suggests that in populous but poor societies, it is not interest alone, or even primarily, that is to be relied upon to insure conformity to the rules of justice, but rather the augmented moral sense—the sense of honor.

It is strange, then, that in the next section (indeed the next paragraph), Hume talks only about interest and its inability to produce conformity in cases of temporal myopia. We were just led to believe that interest is no longer indispensable for conformity to justice; we have the sense of honor to supplement it. So what difference does it make if interest is sometimes hobbled in its motivating power? It looks as if Hume is having the people invent government to solve a problem that has already been solved.

In light of this, I ought to restate the part of the above-described objection pertaining to the power of the moral sentiment to produce action. It really has the form of a dilemma: If the moral sentiment produces conformity to justice, then there is no need to invent government. And if the moral sentiment is inadequate to generate just behavior, then the addition of a duty of allegiance will not solve the problem.

It has been argued here that the sense of honor is the motive that characterizes the honest and faithful person (the person with the virtue of material honesty and the person with the virtue of fidelity to promises, or considering these jointly, the person with the virtue of justice). A person who has "the least grain of honesty, or sense of duty and obligation" will find that his "regard to justice, and abhorrence of villainy and knavery, are sufficient reasons" for him to repay a loan (*T* 3.2.1.9 / SBN 479). Justice is a personal virtue, and the person possessed of it is characteristically moved by the sense of honor, that augmented moral sentiment. It is this motive of which we approve. In the *Treatise*'s section "Of the origin of government", however, we seem to be dealing with a society mainly of amoral individuals, or at least individuals who lack the virtue of justice. The motive of interest alone sustains their conformity to property and contracts, and where interest fails to move them, they fail to conform. What happened to the just individuals and the action-causing force of the sense of honor indicated just a few lines before?

We must also wonder whether, when government is created, any new virtue comes into being analogous to the virtue of justice. If government is a Ulysses contract, it would seem to leave the people with the same interested motives as before. If they violate the rules of justice, the magistrate will force them back into line (somehow), as do the ropes that bind Ulysses. But at the time of temptation, they have no efficacious motive to obey the magistrate, any more than Ulysses has an efficacious motive to resist the sirens; or rather (since they are not literally tied up), what moves them to obey is not virtue, but immediate interest in avoiding the magistrate's penalties. If that is the case, it seems that Hume has no reason to discuss allegiance under the heading of the artificial virtues. Yet Hume seems to think allegiance (which he also calls loyalty) is a character trait of individuals.[5]

IV. SOLUTIONS TO THESE DIFFICULTIES

To determine whether these criticisms are well-founded, we must supplement the account of the *Treatise* with the two essays already quoted and with other elements of the larger *Treatise* account of the artificial virtues. If we fill in the gaps from these sources in the right way, both objections can be refuted. The Humean magistrates have the right sort of emotional levers to enforce the rules of justice and obtain obedience, and allegiance to government is a Humean

---

[5] e.g., Hume groups allegiance with the other virtues that conform to the model provided by feminine chastity and modesty (*T* 3.2.12.1–7 / SBN 570–3). This model involves an inculcated motivating sentiment that is generally approved. It is not just chaste behavior in women that is approved, but the feeling of "repugnance" to illicit advances.

artificial virtue. Indeed, the psychological aspect of the virtue of allegiance is the key to explaining how the device of government can succeed in achieving its ends. Hume's virtue theory is thus well integrated with his political theory, and indeed provides the underpinnings that make the political theory plausible.

Let us take up the objections in reverse order: the question of virtue first, and second, the question of the magistrate's power to engender obedience.

The first clue appears in the 1741 essay "Of the first principles of government". The sentence quoted earlier, in which Hume says that "FORCE is always on the side of the governed", goes on to say that "the governors have nothing to support them but opinion". One opinion that causes obedience to the governors is the belief that this is in the general interest. That, of course, will not solve the myopia problem. But in addition there is opinion of right, which includes both "right to power" and "right to property". The feeling that magistrates have a right to power, and the influence of this attitude on action, Hume says, is greatly enhanced by rulers' claims to belong to an ancient line.

The next clue comes from Hume's late essay "Of the origin of government". After worrying that a man who is an unjust neighbor will have the same motives to be a bad subject of the ruler, he goes on:

Experience, however, proves, that there is a great difference between the cases. . . . [O]ur duty to the magistrate is more strictly guarded by the principles of human nature, than our duty to our fellow-citizens. . . . The persons, who first attain this distinction by the consent, tacit or express, of the people, must be endowed with superior personal qualities of valour, force, integrity, or prudence, which command respect and confidence: and after government is established, a regard to birth, rank, and station has a mighty influence over men, and enforces the decrees of the magistrate. The prince or leader exclaims against every disorder, which disturbs his society. He summons all his partizans and all men of probity to aid him in correcting and redressing it; and he is readily followed by all indifferent persons in the execution of his office. He soon acquires the power of rewarding these services. . . . Habit soon consolidates what other principles of human nature had imperfectly founded.   (*EMPL* 38–9)

We see that it is not force that brings about obedience; and even though reward can come in eventually, it need not at first. Rather, the motives of obedience are respect for and confidence in the magistrate, regard to birth and status, partisanship, probity (the virtue of justice), and eventually, habit. In elevating a magistrate, we make use of the individual's charisma and moral suasion to inspire acts on the part of the people that interest alone was powerless to produce. This personal charisma and moral superiority (or noble birth) bring the multitude to the magistrate's aid in enforcing the rules of justice.

The final clue lies in Hume's parallel descriptions in the *Treatise* of the evolution of the moral sentiment in each of the other artificial virtues. In the development of the sense of honesty or equity (*T* 3.2.2.24 / SBN 499–501), the sense of fidelity (*T* 3.2.5.12 / SBN 523, and both equity and fidelity *T* 3.2.6.9–10 /

SBN 531–4), and the sense of modesty (*T* 3.2.12.7 / SBN 572–3), all of the
following elements are present:

1. A conventional form of behavior is invented.

2. Sympathy, or some similar awareness of the benefits and harms to others,
   evokes moral approval of this convention-defined behavior.

3. Education by parents and the "artifice(s) of politicians" augment this sentiment of approval by associating the behavior with pride, and its opposite with
   shame.

4. Those who have an interest in the cumulative effects of the behavior approve
   it, and the others are "carried along with the stream" (*T* 3.2.12.7 / SBN 572)
   to approve it as well, and to be shocked by transgression.

5. Unlike what is the case in natural forms of human motive formation, those
   who take the convention to heart are guided by general rules which they
   extend beyond the interested reasons for which the convention first arose.

In this way the moral approval and disapproval that naturally arise from the
cumulative beneficial effects of the conventional behavior are transformed into a
moral motive to conform to it oneself, with great strictness, in every instance.

We can, indeed, find four of these features in Hume's account of allegiance
in the *Treatise*. First, government and obedience to it are invented. Allegiance is
one of those artificial virtues that is obviously fabricated, since "all government
is plainly an invention of men, and the origin of most governments is known
in history" (*T* 3.2.8.4 / SBN 542). The only way to maintain that allegiance
was a natural virtue would be to show that it is merely an instance of fidelity
to promises, and Hume argues at length that this is not the case. Second,
we recognize the disobedient acts of others not only as potentially harmful to
ourselves, but "highly prejudicial to the public good", and as a result we feel
"an uneasiness, in considering such seditious and disloyal acts, and . . . attach to
them the idea of vice and moral deformity. 'Tis the same principle, which causes
us to disapprove of all kinds of private injustice" (*T* 3.2.8.7 / SBN 545). Third,
"*Education*, and *the artifice of politicians*, concur in bestowing a farther morality
on loyalty, and branding all rebellion with a greater degree of guilt and infamy"
(*T* 3.2.8.7 / SBN 546). (Note the augmentation of the moral sentiment.) And
fourth, with respect to the moral obligation to submit to government, "general
rules commonly extend beyond the principles, on which they were founded;
and . . . we seldom make any exception to them, unless that exception have the
qualities of a general rule", which is the case for the rare conditions (of oppression
and tyranny by cruel and ambitious rulers) under which revolution is justified
(*T* 3.2 9.3 / SBN 551).

The remaining, and more minor, feature is not articulated in the *Treatise*, or
in the contemporaneous essay "Of the first principles of government". It emerges
explicitly in the later essay "Of the origin of government". In the paragraph

from it quoted above, all those who are neither partisans nor men of probity are carried along by the impulse to obey and support the ruler which has captivated everyone else, until habit takes over for everyone. All are guided by general rules.

Thus for Hume the invention of government goes hand in glove with the cultivation of the moral sentiment, so that the moral sentiment becomes a motive of strict compliance with the convention of government (that is, a motive of obedience to governors). The initial compliance must be otherwise motivated, of course; for the moral sentiment cannot approve obedience until obedience has begun and has started to produce its salutary effects. Interest of the general, shared sort—interest in preserving society—moves the people to select a governor. While this interest may also, sometimes, move them to obey the commands that their ruler issues later, this is not a reliable motive, because of temporal myopia. A variety of complex psychological factors also move the people to obey the governor when the time comes to do so: admiration or awe of his personal virtue or ancestry, the sense of justice, the influence of others, and eventually, habit. Different motives may come into play at different moments. Then sympathy reacts to the widespread benefits of obedience and the harm of disloyalty, giving rise to moral approval and disapproval. The moral sentiment is augmented by education, which links sedition to shame and loyalty to pride. The outcome of the process is a motivating, moral sentiment: allegiance. This is the artificial virtue. It begins from a patchwork of sentiments more fragmented than those that give rise to the other artificial virtues, but it works. The result is not only a new mechanism for appeasing the interested affection, but a new virtuous motive. This augmented moral motive provides a unified object for our further approval, so that the loyal person has a single, characteristic motivating sentiment of which all can approve.

It *seems* as if Hume neglects the cultivation of a new motive in his account of the origin of government because most of his remarks about this are embedded in his lengthy arguments against the thesis that the duty of allegiance is founded for all time on the obligation of promises. The passages quoted above are extracted from those discussions. But in arguing against the contractarians, he also, in passing, gives an account of the origin of the moral obligation of allegiance which perfectly parallels the like accounts for the other artificial virtues. And in so doing, he draws the same conclusion about motives for allegiance that he is committed to for justice (with regard to property and contracts) and chastity.

What Hume does not explicitly say, but what he needs here and no doubt believes, is that the motivating moral sentiment of allegiance, and indeed all the moral sentiments, are *not* subject to temporal myopia. The impulse to keep a promise because to break it would be shameful, or to rebuff an illicit sexual advance because of a repugnance to "gallantry", is an immediate response, not the desire for a means to long-term net gain. In a revealing example, Hume says that temporal myopia poses a problem for marital fidelity, since the pain of a bad reputation is more remote than the pleasure of an illicit sexual encounter;

the solution lies in the "preceding backwardness or dread" of sexual advances that is engendered in a chaste and modest woman, which is an immediate deterrent to dalliance (*T* 3.2.12.5 / SBN 571–2). The feeling that a violation of justice, or of chastity, or of the command of my governor, is itself "base and infamous" (*T* 3.2.3.26 / SBN 500–1) is not a response to a distant prospect; it is an immediate feeling, here and now. Thus there is no distance to obscure it.

This enables Hume's incipient citizens to make the Ulysses contract, and their new magistrate to enforce it. The people bind themselves to obey their new governors by creating conditions under which it will come to seem honorable to obey and shameful to disobey. The new subjects are not induced to obey by force, or by bribery, or in some cases even by long-term interest, but by various immediate impulses (the sense of promissory duty, admiration, the influence of peers) that lead in time, through the workings of sympathy, to the formation of a moral sentiment of allegiance that engenders obedience from the "opinion of right".

One issue remains to be addressed. If the moral sentiment becomes the motivating sentiment of an artificial virtue, and if, as previously argued, that motive is not compromised by our temporal myopia, then why do the people need government in the first place? True enough, their interest could not always move them to conform to the voluntary conventions of justice in the face of tempting riches. But wouldn't their sense of justice fill the gap and keep them on the straight and narrow when interest was incapacitated? What I have said so far only seems to make this difficulty more acute.

To solve this problem on Hume's behalf, we should notice two features of pre-civil society. Hume intimates that the virtue of justice takes hold in at least some people once the society becomes large enough. But he never says it is inculcated in everyone. While the society is poor, it can survive with a manageable balance between just and merely self-interested members, since these two motives will mostly generate the same actions. With an increase in wealth the merely self-interested members will succumb to temporal myopia and indulge in more injustices, and this will wear away at the virtue of the just, who observe many poor role models, and begin to see themselves as the "cully of [their] integrity." One can face sacrifices for the sake of one's conscience if one's conscience is reinforced enough by others, but if many are unjust, setting a poor example and making one feel like a chump, one can begin to lose one's sense of honor on the subject.

The second thing to notice is that even in explaining how the moral sentiment is augmented to engender conformity to *justice*, Hume talks about the influence of politicians. However, there are no politicians in pre-civil society. There are parents and private education, so some cultivation of the sense of honor with respect to promises and property can be carried out. But it is reasonable to infer that the process of making people just, of giving them the virtue of justice, is not completed in pre-civil society. The sense of justice may not be strong enough to cause people to act, or it may not be strong enough in very many people, before politicians come on the scene. Thus we need to make the transition to civil society, not only to insure social stability, but also to perfect the virtue of justice. This is why we still need to invent government, even though the sense of justice can to some extent fill the motivational gaps left by interest: the sense of justice is not yet potent enough to be a consistent motive throughout society without the influence of public leaders and opinion-makers. And in the process of perfecting the individual virtue of justice by creating such leaders, whom we can rely upon to praise honesty and trustworthiness and to blame injustice in order the better to manage us, we also bring into being the additional artificial virtue of allegiance.[6]

We know that for Hume a virtue is constituted by a characteristic motivating sentiment, or a disposition to experience a motivating sentiment. The creation of the personal virtue of justice requires the invention of property and promises, the natural operation of sympathy, and the collusion of parents and politicians to perfect the appropriate motivating sentiment. The completion of this process requires the formation of government and the further invention of the virtue of allegiance. We need public leaders to bring the virtue of justice to full flower (where it does develop—of course not all citizens will be just). To have public leaders is to have government, and the continuing power of government depends upon the development in citizens of a further motivating sentiment, the sense of allegiance. While what induces us to obedience initially is our admiration for our leaders and other influences, ultimately we are moved to obey by our virtue of allegiance, that new motivating sentiment. We find it honorable to obey the laws and decrees of our government, and shameful to flout them. It is this that gives princes their power over us. Thus Hume makes crucial use of his theory of the virtues to account for the power of magistrates and rulers. We see that in this respect Hume's virtue theory is in fact intertwined with his political philosophy. The virtue theory, according to which allegiance to government qualifies as a *bona fide* virtue, identifies the motives of obedience that explain the power of government.

V. AN ASIDE ABOUT CORRUPTION OF THE MAGISTRATES

A problem for Hume's account that should be mentioned but that we cannot entirely solve is how, once a government is instituted, we are to prevent corruption

---

[6] According to the *Oxford English Dictionary*, 2nd edn. (Oxford: Clarendon Press, 1989), xii. 34, 'politician' in this period had the well-accepted meaning of a lawmaker, leader of government, statesman, or leader of a political party. However, Forbes (1977) suggests that 'politician' may also have meant a political opinion-maker, someone who wrote about the science of government and the issues of the day.

of the magistrates by those who wish to commit private injustices with impunity. A magistrate will prevent me from defrauding you, Hume thinks, since the magistrate herself realizes no short-term gain from my act of fraud, and the preservation of society from such injustices is in her immediate interest because of her highly advantaged social position. But it seems that all I must do is offer the magistrate a bribe to look the other way; then she has a near-term interest in tolerating and not punishing my injustice to you. And she, like everyone else, is vulnerable to temporal myopia. Thus in the end, a critic might argue, government will not enforce the rules of property and contract, but will only make violations more expensive for the perpetrators.

Hume offers no explicit solution, but he has some resources between the lines. First, we have seen evidence that Hume thinks the first magistrates, who are selected by a previously unruled populace, will be chosen in part for their integrity. This might make them immune to corruption, or nearly so. If we are right that the virtue of probity (justice) involves feeling a direct repugnance to any violation of the rules of property and contract, then the magistrate of superior integrity would have difficulty overcoming such repugnance for the sake of profit. And perhaps superior prudence (another feature for which the first rulers are selected) entails a less than average degree of temporal myopia. While Hume thinks this weakness is endemic in human nature, he does not think it has the same severity in every individual. "What we call strength of mind, implies the prevalence of the calm passions above the violent," and some people possess this virtue, which enables them, some of the time though not always, to "counter-act a violent passion in the prosecution of their interests" even when those interests are more remote (T 2.3.3.10 / SBN 415).

These considerations, however, do not solve the corruption problem for subsequent magistrates, who come to their position by noble birth or some other routine manner of succession, rather than personal superiority. Hume may think that should it become known that a magistrate (especially a *judge*) is not enforcing the rules of justice, the people would promptly replace her, since such enforcement is the only reason to provide her with the perquisites of office.[7] But he surely realizes that fear of adverse public reaction would not be sufficient to prevent all graft (especially since some could be kept secret). To some extent Hume may envision the magistrates or rulers as occupying a position of such relative wealth that those they govern will not have adequate means to offer them a sufficiently attractive bribe. It will be far more in the governors' interest to preserve the peaceful functioning of their domains than to accept some paltry ill-gotten gains from their subjects in exchange for ignoring misdeeds that are likely to make precarious the governors' enjoyment of their extensive lands and goods. The enjoyment of wealth, after all, requires that many servants, peasants, and other subordinates perform their cooperative tasks

---

[7] See Miller 1981: 83.

reliably and peaceably, something that will not occur if they are busy robbing one another. It would take a huge bribe to make someone accept a risk of disrupting this arrangement, and the common people will not be able to afford it. And finally, though I claim no textual evidence for this speculation, perhaps Hume considers a certain amount of low-level, unchecked corruption of the nobility the inevitable cost of the blessings of government. Clearly when it comes to rulers "transported by their passions into all the excesses of cruelty and ambition", especially those with "supreme power", Hume thinks it becomes worse to have government than to lack it, and indeed under those conditions he thinks revolution is justified. But a bit of bribery here and there would not have such an effect, and he may think it irremediable. We need not worry that it will escalate into rapaciousness, for princes will be deterred from "enormous tyranny and oppression" (*T* 3.2.10.16 / SBN 563) by the threat of revolution.

VI. EXTENDING THE NOTION OF AN ARTIFICIAL VIRTUE?

We have examined three of Hume's artificial virtues in detail (honesty, fidelity to promises, and allegiance to government), and made some observations about another (chastity and modesty in women), noting the overall picture that emerges from them. The artificial virtues are genuine traits of character as Hume understands those: dispositions to feel certain (characteristically) motivating passions. They are also genuine virtues, since sympathy causes us to approve these dispositions on considering them from the common point of view. But unlike the natural virtues, the sentiments they consist of are moral ones. And also unlike the natural virtues, they are socially fabricated mental qualities. It is not only the rules that govern our behavior with regard to property or marriage that are fabricated; the very character traits themselves (honesty, fidelity, and so on) are socially constructed as well. In each case there is some practical problem that arises in human social life (how to cooperate for mutual aid and prosperity, how to overcome the deterioration of justice in a society with a large and thriving economy, how to insure that fathers support their children) which reveals the natural human sentiments to be deficient, for by themselves they are unable to provide a solution. As a species we have certain disabilities. However, we are an "inventive species" and a highly social one, so we use our capacities for tacit agreement, convention, and rule-following, plus the suasion of parents and leaders and the malleability of our feelings, first to provide a practical mechanism for beginning to solve the problem, and ultimately to provide a new emotional disposition that compensates for what is "incommodious in the affections" and yields a more enduring solution. The artificial virtues are both conventional and emotional prostheses that remedy our natural defects.

Once on the trail of prosthetic virtues, Hume continues to find more. In the last section of the *Treatise* he finds that he cannot discuss the natural virtues of self-confidence and modesty (in a different sense, that of having an accurate opinion of our personal weaknesses) and the natural vice of conceit without identifying yet another artificial virtue, that of good manners or good breeding (*T* 3.3.2.10 / SBN 597–8). That virtue proves to be a disposition to conceal our pride in our own merits and accomplishments, even if it is well-founded (for we cannot know whether it is or not), and to exhibit demeanor in company that expresses deference toward others in proportion to their social rank. The problem for which this trait provides a solution is that each of us tends to be rudely shocked by the pride of others, particularly where it is ill-founded, and because of our natural tendency to think well of ourselves, we cannot be sure that our own pride does not exceed our actual merits. (Hume takes it as an empirical fact that outward signs of the inflated pride of others are very irritating; he explains it in terms of his theory of ideas and impressions, sympathy, and another phenomenon that he calls "comparison" (*T* 3.3.2.1–7 / SBN 592–6).)[8] Rather than irritate others and endure constant friction with them, we establish conventional "ranks of men", and we learn to hide our self-esteem and show a humble exterior to all those who outrank us and even to our equals.

This might lead one to wonder whether there are other artificial virtues already developed, or other human problems that are now unsolved but could be solved by the fabrication of a new artificial virtue. There is nothing in Hume's theory to rule out either possibility. In particular, if there are other ways in which our natural sentiments or dispositions to act prevent us from solving a practical problem, those might be suitable arenas for development of a new artificial virtue. Changing circumstances might reveal a deficiency in human nature that keeps us from solving some new problem; and the prospect of fabricating a new virtue to compensate for this is intriguing. Let us briefly consider an example.

In discussing the need to invent property, Hume emphasizes the moderate scarcity of certain material goods relative to people's desires. Only goods that are scarce relative to what human beings want produce the sorts of conflict that can be avoided by creating the convention of ownership and its concomitant virtue. There is no need for ownership of air or water, he observes, because each person can obtain all the air and water she desires without preventing any others from obtaining all that they desire (*T* 3.2.2.17 / SBN 495). Although this was not true of water in arid regions even prior to Hume's lifetime, it was true of air. But it is true no longer; there are ways of using the air that reduce the ability of others to obtain the air they need or want. However, introducing ownership of air does not look like a promising solution. Of course, this is the tip of a very vast iceberg. There is a human problem of which we are acutely

---

[8] For a brief explanation of comparison and how it works to create annoyance with the obvious conceit of others, see Cohon 2006*b*: 269–70.

aware today that was not evident to Hume: the problem of environmental degradation, damage, or depletion, including the human contribution to global climate change. A Humean analysis of the role of our natural sentiments in these problems provides an illuminating example of the need for a new artificial virtue and how it might work.

More than one natural sentiment or condition is involved in the problem, and even some of the natural *virtues* work against us here, just as the partiality of virtuous family attachment worked against solving the problem of moderate scarcity of detachable goods. Our avidity and confined generosity (which are not, of course, virtues for Hume, but in moderate amounts are not vices, because they are to be expected in human nature) incline us to exploit resources as fully as we can to profit ourselves and our families and friends; but of course this results in over-fishing, destruction of eco-systems, depletion of fossil fuels, and the like. Greed and limited generosity also lead us to buy the cheapest vehicles and fuels rather than use more expensive technology, and thus to continue to release greenhouse gases into the atmosphere. Even when we realize that our present enjoyments are leading to greater long-term harms for our offspring and perhaps even for ourselves, our (natural and incurable) temporal myopia prevents these concerns from altering our pursuit of short-term pleasure or advantage. Now there are already some virtues of character that incorporate concern for the longer-term future, but even one of those very virtues thwarts us here. Frugality is a natural virtue for Hume, one that we approve because it is advantageous to its possessor, insuring that his property will suffice for his needs over the course of his life. But in cases where the more environmentally responsible products cost more, frugality with one's own property can lead individuals in large groups to act in ways that harm the group over time by damaging its environment.

Hume would analyze this situation as presenting a coordination problem and a problem of motive. It will not solve the problem for one person to act in environmentally sound ways, any more than it would solve the problem of conflict over goods for one person to refrain from the goods of others; people will act this way only in the reasonable expectation that others will behave similarly, and only widespread cooperation will solve the problem. But widespread cooperation requires motivating sentiments that can be counted on in many different circumstances. Anything we say about what solution Hume might propose to our environmental problems, given his moral and political philosophy, is going to be highly speculative, of course, and there are insufficient grounds to offer any detailed analysis or proposal. But we can make some general, if slightly fanciful, observations.

One strategy that emerges from Hume's discussion of the invention of government is that people can commit themselves to make a sacrifice later for the even longer-term public good. Another is that a few individuals can be selected who are given a direct interest in the creation and preservation of the conventions that serve that distant benefit. This is all consistent with various governmental strategies that are already being implemented in different places to encourage the development and use of, for example, renewable energy sources and fuels that do not add carbon dioxide to the atmosphere. People in democratic states vote to implement fairly severe restrictions on emissions that will go into effect several years in the future, for example; and they create positions of authority in their governments to enforce the rules, making such enforcement the "immediate interest" of those appointed to these posts. So long as it is only avidity (specifically) or even self-interest (more generally) that moves people to change their behavior and conform to environmentally sound practices, the convention will not be stable, for everyone will have some opportunity to violate the rules without penalty, and everyone will sometimes believe that one small violation will do no harm to the environment while it will benefit the violator. The sense of allegiance to government, though, will provide more immediate and reliable incentives to comply, once this is mandated by government. And it would help to inspire further cooperation if persons analogous to the first charismatic governors, individuals known for "probity" or "valour" or even noble birth, would take positions of leadership in these efforts.

What is ultimately needed, a Humean would say, is a change of heart throughout the population. Once enough environmentally sound practices are in place, their benefits for everyone in those communities will become evident, and sympathy will lead all observers to approve the practices that yield these benefits. (Although sympathy with those now living communicates the most vivid pleasures and pains, we should not disregard the role of sympathy with future generations, once the effects on them can be extrapolated, for we can sympathize with all human beings, and particularly with those to whom we bear a causal relationship.) At this point the levers of pride and shame need to be deployed: parents and politicians and all others with influence need to praise environmental responsibility as honorable and to blame environmental carelessness and neglect as shameful and base. The "ductile minds" of the young need to be shaped by such praise and blame. This would augment people's moral approval of conformity to make it a motivating sentiment. Once the motive to conform to environmentally beneficial practices becomes moralized, we will come to have a new virtue—call it "environmental responsibility". With such a trait, people's motives to avoid the use of polluting fuels and reduce their carbon emissions (and so on) will not depend upon their interests always being served thereby, since they will do so because they wish to behave in ways that they can be proud of and do not wish to do anything shameful. So people will not be sensible knaves with regard to the environment, but will have reliable motives of compliance. And their motives will also be immune to temporal myopia, since the feelings of pride and shame will be immediate. A concern for reputation will reinforce the moral motive once it becomes common throughout society to condemn those who do not follow the useful practices, and the fear of ill-repute too is a concern that bypasses temporal myopia; my harm to the environment may not be felt for decades, but my bad reputation will sting me now.

If what was argued earlier in this chapter is right, a new artificial virtue can also arise piecemeal. We have seen that justice does not take root in everyone at once, and requires the invention of government (and so the emergence of eloquent politicians) before it can be fully internalized by most people. Similarly, a virtue of environmental responsibility might take shape in fits and starts, some individuals developing a moral motive while others are still moved mainly by material incentives or the threat of sanctions. But ultimately it could become quite widespread if public opinion-makers cultivate it properly.

There may be limits to the degree to which the human problems posed by the misuse of the natural environment are in fact amenable to solution by means of a Humean prosthetic virtue. With the introduction of property there is instant feedback: when people violate the rules of property in a simple pre-civil society, cooperation breaks down immediately. So they learn to follow the rules nearly all the time, and then there is a working system whose benefits are very evident, and of which it is consequently easy to approve. The sticking point for environmental responsibility, if there is one, is likely to be the difficulty of seeing the benefits and harms that arise from different practices directly enough and soon enough to make such approval possible. The harm that comes from bad practices may come so late that those who did the damage do not live to see its consequences. The benefits of environmentally responsible practices may not become evident quickly enough for the general population to observe them and be led by sympathy to approve what produced them, and so to form a new virtue that transforms their own practice as well, before too much damage is already done. The benefits and harms may also be too diffuse or too distant from their causes; it may not be clear enough which wasteful or damaging practices (or which responsible practices) caused which harms (or benefits) in which places. So there may not be any direct feedback to the participants to keep them going or let them know they are causing trouble, and there may not be a community of thriving compliers whose happy result we can observe and approve. This would explain why the human race has not already fabricated an environmental virtue. It was not clear to our ancestors what they were doing to their own environment or how they might avoid doing it, although we now know that some of them turned fertile lands into deserts by their farming and grazing activities. But there certainly are some environmentally damaging practices that create obvious harm and loss, and some practices that clearly protect against such harm and loss, so there are surely some materials on which the Humean process of virtue fabrication can work. And at present we have capacities for scientific prediction of the impact of our behavior on the environment that we did not have in the past. Such information *might* enable us to create a new environmental virtue that could work fairly well to sustain beneficial practices, with one important proviso. We must be able to imagine ourselves to occupy the appropriate common point of view, that of all those who are or might be affected by our practices down through the generations, and we must be able to receive by sympathy their pleasure or pain. And that is quite a difficult exercise of imagination and feeling.

9

Criticizing Hume's List of Virtues and Vices

We have seen that when everyone in a society contemplates traits of character "in general" and from the common point of view, according to Hume, they approve some traits and consequently label them virtues, and disapprove others and label them vices. This leaves some readers unsatisfied, because it does not address certain fundamental normative issues. The worry can take a variety of forms. In this final chapter we will focus on whether Hume countenances any warranted criticism of the list of virtues and vices that results from this process of feeling moral sentiments from the common point of view, and if so, what the content of this criticism can be. The matter is closely connected with the issue of what, in Hume's theory, constitutes the basis of norms. Ultimately I will argue that for Hume there *is* a normative check on our sentiments, though not enough to warrant all the criticisms that one might like to make of the resulting list of virtues and vices. At the end I will briefly suggest a slight extension of Hume's standard that is in his spirit and supports somewhat more criticism.

I. DESCRIPTIVE PSYCHOLOGY ALONE OR NORMATIVE ETHICS?

Early in Book 3 of the *Treatise* Hume says "An action, or sentiment, or character is virtuous or vicious: why? because its view causes a pleasure or uneasiness of a particular kind. In giving a reason . . . for the pleasure or uneasiness, we sufficiently explain the vice or virtue" (*T* 3.1.2.3 / SBN 471). As we noted at the start of Chapter 6, here it sounds as if he thinks he can perform a descriptive and a normative task at once: in explaining how traits cause our approval under suitable conditions for reflection, he thinks he also shows that these traits are (truly) virtues. He then gives a detailed natural history of the moral sentiments, tracing the causal origin of our moral approval of each of the various virtues to the phenomenon of sympathy. He makes similar moves in the moral *Enquiry*, though often talking of "fellow-feeling" or "humanity" instead of "(natural) sympathy". But it is not immediately clear whether he really does offer us a normative ethical theory or merely an empirical description of the psychology of moral judgment. Does he actually (claim to) discover which traits *are* virtues, or only which traits we *take* to be virtues? To say a trait really is a virtue, and is not merely believed to be one, is to say it is a trait that it is good to have and bad to lack, a trait we should cultivate in ourselves and inculcate in our children, a trait we *should* approve and admire. Clearly Hume does mean to say that the traits on his list are the ones we approve; but does he mean to say they are the ones we *should* approve?

A significant number of commentators treat Hume as a mere descriptive psychologist of moral thought; but others claim or assume that he also presents a normative ethical theory.[1] Hume's own texts are maddeningly ambiguous on this matter, sometimes seeming merely to describe uncritically how "we" feel about character traits, sometimes offering criticism of received moral opinion, sometimes seeming to argue that widely shared sentiment is the final arbiter of all norms of virtue. The moral *Enquiry* in particular baffles the reader on this point with its easy transition from what looks like mere description of human responses without assessment to what looks much more like advocacy. Consider an example of this apparent transition from mere psychological description to endorsement (and back again):

This constant habit of surveying ourselves, as it were, in reflection, keeps alive all the sentiments of right and wrong, and begets, in noble natures, a certain reverence for themselves as well as others; which is the surest guardian of every virtue. The animal conveniencies and pleasures sink gradually in their value; while every inward beauty and moral grace is studiously acquired, and the mind is accomplished in every perfection, which can adorn or embellish a rational creature.

Here is the most perfect morality with which we are acquainted: Here is displayed the force of many sympathies. Our moral sentiment is itself a feeling chiefly of that nature: And our regard to a character with others seems to arise only from a care of preserving a character with ourselves.   (*EPM* 9.10–11 / SBN 276)

What he says in criticizing certain people's lists of virtues and vices, such as the monkish virtues and the Christian doctrine of humility, strongly suggests that he thinks not only that we (human beings generally) do not really approve what those theorists advocate, but that their judgment is mistaken, and that our actual, widely shared approvals and disapprovals, when formed under the right conditions, determine what really is and is not a virtue—not only what is approved, but what should be.[2] Thus for example, he says in the Conclusion of

---

[1] Among the many commentators who treat Hume's theory as merely descriptive are Darwall (1994: 61), Mackie (1980: 5–6), and Santayana (1905–6: 213). By contrast, many take it for granted that Hume advocates particular virtues and vices: e.g., Baier (1991: *passim*, but see, e.g., her discussion of pride in ch. 9). Shaver (1995) is one of the few who argues for this thesis, and though his reasons are different from mine, I have learned from him. He explains how there can be norms of moral judgment in an empiricist theory in a way analogous to that in which there are norms of causal judgment in Hume's theory. (The Santayana reference comes from his article.)

[2] The remarks about the monkish virtues (*EPM* 9.3 / SBN 270), quoted below, are more definite. With respect to the Christian religious "declaimers" who say that humility is a virtue, he is more

the moral *Enquiry* that after the arguments he has already presented, if he can also show that virtue serves the happiness of the virtuous person, "we shall have the satisfaction to reflect, that we have advanced principles, which not only, it is hoped, will stand the test of reasoning and enquiry, but may contribute to the amendment of men's lives, and their improvement in morality and social virtue" (*EPM* 9.1 / SBN 268). A theory that merely describes how and why we take certain qualities of mind to be virtues without taking a normative stand is not one we can expect to bring about moral improvement. A theory that reveals the actual virtues and vices and then shows virtue to be in our interest, however, can expect to make people better. Although I once thought Hume's project was merely descriptive, I now think the textual evidence shows otherwise.[3]

In any case, I shall read Hume as offering a normative account of the virtues and vices, as well as a descriptive psychology of the workings of moral sentiment. Although it is not his purpose to exhort or entice us to become virtuous—to paint virtue in its most attractive colors—that does not mean that his moral philosophy is value-free. As an anatomist (rather than a painter), he does not merely tell us what we *think* is good, but analyzes what is really good. He believes that the traits on his list really are virtues.[4]

II. THE UNIFORMITY OF MORAL EVALUATION

On what basis could Hume argue that we should have certain traits and not others? Presumably the grounds for this are the sentiments we feel: the phenomenologically distinctive pleasure or uneasiness we experience upon contemplating a quality of someone's mind. The closest thing to a definition of

guarded. "Whether this virtue of humility has been rightly understood, I shall not pretend to determine. I am content with the concession that the world naturally esteems a well regulated pride" (*T* 3.3.2.13 / SBN 600).

[3] Although I sometimes refer to Hume's ethical philosophy as a normative ethical *theory*, I do not mean to invoke any of the connotations the word 'theory' has acquired in the work of the anti-theory movement in ethics, or to insist that Hume's philosophy is an ethical theory in their sense. Baier, e.g. (1985*a* and 1985*b*), understands a "normative moral theory" as involving a hierarchy of principles (i.e., rules), as purporting to describe structures of the universe as scientific theories do, and as purporting to correct our motives and sentiments by means of (purely intellectual) reason. Her examples are Kantian and utilitarian views, and she (rightly) denies that Hume's view is of this kind. I mean none of this by the term. What I mean by a normative ethical or moral theory is an account of what is ethically good or bad that is capable of correcting our actual practices and sentiments rather than merely describing them. Given Baier's own view that for Hume the correction of motives, sentiments, and habits "can be done by sentiment and custom" (ibid. 238), I think she would agree that Hume's ethics is a normative ethical theory in my sense.

[4] Here I agree with Shaver (as against, e.g., Darwall 1994) that the distinction between the anatomist and the painter has been wrongly thought to distinguish description from normative theory. It is, rather, a distinction between analysis and exhortation. Today we would call it the distinction between the engineer (or perhaps reverse engineer) of a product and its advertiser. The product is genuine virtue. The engineer enumerates its parts and how they work together; the advertiser entices us to buy it.

virtue that Hume gives occurs in such passages as the following. In the *Treatise* he says, "Every quality of the mind is denominated virtuous, which gives pleasure by the mere survey; as every quality, which produces pain, is called vicious" (*T* 3.3.1.30 / SBN 591), and as we have already seen, "An action, or sentiment, or character is virtuous or vicious, why? because its view causes a pleasure or uneasiness of a peculiar kind" (*T* 3.1.1.3 / SBN 471). In the moral *Enquiry* he says, "It is the nature and, indeed, the definition of virtue, that it is a quality of the mind agreeable to or approved of by every one, who considers or contemplates it" (*EPM* 8.1 / SBN 261 n. 1). If in all his descriptions of our moral reactions he is telling us which traits are genuine virtues, then it would seem that the normativity (the traits' being genuine virtues) arises from the approval itself.

We know this does not mean that every individual has a personal ethical standard different from everyone else's. Human nature is basically uniform, so we all have the same emotional equipment. The varied and conflicting feelings of different people result from the different impact that things, including traits of character, have on us as distinct individuals leading our separate lives, and from the different points of view from which we observe things. We saw in Chapter 5 how these differences are smoothed out in moral evaluation. We can disregard the good or harm a particular character trait might do to our own interests when we assess it "in general" as a virtue or a vice. And when we imagine ourselves to occupy the common or general point of view, we consider the effects of the trait we are about to judge on all those on whom it has an impact, and we acquire their resulting (imagined) feelings by sympathy. (For the natural virtues an imagined position of closeness to the person under evaluation suffices; for the artificial virtues we must consider the impact of the trait on society.) Moral evaluations are indeed the product of the sentiments we feel, but only of those we feel when we disregard our own interests and adopt the common point of view. (Call these the feelings we experience on *unbiased consideration*.) Adopting the common point of view is a procedure we can follow; and if we perform it correctly, what results is a moral evaluation. For Hume the uniformity of human nature and the use of the common point of view enable all of us to reach the same moral assessment of any character trait. There is thus a shared, inter-subjective standard of good and evil. It is a little misleading to call Humean moral evaluation objective, since it is based on felt sentiment, but there is a very high degree of convergence in all moral assessments that are properly formed. (This position is tempered somewhat in "A Dialogue", but not, I would argue, fundamentally. We consider that work more below.)

So moral evaluation is not a matter of feeling just any old sentiment. But there seems to be no further appeal from the sentiments of approbation and disapprobation that we feel when we give a trait our unbiased consideration. What we approve under those conditions is a virtue, and what we disapprove is a vice. It appears that these feelings are the sole basis of normativity in Hume. (We will consider later whether this is so.)

One way to read this reliance on sentiment as the foundation of norms is to understand Hume as a *normative hedonist*, to coin a term. We might read him as holding that what we *should* be or do is determined by our feelings of pleasure and pain, with different sorts of "shoulds" supported by different sorts of pleasures and pains. Thus perhaps Hume holds the view that pain as such and in itself is necessarily bad and pleasure necessarily good, and so these feelings can ground normative judgments. Perhaps he also thinks that only pleasure and pain can ultimately ground any normative truth. That is one way to construe a famous passage in the moral *Enquiry*:

[T]he ultimate ends of human actions . . . recommend themselves entirely to the sentiments and affections of mankind . . . . Ask a man, why he uses exercise; he will answer, because he desires to keep his health. If you then enquire, why he desires health, he will readily reply, because sickness is painful. If you . . . desire a reason, why he hates pain, it is impossible he can ever give any. This is an ultimate end, and is never referred to any other object.
Perhaps, to your second question, why he desires health, he may also reply, that it is necessary for the exercise of his calling. If you ask, why he is anxious on that head, he will answer, because he desires to get money. If you demand, Why? It is the instrument of pleasure, says he. And beyond this it is an absurdity to ask for a reason. [. . .] Something must be desirable on its own account, and because of its immediate accord or agreement with human sentiment and affection.   (*EPM*, App.1.18–19 / SBN 293)

Hume may mean this as an account of what qualifies as an ultimate normative reason—an ultimate justification—for anything. In light of this, the ultimate justification for a *moral* judgment will be its "immediate accord or agreement" with the moral sentiments in particular, those pleasures and pains we feel on unbiased consideration of a quality of mind. This, at least, is a plausible initial interpretation.

III. THE PROBLEM OF CRITICIZING WIDESPREAD MORAL OPINION

A. The Errors Hume Allows For and Those He Does Not Allow For

If this is Hume's position, then it leaves us in some difficulty if we wish to criticize the widespread moral opinions held in an era or a society.

Hume certainly countenances some forms of criticism and identifies some kinds of errors we can make in moral evaluation. Not everyone is a perfectly competent moral judge all the time. First, someone may be unable to screen out selfish concerns and may, for example, erroneously dub an enemy a villain (*T* 3.1.2.4 / SBN 472). More experience and refinement will enable such a person to perform the procedure better. Or someone may fail to imagine the impact of some trait on, for example, foreign people far away and mistake her own local reaction to it for a moral sentiment (*T* 3.3.1.16 / SBN 582). Here too the person fails to carry out the procedure properly. But in these cases the resulting feeling is not really a moral one, or at least the resulting opinion is not a moral judgment. Because she has failed to screen out self-interest, or failed to take up a truly common point of view, the evaluator mistakes a non-moral feeling or judgment for a moral one, and that is how errors occur. Apart from such errors, however, when human beings adopt the common point of view and discover what they feel, they discover the virtues and the vices. They always get it right (given our initial interpretation). Thus one cannot say truly that everyone in a society or an era, even after unbiased contemplation, has the wrong feeling about a trait, or makes the wrong moral assessment of it. If their feeling succeeds in being a moral evaluation at all, it is a correct moral evaluation.

If this is so, then we must grant Hume his list of virtues and vices, at least if he is correct that the traits he lists are in fact widely or characteristically approved and disapproved under unbiased consideration. Of course, Hume might report incorrectly on what everyone or nearly everyone feels—he might be a bad pollster, putting traits on his list that are not in fact widely approved or disapproved. But that does not appear to be the case. Britons of Hume's own day, at least, and many more peoples in other times and places, probably did indeed approve and disapprove the traits he lists when they considered them in the way he specifies. We today agree with them in approving justice, benevolence, friendship, and gratitude under unbiased consideration. But in addition, Hume's countrymen and others surely also disapproved any sort of sexual assertiveness in women, and approved that "backwardness or dread" of flirtation or sexual advances that we considered in Chapter 6, "a repugnance to all expressions, and postures, and liberties, that have an immediate relation to that enjoyment" (*T* 3.2.12.5 / SBN 572), while approving a more active interest in sex and a looser disposition to chastity for men.[5] They did in fact find the greatness of conquering warriors so "dazzling" that they approved the trait of military valor in spite of its historical contribution to "the devastation of provinces" (*T* 3.3.2.15 / SBN 601). (People have always done so and still do.) They approved a weaker standard of justice for princes than for private individuals, and felt indulgence toward princes' tendency to violate treaties when it suited their interests (*T* 3.2.11.3 / SBN 568). They may even have approved (as Hume argues they did) pride proportioned to one's merits together with its habitual concealment behind a veneer of insincere deference toward others (*T* 3.3.2.11 / SBN 598). And although the ancient Greeks approved homosexuality (a phenomenon that Hume thinks can be explained away), Hume

---

[5] " 'Tis contrary to the interest of civil society, that men shou'd have an *entire* liberty of indulging their appetites in venereal enjoyment: But as this interest is weaker than in the case of the female sex, the moral obligation, arising from it, must be proportionably weaker. And to prove this we need only appeal to the practice and sentiments of all nations and ages" (*T* 3.2.12.9 / SBN 573).

and his contemporaries throughout the world disapproved that trait with some vehemence. Thus, according to Hume's inter-subjective standard of good and evil, a double standard of sexual morality for men and women was the right one (at least in the eighteenth century), dishonesty is not always a vice in princes, the valor of conquerors and the pretense of humility in social settings are virtues, and homosexuality is a vice.[6]

A sympathetic reader of Hume might agree that moral evaluation is the product of unbiased feelings of approval and disapproval, yet might wish to criticize Hume for his endorsement of these or other particular traits as virtues and vices. Such a reader might wish to argue that some traits on Hume's list, or on a list generated by the members of various societies' carrying out Hume's procedure, are not virtues after all, because they are exploitative, or frivolous, or the result of indoctrination by the ruling class or unfounded cultural squeamishness, or the like. Our question is how, if at all, such a criticism might coherently be made. Can we grant Hume his overall ethical theory yet object that he was wrong about modesty in women and men or about homosexuality or military valor, or indeed about any particular trait?

In the same vein, Hume's theory appears to leave room for changes in moral opinion but not for social error and correction. If the general attitude shifts over time, the verdict of Hume's philosophy on that shift seems to be not that the people of one era were correct in their moral evaluation and those of another were mistaken, but rather that a trait that was a vice or a virtue ceased to be one, or a trait that was not a vice or a virtue became one. Thus strict female chastity of the kind that Hume's contemporaries endorsed was a virtue then, but is no virtue now. And perhaps a great sensitivity to the requirements of caste was once a virtue in India and is no longer. But, the sympathetic reader is likely to say, Hume of all people should be able to give some grounds for saying that certain old ethical prejudices were in fact mistaken.[7]

B. Errors about Causal Facts

A crucial issue we should consider is whether there is room to make a type of criticism Hume says too little about: that the moral sentiment we feel on a given occasion is defective or incorrect because it is evoked by false causal beliefs, or would not be evoked if we had certain true causal beliefs that we lack. The beliefs in question are about the beneficial or harmful effects that a character trait has on its possessor, her associates, or society in general. In the *Treatise*

[6] These are only examples, of course, meant to draw attention to traits on Hume's list about which a reader might disagree. One might instead agree with Hume about some or all of these (perhaps the pretense of humility in social settings *is* a virtue) but disagree with others on the list.

[7] Hume in particular should be able to, because of passages where he says, in effect, that though we must not be censorious of those of earlier eras who followed the prejudice of their times, we now know better about certain traits and practices. We take up these passages below.

Hume really does not tell us the status of moral sentiments that are triggered as a result of some widely held false causal belief, although clearly this can happen. (In the moral *Enquiry* there is some explicit discussion.)[8] Just recall how moral sentiments are generated according to Hume's theory. It is because we all know that honesty with respect to property serves the social good that we approve that trait, and that that trait is a virtue. We imagine the pleasure of everyone in society who thrives under an orderly system of ownership, we acquire their pleasure through sympathy, and it becomes our feeling of moral approval. If we all falsely believe that some other trait—such as an unwavering obedience to a caste system—similarly serves the social good, we will approve that trait, as the result of similar workings of imagination and sympathy. We will imagine, for example, the peace and order of a society in which the trait is common, and the consequent happiness of its members; and sympathy will transfer that imagined happiness to us, giving rise to moral approbation. Or we will (incorrectly) imagine the disruption and social upheaval we believe would be common in a society whose members lack this trait, and its citizens' resulting insecurity, and sympathy will transmit their imagined uneasiness to us to create moral disapproval of all who lack this trait. Just as sympathy can transfer to us the imagined pleasures we believe would come to the hypothetical beneficiaries of some trait whose possessor is actually walled off in a dungeon (*T* 3.3.1.19 / SBN 584), so it can transfer to us the imagined pleasures we falsely believe would accrue to people as a result of their ingrained caste-consciousness. (Perhaps we sympathize with imaginary pleasures, or perhaps with real pleasures that we mistakenly believe are caused by this trait but are caused in some other way.) But would the trait therefore be a virtue? For all Hume says in the *Treatise*, it may seem that it would, even if all of us in our society are mistaken about what effects unthinking caste-consciousness would have. (Perhaps we do not realize that it leads to great oppression and misery, or lack of innovation and stagnation.) For in the *Treatise* he only says we must set aside selfish concerns and correct for the distortions to which sympathy is vulnerable. He does not say that all our relevant believed ideas must be true. It appears to follow that traits falsely thought to bring benefit, and consequently approved from the common point of view, are indeed virtues.

There is an analogous problem pertaining to missing true beliefs. If we do not know that a certain trait has beneficial or doleful effects, it will not be inscribed on our list of virtues or vices, since even when we adopt the common point of view, we will not imagine it causing any weal or woe, and so sympathy will not transfer to us any pleasant or painful feelings toward that trait. As far as I can see, Hume does not require that in order to make moral evaluations we must all have full information. But if he does not, there are bound to be beneficial traits that are not approved and harmful ones that are not disapproved.

---

[8] It was reading an earlier version of Driver's (2004) article that led me to realize how little Hume really says about this issue and how important it is.

It is tempting to say that Hume's response to this is simply that our assessments made under unbiased consideration stand, regardless of the factual errors or ignorance that brought them about. But there are reasons to think both that Hume has resources to avoid this conclusion and that this is not what he intends to say.

There are hints even in the *Treatise*. Certainly when our beliefs change, our moral evaluation of a person's action also changes (*T* 3.2.1.3 / SBN 477–8), although in the case where he mentions this, the belief is about the agent's motivating sentiment (and so about which trait he has) and not about whether the trait is a cause of weal or woe. He also says in a different context that a passion may be called unreasonable (though in a vulgar sense) because it is founded on a false belief (*T* 3.1.1.12 / SBN 459).

In the moral *Enquiry* there is stronger evidence that he thinks moral evaluations based on false causal beliefs are unwarranted and should be corrected. There he argues that reason plays a large role in moral evaluation: "in order to pave the way for [the moral] sentiment, and give a proper discernment of its object, it is often necessary . . . that much reasoning should precede, that nice distinctions be made, just conclusions drawn, . . . and general facts fixed and ascertained" (*EPM* 1.9 / SBN 173). We need to gather a great deal of information before sentiment plays its part, especially about a trait's impact on society (*EPM*, App.1.2 / SBN 285–6), and the information we gather alters the resulting feelings. Since we use reason to obtain the information, presumably the goal is for the opinions we form to be true. In both the moral *Enquiry* and the (moral) "Dialogue" he talks of factual errors people make that influence their lists of virtues and vices—not errors of mistaking a selfish for a moral evaluation or of failing to take up the common point of view, but errors about the "tendency" of a character trait or practice. People naturally praise giving alms to beggars, thinking it relieves misery. "But when we observe the encouragement thence arising to idleness and debauchery, we regard that species of charity rather as a weakness than a virtue" (*EPM* 2.18 / SBN 180). The ancient Romans approved tyrannicide because they mistakenly believed that fear of assassination would restrain oppressive rulers; in fact, however, "this practice encreases the jealousy and cruelty of princes", and we no longer approve it (*EPM* 2.19 / SBN 180–1). Luxury was regarded as a vice because it was thought to harm society by causing corruption in government, but those who attempt to prove that it increases "industry, civility, and the arts regulate anew our *moral* as well as *political* sentiments" and portray it as "laudable or innocent" (*EPM* 2.21 / SBN 181). Notice that in these three cases Hume does not actually say that the moral judgments themselves were incorrect and needed to be revised, but only that "we" do revise them once we detect the factual error. His language is more pointed with regard to the monkish virtues. The monks approve fasting, penance, and mortification; but "[w]e *justly* . . . transfer them to the opposite column, and place them in the catalogue of vices" (*EPM* 9.1.3 / SBN 270; my emphasis). *Our* classification is the correct one. Although Hume does not say so, he hints that a false causal belief is what triggers the monkish approval of these practices, since it arises from "false religion" (ibid.).[9] But perhaps the monks approve the wrong traits not because of false causal beliefs but because their natural sentiments have been deformed by leading "artificial lives".[10] In "A Dialogue" Hume suggests more strongly that ethical evolutions triggered by false causal beliefs are actually incorrect. The ancients approved of the "Greek loves", which were recommended to them on the grounds that homosexual relationships foster friendship and loyalty ("Dialogue", 28 / SBN 334). We (eighteenth-century Britons) know this causal opinion about friendship and loyalty to be "absurd", and so do not approve such loves. In the language of the *Treatise* (that of the moral *Enquiry* would be similar), because the ancient Greek observers (Hume cites Plato's *Symposium*) falsely believed that homosexuality provided benefit to individuals and to society as a whole, they imagined from the common point of view that those who engaged in it reaped these rewards; and sympathy brought to the observers the participants' imagined happiness, which became the observers' approbation of the trait. But this approbation was a sentiment founded on a false belief, and so their approval of homosexuality did not make it a virtue, even "for them".[11]

Finally, the strongest piece of evidence that Hume thinks that false or incomplete causal beliefs, when involved in the generation of moral sentiments, lead to erroneous moral evaluations comes a bit later in "A Dialogue":

[T]he principles upon which men reason in morals are always the same; though the conclusions which they draw are often very different. That they all reason aright with regard to this subject . . . it is not incumbent on any moralist to show. It is sufficient, that the original principles of censure or blame are uniform, and that erroneous conclusions can be corrected by sounder reasoning and larger experience.   (D 36 / SBN 335–6)

Here Hume finally states that a moral evaluation based on false belief is itself erroneous and needs correction. And though this will involve a vulgar and unphilosophical use of language (for, strictly speaking, sentiments are neither true nor false), we may even call the feeling of approval itself false when it results from insufficient knowledge or false causal belief. As Hume says in the moral *Enquiry*:

[I]n many orders of beauty, particularly those of the finer arts, it is requisite to employ much reasoning, in order to feel the proper sentiment; and a *false relish* may frequently

---

⁹ I am guessing here that the monks believe that their practices please God and lead him to favor their practitioners, a belief that Hume thinks false.

¹⁰ Cf. the discussion of Diogenes and Pascal in "A Dialogue" (D 52–7 / SBN 341–3).

¹¹ I have taken such pains with these passages because while Hume says we do not now approve or disapprove what these other people do or did, he does not say that their ethical evaluations were mistaken. He comes close only in the quoted passage about the monkish virtues. Even in the passage about the "Greek loves" he does not explicitly say that the moral judgment of the Greeks was incorrect. But his tone suggests it, and it is hard to imagine someone of his time and place saying anything else.

be corrected by argument and reflection. There are just grounds to conclude, that moral beauty partakes much of this latter species.   (*EPM* 1.9 / SBN 173; emphasis added)

This way of handling false belief seems either to be inchoate in all Hume's moral philosophy, or at least to emerge in his later writing.[12]

C. Other Kinds of Criticism of Approvals and Disapprovals

We have seen that Hume need not accept the authority of sentiments triggered by false beliefs that a trait causes benefit or harm. But not all moral approval and disapproval is caused by any belief about good or harm to the trait's possessor or to others. Our approval of some traits is caused by the fact that they are immediately agreeable to their possessor or others, and our disapproval of the contrary traits by their being immediately disagreeable. He says this repeatedly in the *Treatise*, the moral *Enquiry*, and "A Dialogue", and it is important. (See, e.g., *T* 3.3.1.27 / SBN 589–90.) If Hume was mistaken in thinking that sexual liberty for women would harm children, but that a modicum of sexual liberty for men would not, then the correction of this causal belief would be expected to alter our moral reactions to different degrees of masculine and feminine chastity; for chastity is an artificial virtue, one whose approval is caused solely by our beliefs about its effects on society. Approval of a natural virtue or disapproval of a natural vice might be triggered either by beliefs of this sort or simply by the realization of its agreeableness or disagreeableness. (Note that even in the latter case sympathy is often involved. I approve the wit of someone far away even though I have no opportunity to enjoy her cleverness, because from the common point of view I sympathize with those who have. But wit is one of those traits approved only because it is immediately agreeable.[13]) We approve kindness in both ways, for it benefits society and is also immediately agreeable both to its possessor and to others. We approve military heroism solely because it is immediately agreeable to its possessor, and his pleasure is irresistibly transferred to all who perceive

---

[12] Though the clear assertion that false causal beliefs can make for incorrect moral judgments comes later, the *Treatise* account of moral judgment is compatible with this thesis. Given this, we should note that Hume's position is not simply that our actual sentiments, as adjusted from the common point of view, make traits virtues and vices. For even the most careful social scientists have some false beliefs about the effects of traits on people's well-being. Rather, Hume's position is that our *well-informed* moral sentiments make traits virtues and vices. Our misinformed sentiments do not.

[13] Darwall (1994: 71) is helpful on the distinction between the agreeable feeling of those who encounter such a trait, which is transmitted to the observer by sympathy, and the feeling of moral approval of the trait, which is the result of this sympathy. But I think Hume's position in the *Treatise* is that our moral approbation of these immediately agreeable traits does not depend entirely upon sympathy, since it arises spontaneously from "particular *original* principles of human nature, which cannot be accounted for" (*T* 3.3.1.27 / SBN 590). But "it has also a considerable dependence on the principle of *sympathy*" as well, since people not directly exposed to the charming trait can share in the approval, which does require sympathy. In any case, the instances in which "this immediate taste or sentiment produces our approbation" are "cases of less moment", such as wit.

it via sympathy, in spite of the fact that it is harmful to society on the whole (*T* 3.3.2.15 / SBN 601). We disapprove conceit and the lack of cleanliness simply because they are immediately disagreeable to others, even if they have no other impact on society than this. "We approve of a person, who is possess'd of qualities immediately agreeable to those, with whom he has any commerce; tho' perhaps we ourselves never reap'd any pleasure from them. We also approve of one, who is possess'd of qualities, that are immediately agreeable to himself; tho' they be of no service to any mortal" (*T* 3.3.1.29 / SBN 590). Note that in approving and disapproving these traits "[w]e must have recourse to a certain sense, which acts without reflexion, and *regards not the tendencies of actions and characters*"—that is, that does not consider their effects on society for good or ill but responds to them spontaneously and directly (*T* 3.3.4.9 / SBN 612; emphasis added).

Now consider homosexuality. Hume and his contemporaries (and quite a few of our own) find it immediately disagreeable.[14] What do they discover when they contemplate this trait from the common point of view? They imagine all who interact with a person with homosexual proclivities, and find that on balance the trait makes people ill at ease. If they think of a particular homosexual of their acquaintance, they might even imagine, quite accurately, that he himself feels profoundly uncomfortable with his own sexual dispositions. (Surely that was often the case in the eighteenth century.) They sympathize with him and with all others who are aware of the trait and partake of their uneasiness about it; and this uneasiness becomes disapproval—authentic Humean disapproval, formed by adopting the common point of view. This makes homosexuality a vice.

No doubt Hume's contemporaries also believed many falsehoods about the effects of homosexuality on society, and correcting these would alter some of their resulting feelings about it. But their antipathy to the trait need not have depended on such beliefs. They might simply have found it disagreeable, as people find conceit disagreeable, regardless of its social effects. It is likely that they would have found it so, since for most people it was very unfamiliar and defeated their standing expectations. And a mere uncomfortable reaction would be quite enough to trigger moral disapproval in the prescribed way, since it would be a spontaneous response of finding something disagreeable. In disapproving this trait, therefore, they would not be misapplying Hume's procedure; they

---

[14] Although Hume does not want to say much about homosexuality ("The Greek loves, I care not to examine more particularly" (D 28 / SBN 334)), he certainly suggests that it is immediately disagreeable: "there is almost as great difficulty . . . to justify the French as the Greek gallantry; except only, that the former is much more natural and agreeable than the latter" (D 32 / SBN 335). (The French gallantry is heterosexual marital infidelity.) He also has Palamedes say, "I think I have fairly made it appear, that an Athenian man of merit might be such a one as with us would pass for incestuous, a parricide, an assassin, an ungrateful, perjured traitor, and something else too abominable to be named"; this last would seem to be "a pederast". Since Hume never claims that homosexual liaisons harm society, it seems that he finds them "abominable" simply in the sense of immediately (very) disagreeable.

would be applying it correctly. None of the errors we have canvassed so far are present here.

It seems we must conclude that, according to Hume's theory, homosexuality was truly a vice in eighteenth-century Britain. That is to say, we must conclude that censure of homosexuals was justified, that children should have been brought up not to be homosexual and to look down on homosexuals, and were rightly brought up if so, and that adults should have sought to overcome any such tendencies they found in themselves and were right to denigrate them in others. But this result will sit badly with many today. For many of us would like to say that the antipathy they felt toward homosexuality was just a cultural prejudice, and not a suitable ground for moral evaluation. Yet, since it was not the result of self-interest, and not the result of the biasing effects of sympathy (for they sympathized even with homosexuals themselves), but would persist even when they adopted the common point of view, and since it was not dependent upon any false beliefs about effects on society, there is no way for Hume's theory to rule out their disapproval of homosexuality as an unwarranted moral evaluation. Consequently, he would have to include homosexuality on his list of vices, simply because his contemporaries found it immediately disagreeable.

We should note that Hume's inclusion of homosexuality on his list of vices is not the result of any error he makes in applying his own moral criterion, as some think Kant's condemnation of lying to a prospective murderer at the door a misapplication of his categorical imperative. Nor is it the result of Hume's moral criterion being difficult to apply to this issue, or of his having had nothing sufficiently specific to say on the matter, as is the case, for example, with Kant on such issues as whether a fetus is a rational being whom it would be wrong to kill, given his conception of a rational being.[15] Hume's moral criterion is quite explicit and easy to apply to the trait of homosexuality, and he even does so in "A Dialogue". What we must do is evaluate the trait from the common point of view, which enables us to feel what is felt by all those affected by the trait, including its possessor. Given the spontaneous reactions to this trait at many times in history, not only of those around its possessor but of the individual himself, Hume's criterion has the clear consequence that the trait is a vice.

Some will demur that this is a poor example, because homosexuality is not a character trait, and so is not suitable for direct evaluation according to Hume's ethical theory. Now in fact Hume cheats a good deal on this requirement, calling things virtues or alleged virtues that are not character traits at all (fasting? silence?); so one response would be to say that here is one more place where he evaluates something that is not a character trait. What he evaluates in "A Dialogue" are homosexual practices, and these, like the monkish practices (and the practices of conforming to the rules of justice, on our interpretation), can

---

[15] See Kant 1976[1797] and 1964[1785]. Thanks to Herlinde Pauer-Studer for pressing me on this issue.

apparently be the topic of reflection from the common point of view. But in fact there is a stronger response. Homosexual orientation (as we would call it today) or proclivities or tastes (as Hume might have said) in fact would qualify quite nicely as a genuine Humean character trait. As we have seen, for Hume a character trait is a characteristic motivating sentiment or disposition to feel certain characteristic motivating sentiments that tend to result in the relevant sorts of actions. The disposition to be attracted to and to fall in love with people of one's own sex fits this description well. So we cannot block the conclusion that careful application of Hume's theory to the sentiments of his contemporaries (and to those of many populations in many times and places) entails that homosexuality is a vice just on the grounds that it is not a Humean character trait.

One response to this result is to say, simply: so much the worse for Hume, and perhaps so much the worse for any sentimentalist moral theory. Hume gives us a normative theory of the virtues and vices, all right; he is not just describing how we feel but endorsing the feelings we have on unbiased consideration. But because he finds the source of normativity in our feelings, he is limited in what corrective mechanisms he can employ to insure that the resulting list of virtues and vices is a palatable one. And in the end certain items are not palatable, and this cannot be helped. As assessed by his sentimentalist theory, homosexuality was indeed a vice in his day; and it will continue to be one in ours, until such time as most people become comfortable with it. If we are dissatisfied with this consequence, then perhaps we should give up sentimentalist ethics.

D. Cultural Relativism

Another response to this result is to say: so much the better for Hume. Readers of Hume who are happy to attribute to him a fairly deep form of cultural relativism will not wish to criticize the list of virtues based on the sentiments of all who consider traits under unbiased conditions. To use another example, suppose bodily self-consciousness and dread of sexual expression among women is approved not on the basis of beliefs about its usefulness in insuring that children are provided for, but just because members of a society find it pleasing and decorous when women cover themselves from head to toe (as in rural Afghanistan and Saudi Arabia), and find a woman who is comfortable showing her arms or face in public to be disagreeably brazen.[16] Those who favor a relativist

---

[16] This is bound to be an oversimplification of real attitudes to feminine modesty. Religious teachings are typically bound up with these customs, and so various causal beliefs that Hume would deem false could be cited as partial causes of the moral attitudes. (In some places, though, the local custom of covering is older than the prevailing religion and has been grafted onto it.) However, women and girls in societies in which women are veiled often say, for example, that they just feel more comfortable covered up, would be embarrassed if anyone saw their hair, and the like. The men say that it would shame their wives and daughters for them to be seen without hair or face coverings. The present example is limited to a case where just such feelings are involved.

Hume will be content to conclude that bodily self-consciousness of the kind that leads a woman to cover herself so completely was indeed a virtue in various places in the past and is so in Saudi Arabia today, because people there, including the women themselves, approve it when they consider it under unbiased conditions, and disapprove its absence. And they will hold that this trait is not a virtue in present-day Europe or the Americas, where people who adopt the common point of view feel no such thing. That is, the relativist will conclude that such modesty was and is normative for women in those times and places where it is or was approved: that it is a trait women should have there and then, one that should be taught to young girls, one for the lack of which censure is or was entirely appropriate.

Others think Hume does not endorse this deep form of cultural relativism for a variety of reasons. They may find cultural relativism itself implausible on general grounds and think Hume too wise a philosopher to have fallen into such error. Or they might be, for example, feminist theorists who argue that even if women in Saudi Arabia do approve that kind of bodily modesty, they are trapped in false consciousness perpetuated by the oppressive patriarchy to keep them subordinate. Thus they might allege an error in moral evaluation here, though not the kind of error that depends upon false causal beliefs about the effects of a trait; and they might hope that Hume could somehow make room for such an error. And finally, so thoroughgoing a form of cultural relativism may not fit Hume's texts.

Hume himself does not seem to be such a thoroughgoing relativist, although he does not raise the issue in precisely these terms. In "A Dialogue" he explains cultural differences as different manifestations of the same basic human sentiments triggered by different circumstances. Where the different conditions of life result in different ethical judgments, Hume seems to endorse each judgment as arising appropriately from the universal moral sentiments under these different circumstances. Where the ethical disagreement is the result of one society laboring under misapprehensions about cause and effect, however, he claims that that society's moral judgments are in error, as we have seen with the Greeks. Some social preferences, too, arise for a different reason: there are two virtues that may be cultivated, but they are in tension with one another, so that the more of one virtue a society cultivates, the less of the other it can maintain. A balance must be struck between them, and different peoples will do this in different ways. Sometimes the tension is between a practice that is useful and a conflicting practice that is immediately agreeable, as in the examples of strict marital fidelity and free interactions between men and women (D 47 / SBN 339). Although "some people are inclined to think" that the English strike the best balance between these, Hume does not actually advocate any one way to do it, but seems to be fairly relativistic (or perhaps pluralistic) about *this*: whichever balance a society strikes is acceptable there, though it can be done better or worse. But this relativism, if that is what it is, is only skin deep. In the most important respects different peoples agree; and where they disagree, for the most part those differences arise from a profound agreement at a deeper level. "In how many circumstances would an Athenian and a French man of merit certainly resemble each other? Good sense, knowledge, wit, eloquence, humanity, fidelity, truth, justice, courage, temperance, constancy, dignity of mind. These you have all omitted," he tells Palamedes, "in order to insist only on the points, in which they may, by accident, differ. Very well: I . . . shall endeavour to account for these differences from the most universal, established principles of morals" (D 27 / SBN 333–4). The "principles" in question are fundamental causal factors, and these are the usefulness or immediate agreeableness of traits of character (D 37 / SBN 336).

And what if people of distinct times and places differ in what they find immediately agreeable? Hume does not seem to entertain this possibility. They may disagree about what is useful if some of them have false causal beliefs, and they may differ about the balance to strike between the useful and the agreeable. But he does not discuss the possibility that they might differ in what they find agreeable. Perhaps he does not think they can. He may suppose that without the influence of "false religion" human nature is simply disposed to find the same traits agreeable everywhere. Or perhaps he simply overlooks this source of conflict. Certainly he does not see it as a basis of cultural relativism.[17]

Is Hume then constrained to say that traits widely found to be immediately disagreeable are vices, even when the uneasiness they evoke is merely an unreasoning distaste? Whether this is so depends ultimately on the basis he offers for his claim that a trait is normative for human beings. We have worked so far with the hypothesis that for Hume that basis is simply the moral sentiment itself; but what basis he offers is in fact a matter of interpretive disagreement. Some interpretations offer him more recourse than we have seen so far.

IV. IS THERE A FURTHER FOUNDATION FOR ETHICAL NORMS IN HUME'S PHILOSOPHY?

If we are right that Hume's ethical theory is not merely descriptive but also normative, then we would do well to reconsider what Hume has to offer as the basis of this normativity. We know it is not reason or the will of God. On what grounds might Hume say not only that we do approve a trait but that we should approve it, and should strive to attain it in ourselves and to inculcate it in our children?

Two main answers have been given to this question on Hume's behalf.

---

[17] For a more systematic discussion of Hume's treatment of the challenge of cultural relativism in "A Dialogue", see Abramson 1999. Abramson sees Hume's conclusion about the trade-offs between useful and agreeable virtues as pluralistic rather than relativistic.

A. The Social Utility Standard

One possibility is that Hume thinks our moral sentiments, even if felt from the common point of view, and even if based only on true causal beliefs with no relevant omissions, may nonetheless be warranted or unwarranted; and what provides the warrant is the social utility of the trait in question. The idea is that approval of a trait is warranted provided the trait has some systematic causal connection to the social good, although that connection may be quite "oblique", as it is for the artificial virtues.[18] There is some textual evidence that Hume does think that social utility is the foundation of norms of virtue, at least in the moral *Enquiry* and thereafter. For example, Julia Driver, who advocates this interpretation, quotes his remark that "wherever disputes arise . . . concerning the bounds of duty, the question cannot . . . be decided with greater certainty, than by ascertaining, on any side, the true interests of mankind" (*EPM* 2.17 / SBN 180).[19]

On this account there is the possibility of a divergence between what we approve and what we should approve—what we judge a virtue and what we should so judge.

This way of grounding normativity may seem simply to repeat the points about false causal beliefs and unknown causal relations; and with regard to all the artificial virtues and some of the natural ones, the point is much the same. If approval is the result of false beliefs about the impact of a trait on human weal and woe, then that approval is unwarranted, and the trait is not a virtue after all. And if members of a society approve a trait on the basis of causal beliefs that are true as far as they go (the trait does cause the benefits it is believed to cause), but they do not know that the trait also causes harms that exceed those benefits, then the approval is also unwarranted, and the trait is no virtue. The analogous conditions—the falsehood of beliefs about social harm and unknown facts about overarching benefit—would invalidate judgments of vice.

---

[18] We briefly considered this possible source of warrant in Ch. 6. Recall that a certain trait may contribute to the social good directly, as when a philanthropist's generosity causes her to ease the suffering of the poor; or it may contribute indirectly, as when the justice of a person of probity does not in fact directly alleviate misery or increase pleasure, but contributes to a practice which, when generally followed, insures the social stability that is indispensable to the common good.

[19] Driver seems to attribute to Hume the social utility standard for warranting our moral sentiments, since she holds that although sentiment provides us with epistemic access to virtues and vices, what a virtue really is, metaphysically speaking, is a trait that conduces to social utility. She says (describing what she takes to be Hume's position), "What actually makes a trait a virtue is that it—generally speaking—leads to various goods (agreeableness and social utility more narrowly defined)" (2004: 180). But her position is more complex than this, since she also claims that Hume would distinguish among experienced moral approvals, some of which (on her interpretation) are true or genuine pleasures and some of which are false ones.

We should also note here that there is no relevant difference (for present purposes) between saying that a trait really is a virtue because it has the property X and saying that the normative warrant of our judgment that a trait is a virtue is its having the property X. The normative claim is embedded in the first statement, that the trait "really is" a virtue.

But there is more to this normative standard. If social utility is the standard for all moral norms, then this standard must apply to those traits we approve because they are immediately agreeable, and not only to those we approve as a consequence of their usefulness. We have seen that a trait's being immediately agreeable or disagreeable is a further source of moral approval and disapproval that operates on the mind separately from judgments of usefulness and harmfulness. For example, the trait of "*good humour* is lov'd and esteem'd, because it is *immediately agreeable* to the person himself"; and the pleasure it brings to observers comes "from a sympathy with his gaiety" (*T* 3.3.4.8 / SBN 611). Here there need be no thought of the impact on society, or on anyone other than the trait's possessor, in order to generate the moral sentiment. (Good humor seems to mean cheerfulness or optimism.) Hume's examples in the moral *Enquiry* of this sort of approval and disapproval are very numerous (see, in particular, section 7). In such cases the norm of social utility and the cause of approval diverge. Their objects may coincide nonetheless, but they need not. If they fail to coincide, this need not be the result of any false belief or ignorance on the part of the community of moral judges. And if they do not coincide, then the moral sentiment that arises from what is immediately agreeable or disagreeable must be corrected by the facts of social utility, according to this interpretation of Hume's normative standard. Thus, if we find homosexuality immediately disagreeable but it does no harm to society, it should be removed from our list of vices; our sentiment stands corrected. If we find a trait such as military glory immediately agreeable, but in fact it brings about "infinite confusions and disorder . . . the subversion of empires, the devastation of provinces, the sack of cities" (*T* 3.3.2.15 / SBN 601), then we must correct the initial judgment and conclude that it is no virtue after all, in spite of the enormous immediate pleasure it gives its possessor and transmits to others via sympathy. So there is considerable room for correction of our moral sentiments on this interpretation, which is one of its attractions.

B. Shortcomings of the Social Utility Standard

Thus the social utility standard enables us to strike some traits from the list of virtues and vices that were placed there even when Hume's procedure was performed properly. It gives considerations of public utility priority over what is immediately agreeable or disagreeable. But unfortunately it is impossible to conclude that this view of normativity is Hume's position. This is because the interpretation allows appeal to utility where Hume does not allow any; it makes him a utilitarian of character traits (and so makes the moral sentiments otiose); and it conflicts with too much of Hume's overall theory of moral evaluation.

There is no evidence that Hume thinks social utility provides a basis for correcting those of our evaluations that result from agreeableness. He not only sees agreeableness as a source of moral sentiment independent of usefulness, but also thinks that agreeableness sometimes trumps social utility, rather than vice versa. This seems to be his conclusion in the *Treatise* about the form of pride that constitutes "[h]eroism, or military glory", in spite of the great harm the warlike leader does to mankind. "The pain, which we receive from its tendency to the prejudice of society," he says, "is over-power'd by a stronger and more immediate sympathy" (*T* 3.3.2.15 / SBN 601).[20] We saw that in "A Dialogue", when he finds that an agreeable practice, if fully developed, cannot coexist with a useful one also fully formed, he suggests that it is simply a matter of preference, local custom, or luck what balance is struck between them. Apparently the two conflicting virtues have equal claim on us. Certainly the demands of social utility do not require us to disregard the claims of the agreeable. If they did, we would be required to seclude women from the society of men so as to prevent intrigue and adultery (the prevention of which is very useful), since the only reason to permit free association between the sexes is the agreeableness of the company of ladies.[21] And there is simply no evidence that Hume treats immediate agreeableness as one, very mild kind of social utility to be weighed against greater and longer-term kinds of utility and disutility to arrive at some net utility that could then be used as a check on our sentiments. Hume treats agreeableness and social utility as independent sources of value. Since they are independent, they can conflict in particular instances, and he does not offer a formula for how the conflict should be settled. It seems that it is settled differently in different cases: sometimes agreeableness dominates social utility, and sometimes the reverse. Hence it is clear that for Hume social utility does not serve as an independent standard by which the verdict that something is a virtue based on its immediate agreeableness can be either endorsed or overruled.[22]

[20] This is an example of the ambiguity described earlier that runs through Hume's moral philosophy. Is he here merely describing the fact that we continue to take military glory to be a virtue, leaving the issue of whether it is one unsettled, or does he think we err when our more immediate sympathy swamps the pain we feel from the tendency of this trait, or does he think the fact that we so take it even after we know the ugly facts settles its status as a virtue? He is not explicit; but the wording in the *Treatise* suggests that he takes it really to be a virtue because the pleasure from its agreeableness overpowers the sympathetic pain from its disutility. His view seems to shift in the moral *Enquiry*, in that he describes military courage as useful as well as immediately agreeable, eliminating the conflict. But he still argues that the trait "has a peculiar lustre, which it derives wholly from itself" rather than from its beneficial tendency. (See *EPM* 7; the quote is from *EPM* 7.11 / SBN 254.)

[21] This is what he says. Obviously he overlooks the great *disutility* to women of being secluded from all the important economic, intellectual, and political activities of the day.

[22] An anonymous referee for Oxford University Press pointed out, rightly I think, that Hume is a pluralist about the sources of value, holding moral goodness to come from four vectors (immediate agreeableness or utility to oneself or others), and denying any set hierarchy of these sources of value, which rules out the possibility of an algorithm for deciding conflicts. I would add that this is another respect in which Hume's perspective is different from our own: he does not feel the pressure, inevitable since the development of maximizing utilitarianism, to offer such an algorithm. The referee suggests, quite plausibly—although I do not investigate this here—that Hume may not think philosophy capable of providing a principled way to adjudicate conflicts between different sources of value.

What is worse, the interpretation according to which social usefulness or advantage provides the normative check on our moral sentiments would make Hume abandon sentiment—even adjusted sentiment—as the defining feature of virtue and vice, which runs contrary to so much in the texts. It would shift him instead to a utilitarianism of character traits. It is not a maximizing utilitarianism, of course, and its primary focus for evaluation is a quality of mind rather than an action. But it is a kind of utilitarianism nonetheless, in that it treats social utility as the essence of moral virtue, and this seriously undercuts Hume's sentimentalism. On such a view our sentiments do not make it the case that a trait is a virtue, but only serve as approximate guides to what is really virtuous—namely, traits that are advantageous to society. If this is so, then the moral sentiments play no necessary role in the constitution of virtue. Even when exercised in light of accurate, relevant information, and even when regulated from the common point of view, the moral sentiments provide only a kind of rough indication of which traits are really virtues and vices, something that might, in principle, be calculated far more precisely without them. If the feature that makes a quality a virtue is simply its social utility, the sentiments only obscure our view.[23]

It is of course open to a sentimentalist to claim that our moral sentiments in fact track social utility. Had Hume thought the moral sentiments were provoked only by social utility and disutility, and not also by those spontaneous responses people feel to wit and conceit and the like, he would have concluded, much as Hutcheson did, that all virtues are in fact traits that promote overall social welfare. But to say this is not yet to adopt the social utility standard of normativity. It is a further substantive move to claim that social utility provides a check on our sentiments and the basis for correcting them; and as long as Hume is fundamentally a sentimentalist, he cannot consistently do so. Recall that our question was on what grounds the deliverances of properly regulated moral sentiments (the resulting list of virtues and vices) might be rejected or overridden or deemed unwarranted. If the general welfare provides such grounds, then it is a trait's impact on the general welfare, rather than the way a trait feels to human observers, that is the standard of moral evaluation.[24]

The most difficult of Hume's claims to square with the social utility interpretation of the foundation of norms, though, is his denial that moral distinctions are relations discoverable by any sort of reasoning, including causal reasoning.

---

[23] Thus although some have read Hume as a utilitarian, this interpretation is strained. Bentham (1948[1776]) famously read Hume and found himself convinced thereafter that "*utility* was the test and measure of all virtue" (51 n. 2). But Bentham realized that to advocate utilitarianism, he did best to drop the moral sentiments entirely from his account of virtue and define it in terms of utility alone. Indeed, he mocks Hume and the other sentiment theorists as advocates of the "principle of sympathy and antipathy" (1988[1781]: 15–16). (Hume is not the sole target of this mockery, but he is implicated in the description of moralists who base all moral evaluation on people's approbation and disapprobation.)

[24] I am grateful to an anonymous referee for Oxford University Press for pressing me on this point.

There are two aspects to this, epistemic and metaphysical. We saw in Chapter 4 that Hume is interested mainly in moral epistemology: he wants to show us that reason alone cannot *discern* moral good and evil, and what he says about the nature of moral properties themselves is largely driven by this concern. Yet he commits himself quite explicitly not only to denying that reason alone can discover moral properties but to denying that moral properties can themselves *be* causal relations discoverable by reasoning. Virtue and vice do not consist in any relations of the kind discoverable by either demonstrative or causal reasoning or the two combined. For example, he says that "the crime or immorality is no particular fact or relation, which can be the object of the understanding: But arises entirely from the sentiment of disapprobation, which, by the structure of human nature, we unavoidably feel on the apprehension of barbarity or treachery" (*EPM*, App. 1.16 / SBN 292–3). But the public utility or disutility of a trait is simply a causal property of that trait that can be discerned by careful use of cause-and-effect reasoning. It does not arise entirely from the sentiment of disapprobation.

Furthermore, the thesis that virtue itself consists in a certain causal relation, the tendency of a trait to increase the general welfare or happiness, conflicts with Hume's contention that moral *awareness* requires the capacity for moral sentiment and cannot be attained by reasoning alone. That is, this interpretation also conflicts with Hume's moral epistemology. Causal reasoning alone can show us which traits tend to the good of society, and no capacity for moral sentiment is needed to apprehend this. There is no reason to think that only sympathetic beings have epistemic access to the effects of gratitude or justice on human welfare; for while beings that lack sympathy will not become aware of the usefulness of a trait by *sympathy*, they can gather data about it from interviews and detached observations of others, and from the study of history.[25] Indeed, according to the *Treatise* account of sympathy, in order for that mechanism to operate, we must first form an idea of what the other person feels; so discursive knowledge of the feelings of others is prior to sympathy, and does not depend on it. Hence we certainly do not need to be sympathetic creatures, and so creatures with moral sentiments, to know the impact of a trait on the happiness of others, and hence, according to the social utility interpretation, to discern that it is a vice or a virtue.[26] Note that this objection does not depend specifically on

[25] Here I challenge one possible interpretation: that for Hume our moral judgments depend on our feelings because only feelings give us knowledge of vice and virtue, but vice and virtue themselves, metaphysically speaking, are not reaction-dependent traits but consist in the tendency to harm or benefit society, a tendency which typically evokes disapproval or approval. See Driver 2004; this appears to be part of her interpretation. Some others who have seen social utility as the standard of virtue in Hume are Rawls (1971: 22 n. 9) and Glossop (1967). Darwall (1994) rejects the utilitarian interpretation, and Sayre-McCord (1995) argues against it.

[26] One might be tempted to object that we only have the ideas of the pleasure and pain of others because we have had impressions of pleasure and pain ourselves. This is quite true. So we must be creatures capable of pleasure and pain ourselves in order to know that a trait is conducive to public

the moral sensing interpretation of Hume's theory of moral judgment or the two-sentiment account of the common point of view defended in this book. An individual who used the social utility standard could distinguish virtue from vice, and so form moral judgments, without ever having experienced any moral sentiments whatsoever. This is a view not reasonably attributed to Hume on any interpretation.

Finally, the social utility interpretation effectively makes Hume a moral realist as I defined this in Chapter 4: that is, one who maintains that ethical properties exist independently of human psychological reactions to the entities (such as people and actions) that are thought to bear these properties. This is impossible to square with the text. Although in that chapter I argued that Hume is not a noncognitivist, but rather thinks that moral judgments can be true or false and represent facts (of a kind analogous to facts about colors and heat and cold), I could not dismiss the rejection of moral realism that he expresses in many passages. Recall how reason "discovers objects as they really stand in nature, without addition or diminution"; while taste, including moral taste or sentiment, "has a productive faculty, and gilding or staining all natural objects with the colours, borrowed from internal sentiment, raises in a manner a new creation" (*EPM*, App.1.21 / SBN 294). Social disutility, however, *is* a particular relation between objects as they really stand in nature. It is not raised anew from the sentiment of approval or disapproval that we feel on apprehending a trait.

Thus the social utility standard is not what Hume has in mind.

C. The Reflexivity (and/or Reflective Endorsement) Standard

We began this chapter by assuming that all normativity, for Hume, resides in our sentiments alone, and that there is no further justification to be had. The social utility standard would constitute a huge departure from this. The second alternative to that simple initial interpretation adheres more closely to sentiment as the basis of norms, yet permits more justification and criticism of people's actual sentiments under unbiased consideration than does the simple view with which we began. We may follow Christine Korsgaard in seeing, in Hume's work, an appeal to reflexivity or broader reflective endorsement as the foundation of normativity.[27] This too makes normativity reside in our feelings, ultimately, although Korsgaard does not put the point this way.

As Korsgaard notes, at the end of the *Treatise*, after Hume has shown that our approval of all the virtues (natural as well as artificial) is caused by sympathy, and thus that it is our deep engagement with our fellow human beings that

---

happiness. But this does not show that we need to be capable of sympathy or moral sentiment (which depends on sympathy). All we need is the ability to form the *idea* of another's pain or pleasure, which is prior to sympathy.

27 Korsgaard 1996: 61–3. Also see Baier 1991: 196–7, 277.

gives rise to moral evaluation, he claims that when we reflect on this fact, we realize that the moral sentiments are derived from a noble source, and we feel approval for the sense of virtue itself. Korsgaard reads this reflexivity of moral sentiment as one source of normativity in Hume's ethics. The moral sentiments (adjusted from the common point of view) give us our list of virtues, and we know this is the right list—these are the traits we should approve—because our moral sentiments, when turned upon themselves, approve their own operation and origin. Korsgaard calls this "normativity as reflexivity". By contrast, if when reflecting on our moral sentiments and their causes we were to disapprove them—perhaps thinking they arise from shameful features of ourselves, or are corrupted by propaganda or other ignoble influences—then our sense of virtue would not be normative for us, and the list of virtues it gives us could not be relied upon as a list of traits we should approve or cultivate. She contrasts the triumphant end of *Treatise*, Book 3, with the melancholy and skeptical end of Book I, where Hume has just turned the understanding upon itself and found it to subvert its own conclusions. Because of these different results of applying a faculty to itself, says Korsgaard, Hume concludes that "scepticism about the understanding is in order, but scepticism about morality is not".[28]

Korsgaard also sees in Hume a wider kind of reflective endorsement of the sense of virtue. Hume bids us reflect on our moral sentiments not only from the perspective of the moral sentiments themselves, but also from the perspective of self-interest. He argues that the life of virtue is also the happiest life. This too is reason to think the list of virtues provided by our moral sentiments is the right one. If our sense of virtue proved dangerous to our well-being, that would be reason to deny that the traits it singles out are ones we should approve and cultivate. For present purposes, though, let us set aside this broader reflective endorsement (evaluation by self-interest as well as the reflexively applied moral sentiment) and just consider reflexivity as the foundation of moral norms.[29]

One may well wonder whether normativity can be established in this boot-strapping way. If human moral sensibility were systematically defective, we would not expect to find the defect by turning that sensibility on itself, any more than we could find the defect in a test instrument (say, a volt meter or thermometer) by using it on itself. But since as empiricists we have no resources beyond our own perceptions, this may be the best we can do. Indeed, there may be, for Hume, no other sense we can make of the claim that the human moral sensibility is defective except to say that it offends against itself or against another human faculty such as self-interest. It is for this reason that we treat Korsgaard's interpretation as a variation on the theme that for Hume all normativity lies

---

[28] Korsgaard 1996: 62.

[29] Korsgaard admires this way of grounding normativity, and mentions only one respect in which she finds it lacking: it cannot account for the normativity of specific moral requirements on *action* as readily as it does for the normativity of traits. (Since for Korsgaard the will is of central importance in ethics, this is no small weakness for her. But it is not our present concern.)

ultimately in feeling. Some sort of "immediate accord or agreement with human sentiment and affection" is the sole and ultimate justification available. But here the accord is with a second-order moral sentiment, as we might put it. What makes the sense of virtue normative for us (and its list of virtues the right one) is that once we know the origin of this sentiment in sympathy we approve *it*. Hume asks us to consider our moral feelings about each of the virtues and about the origin of each instance of approbation in sympathy, and in every case, he says, what we find is good and admirable (*T* 3.3.6.3 / SBN 619).

D. Successes and Shortcomings of the Reflexivity Standard

The reflexivity standard fares better as an interpretation of Hume than the social utility standard. It comports well with Hume's moral epistemology and his rejection of moral realism.

The question to ask about this interpretation is whether it makes room for well-founded criticism of the list of virtues and vices that most people settle on from the common point of view. It says that what makes the sense of virtue normative for us is that once we know its origin in sympathy, we approve it — and our approval of it is a manifestation of the moral sentiment itself. Hume uses the moral sentiment to assess the sense of virtue itself and also to assess its general origin in our concern for and identification with our fellow human beings. The reflection on the origins of the moral sentiments goes beyond what is included simply in adopting the common point of view, for while that requires imagining the effects of a trait on the person's associates, and sympathizing adequately with those effects, it includes no requirement to consider what factors may have caused the trait to produce the emotional responses it does. One could think of the reflexivity standard as requiring the moral spectator to consider an additional set of facts, those about where our moral sentiments come from, and to respond emotionally to that reflection. This addition makes the standard reflexive, since what is evaluated is the moral sentiment, and it is evaluated by the moral sentiment, in response to facts about its origin.

Given this, we can use such reflexive consideration to criticize the list of virtues that results from contemplation from the common point of view. Korsgaard does not discuss applying it in this way, but it can be done. Suppose, for example, that the moral sentiments of all eighteenth-century Europeans (male and female) approve, under unbiased consideration, the sexual "repugnance" and bodily self-consciousness of women that Hume calls modesty. But suppose that when these people track down the origin of their universal approval of female modesty, this sentiment proves to be caused by indoctrination carried out by the domineering priesthood of a false religion (to use an example Hume would recognize), or by false consciousness engineered by a self-serving patriarchy bent on retaining male power (to use a present-day example), rather than by sympathy with children. In such a case the moral sentiment would not approve the origin of the approval of feminine modesty, since there is nothing admirable in this origin. Thus feminine modesty, though approved by everyone then living, would be a seeming virtue but not a real one; the favorable sentiment toward it would prove to be a "false relish" not endorsed by the moral sentiment reflecting on itself. Gratitude and justice, however, would pass the test, since our approval of them indeed arises from sympathy, either directly (with the recipients of gratitude) or indirectly (with the citizens of a society living under rules of justice). Increasing knowledge of what causes approval in society would then enlighten us as to when our first-order moral sentiment (as we might call it) is on target and when it is misguided.

The reflexivity standard may seem otiose in such a case, so I should clarify what it adds to the strictures of the common point of view and the identification of errors in causal belief already found in Hume's work. In our example, if modesty in women played no role in securing the care of children, then there would be no need to appeal to the reflexivity standard to figure out that modesty is not a real virtue; the claim that it is one would be found to be erroneous on the grounds that it depends on a false causal belief. But suppose it turns out to be *true* that female modesty and chastity have in fact functioned together with the institution of marriage to secure (to a reasonably great extent) the care and support of children in eighteenth-century Europe. In that case we are not dealing with an instance of false causal beliefs. But we might still be dealing with a situation in which the moral approval of the trait (modesty in women) is not brought about *by* such beliefs, but rather by something far less attractive, such as indoctrination by the powerful for their selfish ends. (Female modesty might actually have this effect on society although people know nothing about it; or they may realize that it operates this way, perhaps see this as a lucky side-effect of virtue, but do not derive their moral sentiments from any consideration of children at all.) Thus the reflexivity standard could undercut the authority of a moral sentiment even if the approved trait really was socially useful, provided the approval was in fact unrelated to that utility and drawn from a distasteful source. Reflexive evaluation can thus provide a further assessment of a moral evaluation even after the causal facts have been correctly established.[30]

But what of the virtues whose approval is caused only by their agreeableness, rather than their utility, such as wit, charm, and military greatness? We know that for Hume, while many virtues are *both* useful and agreeable, such as kindness and self-confidence, some are approved only because of their agreeableness to those who encounter them. And some are approved for their agreeableness in spite of their actually being harmful, as we saw with the "dazzling" conqueror. Similarly, some vices are disapproved because they are disagreeable, even though they are not harmful to anyone. In practice it is not always easy to separate these

---

[30] Thanks to John Corvino for pressing me on this issue.

different sources of approval and disapproval, but Hume thinks that in principle they are distinct.

The reflexive account of normativity has little to say about this aspect of Hume's theory of the virtues. If our approval and disapproval of these traits is the result of something shameful in our nature, such as susceptibility to manipulation by those bent on holding power unjustly, then the reflexivity standard will not endorse it. But in the cases Hume describes of traits that are immediately agreeable or disagreeable, such as wit and "good humor", on the one hand, and conceit, meanness (the disposition to degrade oneself and fawn on others in pursuit of trivial aims (*EPM* 7.10 / SBN 253)), and dirtiness, on the other, the delight and disgust people feel at these traits is simply natural and spontaneous, not the result either of beliefs about the happiness or unhappiness these traits produce, or of any sort of shameful weakness we have. And the approval produced by an immediately agreeable trait comes to the moral observer by sympathy. If I am unique in finding a trait disagreeable, sympathy with others who are at ease with it may well cancel out my feeling and leave me with no moral disapproval of the trait; Hume does not say this explicitly, but it seems to be a consequence of his mechanism of the common point of view. But if I find my uneasiness reflected back to me by sympathy with everyone else when I adopt the common point of view, my resulting sentiment will qualify as moral disapproval. Hume says that sympathy is a feature of the mind of which the sense of virtue approves on reflection, because it reveals us to be connected at a basic level with the pleasure and discomfort of others. Since, and insofar as, our approval of agreeable traits is caused by sympathy, that approval will receive second-order approval in turn. If we falsely believe that a trait is disagreeable to others when others in fact do not mind it, then correcting our causal information will lead us to correct our moral sentiment, in much the same way as it does for beliefs about usefulness. But if we are right about what pleases and displeases immediately, then nothing will change when the moral sentiment reflects on itself. It will find its own origin in sympathy, of which it approves. The second-order moral sentiment thus will rubber-stamp the first.

Given Hume's actual account of the moral sentiment's own self-examination, then, he is left without grounds to criticize a list of virtues and vices that reflects some of the baseless social prejudices of a time and place. Agreeableness and disagreeableness are often not subject to persuasion. If we all find a trait disagreeable, and if learning that it does no real harm does not make us like it any better, then we will disapprove it. Even if I do not personally find the trait disagreeable, when I enter into the common point of view, I will acquire by sympathy the distaste of others, and so I will still disapprove it. And my moral sentiment turned on itself will find nothing to disapprove in the origin of this disapproval, which is, after all, sympathy.

Thus the reflexivity standard enables Hume to provide grounds for a critique of *some* of the moral evaluations based on mere cultural prejudices: those that arise not from sympathy with a spontaneous natural reaction but from some worse impulse in human nature, such as the desire for dominance or the gullibility of the powerless. But it disappoints the hopes of readers who think that Hume should have some way to reject and correct moral evaluations based on all such prejudices. It cannot warrant any objection to evaluations that arise simply from sympathy with what others find immediately agreeable or disagreeable. If Hume bases normative claims on the self-approval of the moral sentiment as it arises from sympathy, he is left with a certain amount of cultural relativism, perhaps more than he thought. Thus we must grant that for Hume, as long as most people find homosexuality immediately disagreeable, and this is transmitted to the observer via sympathy, it is indeed a vice. As a vice rooted merely in what is immediately disagreeable, rather than in any tendencies to social harm, it is not a very important one; the virtues and vices so grounded fall outside "the great lines of our duty", constituting "cases of less moment" (*T* 3.3.1.27 / SBN 590). But a vice it remains.

It is possible that the reflexivity standard can do a bit more work to unseat some attributions of virtue and vice to immediately agreeable or disagreeable traits. The question of the origins of our sentiments could be pressed further, to ask the source of those spontaneous feelings of delight and disgust with which the moral spectator sympathizes, and the moral sentiment could be brought to bear on *those* origins instead of simply stopping with sympathy. Perhaps some qualities of mind do "produce satisfaction . . . by particular *original* principles of human nature, which cannot be accounted for", as Hume says (ibid.). But surely some of our spontaneous delight and disgust, while not triggered by any thought of utility, is in fact generated by childhood conditioning or child-rearing practices, early trauma, or unconscious forces such as Freudian latency. (For perhaps, for example, Freud is right that an immediate discomfort with homosexuality is the result of the observer's own latent homosexual feelings.[31]) If such origins were unearthed, they might not redound to our credit, and as a result we might disapprove the origin of the pleasure and uneasiness that such traits produce, in which case the reflexivity standard would undercut our judgment that the traits are virtues or vices. There is room to extend the account in this direction. Here, though, I think we have departed from anything Hume says or even suggests. There is some limited evidence that he proposes a reflexivity standard, but that standard, if it is there, is met once approval of a trait is found to result from sympathy. The origins of the immediate pleasure or uneasiness with which we sympathize are not explored, and Hume seems to think they cannot be known.

---

[31] Thanks to Joseph Ellin for suggesting this as a parallel to the speculation that approval of female modesty might be engineered by a power-hungry patriarchy. The Freudian story, however, seems to me only to push the problem back one step, and to leave the reaction to homosexuality an original principle of human nature and unaccounted for. The observer must already feel unconscious uneasiness with his own latent homosexual feelings before these can make him uneasy with another person's homosexuality, and the origin of this uneasiness is thus far unexplained.

V. A HUMEAN SUGGESTION FOR EXTENDING
THE REFLEXIVITY STANDARD

Reflexive evaluation of the moral sentiment and its origin in sympathy is, I believe, as far as we can go with Hume. Nevertheless, reflexivity can be extended in his spirit, but with a more contemporary twist, as above. Or one might do more by going a bit beyond what he says in a different direction, again adhering to his spirit, but widening the scope of reflection rather than digging deeper into the unconscious origins of our feelings. One thing that strikes us about certain widely shared ethical attitudes that we think erroneous is the harm that they do to human lives. I have in mind not the harm that a trait itself does, but rather the harm that is done by the social condemnation and attempted suppression of a trait. Had homosexuality been tolerated, so much human suffering would have been avoided. Had women not been "ruined" when they made the smallest sexual misstep (or seeming misstep—for, as Hume observes, their reputations were sullied on the strength of mere "surmizes, and conjectures" (*T* 3.2.12.4 / SBN 571)), many lives would not have been shattered. Had the magnanimity of conquerors not been admired by the multitudes, many provinces would not have been laid waste.

Hume does not propose any mechanism for taking into account not only the origin of our moral sentiments in sympathy but also the effects of our shared moral evaluations on human weal and woe. But I suggest that this would be a plausible and very Humean check on a list of virtues and vices. The moral sentiment can further reflect on the effects of its own workings in society, and the observer can feel either approval or disapproval of what results. One might say that a real virtue is a trait approved as a result of unbiased consideration, the approval of which is also approved, both because of its admirable origin in sympathy and also because of the consequences for human happiness if people generally approve such a quality of mind and encourage it.

This expansion of what we consider in applying the moral sentiment to itself does not unequivocally prevent all considerations of mere agreeableness from swamping considerations of social utility; nor should it. Take, for example, a trait that is disapproved because people find it unfamiliar and strange, and that consequently evokes spontaneous discomfort in many people; that discomfort is transmitted to all others by sympathy, so that the trait is deemed a vice. And suppose we ask whether this trait is really a vice. In the further reflection now proposed, we will have to consider both this sympathy-based disapproval we receive as a result of people's spontaneous discomfort (and which the moral sentiment endorses) *and* the effects of this widespread disapproval on people's happiness, which is a consideration of the social utility or disutility of judging the trait a vice. If the trait is not harmful but only immediately disagreeable, and the effects of people's judging it a vice arc sufficiently devastating, we have grounds to reject the moral opinion that the trait is vicious. But more mildly negative effects on happiness might be overridden by the fact that people just do find the trait immediately disagreeable. That will still count, because our shared response still reveals our mutual identification and capacity for sympathy, and so evokes our approval.

In viewing the grounds of norms in this way, we take only the smallest step beyond what Hume actually proposes. We stipulate one further reflective task: to contemplate the effects of a widely shared moral opinion on those whose lives are altered by it, and use that as a further way to evaluate whether that opinion is warranted or erroneous. But it gains us a good deal. It enables a Humean to say that even when a trait is found immediately disagreeable by most people, if it is socially harmless, and if blaming it also costs a great deal in human suffering, it is really not a vice and should not be blamed. This provides a check on the immediately agreeable and disagreeable, which, as we have seen, Hume's theory very much needs.

Bibliography

Abramson, K. (1999). Hume on cultural conflicts of values. *Philosophical Studies*, 94, 173–87.

—— (2000). Sympathy and the project of Hume's *Second Enquiry*. *Archiv für Geschichte der Philosophie*, 83(1), 45–80.

Ainslie, D. (1995). The problem of the national self in Hume's *Theory of Justice*. *Hume Studies*, 21(2), 289–313.

—— (1999*a*). Review of the book *Reason and Feeling in Hume's Action Theory and Moral Philosophy: Hume's Reasonable Passion*, by Daniel J. Shaw. *Hume Studies*, 25, 266–9.

—— (1999*b*). Scepticism about persons in book II of Hume's *Treatise*. *Journal of the History of Philosophy*, 37(3), 469–92.

Anscombe, G. E. M. (1981*a*). On promising and its justice and whether it needs be respected *in foro interno*. In *Collected Philosophical Papers*, V. III, Minneapolis: University of Minnesota Press, 10–21.

—— (1981*b*). Rules, rights and promises. In *Collected Philosophical Papers*, V. III, Minneapolis: University of Minnesota Press, 97–103.

Árdal, P. S. (1966). *Passion and Value in Hume's Treatise*, 2nd edn. Edinburgh: Edinburgh University Press.

—— (1977*a*). Another look at Hume's account of moral evaluation. *Journal of the History of Philosophy*, 15, 405–21.

—— (1977*b*). Convention and value. In *Morice* (1997), 51–68.

Baier, A. C. (1979). Good men's women: Hume on chastity and trust. *Hume Studies*, 5, 1–19.

—— (1985*a*). Doing without Moral Theory? In *Postures of the Mind: Essays on Mind and Morals*, Minneapolis: University of Minnesota Press, 228–45.

—— (1985*b*). Theory and reflective practices. In *Postures of the Mind: Essays on Mind and Morals*, Minneapolis: University of Minnesota Press, 207–27.

—— (1988). Hume's account of social artifice—Its origins and originality. *Ethics*, 98, 757–78.

—— (1991). *Progress of Sentiments*. Cambridge, MA: Harvard University Press.

Baillie, J. (2000). *Hume on Morality*. London: Routledge.

Balguy, J. (1991[1734]). The foundations of moral goodness. In Raphael (1991), 389–408.

Baron, M. (2001). Hume's noble lie: an account of his artificial virtues. In Cohon (2001*a*), 273–89. Repr. from *Canadian Journal of Philosophy*, 12 (1982), 273–89.

Bentham, J. (1948[1776]). *A Fragment on Government*, ed. W. Harrison. Oxford: Basil Blackwell.

—— (1988[1781]). *The Principles of Morals and Legislation*. Buffalo: Prometheus Books.

Berkeley, G. (1998[1710]). *A Treatise concerning the Principles of Human Knowledge*, ed. J. Dancy. Oxford: Oxford University Press.

Blackburn, S. (1984). *Spreading the Word*. Oxford: Oxford University Press.

——(1993). Hume on the mezzanine level. *Hume Studies*, 19, 273–88.

——(1998). *Ruling Passions*. Oxford: Clarendon Press.

Botros, S. (2006). *Hume, Reason, and Morality: A Legacy of Contradiction*. New York and London: Routledge.

Bricke, J. (1996). *Mind and Morality*. Oxford: Clarendon Press.

Brown, C. (1994). From spectator to agent: Hume's theory of obligation. *Hume Studies*, 20, 19–35.

——(1998). Is Hume an internalist? *Journal of the History of Philosophy*, 26(1), 69–87.

——(2001). Is the general point of view the moral point of view? *Philosophy and Phenomenological Research*, 62, 197–203.

Capaldi, N. (1966). Hume's rejection of 'ought' as a moral category. *Journal of Philosophy*, 63, 126–37.

——(1975). *David Hume: The Newtonian Philosopher*. Boston: Twayne Publishing.

——(1989). *Hume's Place in Moral Philosophy*. New York: Peter Lang.

Chappell, V. C. (1996). *Hume: A Collection of Critical Essays*. Garden City, NY: Doubleday.

Clarke, S. (1991[1706]). A discourse concerning the unchangeable obligations of natural religion and the truth and certainty of the Christian revelation. In Raphael (1991), 192–225.

Cohon, R. (1988). Hume and Humeanism in ethics. *Pacific Philosophical Quarterly*, 69, 99–116.

——(1994). On an unorthodox account of Hume's moral psychology. *Hume Studies*, 20(2), 179–94.

——(1997*a*). The common point of view in Hume's ethics. *Philosophy and Phenomenological Research*, 57(4), 827–50.

——(1997*b*). Hume's difficulty with the virtue of honesty. *Hume Studies*, 23(1), 91–112.

——(1997*c*). Is Hume a noncognitivist in the motivation argument? *Philosophical Studies*, 85, 251–66.

——(2001*a*) (ed.). *Hume: Moral and Political Philosophy*. Burlington, VT: Ashgate.

——(2001*b*). The shackles of virtue: Hume on allegiance to government. *History of Philosophy Quarterly*, 18(4), 393–413.

——(2006*a*). Hume on promises and the peculiar act of the mind. *Journal of the History of Philosophy*, 44(1), 25–45.

——(2006*b*). Hume's artificial and natural virtues. In Traiger (2006), 256–75.

——(2008). Hume's indirect passions. In Radcliffe (2008), 159–84.

——and Owen, D. (1997). Hume on representation, reason and motivation. *Manuscrito*, 20, 47–76.

Cudworth, R. (1991[1731]). A treatise concerning eternal and immutable morality. In Raphael (1991), 103–19.

Dancy, J. (1998) Moral realism. In E. Craig (ed.), *Routledge Encyclopedia of Philosophy*, London: Routledge. Retrieved from <http://www.rep.routledge.com/article/L059>, 21 Jan. 2008.

Darwall, S. (1994). Hume and the invention of utilitarianism. In M. A. Stuart and J. P. Wright (eds.), *Hume and Hume's Connexions*, Edinburgh: Edinburgh University Press, 58–82.

—— (1995). *The British Moralists and the Internal 'Ought'*. Cambridge: Cambridge University Press.

Davidson, D. (1980). *Essays on Actions and Events*. Oxford: Clarendon Press; New York: Oxford University Press.

Davie, W. (1999). Hume on monkish virtue. *Hume Studies*, 25, 139–53.

Dees, R. H. (1997). Hume on the characters of virtue. *Journal of the History of Philosophy*, 35(1), 45–64.

Driver, J. (2004). Pleasure as the standard of virtue in Hume's moral philosophy. *Pacific Philosophical Quarterly*, 85, 173–94.

Falk, W. D. (1975). Hume on practical reason. *Philosophical Studies*, 27, 1–18.

—— (1976). Hume on is and ought. *Canadian Journal of Philosophy*, 6, 359–78.

Fine, A. (1998). Scientific realism and antirealism. In E. Craig (ed.), *Routledge Encyclopedia of Philosophy*, London: Routledge. Retrieved from <http://www.rep.routledge.com/article/Q094 >, 21 Jan. 2008.

Flew, A. (1963). On the interpretation of Hume. *Philosophy*, 38, 178–81.

—— (1986). *David Hume: Philosopher of Moral Science*. Oxford: Basil Blackwell.

Foot, P. (1963). Hume on moral judgment. In D. Pears (ed.), *David Hume: A Symposium*, London: St Martin's Press, 74–80. Repr. in Cohon 2001a.

Forbes, D. (1975). *Hume's Philosophical Politics*. Cambridge: Cambridge University Press.

—— (1977). Hume's science of politics. In Morice (1977), 39–50.

Garrett, D. (1997). *Cognition and Commitment in Hume's Philosophy*. Oxford: Oxford University Press.

Gauthier, D. (1979). David Hume, contractarian. *Philosophical Review*, 88, 3–38.

—— (1992). Artificial virtues and the sensible knave. *Hume Studies*, 18, 401–27.

Geach, P. T. (1958). Inperatives and deontic logic. *Analysis*, 18, 49–56.

—— (1965). Assertion. *Philosophical Review*, 74, 449–65.

Gibbard, A. (1990). *Wise Choices, Apt Feelings*. Cambridge, MA: Harvard University Press.

—— (2003). *Thinking How to Live*. Cambridge, MA: Harvard University Press.

Gill, M. (2000). Hume's progressive view of human nature. *Hume Studies*, 26(1), 87–108.

—— (2006). *The British Moralists on Human Nature and the Birth of Secular Ethics*. Cambridge: Cambridge University Press.

Glossup, R. (1967). The nature of Hume's ethics. *Philosophy and Phenomenological Research*, 27, 527–36.

Goldman, A. (1970). *A Theory of Human Action*. Princeton: Princeton University Press.

Haakonssen, K. (1981). *The Science of a Legislator: The Natural Jurisprudence of David Hume and Adam Smith*. Cambridge: Cambridge University Press.

Hampton, J. (1995). Does Hume have an instrumental conception of practical reason? *Hume Studies*, 21(1), 57–74.

Hare, R. M. (1952). *The Language of Morals*. Oxford: Clarendon Press.

—— (1963). *Freedom and Reason*. Oxford: Oxford University Press.

Harman, G., and Thomson, J. J. (1996). *Moral Relativism and Moral Objectivity*. Cambridge, MA, and Oxford: Blackwell Publishing.

Harrison, J. (1976). *Hume's Moral Epistemology*. Oxford: Clarendon Press.

—— (1981). *Hume's Theory of Justice*. Oxford: Clarendon Press.

Hobbes, T. (1996[1651]). *Leviathan*, ed. R. Tuck. Cambridge: Cambridge University Press.

Hudson, W. D. (1964). Hume on is and ought. *Philosophical Quarterly*, 14, 246–52.

Hume, D. (1932). *The Letters of David Hume*, ed. J. Y. T. Greig. Oxford: clarendon Press.

——— (1967[1745]). *A letter from a gentleman to his friend in Edinburgh*, ed. E. Mossner and J. V. Price. Edinburgh: University of Edinburgh Press.

——— (1975[1748, 1751]). *Enquiries concerning Human Understanding and concerning the Principles of Morals*, 3rd edn., ed. L. A. Selby-Bigge. Oxford: Clarendon Press.

——— (1978[1739–40]). *A Treatise of Human Nature*, 2nd edn., ed. L. A. Selby-Bigge and P. H. Nidditch. Oxford: Clarendon Press.

——— (1983[1778]). *The History of England from the Invasion of Julius Caesar to the Revolution in 1688*. Indianapolis: Liberty Fund.

——— (1985[1777]). *Essays, Moral, Political, and Literary*, ed. E. F. Miller. Indianapolis: Liberty Fund.

——— (1985[1757]). Of the standard of taste. In E. F. Miller (ed.), *Essays, Moral, Political and Literary*, Indianapolis: Liberty Fund, 226–49.

——— (1992 and 1995[1757]). *Four Dissertations and Essays on Suicide and the Immortality of the soul*, ed. J. Immerwahr, J. V. Price, and J. Fieser. South Bend, IN: Thoemmes Press.

——— (1998[1751]). *An Enquiry concerning the Principles of Morals*, ed. T. L. Beauchamp. Oxford: Oxford University Press.

——— (2000[1739–40]). *A Treatise of Human Nature*, ed. D. F. Norton and M. J. Norton. Oxford: Clarendon Press.

——— (2006[1748]). *An Enquiry concerning Human Understanding*, ed. T. L. Beauchamp. Oxford: Oxford University Press.

Hunter, G. (1962). Hume on is and ought. *Philosophy*, 37, 148–52.

——— (1963). Reply to Professor Flew. *Philosophy*, 38, 182–185.

Hursthouse, R. (1995). Applying virtue ethics. In R. Hursthouse, G. Lawrence, and W. S. Quinn (eds.), *Virtues and Reasons: Philippa Foot and Moral Theory*, Oxford: Oxford University Press, 57–75.

——— (1999). *On Virtue Ethics*. Oxford: Clarendon Press.

Hutcheson, F. (1971). *Collected Works of Francis Hutcheson*, ed. B. Fabian. Hildesheim: Georg Olms.

Jacobson, A. J. (2000) (ed.). *Feminist Interpretations of David Hume*. University Park, PA: Pennsylvania State University Press.

Jensen, H. (1977). Hume on moral agreement. *Mind*, 86, 497–513.

Kant, I. (1964[1785]). *Groundwork of the Metaphysic of morals*, 3rd edn., trans. H. J. Paton. New York: Harper & Row.

——— (1986[1797]). On a supposed right to lie from philanthropy. In *Immanuel Kant: Practical Philosophy*, trans. M. Gregor, Cambridge: Cambridge University Press, 611–15.

Karlsson, M. (2000). Rational ends: Humean and non–Humean considerations. *Sats—Nordic Journal of Philosophy*, 1(2), 15–47.

——— (2001). Cognition, desire and motivation: "Humean" and "non-Humean" considerations. *Sats—Nordic Journal of Philosophy*, 2(2), 30–58.

King, J. (1999). Pride and Hume's sensible knave. *Hume Studies*, 25(1–2), 123–37.

Korsgaard, C. M. (1996). *The Sources of Normativity*. Cambridge: Cambridge University Press.

_____ (2001). The general point of view: love and moral approval in Hume's ethics. In Cohon (2001*a*), 231–69. Repr. from *Hume Studies*, 25(1,2) (1999), 3–41.

Kripke, S. A. (1972). Naming and necessity. In *Semantics of Natural Language*, ed. D. Davidson and G. Harman, Dordrecht: D. Reidel Publishing Company, 253–355.

Kuflick, A. (1998). Hume on justice to animals, Indians and women. *Hume Studies*, 24(1), 53–70.

Levey, A. (1997). Under constraint: chastity and modesty in Hume. *Hume Studies*, 23(2), 213–26.

Livingston, D. W. (1984). *Hume's Philosophy of Common Life*. Chicago: University of Chicago Press.

Locke, J. (1955[1689]). *A Letter concerning Toleration*. New York: Macmillan.

_____ (1959[1690]). *An Essay concerning Human Understanding*, ed. A. C. Fraser. New York: Dover Publications, Inc.

_____ (1986[1690]). *Second Treatise on Civil Government*. Buffalo: Prometheus Books.

Loeb, L. E. (1977). Hume's moral sentiments and the structure of the treatise. *Journal of the History of Philosophy*, 15, 395–403.

_____ (2002). *Stability and Justification in Hume's Treatise*. Oxford: Oxford University Press.

McDowell, J. (1979). Virtue and reason. *Monist*, 62, 331–50.

MacIntyre, A. C. (1959). Hume on 'is' and 'ought'. *Philosophical Review*, 68, 451–68.

McIntyre, J. L. (1990). Character: a Humean account. *History of Philosophy Quarterly*, 7, 193–206.

McNaughton, D. (1998). *Moral Vision*. Oxford: Blackwell Publishing.

Mackie, J. L. (1977). *Ethics: Inventing Right and Wrong*. Harmondsworth: Penguin.

_____ (1980). *Hume's Moral Theory*. London: Routledge.

Magri, T. (1996). Natural obligation and normative motivation in Hume's *Treatise*. *Hume Studies*, 22(2), 231–53.

Mandeville, B. (1988[1732, 1924]). *The Fable of the Bees*, with commentary by F. B. Kaye. Repr. Indianapolis: Liberty Press/Liberty Classics.

Miller, D. (1981). *Philosophy and Ideology in Hume's Political Thought*. Oxford: Clarendon Press.

Millgram, E. (1995). Was Hume a Humean? *Hume Studies*, 21, 75–93.

_____ (1997). Hume on practical reasoning. *Jerusalem Philosophical Quarterly*, 46, 235–65.

Morice, G. P. (ed.) (1977). *David Hume: Bicentenary Papers*. Austin: University of Texas Press.

Morris, W. E. (2008). Hume's epistemological legacy. In Radcliffe (2008), 457–76.

Norton, D. F. (1982). *David Hume: Common-Sense Moralist, Sceptical Metaphysician*. Princeton: Princeton University Press.

_____ (1985). Hume's moral ontology. *Hume Studies* (special volume), 189–214.

_____ (1993*a*). *The Cambridge Companion to Hume*. Cambridge: Cambridge University Press.

_____ (1993*b*) (ed.). Hume, human nature, and the foundations of morality. In Norton (1993*a*), 148–81.

Nowell-Smith, P. H. (1954). *Ethics*. Melbourne: Penguin.

Owen, D. (1994). Reason, reflections and *reductio*. *Hume Studies*, 20, 195–210.

_____ (1999). *Hume's Reason*. Oxford: Oxford University Press.

_____ (2000) (ed.). *Hume: General Philosophy*. Burlington, VT: Ashgate.

Penelhum, T. (1975). *Hume*. London: Macmillan.

_____ (1992). *David Hume: An Introduction to his Philosophical System*. West Lafayette, IN: Purdue University Press.

Persson, I. (1997). Hume—not a 'Humean' about motivation. *History of Philosophy Quarterly*, 14(2), 189–206.

Pitson, A. E. (1996). Sympathy and other selves. *Hume Studies*, 22, 255–71.

_____ (2002). *Hume's Philosophy of the Self*. London: Routledge.

Postema, G. (1998). Hume's reply to the sensible knave. *History of Philosophy Quarterly*, 5, 23–40.

_____ (2005). Cemented with diseased qualities: sympathy and comparison in Hume's moral psychology. *Hume Studies*, 31(2), 249–98.

Pritchard, H. A. (1949). The obligation to keep a promise. In *Moral Obligations*, Oxford: Clarendon Press, 169–79.

Putnam, H. (1973). Meaning and reference. *Journal of Philosophy*, 70(19), 699–711.

Radcliffe, E. S. (1994*a*). Hume on motivating sentiments, the general point of view, and the inculcation of "morality". *Hume Studies*, 20(1), 37–58.

_____ (1994*b*). Hume on passion, pleasure, and the reasonableness of ends. *Southwest Philosophy Review*, 10, 1–11.

_____ (1997). Kantian tunes on a Humean instrument: why Hume is not really a skeptic about practical reasoning. *Canadian Journal of Philosophy*, 27, 247–69.

_____ (1998). How does the Humean sense of duty motivate? *Journal of the History of Philosophy*, 34, 47–70.

_____ (1999). Hume on the generation of motives: why beliefs alone never motivate. *Hume Studies*, 25(1–2), 101–22.

_____ (2000). *On Hume*. Belmont, CA: Wadsworth.

_____ (2008) (ed.). *A Companion to Hume*. Malden, MA, and Oxford: Blackwell Publishing.

Railton, P. (1986). Moral realism. *Philosophical Review*, 95.

Raphael, D. D. (ed.) (1991). *British Moralists 1650–1800*, i. Indianapolis: Hackett.

Rawls, J. (1971). *A Theory of Justice* Cambridge, MA: Harvard University Press.

_____ (2000). *Lectures on the History of Moral Philosophy*, ed. B. Herman. Cambridge, MA: Harvard University Press.

Read, R., and Richman, K. A. (2000) (eds.). *The New Hume Debate*. New York: Routledge.

Robins, M. (1984). *Promising, Intending and Moral Autonomy*. Cambridge: Cambridge University Press.

Santayana, G. (1905–6). *The Life of Reason*, New York: Scribner's.

Sayre-McCord, G. (1988) (ed.). *Essays on Moral Realism*. Ithaca, NY: Cornell University Press.

_____ (1994). On why Hume's general point of view isn't ideal—and shouldn't be. *Social Philosophy and Policy*, 11, 202–28.

_____ (1995). Hume and the Bauhaus theory of ethics. *Midwest Studies in Philosophy*, 20, 280–98.

Scanlon, T. M. (1990). Promises and practices. *Philosophy and Public Affairs*, 19, 199–226.

——(1998). *What We Owe Each Other*. Cambridge, MA: Harvard University Press.

Schneewind, J. B. (1990). The misfortunes of virtue. *Ethics*, 101(1), 42–63.

——(1998). *The Invention of Autonomy*. Cambridge: Cambridge University Press.

Searle, J. (1962). Meaning and speech acts. *Philosophical Review*, 71, 423–32.

——(1964). How to derive "ought" from "is". *Philosophical Review*, 73, 43–58.

——(1969). *Speech Acts*. Cambridge: Cambridge University Press.

Shaver, R. (1995). Hume's moral theory? *History of Philosophy Quarterly*, 12(3), 317–28.

Shaw, D. (1998). *Reason and Feeling in Hume's Action Theory and Moral Philosophy: Hume's Reasonable Passion*. Lewiston, NY: Edwin Mellen Press.

Smith, M. (1987). The Humean theory of motivation. *Mind*, 96, 36–61.

——(1994). *The Moral Problem*. Oxford: Blackwell Publishers.

——(2004). *Ethics and the A Priori*. Cambridge: Cambridge University Press.

Smith, N. K. (1941). *The Philosophy of David Hume*. London: Macmillan.

Snare, F. (1991). *Morals, Motivation and Convention*. Cambridge: Cambridge University Press.

Stewart, C. (1976). The moral point of view. *Philosophy*, 51, 177–87.

Stewart, J. B. (1992). *Opinion and Reform in Hume's Political Philosophy*. Princeton: Princeton University Press.

Stocker, M. (1976). The schizophrenia of modern moral theories. *Journal of Philosophy*, 73(14), 453–66.

Stroud, B. (1977). *Hume*. London: Routledge.

——(1993). "Gliding" or "staining" the world with "sentiments" and "phantasms". *Hume Studies*, 19, 253–72.

Sturgeon, N. (2001). Moral skepticism and moral naturalism in Hume's *Treatise*. *Hume Studies*, 27(1), 3–83.

Swain, C. (1992). Passionate objectivity. *Noûs*, 26(4), 465–90.

Taylor, J. (2001). Justice and the foundations of social morality in Hume's *Treatise*. In Cohon (2001*a*), 205–30. Repr. from *Hume Studies*, 24 (1998), 5–30.

——(2002). Hume on the standard of virtue. *Journal of Ethics*, 6, 43–62.

Traiger, S. (ed.) (2006). *The Blackwell Guide to Hume's Treatise*. Oxford: Blackwell Publishing.

Tweyman, S. (1974). *Reason and Conduct in Hume and his Predecessors*. The Hague: Martinus Nijhoff.

Watson, G. (1990). On the primacy of character. In O. Flanagan and A. O. Rorty (eds.), *Identity and Morality: Essays in Moral Psychology*, Cambridge, MA: MIT Press, 449–69.

Waxman, W. (1994). *Hume's Theory of Consciousness*. Cambridge: Cambridge University Press.

Whelan, F. (1981). *Order and Artifice in Hume's Political Philosophy*. Princeton: Princeton University Press.

Wiggins, D. (1998). A sensible subjectivism. In *Needs, Values, Truth*, 3rd edn., Oxford: Clarendon Press, 185–214.

Williams, B. (1981*a*). Internal and external reasons. In *Moral Luck*, Cambridge: Cambridge University Press, 101–13.

_____ (1981*b*). Persons, character and morality. In *Moral Luck*, Cambridge: Cambridge University Press, 1–19.

Wollaston, W. (1991[1724]). The religion of nature delineated. In Raphael (1991), 237–58.

Wright, J. P. (1983). *The Skeptical Realism of David Hume.* Minneapolis: University of Minnesota Press.

Index